First Pennsylvanians

THE ARCHAEOLOGY OF NATIVE AMERICANS IN PENNSYLVANIA

Kurt W. Carr
and
Roger W. Moeller

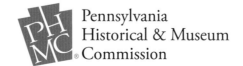

Pennsylvania
Historical & Museum
Commission

Pennsylvania Historical and Museum Commission
Harrisburg, Pennsylvania 17120-0024
www.phmc.state.pa.us

First edition 2015

Printed in the United States of America
10 9 8 7 6 5 4 3

Jonathan Frazier, *Illustrator* (unless otherwise credited)

Kimberly L. Stone, *Designer*

Cover: Typical Algonquian Indian village, circa 1500 AD, by Robert Thom
MICHIGAN INDIANS: ALGONQUIAN VILLAGE ABOUT 1500 A.D., ©1964 MICHIGAN BELL TELEPHONE COMPANY (NOW AT&T MICHIGAN), THE HISTORY OF MICHIGAN IN PAINTINGS SERIES.

Back cover: Late Prehistoric Monongahela pot from the Martin site (36Fa87)
THE STATE MUSEUM OF PENNSYLVANIA/PHOTO BY DON GILES

Library of Congress Cataloging-in-Publication Data

Carr, Kurt William, 1949-
    First Pennsylvanians : the archaeology of Native Americans in Pennsylvania / Kurt W. Carr, Roger W. Moeller.—First edition.
        pages cm
    Includes bibliographical references and index.
    ISBN 978-0-89271-150-5 (pbk.)—ISBN 0-89271-150-7 (pbk.)
    1. Indians of North America—Pennsylvania—Antiquities. 2. Indians of North America—Pennsylvania—History—To 1500. 3. Pennsylvania—Antiquities. I. Moeller, Roger W. II. Pennsylvania Historical and Museum Commission. III. Title. IV. Title: Archaeology of Native Americans in Pennsylvania.
E78.P4C37 2014
974.8'01—dc23
                                                            2015011659

CONTENTS

PREFACE

This is the story of Native Americans in Pennsylvania—the first Pennsylvanians. The story begins in prehistoric times, extends to the present, and focuses on what is known through the science of archaeology. It is organized by time periods and the three major drainage basins—the Ohio/Monongahela, the Susquehanna, and the Delaware—in the Commonwealth. Follow in the footsteps of this book and discover the archaeology of the first Pennsylvanians— and Pennsylvania's far-reaching past. The earliest Pennsylvanians arrived here during a time span referred to as prehistory, a period categorized as the time before written records. In Pennsylvania, archaeological sites and artifacts date to at least 16,250 years ago. Within this span of time are periods that archaeologists use to help distinguish changes in human technology, population, subsistence, culture, and behavior. They are the Paleoindian, Archaic, Transitional, Woodland, and Contact periods. These periods represent changes over time from when Ice Age people foraged on the edge of the glaciers through to the early days of European contact and settlement.

ACKNOWLEDGMENTS

First Pennsylvanians: The Archaeology of Native Americans in Pennsylvania was written over a period of five years, during which many talented individuals generously contributed to its creation, development, and production. It is part of a series on Pennsylvania archaeology supported by the Transportation Enhancement program funded by the Federal Highway Administration, U.S. Department of Transportation, and the Pennsylvania Department of Transportation (PennDOT). I am especially indebted to Ira Beckerman, Cultural Resources Group Leader, and Christine Kula, Senior Archaeologist, Central Office, of PennDOT. The printing of this book was funded by Westmoreland County through an agreement with the Federal Emergency Management Agency, Region III.

Initially, Brenda Barrett, former Director of the Bureau for Historic Preservation (BHP) of the Pennsylvania Historical and Museum Commission (PHMC), encouraged the launch of this project. In addition to affording me the necessary time to research and write, Jean Cutler, former Director of BHP, was persistent in making this project one of my highest priorities. Diane B. Reed, former Chief of PHMC's Division of Publications and Sales, was of tremendous assistance in the initial organizing of this project. Ted R. Walke, former Chief of the Division of Publications and Sales, created a vision for this book and his enthusiasm reinvigorated the project.

The staff of The State Museum of Pennsylvania's Section of Archaeology has made significant contributions to this volume over the past five years. David Burke and Elizabeth A. Wagner, Collections Assistants, and Andrea Johnson Carr and Paul Pluta, Laboratory Technicians, have reviewed at least one draft and suggested numerous changes. Elizabeth Wagner was instrumental in formating many of the images. Curator Janet Johnson has been helpful in suggesting artifacts from the collection for illustrations and also in editing. She has been especially adept in keeping the office running smoothly while I worked on this book. Jim Herbstritt, Historic Preservation Specialist, suggested artifacts for use as illustrations and directed our gifted freelance illustrator, Jonathan Frazier, in accurately portraying artifacts and scenes of Native American life in his distinctive drawings. Jim was also my go-to expert on Pennsylvania archaeology. Jonathan did a yeoman's job and patiently worked with artifacts and human figures in developing the millennia-old settlement pattern scenes.

His illustrations have added significantly to the educational value of this publication. *First Pennsylvanians* is enhanced by the artifact photography, most of which was undertaken by Don Giles of The State Museum. His work is sincerely appreciated. Chief of PHMC's Marketing and Media Services Howard M. Pollman, editors Michael J. O'Malley III and Kyle R. Weaver, graphic designer Kimberly L. Stone, and proofreader Brett Keener have been inspiring and extremely accommodating. Their editing and design skills immeasurably improved the final book.

For their support of scholarship, educational initiatives, and public outreach programs, I heartily thank James M. Vaughan, PHMC Executive Director; David W. Dunn, Director of The State Museum; and Bradley Smith, Curatorial Administrator of the Bureau of the State Museum.

To ensure the accessibility of this material to as broad an audience as possible, many thanks are due Kevin Wagner, Social Studies Program Chair, 6–12, Carlisle Area School District, who, as an independent educational consultant, reviewed the draft and offered helpful suggestions.

Finally, my wife Judy, and children Ryan, Megan, Eric, Erin, Norman, Katharine, and Theresa have persevered while I spent evenings, weekends, holidays, and vacations working on this project. I could not have finished without their support and understanding. I hope that my grandchildren Aubrey, Olivia, William, Laura, Camila, and others that may come along, will enjoy the lively first-person narratives.

Kurt W. Carr, Ph.D.
Senior Curator of Archaeology
The State Museum of Pennsylvania
Harrisburg, Pennsylvania

This book evolved over the years from my initial manuscript, aided greatly by my wife Judy's insights as a secondary education reading consultant. Kurt had the advantage of a large staff in a museum environment to make suggestions for the revisions, and I am extremely pleased with the final version incorporating my responses to their questions.

Roger W. Moeller
CEO
Archaeological Services
Bethlehem, Connecticut

INTRODUCTION

The Commonwealth of Pennsylvania possesses a long and enviable history of conducting archaeological investigations. In fact, the state has had an agency responsible for interpreting the past since 1905.

Initially there were two state agencies involved in archaeology. The State Museum of Pennsylvania was formed in 1905, followed by the creation of the Pennsylvania Historical Commission (PHC) eight years later, in 1913. The State Museum immediately began acquiring collections from amateur archaeologists. PHC was originally interested in erecting historical markers. Significantly, thirteen of the twenty-seven markers erected between 1924 and 1926 commemorated Native American sites.

During the 1920s and 1930s, PHC sponsored a number of archaeological investigations. In 1945, The State Museum and PHC were combined to create the present-day Pennsylvania Historical and Museum Commission (PHMC). Since then, archaeological field work and research have continued, led by talented PHMC staff. Much of the work from 1960 to 1980 emphasized research in the Susquehanna Valley, especially the analysis of prehistoric and historic Native American farming communities. From the early 1980s until 2005, the focus was on historic archaeology, especially at sites owned or formerly owned by PHMC, including Fort Loudoun, Franklin County; Fort Augusta and the Joseph Priestly House, both in Northumberland County; Eckley Miners' Village, Luzerne County; and Ephrata Cloister, Lancaster County.

PHMC's archaeology programs have significantly expanded during the past twenty years and offer a variety of educational, research, and historic preservation opportunities for everyone. PHMC's website, www.phmc.state.pa.us, facilitates research, educates, and informs the public about Pennsylvania archaeology. Students, teachers, and avocational archaeologists can find popular summaries, curricula, a list of resources, and a video tour of the Hall of Anthropology and Archaeology at The State Museum of Pennsylvania on the website. Professional archaeologists are able to consult report abstracts, watershed syntheses, and PHMC guidelines, policies, and forms, as well as summaries of reports and new research being conducted throughout the Keystone State. The website also identifies PHMC staff members that can respond to specific inquiries and discuss particular interests.

The State Museum's Hall of Anthropology and Archaeology provides a comprehensive (and graphically appealing) tour of Pennsylvania archaeology and cultural history from the Paleoindian period through the nineteenth century. The museum features exhibits on archaeological laboratory and field methods, prehistoric technology, historic archaeology, PHMC excavations, dioramas depicting the evolution of prehistoric lifeways in Pennsylvania, and a reconstructed Delaware Indian village.

October is annually observed as Archaeology Month in Pennsylvania, with educational programs taking place around the state with assistance from PHMC and its partners, the Society for Pennsylvania Archaeology, the Pennsylvania Archaeological Council, and the Pennsylvania Department of Transportation. Excavation demonstrations and experiments in the replication of artifacts are held for the public during Archaeology Month. These activities draw public attention to the importance of archaeological resources and the need to protect them.

PHMC offers individual educational experiences in archaeology. Internships in archaeology are available for students with a wide range of academic interests. For the general public, we accept volunteers. Opportunities for fieldwork, data analysis, mapping, and collections management are available in many of PHMC's archaeology programs. Depending on the budget, the agency's Scholars in Residence program awards stipends to independent scholars to conduct research that will enhance the understanding and interpretation of the PHMC's collections.

PHMC's archaeological collections contain a wealth of valuable information. Established in 1905, The State Museum has collected more than four million artifacts that it manages on behalf of the citizens of Pennsylvania. These collections are the result of excavations conducted by Commission staff and include private donations from individuals and educational institutions. Other collections have been acquired as a result of archaeological investigations required by historic preservation laws. The collections continue to grow, and donations of mapped and documented artifacts are always welcome. Documentation associated with these collections includes photographs, excavation records, maps, and more than seventeen hundred unpublished manuscripts, available exclusively at PHMC. Access to these collections requires a written proposal submitted to the Section of Archaeology of The State Museum. PHMC manages a loan program, making artifacts and objects available to institutions and organizations for research purposes and exhibitions. A general list of collections and a bibliography of unpublished manuscripts are available on PHMC's website.

Grant assistance may be available, depending on the economy and PHMC's budget, to support activities promoting or enhancing the understanding of Pennsylvania's prehistoric and historic archaeological resources for public benefit. Projects eligible for funding include public education programs, surveys, artifact analyses, development of regional site sensitivity models, preparation of syntheses, field schools, and excavation projects. These activities cannot be associated with state or federal compliance projects.

The review of federal and state projects, authorized by the National Historic Preservation Act of 1966 (As Amended) and the Pennsylvania History Code, is the primary archaeology program managed by PHMC's Bureau for Historic Preservation (BHP). These laws require state and federal agencies to take into consideration archaeological resources during the planning process for construction projects. They also ensure that mitigation is conducted for sites destroyed or adversely affected by state and federal actions.

Recording archaeological sites aids in their protection. The Pennsylvania Archaeological Site Survey (PASS) files have been converted to a geographic information system (GIS) known as the Cultural Resource Geographic Information System (CRGIS). CRGIS is a map-based inventory of more than 125,000 historic properties, 5,000 archaeological surveys, and the PASS files combined into one electronic system. These resources are constantly updated and can help communities and local governments develop plans and streamline project reviews. It is available online at http://phmc.info/pacrgis. PHMC also promotes the listing of significant archaeological sites on the National Register of Historic Places. Guidelines for adding archaeological sites, as well as buildings, structures, objects, and districts, to the National Register are posted on PHMC's website.

The State Museum Store offers many popular and technical publications, including titles on Native American prehistory, Native American cultures, and archaeology in the Commonwealth. Visit PHMC's online bookstore at www.shoppaheritage.com for a wide array of books and publications.

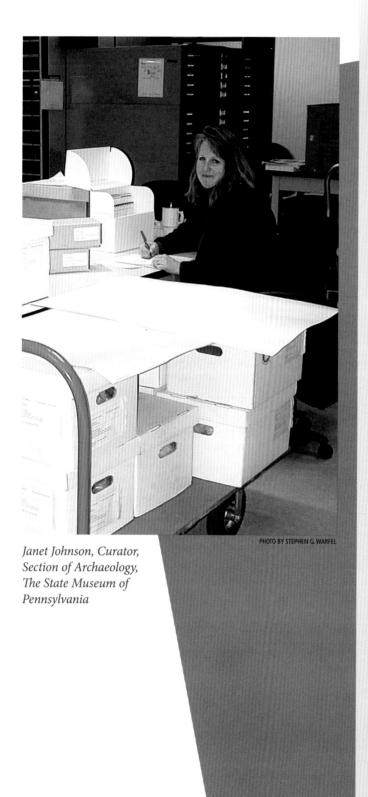

PHOTO BY STEPHEN G. WARFEL

Janet Johnson, Curator, Section of Archaeology, The State Museum of Pennsylvania

IN ADDITION TO PRESENTING SPECIFIC TRAITS OF EACH ARCHAEOLOGICAL TIME PERIOD FOR WATERSHEDS IN PENNSYLVANIA, THE AUTHORS HAVE PREPARED A GLIMPSE OF THE DAILY LIFE OF NATIVE AMERICANS. THE ACADEMIC ACCOUNT OF LIFE BASED UPON THE ARCHAEOLOGICAL DATA LACKS ONE THING: A HUMAN VOICE. RATHER THAN PRESENT AN ETHNOGRAPHIC (SCIENTIFIC DESCRIPTIONS OF THE CUSTOMS OF PEOPLES) MODEL DERIVED FROM A SIXTEENTH-CENTURY EUROPEAN SOURCE UNTRAINED IN ANTHROPOLOGICAL OBSERVATION, WE HAVE CREATED FIGURES WHO WILL RELATE THEIR OWN STORIES IN THEIR OWN WORDS FOR DIFFERENT TIME PERIODS BASED ON THE ARCHAEOLOGICAL RECORD. WE HAVE ALSO ASKED COLLEAGUES TO SHARE THEIR PERSONAL STORIES. HERE IS THE FIRST OF MANY VOICES YOU WILL ENCOUNTER.

I AM AN ARCHAEOLOGIST.

If we are the sum total of our life experiences, then I have no doubt my childhood led me to become an archaeologist. I credit my father for exposing me to cultures from around the world through his travel while serving in the U.S. Air Force. His enthusiasm for sharing the customs of foreign places with his family would often lead to an evening supper created to replicate a meal from some distant place. Sometimes he brought gifts of dolls dressed in native garments or clothing, including a colorful Japanese kimono, for my two sisters and me. The photographs of faraway lands always included people, and there were stories connected to each of their faces. The military also provided me with academic experiences that were more diverse than those of many of my peers. There were Spanish lessons in the third grade, a Chinese dragon large enough for the entire class to walk beneath it, and show-and-tell stories of objects brought home by other fathers as they traveled the globe.

Military family moves led to new friends, new places, new experiences. From the West Coast to the Hawaiian Islands to the Deep South, these places offered exciting cultures to experience. My father retired from service while I was in my teens, and we moved to our family farm in rural Pennsylvania that has been the homestead for more than one hundred years.

Farmlands, hills, streams, and old outbuildings soon became my refuge. They led to hours of exploration and discovery. There were rocks, fossils, and old abandoned farm equipment and implements. The plowing of the fields in spring uncovered rocks and tools that my grandfather said the Indians had left behind. My grandfather's office resembled a small museum with family heirlooms, but it also contained a display case of points and stone tools collected by my ancestors on this land.

I read history books and *National Geographic* and watched television programs about Indians, but none of these had pictures of artifacts like those in grandfather's office. Visits to museums on family vacations provided some answers, but I wanted to learn more about the people who had lived here before my family.

College was an opportunity to explore unfamiliar subjects and satisfy my curiosity about nature, people, and history. I began taking geology and soils classes, learning about changes to the earth over millions of years and how these changes are revealed in the rocks and soils around us. I studied the history of ancient civilizations and the cultures of people that my father had not experienced. I began to recognize the key to understanding past behavior would be through the artifacts left behind by these people. A summer field school in archaeology along the Clarion River provided some of the training and experience to learn about peoples who inhabited our excavation site as many as eight thousand years ago. Holding artifacts that had been touched or made by these people was an incredible experience. I had been bitten by the archaeology bug, and there was no turning back. I continued to pursue every course available in archaeology and was selected for an internship under Barry C. Kent, the State Archaeologist, at the Pennsylvania Historical and Museum Commission in Harrisburg. Dr. Kent also served as a curator for the William Penn Memorial Museum, now The State Museum of Pennsylvania. The opportunity to work with thousands of artifacts from throughout the state and conduct research further fired my desire to become an archaeologist.

I had always enjoyed family visits to museums, but here I had the remarkable good fortune to learn how to properly care for artifacts. Graduate courses in history and archaeology, as well as another internship with Dr. Kent, were essential to developing my career choice.

Life experiences took a turn when I married and moved to Virginia. My husband and I settled near Williamsburg, which allowed frequent visits to its outstanding historic displays as well as numerous tours of other sites in the area rich in human development. My interest in history and archaeology was shared by my husband and young sons, and the goal of one day returning to the archaeology workplace remained constant. The desire to return to Pennsylvania and an opportunity to settle in the Harrisburg area encouraged me to pursue my desire and led me to seek a position with The State Museum.

I accepted a temporary position assisting with a massive inventory project of archaeological collections for compliance with new federal regulations. This position led to a permanent part-time position, and after several years I was able to secure my present full-time position as curator in the museum's Section of Archaeology. My duties are as varied as my life experiences and enable me to continue learning and growing. Many of my daily tasks deal with management of a collection in excess of four million artifacts that require monitoring of environmental conditions, database management, research, and loan requests. Participation in field investigations of both historic and prehistoric sites in Pennsylvania permit me to experience the excitement of once again discovering an artifact not seen or used by others for hundreds or thousands of years. It reminds me of the significance of properly curating these artifacts so that following generations will be able to examine and research this evidence of human behavior. Opportunities to meet and assist researchers are a rewarding component of my position. Their interests in researching artifacts range from historic to the earliest prehistoric sites in Pennsylvania. Their willingness to share information gleaned from research of collections housed at other institutions proves to be undeniably gratifying.

Museum curators also function as interpreters between artifacts and the public. We develop programs and exhibits to enable the public to explore artifacts as a tool to understanding human behavior of both the recent past and ancient peoples. Presentations at schools and public venues are geared towards fostering an appreciation not only for preserving our past, but also for protecting our precious archaeological resources. Archaeology is a science, and one that is still evolving. Our understanding of human behavior continues to grow as new methods of analysis are developed. Collections that have been curated for decades are once again the sources for ongoing research of a culture long gone with no written record to pass on to following generations.

Archaeologists come from a wide variety of backgrounds. Our training is as diverse as the life experiences we bring to the profession, but we all share common traits of curiosity of human diversity, the joy of holding interesting artifacts that have passed through hands of an earlier person hundreds or thousands of years ago, and the desire to discover new information about our past. If we are indeed a total sum of our life experiences, my total sum is still increasing as I continue to grow in my profession as an archaeologist.

Janet R. Johnson, Curator, Section of Archaeology
The State Museum of Pennsylvania

Drainage Basin

A drainage basin is a land region from where a flowing body of water receives water runoff and groundwater flow. Within these regions are watersheds. A watershed, such as the Ohio/Monongahela, Susquehanna, and Delaware Rivers, represents all of the stream tributaries that flow to some location along the stream channel. These lifelines of water provide archaeologists with a "road map" to understanding how Native Americans lived and migrated in Pennsylvania. Europeans and Native Americans used drainage basins differently. Europeans frequently used rivers as boundary markers, but to Native Americans, they were the equivalent of today's Main Streets.

Most of Pennsylvania's present topography has been formed by erosion, the down-cutting of the landscape. Tens of millions of years ago, mountains were building due to continental drift, but that has generally stopped. Most erosion in Pennsylvania is caused by rivers and streams that are gradually wearing down rocks and washing the sediments to the ocean. As they erode down through bedrock, they form valleys. Along large streams and rivers there typically is a broad flat area called a floodplain. The floodplain is the result of sediments, or soil, being deposited after rivers overflow their banks as a result of increased rainfall. During a heavy rain event, water erodes soil from the uplands, rapidly moving it down steep slopes. It usually slows and spreads when it reaches the relatively flat valleys. With each flood, a thin layer of soil is deposited over the floodplain. Over hundreds and thousands of years, the floodplains in Pennsylvania along the major rivers have grown to more than ten feet thick. The tools (now artifacts) dropped by people living on floodplains are buried by flood deposits. Terraces, slightly higher areas bordering floodplains, are essentially older floodplains from when the river was at a higher elevation.

The drainage basins of Pennsylvania each have special characteristics that affect the archaeology of the basin. The Ohio/Monongahela/Allegheny drainage basin is connected to the Mississippi River and the Gulf of Mexico. The archaeology of this basin is more related to the central United States than the Commonwealth's other basins. In contrast, the archaeology of

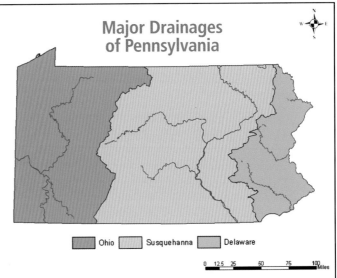

Major Drainages of Pennsylvania

Ohio   Susquehannas   Delaware

0 12.5 25 50 75 100 Miles

the Susquehanna and Delaware drainages is more related to the Southeastern United States and New England.

Drainage basins affect where people live, and they produce different types of archaeological sites. The Ohio/Monongahela/Allegheny drainage basin is generally more entrenched and the floodplains are frequently small and narrow. They are not as frequently stratified or used as village locations. In this basin, major Native American farming villages are frequently located on hilltops. In contrast, the floodplains of the Susquehanna and Delaware basins are frequently broad, offering ideal locations for early Native American farming communities. In addition, archaeological sites in the Susquehanna and Delaware basins are more frequently buried by seasonal flooding, resulting in the development of stratified sites where Native American camps are buried on top of one another—similar to a layer cake. Finally, both the Susquehanna and Delaware have direct access to the Atlantic Ocean and annual migratory fish. This resource was heavily exploited and is commonly found in the archaeological record.

The prehistoric people who lived within the borders of what is now Pennsylvania obviously did not recognize state boundaries. The archaeology of Pennsylvania is closely related to that of adjacent states. Known as the Middle Atlantic region, it includes Pennsylvania, New York, New Jersey, Delaware, Maryland, Virginia, and West Virginia.

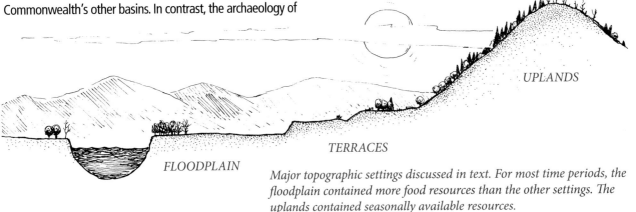

UPLANDS

TERRACES

FLOODPLAIN

Major topographic settings discussed in text. For most time periods, the floodplain contained more food resources than the other settings. The uplands contained seasonally available resources.

Chapter 1

Archaeology: Uncovering Prehistory

The Anthropology of Past Cultures

Anthropology is the study of human cultural behavior in all times and places. Archaeology is one of four subdisciplines within anthropology. It is the scientific study of past human behavior through the systematic recovery and analysis of material remains. It is probably most famous for studying the pyramids of Egypt, the Mayan temples of Mexico, or three-million-year-old pre-human remains in Africa. Archaeology is also the study of Native American fishing sites along the Delaware River, six-hundred-year-old farming towns along the Monongahela River, Revolutionary War soldiers' lives at Valley Forge, and ordinary farm life 150 years ago in central Pennsylvania.

Archaeology seeks to identify patterns in human activity—how people lived in the past and how they adapted to their environment. Archaeologists assume that human culture represents a technological, social, and ideological adaptation to the environment. Just as groups (or packs) of wolves use their teeth and speed and cooperate with one another to acquire food and reproduce, humans use technology, living in groups, and their belief systems to do the same. Culture provides humans with a set of rules for behavior and a strategy for how they can adapt to their natural and cultural environment.

Searching for Answers

Paleontology and archaeology are frequently confused, but archaeologists do not dig up dinosaurs or search for fossils. These are the goals of paleontologists, who study plant and animal life of the past. Archaeologists seek to explain how cultures function and adapt to their environment and how and why cultures change. It is the only science that studies changes in human societies over thousands of years.

- How did humans adapt to living during the Ice Age?
- Why did humans change from hunting and gathering to growing their own food?
- What are the conditions that caused people to migrate together and build large cities?
- What are the factors in the development of the world's major religions?

THE STATE MUSEUM OF PENNSYLVANIA/PHOTO BY DON GILES

Archaeologists (above) excavate artifacts to understand how people lived in the past.

Paleontologists (left) excavate fossils to understand past animal and plant life.

ROBERT SULLIVAN

1

Subdisciplines of Anthropology

Anthropology is the study of human cultural behavior in all times and places. It is divided into four subdisciplines: cultural anthropology, physical anthropology, linguistics, and archaeology. *Cultural anthropology,* known also as ethnology, is the study of existing cultures or cultures from the recent past. It studies their technology, how they obtain food, how they are organized into groups, the different social roles of males and females, their religion, and all other aspects of human group behavior. It seeks to identify the similarities and the differences between cultures. The ultimate goal is to be able to explain how cultures operate and how they will change.

Physical anthropology is the study of the relationship between human biology and human cultural behavior. The two main subfields are the study of human evolution and human variation: How did humans evolve over the past ten million years and why are there so many different colors and shapes of humans? A recent specialization is forensic anthropology, which focuses on the analysis of human skeletal remains for legal purposes. This is frequently used at crime scenes and mass gravesites.

Linguistics is the study of the relationship between language and human cultural behavior. The two main subfields are the study of the history of languages and the description of languages, or how languages are structured. All humans have a complex language that can express concepts they need to live in their environment. There are no simple or primitive languages. It is becoming increasingly clear that the human brain is "wired" for language—both the ability to project a complex series of sounds (or words) and the ability to receive (or hear) and interpret those sounds.

Archaeology is the scientific study of past human behavior through the systematic recovery and analysis of material remains. The study of archaeology began in the nineteenth century with the discovery of spectacular temples and tombs in the Middle East and South America. At the time, archaeologists were primarily interested in understanding the development of technology, statues, pottery, and classical architecture, which is considered classical archaeology. In the twenty-first century, archaeologists focus on human behavior. A great deal of time is spent analyzing artifacts and material culture, but the goal is to understand how people behaved in the past and why their cultures changed.

The only science able to explain these developments is archaeology. It is important to the future of humanity that these changes are understood because it helps explain how and why these changes occurred. According to Project Archaeology, a joint endeavor of the U.S. Department of the Interior's Bureau of Land Management and Montana State University, "Understanding the human past is essential for understanding the present and shaping the future." (Project Archaeology gives students a basic understanding of how archaeology works and teaches them to respect and protect the nation's rich cultural heritage by using two quality guides, *Intrigue of the Past: A Teacher's Activity Guide for Fourth through Seventh Grades* and *Project Archaeology: Investigating Shelter.*) Ultimately, archaeologists seek to predict the nature of cultural change.

Painting a Picture of Life

Archaeology paints a picture of how people once lived. Using information recovered from the ground, archaeologists scientifically reconstruct the histories of societies that do not have written records. Since the beginning of human culture, three million years ago, more than 98 percent of human cultural development occurred before the invention of writing. Archaeology is the only scientific discipline that can reveal what happened prior to written records. Writing was invented about five thousand years ago, but for much of the time since then, it generally applied to, and revealed, the wealthy and religious members of a culture. Most Native Americans, for example, never had a written language. Archaeology provides them with a scientifically based history and a cultural heritage. The same is true for many modern marginalized populations. Archaeology enriches the heritage of former slaves and early immigrants who were insufficiently documented because of their lack of social standing. The goal of archaeology is to improve the human existence. For archaeologists, "learning about cultures, past and present, is essential for living in a pluralistic society and world."

Cultural anthropologists study how humans live in a cultural setting in the present. They seek to understand how different cultures operate and how they adapt to the environment. Anthropologists have studied hundreds of different cultures that exist in the world today or in the recent past. They have described these cultures in great detail. They compare and contrast these cultures to better understand how humans live—why we live differently and also why there are common characteristics.

Scene from an Algonquian village. Archaeologists reconstruct how people lived in the past.

Archaeologists study and interpret the anthropology of past societies with an emphasis on why and how cultures operate and why they change. Archaeologists are social scientists. They use the information gathered by anthropologists who study existing cultures to develop a general picture of the ways different types of cultures function. Much archaeology focuses on cultures prior to the development of farming, with people who only hunted animals and collected roots, seeds, nuts, and berries. This form of obtaining food is called foraging. By studying living foraging groups, anthropologists have identified similar patterns in their family organization and religious beliefs. Archaeologists combine the analysis of artifacts and these similarities to help describe prehistoric foragers. Using modern cultures to interpret archaeological situations is called *ethnographic analogy*.

Voices of a Culture

As a word of caution, there are sometimes several different descriptions, or voices, that can be used in the description of archaeological cultures. The description of relatively recent cultures (within the past one thousand years) can particularly vary, depending on the relative role of oral traditions such as storytelling. Cultures with writing maintain their history, cultural traditions, and religion in written records and now electronically. Cultures without writing maintain their history, cultural traditions, and religion through oral tradition—by word of mouth. We may call these myths or legends, but they are just as real as actual events are to the speakers. In fact, some people reject archaeology and the scientific approach to the interpretation of the

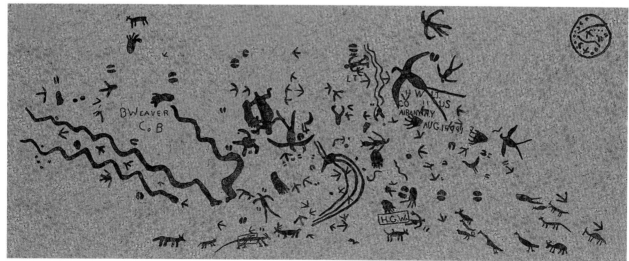

Little Indian Rock in the Susquehanna River, Lancaster County.

past. When they want to learn about the past, all they need to do is ask their parents or grandparents.

Some archaeologists focus on the broad issues of cultural evolution such as the development of agriculture or city life. What are the basic technological, behavioral, and environmental requirements for these major developments? Other archaeologists focus on the individual's role or changes in the relationship between men and women in the development of agriculture. These represent very different descriptions of the same event. Actually these approaches complement each other and the different types of descriptions result in a more detailed analysis and understanding.

Archaeologists Study Time

Archaeologists study how and why cultures change over time. This is done by analyzing artifacts. Artifacts are the physical remains of human activity such as pottery, spearpoints, plant and animal remains, and even dwellings. Archaeologists generally divide time into the historic period and the prehistoric period, even though they are continuous. Prehistory is the period of time before a culture acquired a written language. *Historical archaeology* is the archaeology of people who have a written language or have been documented by a written record. Historical archaeology includes the archaeology of the Mayans, Rome, William Penn's country estate, Fort Pitt in Pittsburgh, and the first oil wells in Crawford County. However, for each of these cultures, archaeology plays a different role. Much of the Mayan writing only applies to the wealthy or religious class and archaeology can contribute greatly to our understanding of the rest of the culture. In contrast, the written record is extensive concerning the world's first

PHOTO BY TED WALKE

Little Indian Rock may have been the location where Native Americans documented their culture using symbols we can no longer interpret.

successful oil well, sunk by Edwin L. Drake at Titusville, Venango County, Pennsylvania, in August 1859. However, there is still much to be learned because the written record reflects a biased opinion.

In the United States, much historical archaeology has been conducted at early colonial period sites such as Williamsburg, Virginia, and Pennsbury Manor, Independence Hall, and Valley Forge in Pennsylvania. This archaeology has added significantly to the understanding of the founding of our country. It provides us with the material remains of our national and cultural heritage. However, a common question concerning historical archaeology is, "What can archaeology tell us about our own culture that we do not know through the written record?" The answer is "plenty."

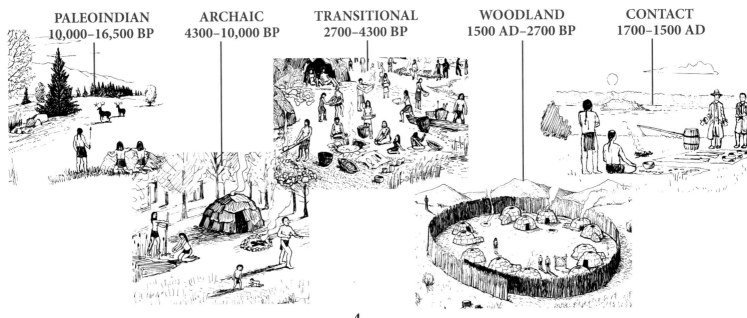

PALEOINDIAN	ARCHAIC	TRANSITIONAL	WOODLAND	CONTACT
10,000–16,500 BP	4300–10,000 BP	2700–4300 BP	1500 AD–2700 BP	1700–1500 AD

Archaeologists working at Valley Forge have improved our understanding of the lives of Revolutionary War soldiers.

The Walking Purchase treaty between William Penn and the Delaware Indian tribe dating to 1686 (below). The Indian reading of the agreement and that of the English were quite different. The Indians expected the land to be measured by a casual walk lasting a day and a half with their old friend William Penn. In 1737, William's son Thomas Penn used trained runners to measure the land. He acquired an area along the Delaware and Lehigh Rivers 65 miles long, encompassing the present-day cities of Easton, Bethlehem, and Allentown. The Delaware felt cheated and joined the French in the French and Indian War.

Who Tells the Story?

Our culture documents people and events through books, newspapers, television, and the Internet, but there is often a distinct difference between what has occurred and what is written. Modern media frequently puts a "spin" on a story that reflects an editorial bias. Historians writing hundreds of years ago were no different; they described the world around them from their own point of view. Historical archaeology helps determine the difference between an individual's personal view and what really happened. It provides a more objective view of historic events than the written record alone. As we go back in time, there is less documentation about cultures; moreover, it frequently applies only to the most prominent members of a society. Archaeology helps enhance our understanding of the average person and marginalized groups who are frequently not represented in the written record.

There are times when the written record is inadequate for telling the story about a culture. For example, Mayan hieroglyphics have limited value for understanding the common working class. Other cultures writing on behalf of another people, such as English and French traders describing the Native Americans of Pennsylvania, do not sufficiently record their complete history. The time period when Europeans were documenting Native Americans is called the Contact, or the Proto-Historic, period. The European view of Native American culture was very biased because many considered Native Americans to be "savages." Archaeology is extremely important in examining this period because European descriptions are inaccurate.

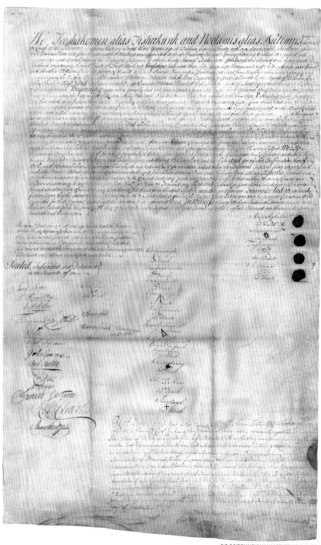

Historical and Archaeological Evidence: What's the Difference?

Stephen G. Warfel, Senior Curator of Archaeology (retired), The State Museum of Pennsylvania

Stephen G. Warfel

History and archaeology are gateways to the past. Each enables us to understand and connect with people who lived before us. In our quest to discover and understand the nature of life in earlier times, we must remember that both sources of information have strengths and weaknesses. The historic record, comprised of items such as legal documents, diaries, letters, maps, paintings, photographs, and oral histories, is intentional. These sources are written or produced for a purpose. They often capture incredible detail about former people, events, and activities, but are sometimes tainted by the subjectivity of their authors and subjects. Moreover, because literacy, land ownership, and the right to hold public office were reserved for affluent white males in colonial America, large segments of society, such as women, minorities, and poor white men, were underregistered or simply not recorded. Consequently, the historic record of the past may be inaccurate or incomplete.

The archaeological record, on the other hand, is an unintentional history of past behavior and events. It consists of refuse—bits and pieces of objects made and/or used by people and eventually discarded. Those who disposed of their trash long ago never intended for it to be found, analyzed, or understood. Because all humans generate refuse, archaeological evidence is often considered to be "democratic" or "fair." Yet, not all materials survive the ravages of time. As a result, interpretations based on artifacts alone may be biased by what has or has not been preserved and found.

Obviously, the best way to learn about people who lived during the period of recorded history is to combine the results of historic and archaeological research. Where the testimony of sources agrees, confirmation or "truth" can be assumed. Where disagreement occurs, we are forced to ask why, prompting reevaluation of existing evidence and renewed search. Importantly, because historical and archaeological data are independent, that is they do not rely on one another, one body of evidence can be used to test the other.

Research conducted between 1993 and 2003 by The State Museum of Pennsylvania at Ephrata Cloister, an early religious commune in Ephrata, Lancaster County, clearly illustrates distinctions made between the historic and archaeological records. (Ephrata Cloister is administered by the Pennsylvania Historical and Museum Commission as one of twenty-five historic sites and museums along the Pennsylvania Trails of History®.) Ephrata community histories, including one written by two members in 1786, indicate members practiced self-denial with hopes of achieving union with God. Ownership of personal property was "declared sinful." However, archaeological investigations unearthed nearly thirty pieces of earthenware pottery, bearing personal initials scratched into their fired clay bases. Some members obviously felt the need to identify and mark objects as personal possessions.

Other artifact types, such as clay smoking pipe pieces and liquor bottle fragments, support documentary claims. Neither artifact type was found in as great a quantity as normally observed on sites of the same time period. Apparently many members did abstain from the use of tobacco and alcohol.

When historical and archaeological evidence are combined, we gain a more honest understanding of life at Ephrata Cloister. Although peculiar, the men and women who participated in the Ephrata experiment were quite ordinary. Because of human weaknesses, members did not always succeed in conducting their behavior according to rigid standards established for the community. This conclusion exists in stark contrast to romanticized views of life recorded by community members and historians alike.

Students map the remains of a 1745 cellar at Ephrata Cloister, Lancaster County.

*Edward Weber & Co. (American, fl. 1835-1851), Detail, **Broadside of William Penn's Treaty** c. 1840-1850, lithograph with watercolor. If Indians had painted this picture, would they have portrayed themselves in this manner?*

It's All About Time

Prehistory applies to 98 percent of the span of human existence, and archaeology is the only method for understanding cultural behavior during this time. To describe periods of time, archaeologists use the terms BP, Before the Present; BC, Before Christ; AD, After Christ (anno Domini); BCE, Before the Common Era; and CE, Common Era. Until 1950, there were few methods to accurately date archaeological sites; much of it was based on events from the Old World, especially changing pottery styles in Egypt. (The term Old World is used to identify Europe, Asia, and Africa before the discovery of the North and South America continents. The term New World is used to refer to North and South America after European explorations.) Dates were expressed as BC and AD in relation to the Christian calendar and specifically a well-documented event, the life of Christ. With the advent of radiocarbon dating, dates were expressed in years before the present. Since the present is always changing, archaeologists have agreed that BP actually means years before 1950. Over the years, there has been a gradual change to the use of the phrase "years before the present," but many archaeologists continue to use BC and AD. In an effort to reduce the ethnic and religious connotations of BC and AD, the use of BCE and CE have been adopted by a number of professional journals. Archaeologists believe this additional set of abbreviations confuses the public and are quick to point out that we are still using the Christian calendar. In this publication, we use BP.

This publication covers the archaeology of Native Americans in Pennsylvania, most of which occurred during prehistoric times. Archaeologists have divided Native American culture history in Pennsylvania into five major time periods:

- **Paleoindian**   10,000–16,500 BP
- **Archaic**   4300–10,000 BP
- **Transitional**   2700–4300 BP
- **Woodland**   1550 AD–2700 BP
- **Contact**   1550–1750 AD

The Archaic and the Woodland periods are further divided into Early, Middle, and Late periods. In the Ohio drainage, the Late Woodland period is brief and is followed by the Late Prehistoric period. All of these period designations generally correspond to changes in distinctive tools and other kinds of artifacts and the way food was gathered. Archaeologists assume there were also changes in the way people organized their families, their bands or tribes, and their religions. But archaeologists frequently cannot document all of the specific changes.

How Old is It?

Determining the age of artifacts and archaeological sites is essential to the study of archaeology. There are several ways that this can be done and the methods are becoming increasingly sophisticated and accurate. The simplest and most common method is based on *stratigraphy*, the layering of soils and rock in the earth.

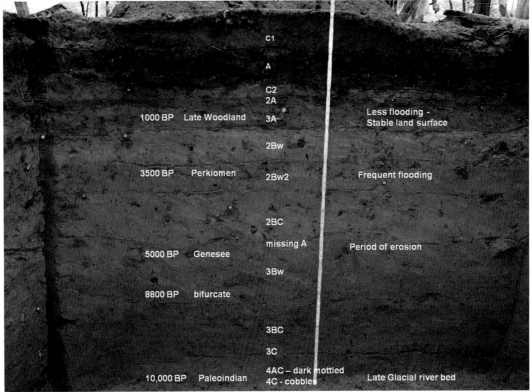

	C1	
	A	
	C2	
	2A	
1000 BP Late Woodland	3A	Less flooding - Stable land surface
	2Bw	
3500 BP Perkiomen	2Bw2	Frequent flooding
	2BC	
	missing A	Period of erosion
5000 BP Genesee	3Bw	
8800 BP bifurcate		
	3BC	
	3C	
10,000 BP Paleoindian	4AC – dark mottled 4C - cobbles	Late Glacial river bed

The layering of soils (stratigraphic profile) at the Nesquehoning site, Carbon County. The soil color and texture help archaeologists determine the environment under which the soils were deposited by floodwaters.

The layers of soil at the top of an archaeological site are more recent than those below. This is called stratigraphic dating, which is a relative form of dating. Archaeologists do not know the number of years before the present and realize deeply buried artifacts do not always signify a great age. They do, however, understand that one artifact or layer of artifacts is deeper and older than those above it.

In Pennsylvania, there has been an intensive analysis of the stratigraphy of archaeological sites over the past twenty years and significant patterns have been identified. Much of this work has been conducted by geomorphologists. These scientists study soil stratigraphy and the formation of landforms (topographic features) such as floodplains, terraces, sand dunes, wetlands, and streams. Except for the area covered by the glaciers in the northern part of the Commonwealth, the topography (ridges and valleys) and ground surface have not changed significantly since humans arrived over fifteen thousand years ago. Contrary to popular belief, soil is not naturally developing and covering artifacts. For soil to cover artifacts, it must be transported from another location. Most artifacts that were dropped one thousand or even ten thousand years ago are lying close to where they fell, at or near the present ground surface. Although separated by thousands of years of time, little soil has developed to bury and separate artifacts of great differences in age. Modern agricultural practices, specifically plowing, have mixed these artifacts together

and covered them with several inches of soil, but it has not moved them a significant horizontal distance.

In the eastern United States, there are several ways that artifacts can be buried by natural processes. Artifacts dropped by Native Americans next to a hill can be covered by soil slowly washing down the slope, which is referred to as *colluvium*. Artifacts in areas with little vegetation and high winds can be buried by wind-blown deposits, or what are called *aeolian deposits*. The most common mechanism for burying artifacts is soil carried by rivers, known as *alluvial deposits*. With a heavy rain, a stream or river floods or overflows its banks. During this process, it carries soil that is deposited in layers on the surrounding land.

Wherever there are floodwaters and people dropping artifacts, archaeological sites are being buried. As each culture drops artifacts, they are buried and separated by a layer of soil from subsequent or later artifacts. Archaeologists at a site in Perry County along the Susquehanna River were able to document more than ten thousand years of visits by humans to a depth of twelve feet and more. Archaeological sites containing layers of buried artifacts are said to be *stratified*. These are significant sites because they contain the archaeological history or cultural sequence of a region. At these sites the environmental characteristics are the same and this allows for the easy comparison of cultures.

Dating based on stratigraphy is called relative dating because the exact age in years from the present is not known. Absolute dating methods result in a date measured in years before the present. The most common type of absolute dating in Pennsylvania is carbon 14 (c-14) or radiocarbon dating (or ^{14}C yr BP). The ability to accurately date artifacts before the present was an enormous advance for archaeological research. Discovered in 1949 by Willard Libby and J. R. Arnold, it represented the first time that archaeological materials could be accurately dated in the eastern United States. Radiocarbon dating must be used on organic materials (plants or animals) and it can be used on materials that are up to approximately fifty thousand years old. It can be used to date human existence in the New World.

Radiocarbon dating represented the first time that prehistoric archaeological materials could be accurately dated in much of the world. It was a spectacular discovery and it revolutionized archaeology. With refinements to the method, especially over the past twenty years, archaeologists can now determine the age of objects in years Before the Present (BP) and accurately determine the age of significant events such as the beginning of agriculture or the entrance of humans into the New World. They can compare cultural sequences in widely separated regions of the world and, most significantly, measure the rates of cultural change.

What is Geoarchaeology? Frank Vento, Ph.D., Clarion University of Pennsylvania

Geoarchaeology is a multidisciplinary approach that uses geologic principles and geologic field and laboratory methods to aid in the reconstruction of an archaeological site and determines how it was formed, including the climatic conditions under which it was created. This helps archaeologists determine past environments, the age of the sites, and the appropriate methods of excavation. Geoarchaeological investigations at archaeological sites provide a wide range of both field-based and postfield analyses.

An important aspect of archaeological excavations is the detailed mapping of the sediment layers, or *soil horizons*. Soil is the unconsolidated material that is situated above bedrock. Soil consists of particles characterized by size: sand (2.00mm–0.05mm), silt (0.05mm–0.002mm), and clay (less than 0.0002mm). Typically, the layering of the soil, or the *soil profile*, at an archaeological site is described based on the walls of the excavation unit, but drilling and even backhoe trenches can be used to expose a soil profile. Geoarchaeologists generally recognize three major layers in a soil profile, which are identified as the A, B, and C horizons. The C horizon is the layer at the bottom from which the soil originally formed, typically during the chemical and physical breakdown (or weathering) of the bedrock. The A horizon, or uppermost layer, is a relatively stable layer that contains a high concentration of organic material. The B horizon is a mineral zone that in the Middle Atlantic region is typically brown, tan, or reddish in color. B horizons form under A horizons. They are zones where fine particles of clay and other minerals gradually move down from the upper A horizon.

In alluvial settings, B horizons are typically thick and represent long periods of frequent small floods. A horizons usually represent longer time periods when the frequency of flooding is low and organic material (in the form of dead vegetation) is allowed to accumulate on the surface. A horizons can become buried or washed away. For example,

Frank Vento   PHOTO BY KURT W. CARR

during a flood, large amounts of sediments may be deposited in the floodplain. This process could bury the existing A horizon and allow the formation of a new A horizon to begin. The rate of flooding could also increase and organic material would not be able to accumulate as the profile thickens and, consequently, no A horizon would form. B horizons evolve over time and become more developed. There is a change in the color and structure of B horizons and geomorphologists use these factors to determine the ages of soils and the artifacts they contain. In some cases, the A horizon, dark in color because of its high organic matter content, is underlain by a lighter (gray to white) horizon designated as the E horizon. The E horizon typically forms where there has been intensive leaching (eluviations) of the iron and aluminum from carbonic and humic acids moving downward from the overlying rich organic A horizon. The E horizon is a postdepositional or diagenetic horizon. Understanding the depositional processes responsible for the emplacement of a site's sediment package or soil profile is critical in reconstructing how the site formed or changed over time. In geomorphological terms, archaeological sites can be divided into two categories: surface sites and buried or stratified sites. The stratigraphic profiles present at these two types of sites are often extremely different and pose various challenges to geoarchaeological investigations. *Surface sites* are typically situated in upland settings where little or no soil has been deposited. In this setting, the artifacts are essentially lying at the present ground surface in the A horizon. Artifacts that were dropped one hundred or ten thousand years ago are found together. Agricultural activity, such as plowing, may have pushed them to a depth of more than twelve inches, and tree roots and animal burrowing, called *bioturbation*, may also have contributed to the mixing. These soils are called residual soils because they formed from the in situ (or in place) weathering of bedrock. In residual soils, the profile is relatively simple and usually consists of A, B, and C horizons. This is by far the most common profile for archaeological sites in Pennsylvania.

Stratified sites are formed where sediment is being deposited. There are three processes: *alluvial deposition,* sediment deposited by water such as during floods; *aeolian deposition*, sediment deposited by wind; and *colluviums*, sediment and soil deposited by gravity or downslope movement. Alluvial deposition is the most common process that causes the burial of archaeological materials. Windblown sediments are sometimes found along the terraces of the Delaware and Susquehanna Rivers. Colluvial soils are frequently found at the bases of slopes. Stratified sites can be deep and the stratigraphy complex. Typically, stratified sites along the Susquehanna River measure more than twelve feet deep and are characterized by a series of stacked A and B horizons or often truncated B horizons where the A horizon has been washed away by later flooding. In many cases, the sequence of A and B horizons can be correlated with soil horizons at other sites both in a given drainage basin and in adjoining basins. These correlations reflect basinwide or regional flood events such as hurricanes. These can be used to reconstruct past climates and assign dates to cultural occupations.

This type of data might provide information that during the period 10,000 to 8000 BP, prehistoric occupation at the site was on a river floodplain while later occupations were in fine sands deposited by aeolian activity. This change in depositional processes may also reflect a change in climate. Geoarchaeologists are often involved in determining, through soil analysis and landform development, the paleoenvironments present during occupation of a site. A change in the rates of soil deposition may indicate changes in precipitation rates or vegetation cover.

Geoarchaeologists often employ the use of geophysical prospection—ground-penetrating radar, resistivity, and magnetometer—to identify buried archaeological features. These types of field studies can often reduce the amount of field work required by defining buried cultural features. This is especially useful at historic and classical sites where the buried features are often large walls or deep wells, which are more easily identified by geophysical methods than, for example, an isolated and buried prehistoric fire pit. Geoarchaeologists might also employ postfield analysis of the site's soils and sediments to provide information on its function. Geoarchaeological research can produce critical information, not only for understanding, but also for predicting the changing pattern of settlement and land use over time through paleoenvironmental reconstruction of past landscapes.

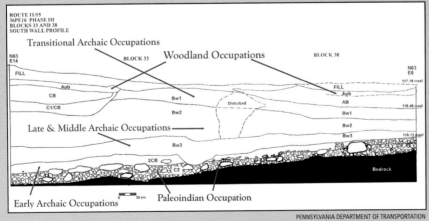

The soil profile at the Wallis site (3Pe16). The Wallis site is stratified and documents over 10,000 years of Native American camp sites.

PENNSYLVANIA DEPARTMENT OF TRANSPORTATION

How Carbon 14 Dating Works

Carbon 14, an isotope, is formed when rays from the sun bombard nitrogen molecules in the atmosphere. It acts like other elements, such as oxygen or iron, but it is radioactive and therefore unstable. It behaves similarly to the stable or nonradioactive form of carbon. All living things contain the stable form of carbon, carbon 12, and the unstable form of carbon, carbon 14. As long as plants and animals are living, they absorb carbon 14, thereby introducing it into the cells of the body. However, when an organism dies, no new carbon 14 is incorporated into the body. At the same time, the stable form of carbon remains unchanged in the body. Because carbon 14 is unstable, it returns over time to a stable form of nitrogen. In 5,730 years, one-half of the original amount of carbon 14 in an organism will revert to nitrogen, which is called the carbon 14 half-life. Through Willard F. Libby's 1949 discovery of carbon dating, the ratio of stable carbon to unstable carbon can be measured and a date can be calculated to determine the age of the carbon at the time of death. Essentially, this is how carbon dating works.

A drawback with c-14 dating is that it can only be used on organic material such as wood, bone, or shell, materials that were once parts of plants and organisms. It cannot be used to directly date stone spearpoints or pottery, which are by far the most common artifacts from prehistory that have survived. Archaeologists must date the organic materials directly associated with these non-organic artifacts. For example, scientists date the charcoal from the cooking hearth where the broken pot was found and not the pot itself.

A projectile point from the Central Builders site in Northumberland County was associated with charcoal from a cooking hearth that radiocarbon dated to 9165 + 210 BP. What does this mean? First, the University of Arizona performed the analysis and the sample number was 10053. The letters "BP" are an abbreviation for Before the Present. That is not entirely correct, however, because it actually means before the year 1950. Since the present is always changing, Libby decided to use a standard date of 1950 (the year after his discovery of the carbon 14 method) as the present. The date of the charcoal is 9,165 years before 1950, but that is not precisely accurate. The University of Arizona's laboratory took several measurements of the amount of carbon 14 and carbon 12 remaining in the sample and the number 9165 is the average of these measurements. This results in a plus or

PHMC THE STATE MUSEUM OF PENNSYLVANIA/PHOTO BY DON GILES

This spearpoint was found at a depth of more than eight feet and was associated with a hearth containing charcoal dated to 9165+/-210 BP.

minus factor, or standard deviation, produced by the laboratory calculations. By using one standard deviation, there is a 68 percent chance that the actual date falls between 9375 and 8955 BP. Usually, archaeologists are looking for a 95 percent rate of probability and that means the date is somewhere between 9580 and 8745 BP. This is a range of 835 years, but this plus or minus factor has been greatly reduced by refining the radiocarbon dating method.

In the past, carbon 14 dating required large samples of organic material, but a new process, accelerator mass spectrometry (AMS), allows for extremely small samples to be accurately dated. These materials include seeds or the carbonized organic remains of a burned meal adhering to the inside of a clay cooking pot. With the implementation of this new procedure, the plus or minus factor for the above date may be reduced to less than forty years.

Another problem with radiocarbon dating is contamination, specifically the accidental introduction of old or new carbon. Consequently a great deal of care must be used when collecting samples. Further, charcoal is light in weight and can be easily moved around by wind and water. The same flood deposits that cover artifacts at a stratified site along a river can bring in old charcoal eroded from a site or nonsite upstream. This results in a radiocarbon date that does not accurately reflect the date of the deposit. This type of contamination can be partially offset by obtaining multiple radiocarbon dates from a site. Radiocarbon dates are relatively inexpensive, approximately $300 for a standard date to more than $600 for an AMS date. When the charcoal is available, it is not uncommon for archaeologists

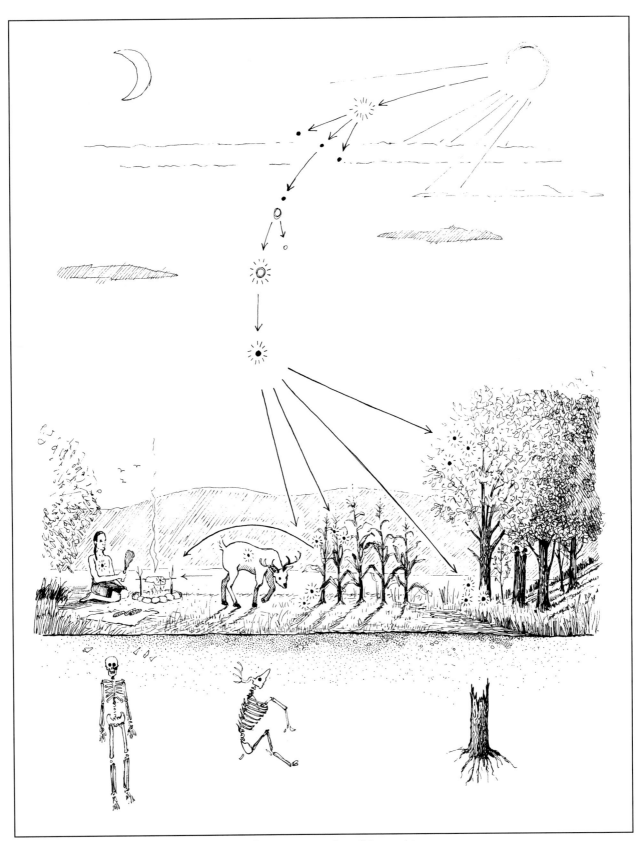

The incorporation of radiocarbon formation and its merging within all living things.

to obtain numerous dates from the same site or cooking hearth. Archaeological analysis is a process of identifying patterns and radiocarbon dates are a means to an end in reaching that part of the patterning. If all of the artifacts and stratigraphy point to a date of 5000 BP and the radiocarbon date is 20,000 BP, there is probably something wrong with the radiocarbon date.

Changes in the intensity of sunspot activity, the burning of fossil fuels, and the testing of nuclear weapons can potentially skew the accuracy of carbon 14 dating. This has resulted in two problems. First, dates less than three hundred years old are highly suspect as to their accuracy, and other comparative methods must be used to date artifacts from this period. Second, the amount of carbon 14 in the atmosphere has changed over time. This was discovered through dendrochronology, the sequencing and dating of tree rings. Using AMS to date individual tree rings, it has been discovered that the radiocarbon years do not exactly correlate with tree ring dates (or calendar dates). We know that tree rings in most climates are formed on an annual basis—one ring for each year. However, when a known tree ring sequence is dated using radiocarbon methods, the dates are not the same. For example, when calibrated for tree ring corrections, radiocarbon dates of around 3500 BP are shown to be several hundred years too old. Conversely, tree ring corrections applied to radiocarbon dates of 11,000 BP (11,000 14C yr BP) are nearly two thousand years too young. Formulas are being developed to convert radiocarbon years to calendar years but the system still requires greater refinement. In the meantime, archaeologists continue to employ both systems of calendar years (cal yr BP) and radio carbon years (14C yr BP). This most likely will be resolved in the next several years but presently it is confusing for both the professional archaeologist and the general public.

Archaeologist David Hurst Thomas contends "radiocarbon dating is the workhorse of archaeology." It produces reasonably accurate dates, to within a few decades, and it allows us to compare a variety of significant technological and cultural events.

Diagnostic Artifacts and Written Records

Radiocarbon dating has been used for more than sixty years. Many different types of artifacts have been dated and it has been found that certain artifact styles consistently have the same date. Modern cultures have distinctive styles of clothing, automobiles, and toys. Photographs and other images that are 150 years old can be dated by these distinctive items. From earlier times, stone spearpoints or pottery made by Native Americans can be especially distinctive in their shape and are also used to date artifacts to specific time periods. This allows archaeologists to use these distinctive artifact styles to date sites when no organic material is available for radiocarbon dates. Artifacts that can be dated in this fashion are called *diagnostic artifacts*. It is a quick and easy way of dating sites, but it is not always foolproof. Unfortunately, many spearpoint styles were in use for thousands of years and are not of much help in determining the age of a site. For the Woodland period, beginning three thousand years ago in Pennsylvania, pottery decoration provides information on a site's age. Pottery styles are sensitive to cultural changes and many styles have been well dated. Pottery is generally a better indicator of age than projectile points.

Historic sites, or sites for which written records exist, are most frequently dated using artifacts. The burning of fossil fuels and nuclear testing has adversely affected the radiocarbon dating process and does not work well for recent times. Historic sites are most frequently dated using distinctive artifacts such as pottery styles. Manufacturing techniques are another method for dating common materials such as nails, bottles, firearms, and other artifacts that have obviously evolved over the historic period. There is extensive literature that provides information on how manufacturing techniques changed, and artifacts can be very precisely dated using this information rather than radiocarbon dating. For example, changes in ceramics included the type of paste and decoration as certain styles gained or lost popularity. These techniques generally allow for a more precise dating of historic artifacts than prehistoric artifacts.

Projectile Point Types and Pottery Types: How are They Developed and What do They Tell Us?

The goal of artifact analysis is to identify patterns and solve research problems. When archaeologists return from a field excavation of a prehistoric Native American site, they generally return with hundreds, often thousands of artifacts. These artifacts need to be described so they can be compared to artifacts from other sites and so other archaeologists can best understand what was found at this site. Because it is not practical to describe every artifact in detail, they are usually organized by common characteristics and described in groups. For example, they may be grouped by material types such as stone, bone, and pottery. There may be additional subgroups within these groups. The stone artifacts might be divided into specific lithic material types such as argillite, chert, jasper, quartz, quartzite, and metarhyolite, or separated into tools and simple flakes from the production of tools.

A great deal of experimentation has been conducted with modern flint knappers, and we know that characteristics of the flakes can be used to generally identify different knapping techniques. The bulb of percussion is particularly important (see the sidebar on the making of stone tools on page 55). Flakes with thick bulbs of percussion and relatively few dorsal flake scars represent the early stages of making stone tools. Flakes with wide and relatively thin bulbs of percussion, many dorsal scars, and lipping on the striking platform represent the final stages of stone tool production. These two groups represent two different artifact types. In this case, the explanation for the differences between these two is related to stone tool technology. Most of the differences discussed in this book will be cultural and temporal rather than functional.

An *artifact type* is a set of attributes (or characteristics) that are diagnostic of a certain class of artifacts and serve to differentiate that class from all others of similar magnitude. The attributes used to define an artifact type reflect the rules of production concerning how the artifact should be made. It is assumed that when Native Americans (or any cultural group) made artifacts, they followed rules of production that were formally or informally learned. James Deetz defined the rules of production as the "mental template," the culturally determined idea concerning the shape of an artifact. Artifact types that are similar were created by a similar set of rules, or mental template, and may represent the same or a closely related culture. However, there are functional reasons for similarities in the artifact types and the mental template. Artifact types are not necessarily based on attributes that were important to the native; instead, attributes are chosen by the archaeologist to solve research problems.

Projectile points and pottery are the two most common artifact categories archaeologists use to define artifact types. These exhibit attributes that are likely to reflect cultural rather than functional differences. Projectile point types are defined based on attributes such as the shape of the base and blade; the type of notching, and the length, width, and thickness of the point. Early in the history of archaeological research, it was observed that during certain time periods there was only one projectile point type being used. Since these shapes were culturally determined, it was assumed that every culture had its own spearpoint style. Using stratified sites, projectile point sequences (the evolution of shapes over time) were developed by region, illustrating how types changed over time. These types were useful to archaeologists because they helped date sites when radiocarbon dating was not available. As archaeologists excavated more sites using better methods, however, it became apparent that during some time periods, several projectile point types were being made. In addition, archaeologists realized there existed a range of allowable variation within types. In some cases, the rules of production were specific and in some cases they were more general. Some projectile point types were used for relatively short periods of time and their shapes include a limited range of variation. Other types were made for thousands of years and are not useful as temporal markers.

The most detailed typologies used by archaeologists have been developed for pottery. Pottery is a flexible medium, allowing for many different designs to be executed in the soft clay. It is an additive technology in that design elements are added to the clay and if mistakes are made they can be corrected. Pottery is also believed to be a good reflection of the rules of production and the mental template. In the Middle Atlantic region, there are many attributes that are used to define pottery types, such as the shape of the pot, body treatment (cordmarked, netmarked, and smooth) and designs (incising and stamping) on the rim and collar. The additive technology of pottery is in contrast to the subtractive technology of stone tool technology. A block of stone is reduced in size and shaped to make a tool. If mistakes are made, they cannot be corrected. When they are discarded, they will become part of the archaeological record. This process increases the range of variation for stone artifacts and is less of a reflection of the rules of production and the mental template.

Although pottery has advantages over projectile point types for defining temporal and cultural differences, the complexity of pottery designs creates a different set of issues when attempting to explain differences between two or more types. These could be functional, temporal, or cultural. In addition, they could represent differences between social groups such as clans or families. Therefore, mapping the horizontal and vertical distribution of these types and identifying patterning would be very important in making the best interpretation.

A Summary of Indian Lifeways in Pennsylvania

CULTURAL PERIODS	DATES	PROJECTILE POINTS	OTHER CHARACTERISTICS
CONTACT Susquehannocks and other historically recorded tribes	1550–1750 AD		Native tools replaced by European equivalents, warfare for control of the fur trade, breakdown and dispersal of native populations.
LATE WOODLAND	900–1550 AD		Great variety of pottery shapes and decorations, numerous and elaborate pipe forms, celts, variety of bone tools, bows and arrows, stone hoes, agriculture, large stockaded villages, cemeteries, tribal social organization.
MIDDLE WOODLAND Hopewell	1100–2100 BP		Pottery, celts, pipes, gorgets, trade systems, a few burial mounds in western Pennsylvania, some year-round villages.
EARLY WOODLAND Adena	2100–2700 BP		Earliest ceramic vessels, gorgets, $^3/_4$–grooved axes, earliest smoking pipes, trade, some burial ceremonialism, semipermanent villages.
TRANSITIONAL	2700–4300 BP		Soapstone bowls, stone picks for working soapstone, broadspears worked into a variety of hafted tools, lithic exchange systems, food gathering emphasized major river systems.
ARCHAIC	4300–10,000 BP		Full– and $^3/_4$–grooved axes, adzes, atlatl (spear-thrower weights), mullers, pestles, mortars for grinding seeds and nuts, stone drills, relatively small areas were needed for food gathering.
PALEOINDIAN	10,000–16,500 BP		High–quality stone used for making tools, small scrapers for working hides, gravers for drilling or engraving bone, knives, nomadic big game hunters in a glacial environment who exploited caribou and elk.

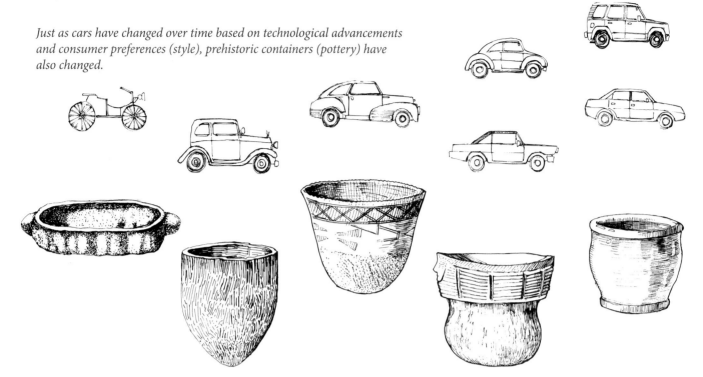

Just as cars have changed over time based on technological advancements and consumer preferences (style), prehistoric containers (pottery) have also changed.

Archaeological Data: Artifacts, Features, and Ecofacts

The basic data of archaeologists—what they primarily deal with—are artifacts, features, ecofacts (environmental evidence), and sites. Although they use documents to reconstruct the past, most of their data comes from artifacts. *Artifacts* are the material remains of human behavior. They include Native American stone arrowheads, clay cooking and storage vessels, and bone sewing needles, but also more recent objects such as medicine bottles, belt buckles, and children's toys. They also include broken pieces of window glass, scraps of bone, and the chips of stone from making tools. Usually these objects are broken (archaeologists have been cited as studying other people's garbage). Artifacts can be used to date archaeological sites, but they also reveal much about activities that occurred at these locations. Sites characterized by spearpoints, knives, and hide scrapers probably functioned as hunting camps. Sites with cooking hearths and seed-grinding stones most likely operated as plant food processing sites. Sites with houses, cooking hearths, spearpoints, grinding stones, and cooking and storage pots may have served as base camps or villages.

Some types of artifacts survive longer than others. Artifacts can be divided into two groups based on their material: organic and inorganic. *Organic artifacts*, such as leather, paper, basketry, wood, bone, antler, and teeth are made from materials that once contained living elements. In most of North America, these materials decay quickly and are rarely preserved in the archaeolog-

ical record. *Inorganic artifacts*—stone, glass, clay ceramics, and metals—are the most commonly found materials in the archaeological record. Under normal conditions, stone, clay, and glass artifacts survive indefinitely. Many types of metals also survive for long periods, with the exception of iron and steel, which oxidize or rust and return to their original elements.

Organic artifacts have been preserved under extraordinary conditions, particularly extreme drying or cold. The dry deserts of Egypt allow for the preservation of wooden artifacts and basketry and contribute to the complete preservation of human remains in the form of the famous Egyptian mummies. The same is true in the American Southwest where baskets, sandals, and bows and arrows are commonly found. Extreme cold has similar results, and Inuit (Eskimo) artifacts, including human remains, have also been recovered completely preserved. These environments are rare in the eastern United States and practically nonexistent in Pennsylvania. There are few organic artifacts in Pennsylvania that are more than one thousand years old. If organic artifacts are partially burned, they will be preserved longer. Rock shelters and caves frequently preserve organic artifacts by keeping them dry. Two sites in Pennsylvania—the Meadowcroft Rockshelter in Washington County and the Sheep Rock Shelter in Huntingdon County—have large quantities of preserved bone and also basketry, clothing, and wooden artifacts such as a canoe paddle.

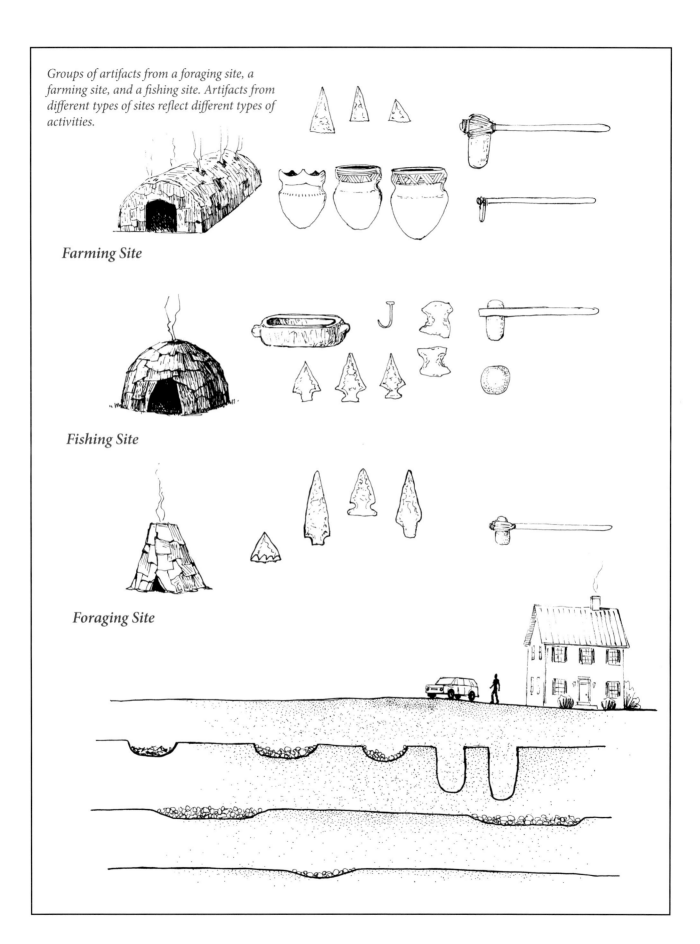

Groups of artifacts from a foraging site, a farming site, and a fishing site. Artifacts from different types of sites reflect different types of activities.

Farming Site

Fishing Site

Foraging Site

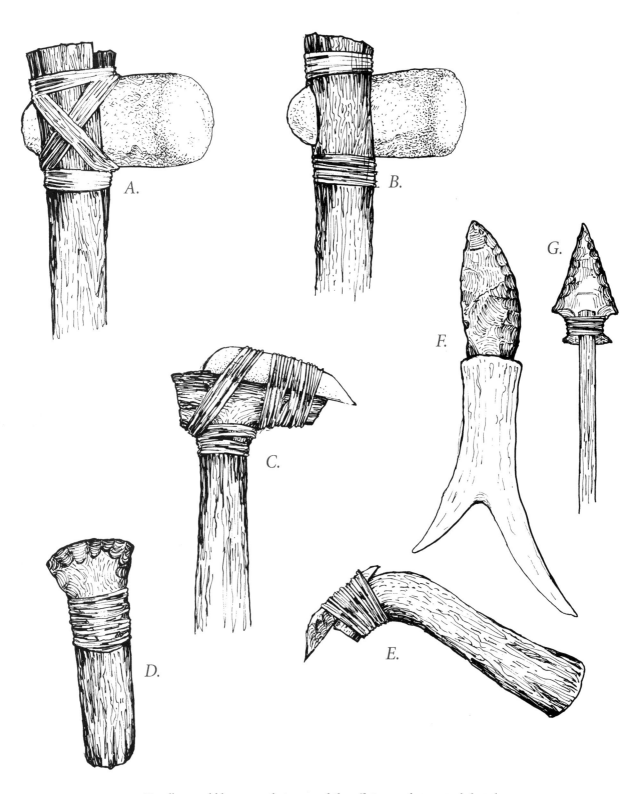

Handles would have greatly increased the efficiency of stone tools but they are rarely preserved in the archaeological record. A. Hafted grooved axe for woodworking. B. Hafted celt for woodworking. C. Hafted scraper for the final cleaning of hides. D. Hafted adze for woodworking. E. Hafted scraper for the initial cleaning of hides. F. Hafted knife. G. Hafted spearpoint.

Charred basketry from Meadowcroft Rockshelter, Washington County.

Braided bark and cordage from Sheep Rock Shelter.

Archaeologists also study *features*. Archaeological features are caused by human behavior but they cannot be removed from the field. They include wells, privies, fire hearths, garbage pits, burials, and artifact clusters. Features are important for the relationships among the artifacts they contain. Features are frequently formed when holes are dug in the ground and the dark topsoil is mixed with the light subsoil. Many features are similar to sealed time capsules; they contain a collection of artifacts deposited over a relatively short time period and they represent the same activity.

The so-called trash pits that are so common at Native American sites are a remarkable source of data. The organic material and charcoal originally placed in these features frequently alters the soil chemistry, resulting in better organic preservation than the surrounding soils. They typically contain food remains, broken tools used to process food, and broken pots in which food was cooked. Since these features are rich in data, special techniques are used to recover as many remains as possible.

Water screening is a process by which soil is placed on a very fine meshed screen—about the size of a window screen—and washed away with water. Small artifacts such as shell beads, small chips from stone tool production, and animal bones can be collected in this manner. *Flotation*, ideally used in connection with water screening, is a technique used to collect seeds and nut fragments that have been partially burned. There are a variety of devices and chemicals used to separate the charred remains from the soil but they are based on the principle that soil sinks and the carbonized remains float. This technique has been instrumental in recovering tremendous amounts of data on prehistoric diets.

Post molds are yet another type of feature important at Native American sites. Posts or stakes were placed in the ground to support tents, dwellings, stockade walls, cooking structures, and drying racks. Post molds are created when a post is driven into the ground and the

The Marshall's Creek mastodon was preserved in a bog for nearly 12,000 years.

posts rot, or are pulled out and dark topsoil falls into the hole or the posts burn in place. They appear as dark stains or "dots" measuring between two and four inches in diameter in the soil. It is a matter of connecting these dots to identify the structures.

Archaeologists also study *ecofacts*, data which tells us about past environments. Preserved animal bones, plant remains, and even pollen spores enable archaeologists to begin painting a picture of past climatic conditions. Reconstructing the environment is important because it represents the stage on which cultures evolved. The greatest environmental change occurred at the end of the last Ice Age, ten thousand years ago, when temperatures rose an average of ten degrees. Since the Ice Age, there have been several changes in temperature and rainfall that significantly affected human culture. Unfortunately, organic remains are rarely preserved from that period. In Pennsylvania, the most common environments for finding ecofacts are caves, rock shelters, sinkholes, bogs, and swamps. Waterlogged artifacts buried in swamps and bogs are settings that do not contain oxygen but preserve organic materials by preventing insects from eating the remains. These settings are rare but extremely important. In some cases, they have preserved entire tree trunks and all types of plant remains that make it possible to reconstruct past environments. The bogs and lakes of northern Pennsylvania have preserved Ice Age animals. More than 85 percent of a mastodon skeleton was found in Marshall's Creek, Monroe County, in 1965, and is completely mounted and on exhibit at The State Museum of Pennsylvania in Harrisburg.

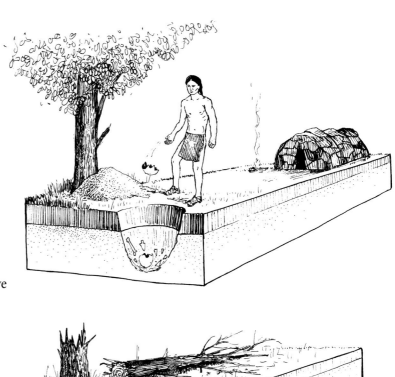

The formation of a prehistoric pit feature. Holes were dug by prehistoric peoples for a variety of reasons such as food storage or food preparation. However they were usually filled with surrounding dirt and discarded artifacts. Commonly called trash pits, they were not originally dug for that reason.

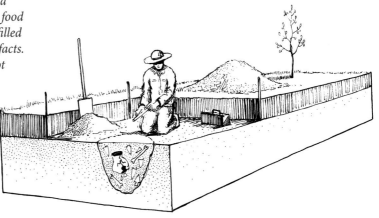

All About Flotation   Roger Moeller, Proprietor, Archaeological Services

The flotation process used by archaeologists is rather simple. The best flotation tub is a square galvanized and handled 12-gallon wash tub with the bottom replaced by 1/16–inch hardware cloth. Standing in flowing water with the tub submerged to within 3 inches of the rim, slowly pour soil into the tub while agitating the tub in a circular pattern. When all the finely grained soil has passed through the screen, skim the floating materials with a tea strainer and place them onto a drying pan. After the floating material has been skimmed, lift the tub out of the water and pour the heavy portion onto the same or separate drying pan. When the materials have dried, sort them into seeds, bones, lithics, charcoal, and other categories. Each different item is identified and quantified. This aspect may sound simple, but it is not.

Unfortunately these good intentions and hard work are more than likely to produce, at best, inconsistent truisms if the samples are too small, not intensively or systematically collected, or culturally biased. The keys to the flotation trap are that random samples produce random results, small samples produce small results, and culturally biased samples produce meaningless results. Stratigraphy must be obeyed, and holistic studies are the only viable solution. Flotation is of undeniable importance in determining the qualitative nature of data present. Without it, data interpretation is severely handicapped or, even worse, misleading. Excavations at one site prior to the use of flotation recovered only a small quantity of bone. The assumption was made that the acidic soil had long since destroyed all but the large, heavy bones. Flotation showed a variety of small mammals, fish, birds,

amphibians, and a much wider distribution of mussels, which had only been inferred previously. Even though they may represent only a small fraction of the total bone recovered by weight, the species they represent played a role in aboriginal subsistence and must be taken into account.

There is also the smaller debitage, which is indicative of close retouch or reworking of artifacts. Missing such data would distort the range of manufacturing and maintenance tasks undertaken. The identification of seed remains provides the necessary data for determining diet, seasonality, econiches exploited, reasons for the encampments, and possible techniques for food preparation and preservation. Without flotation very few seeds would ever be recovered during excavation. However, flotation should never be conducted solely to recover ecofacts for seasonality studies. There are too many other factors to be considered first to establish the integrity of the sampling context before one can use any of the information recovered.

The discarded soil matrix and control samples from seemingly noncultural zones should be analyzed as closely as the cultural samples. What seems intuitively obvious in the field when the context was positive should be quantified and described for those contexts of unknown integrity. What is not found can be as important as what is found. The recent contaminants (called background noise) can yield data crucial to interpreting the occupation. One's interpretation can be biased by the nature of the flotation sampling regime. To understand what should be done, one must begin by defining a meaningful cultural context, proceed with the appropriate equipment, conduct an intensive analysis of all materials found in the dried flotation samples, and interpret everything within a holistic framework.

Everything present means something in relation to everything else. Flotation sampling should be thought of in the same light as soil coring. There must be a precise level–by–level record of the soil strata that can be examined for color, texture, nature of inclusions, and cultural materials. Many samples are taken since there is no reason to assume that the strata or contexts are identical everywhere on the site. The precise location of the sample is mapped to facilitate its correlation with other observations, artifacts, and ecofacts to aid in the analysis and interpretation of the site.

Flotation is by far the most economical and efficient technique yet devised for the large-scale recovery of small-scale remains from archaeological deposits. At one site all the thousands of carbonized seeds, most of the identifiable bones, and a small percentage of the thousands of artifacts examined, counted, and classified were collected by flotation.

PHOTO BY ROGER MOELLER

Flotation and water screening are techniques for recovering very small artifacts. Organic materials reflecting prehistoric food remains float and are skimmed from the top.

Archaeological Data: Sites and Settlement Patterns—Where People Live

Archaeological sites are simply defined as concentrations of artifacts separated from other concentrations of artifacts. They exist where people once lived, worked, and played. They can be as small as a favorite fishing spot or as large as a historic city with thousands of inhabitants. Our own culture is represented by many sites. The cities of Philadelphia, Pittsburgh, and Erie are significant archaeological sites, as are their suburbs, farms in the country, convenience stores along highways, and vacation homes in the mountains. These sites are critical to understanding how humans behave and the nature of modern culture of Pennsylvania. The same is true for past cultures; we need to understand Native American village sites, fishing sites, hickory nut collecting sites, places where they gathered reeds for baskets and rock for stone tools, and locations where they buried their dead. These create a picture of how a culture functioned in the past. These sites are interrelated and illustrate how a culture adapts to its natural and cultural environment. The distribution of these sites across the landscape is called a *settlement pattern.*

Archaeologists study settlement patterns for two reasons. First, as the distribution of sites changes through time, archeologists can identify changes in how a culture exploited their environment or the adaptive strategy of a culture. For example, the change from hunting and gathering to farming is clearly reflected in a settlement pattern. Second, archaeologists have studied settlement patterns for a long time and have learned where certain types of sites can be found. Native American camps and village sites, for instance, are usually found along wide flat floodplains, especially where small streams feed into rivers. Their farming villages are found in areas of highly fertile soils. When hunting animals or foraging for seeds, nuts, berries, or roots, they sometimes left the floodplains and moved to swamps and bogs or to upland springs. These factors—floodplains, high-fertility soils, swamps, bogs, and springheads—are indicators of where prehistoric archaeological sites might be found in Pennsylvania. A different set of factors is used for historic sites such as convenient transportation routes and mineral resources. Put together, these factors are used to develop what archaeologists call predictive models. This is a tool that indicates the probability of finding an archaeological site in a given location (for example, along a proposed new highway location). Archaeologists use predictive models when they search for particular types of sites or sites that may be impacted by state or federal construction projects.

Archaeological sites are the only record of the prehistoric past, and they are essential to understanding the historic past. They are a nonrenewable resource that is being destroyed at an alarming rate. Recording archaeological sites helps to protect them. The Pennsylvania Historical and Museum Commission (PHMC) encourages the recording of archaeological site information on Pennsylvania Archaeological Site Survey (PASS) forms. Thousands of avocational and professional archaeologists have shared site locations with PHMC, resulting in more than twenty-two thousand sites having been recorded in PASS files. (Information for recording sites can be found at www. phmc.state.pa.us.) Once a form has been submitted to PHMC, a *PASS number* is assigned. This number can be written on artifacts from the site so that there will always be a record of where they were found. Recording sites with PHMC does not affect the landowner's rights and ability to develop or even destroy the site.

The PASS number, which is based on a nationwide system called the Smithsonian, or trinomial system, is divided into three parts. The first part is Pennsylvania's alphabetical position within all of the states before Alaska and Hawaii became states. The second part is the county designation, and the third part is the next number available in that county. For the PASS number 36Da20, 36 is the alphabetical position of Pennsylvania, Da. is the designation for Dauphin County, and 20 is the twentieth site recorded in the county. In addition, artifacts are marked with a catalog number, which is a code for its location within the site.

Artifacts are labeled with the archaeological site number—36Da20—and a catalog number specifying the location within the site. The ink is coated so it will not easily rub off.

The settlement pattern of a Native American band illustrating the different locations of campsites and the resources they were exploiting. The numbers of people or families at these sites changed based on the type of resources being exploited. The floodplain areas near the river typically contained large quantities of food resources. Upland areas generally contained fewer but sometimes seasonally concentrated resources.

How do we know where to dig?
Why do archaeologists dig square holes?

One of the most common questions asked of archaeologists is, "How do you know where to dig?"

The simple answer is that artifacts and archaeological sites are not randomly distributed across the landscape or within a single field. They follow patterns that reflect human preferences and behavior. People live where they can have access to food, water, transportation, and important resources. The nature of "important resources" may change through time and this will cause a change in settlement patterns. Depending on the type of site that is being researched, the settlement pattern directs where to excavate. Prior to agriculture, swamps and bogs were favorite campsites in Pennsylvania for collecting roots, berries, and waterfowl. With the development of agriculture, high-fertility soils became more important. Prehistoric settlement patterns reflect these preferences. When archaeologists are searching for archaeological sites, they look in areas where resources would have been plentiful. They spend much time mapping archaeological sites by different time periods to better understand how a culture lived and adapted to its environment based on where these sites are found.

Archaeologists interpret behavior by identifying cultural patterns—how artifacts and features are distributed within a site. To identify patterns, artifacts and features must be mapped. Archaeological field work is all about mapping. Another comment that archaeologists frequently hear is, "Your excavations are so neat and square." Archaeologists excavate based on a grid system, which is why they excavate in square holes called excavation units. For comparative purposes, the excavation units are

a standard size, usually measuring one meter, or 3 feet, on a side. Ideally, all artifacts are mapped using the grid system. Using a surveyor's transit or a total station (a computerized laser transit), the location of artifacts and features can easily and accurately be transferred from the ground to the graph paper. From these maps, the outline of house foundations, fire hearths, trash pits, and tent posts can be easily identified. The same is true for clusters of artifacts representing plant food processing and the butchering of animals. These maps are used to describe and interpret the activities that occurred at a site. More importantly, using electronic maps, the relationship between different types of artifacts and features can be electronically analyzed.

Although the goal is to map every artifact, this requires time-consuming and careful excavation. Most archaeologists map large artifacts—those measuring more than two inches—and once mapped, they scoop out soil containing the smaller artifacts and recover these by screening the soil through fine-mesh hardware cloth, usually 1/4 inch in diameter. This means that we do not know their exact location, but depending on the size of the excavation unit, we know to within one meter, or 5 feet, of where the artifact was dropped.

Stratified sites, where artifacts have been buried in multiple layers, are relatively unique and very

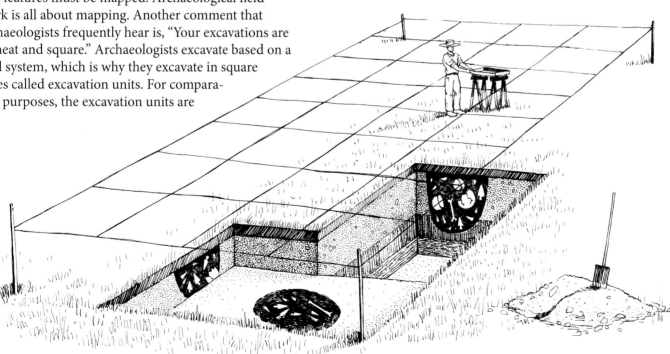

The grid is used for mapping the artifacts and features recovered from a site. They are mapped both vertically and horizontally.

important. Archaeologists describe these layers as living floors or occupation floors. They represent the ground surface on which people were living at the time of the occupation. They are surfaces where the artifacts have not moved since they were originally dropped hundreds or thousands of years ago. The patterns of artifacts and features have not been significantly altered and are closely correlated to prehistoric behavior. Mapping the three-dimensional location, or *provenience*, of artifacts is important. It is also important to map each cultural occupation or visit to the site separately, so individual visits or occupations

PHOTO BY JIM HERBSTRITT

A mapping frame is used to depict the location of artifacts and features within the grid.

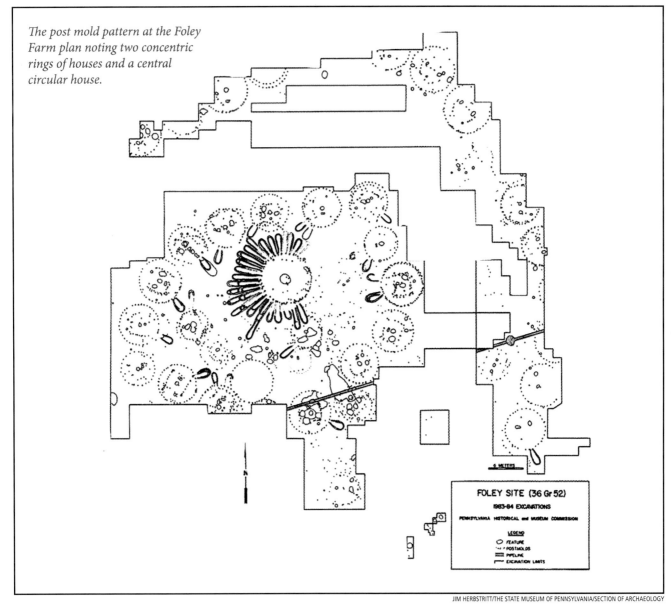

The post mold pattern at the Foley Farm plan noting two concentric rings of houses and a central circular house.

FOLEY SITE (36 Gr 52)

1983-84 EXCAVATIONS

PENNSYLVANIA HISTORICAL and MUSEUM COMMISSION

LEGEND
○ FEATURE
POSTMOLDS
PIPELINE
EXCAVATION LIMITS

JIM HERBSTRITT/THE STATE MUSEUM OF PENNSYLVANIA/SECTION OF ARCHAEOLOGY

A transit is used to set stakes for locating the grid. At Meadowcroft Rockshelter, a total station (computerized transit) was used to map artifacts, features, and the stratigraphy. The use of this instrument is much more accurate and faster than traditional methods.

Archaeologists use whatever tools are necessary to scientifically recover artifacts and features.

are not mixed. Frequently, the visits are not separated by much soil and the cultural layers are not visible. In these situations, the excavation units are excavated in arbitrary levels. The goal is to excavate single cultural visits so the levels are relatively thin, either 3 inches or 5 centimeters in thickness.

Tools archaeologists use to excavate or move soil range from small brushes and pointed bamboo sticks (better than dental picks because they are less likely to damage fragile artifacts) to bulldozers and backhoes. Included in this broad range are various sizes and shapes of trowels, shovels, hoes, a variety of mechanical and hand-operated screens, and an array of measuring tapes.

Archaeological Interpretation—Foraging and Farming Societies

For most of the time that Native Americans lived in Pennsylvania, they hunted, fished, and collected plant foods such as roots, seeds, nuts, and berries. This method of obtaining food is called *foraging*. Foragers lived in mobile family groups called *bands* consisting of grandparents, parents, and children. They were nomadic and moved their camps many times during the year. The camps were moved to the location of seasonally abundant foods such as hickory nuts, sunflowers, fish, or migrating caribou. Foragers camped at these locations until the resources were depleted and then they moved to a new food source. Sometimes, the resource would not support a large group and the band would divide into several smaller families. These different sites, involving the different-sized social groups, created the settlement patterns discussed above. The average band size was twenty-five individuals. The bands were made up of several individual nuclear families and easily reorganized into smaller groups (microbands; ten individuals) or larger groups (macrobands; fifty individuals). Band organization was very flexible, and this flexibility was the key to the success of foraging bands. They could organize their size to maximize their exploitation of resources.

Although Native Americans were growing squash in small gardens more than four thousand years ago, it was not until approximately one thousand years ago in Pennsylvania that corn, beans, and squash were the main source of food. It is often difficult for archaeologists to determine the specific foods people ate at an archaeological site because the remains of the meals are usually not preserved. Sometimes charred animal bones, freshwater mussel shells, or partially burned hickory shells are found at a site and it is assumed that these foods were eaten at many other sites during the same time period. To better understand how foragers lived, we also study what foragers ate in the historic past or eat today. Based on the foraging societies that anthropologists studied in the nineteenth and twentieth centuries, the major portion of their diet in temperate climates such as Pennsylvania is always from plant foods instead of hunted animals or fish. In fact, usually over 60 percent of their diet consisted of roots, nuts, seeds, and berries. These foods are generally easy to collect, seasonally abundant, and more easily preserved than animal protein. Usually they were collected by women. It is ironic that archaeologists spend as much time analyzing spearpoints, typically produced by men, but most foods were collected with wooden digging sticks used by women. The wooden digging sticks are rarely preserved in the archaeological record.

Archaeologists spend a lot of time studying foraging societies as they were recorded by early explorers and anthropologists. Understanding how foragers lived gives us the ability to add life to the inanimate artifacts from archaeological sites that are thousands of years old. It provides a better picture of their family organization, politics, and religious beliefs. There is a great deal of variation in these societies, but one common characteristic is that foragers are generally an egalitarian people. This means they usually believed people were equal and deserved equal treatment. There were hardly any differences in wealth or status. Everyone—men, women, and children—were considered equal. The basic social unit was the nuclear family—meaning they included a woman, a man, and their children. Nuclear families could operate independently from one another; sometimes the band was organized around a group of sisters or brothers, but this was quite flexible.

There were usually only two prominent social roles within a forager society, a headman and a shaman. Neither of these individuals received any benefits by holding this position, and the responsibility was frequently considered a burden. The headman was the leader or spokesperson of the band. He was not considered a chief, who gave orders to his people. He suggested and helped organize activities, but most of the decisions were a result of group consensus. The population was low in numbers, and everyone knew what to do and when to do it. There was no need to organize or control a large workforce. Although it is difficult to identify individual personalities in the archaeological record, archaeologists know there are individuals in band societies (and in all societies) who

are charismatic leaders or have strong personalities. These individuals most likely existed in the past and may have been important in developing and controlling trade, introducing new technologies, or accepting the domestication of plants. We can acknowledge their existence but identifying specific examples in the archaeological record is difficult.

The shaman was the spiritual leader of the band, and he or she also led the curing ceremonies. When an individual was sick, the shaman led the group in healing the individual. A person with a toothache would be in pain and the shaman would deal with that symptom using a variety of herbs and medicinal plants. But the toothache was believed to have a spiritual basis; the individual may have insulted an ancestor, rejected a lover, or acted in an inappropriate way, with which the shaman would also deal.

As populations grew, people became more dependent on cultivated plants and remained in one place for longer periods of time. There then became a need to organize larger groups in order to clear the fields for planting, weeding, and harvesting crops. While cultivated crops often denoted land ownership, the land was owned by the group, not individuals. In addition, it could not be bought or sold in the European sense. Living in the same place year-round with large numbers of people also required increased social controls. In some areas, this resulted in the development of what anthropologists call tribal organization. Tribes were organized by family groups, frequently all related through the male or female line. They were less

Band organization was very flexible and could change size from single nuclear families to macrobands consisting of many families. The size of the band was usually determined by the resources being exploited.

flexible in their organization. Tribal organization was also egalitarian and decisions were based on developing a consensus among the families. Just as in band organizations, there were usually only two prominent roles: the headman and the shaman. Native American tribes would have a member who was a chief, but this individual worked with a governing council and did not receive benefits from this position. The chief operated by developing a consensus among the people.

How many Indians lived in Pennsylvania during Prehistoric times?
Or, Understanding the Role of Population Density in Cultural Evolution

Why do cultures change and evolve?

Archaeologists are not completely certain of a specific answer but have learned the answer is complex. For foraging societies, climate change, inventions, and the introduction of new ideas or technologies from neighboring societies can result in cultural change. But what are the reasons for major changes, such as the adoption of agriculture, the move to cities, or the development of monumental architecture such as the pyramids? These all require more work than simply foraging for food. Why would humans go to such an effort?

Up until the 1950s, archaeologists believed that culture evolved in stages. For example, beginning with the simplest hunters and gatherers, these groups evolved into more advanced foragers who evolved into horticulturists who evolved into agriculturists who moved into cities and built large religious centers. The prime motivator in this sequence—the cause for the change—was what was seen as progress. Human culture was striving to improve, to become more technologically efficient.

Archaeologists now define culture as an adaptation to the environment. It is not necessarily improving or getting better, it is adapting to its surroundings. Climate, flora and fauna, technology, social organization, relations with neighboring groups, and history are all part of the adaptation.

Another variable that is not frequently discussed but is generally recognized as an important motivating factor in cultural change and cultural evolution is human population density. Some archaeologists believe population density is the most important variable in cultural evolution. As population density increases, humans are motivated to increase technological efficiency to extract more calories from the environment to feed more people. With increasing population density there are also changes in social organization and religious beliefs. The most striking example of the effects of increasing population density and cultural evolution is the addition of domesticated plants and farming to the adaptation. Traditional wisdom tells us farming allowed for an increase in population. In other words, farming came first and caused the population to increase. This was a relatively rapid event that has been called the agricultural revolution.

Some archaeologists argue that people were forced to use domesticated plants to feed a population that could no longer extract sufficient calories from the environment using a foraging subsistence system. In other words, large populations developed prior to the use of domesticated plants. In this scenario, as population density reached a point where simple foraging could no longer extract sufficient calories from the environment, changes in technology or hours spent foraging were used to increase calories. Eventually, however, these stopgap measures were insufficient and people began to supplement their diet with domesticated plants. As the population continued to increase additional domesticated foods were added to the diet and eventually a major percentage of the diet consisted of domesticated foods. In this case the development of agriculture was a relatively slow process.

Climate and the diffusion of ideas from other cultures were important and may have affected the speed of this process but increasing population was the most important variable. To prove that population growth is a prime cause in cultural evolution, we must be able to demonstrate that population density is increasing to a critical point prior to technological development—and herein lies the problem. How do we determine absolute population size or even relative population density prior to written records?

Formulas based on ethnographic studies can be used to determine the number of people living in a house based on floor space. It is a matter of measuring the amount of floor space in a village to determine the number of people living in a group, followed by calculating the number of people living in contemporary villages. There are problems with this method (see the Late Woodland village sidebar) but at least it will result in a rough approximation.

What do we do for the period before the time people lived in relatively permanent hamlets and villages? How do we determine the number of people living in a nomadic hunting and gathering camp, especially when they occupy several camps each year and the number of people occupying these camps changes based on available food resources? In Pennsylvania two thousand years ago, there are very few examples of houses that have survived the ravages of time so it is impossible to extend this method very far into the distant past.

Another method that archaeologists use to reconstruct prehistoric demographics is to count the number of archaeological sites per time period. Sites can be roughly dated in time based on projectile point types and pottery types.

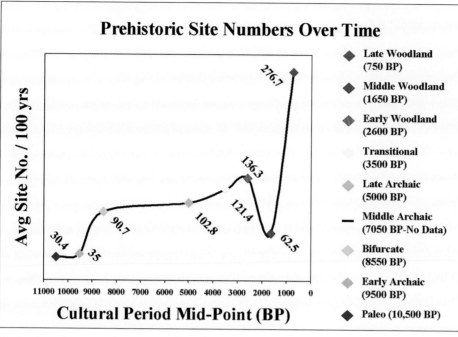

Prehistoric Site Numbers Over Time

Avg Site No. / 100 yrs

276.7

136.3

121.4

102.8

90.7

30.4

35

62.5

Cultural Period Mid-Point (BP)

11000 10000 9000 8000 7000 6000 5000 4000 3000 2000 1000 0

◆ **Late Woodland**
(750 BP)

◆ **Middle Woodland**
(1650 BP)

◆ **Early Woodland**
(2600 BP)

◇ **Transitional**
(3500 BP)

◆ **Late Archaic**
(5000 BP)

— **Middle Archaic**
(7050 BP-No Data)

◇ **Bifurcate**
(8550 BP)

◆ **Early Archaic**
(9500 BP)

◆ **Paleo (10,500 BP)**

Native American population curve based on the number of archaeological sites per time period for Pennsylvania.

The above graph begins with the number of Paleoindian sites based on the 304 sites that have produced fluted projectile points. The increase to the Early Archaic period (n=344 sites) is not great. With the emergence of the oak deciduous forest nine thousand years ago, there is a sharp increase in Middle Archaic sites and it is assumed that this correlates with a significant increase in human population. This is followed by four thousand years of steady growth adapting to a warm and wet deciduous forest. At about four thousand years ago, during the Late Archaic and Transitional periods, the rate begins to increase more rapidly. Between one thousand and two thousand years ago there appears to be a sharp population decline; however, most archaeologists believe this is not real. There are not many distinctive projectile point or pottery types for this time period (the Middle Woodland) so these numbers are artificially low. After this time, however, there is a markedly sharp rise in population during the Late Woodland period when agriculture was developing throughout much of Pennsylvania. The graph needs to be broken into finer time periods but clearly there is evidence for a population increase prior to the adoption of agriculture.

Many, if not most archaeologists, do not accept this method as a valid procedure for documenting population change. We know that some projectile point types cover a broad time range and some types crosscut other time periods. An example of this typological crosscutting is the triangular projectile point type. It is typically associated with the Late Woodland period where such objects were used as arrow points. However, triangular forms were also used during the Late Archaic period as spearpoints and there does not seem to be any way to determine the difference between these and their later counterparts. Therefore, the Late Archaic numbers are likely too low and the Late Woodland numbers are likely too high.

Population density is clearly an important variable in the equation of determining cultural change. However, until archaeologists develop better methods for determining prehistoric population density, the effects of this variable will largely remain speculative.

The Archaeologist's Educational Toolbox

People are usually attracted to the science of archaeology by their interests in other cultures, history, technology, ecology, and geology. Most enjoy working outdoors. In the United States, archaeology is taught in colleges and universities as a subfield of anthropology. To be an archaeologist requires a curiosity about the past. It is similar to reconstructing a jigsaw puzzle or a crime scene.

Although there are jobs that do not require a college degree, most archaeology technicians also have a BA degree in anthropology. This field provides graduates with a background in a variety of other, non-Western, cultures. This is helpful when describing archaeological cultures. Many archaeologists find a rewarding career working at excavations, in museums, or in research laboratories. Fieldwork requires some physical strength but mostly patience. Fieldwork frequently involves excavating small artifacts, such as broken stone tools and bottle glass, for hours at a time using small utensils such as dental picks and brushes. This fieldwork is usually conducted during the heat of summer amid biting insects. Fieldwork also requires scientific precision. All artifacts and features are mapped in three dimensions.

Exavating a charred sapling using a sharpened bamboo splint to reduce damage to the fragile artifact. The sapling is from a keyhole structure (storage structure) at the Quaker Hills Quarry site, 36La1100.

Although you may be working under adverse conditions, it is important to remember that someone in the past was sitting in the same spot, worrying about his or her next meal, whom they would marry, and whether their parents would approve. Training in the study of soils, surveying, and photography is also important for field technicians.

Processing artifacts in a laboratory is usually done under better environmental conditions, but it also requires patience, neatness, organization, and scientific precision. Each artifact must be carefully washed, marked, and assigned a catalog number identifying its location, or provenience, in an archaeological site. Most artifacts, such as stone tools and ceramics, are relatively durable, but bone, wood, shell, leather, and metal artifacts may be in poor condition. These need stabilization through a variety of conservation techniques to prevent further deterioration. Working in a research laboratory at a university or a museum, archaeologists frequently become specialized in the analysis and/or preservation of one type of artifact such as stone tools or ceramics.

One of the main jobs in a museum is managing collections and curating artifacts—that is, making sure that the artifacts do not continue to decay and organizing them so that they can be used by other researchers or placed on exhibit. Museum archaeologists are also usually involved in creating and updating exhibits. Finally, whether a researcher or curator, all archaeologists are involved in public outreach. In

North America, a huge amount of information has been excavated over the past several decades, and it is difficult to synthesize it all and translate technical reports into something useful and interesting to the public. Further, archaeological sites are being destroyed at an alarming rate, and archaeologists are constantly trying to preserve the information and the sites. Archaeologists frequently speak to civic and professional organizations, school groups, public agencies, and politicians to disseminate information and argue for the preservation of archaeological sites and data.

Many archaeologists specialize in different geographical regions; they frequently emphasize the study of either prehistoric cultures or historic cultures. Within these two broad time periods, they specialize in a region and/or a particular type of adaptation, such as hunting and gathering bands, agriculture societies, complex civilizations, and industrial sites, among others. Many spend their careers in the management and care of collections. However, some archaeologists engage in all of these endeavors.

As in most careers, the most interesting and financially rewarding ones require a MA degree or doctorate. These are the individuals who plan, execute, and report on archaeological research. They also supervise the curation of millions of artifacts and create and build new exhibit galleries.

Andrea Johnson Carr, archaeological lab assistant, PHMC

Field Tech: Life on the Trowel's Edge of Discovery Andrea Johnson Carr

The majority of jobs in archaeology are at the technician level. It may sound mundane, but technicians are the backbone of the profession. They are the ones literally in the trenches, surveying, excavating, and recording sites. The following are some of my thoughts and observations about my years as an archaeological technician.

Moving from project to project, a field archaeologist needs to adapt to different living and working conditions. Accommodations range from roughing it with sun showers and sleeping in a tent to extended stays in major hotels with a generous food stipend. Days can be physically grueling, and while you tend to acclimatize to the weather conditions quickly, it can be unforgiving at times. I've worked during record-breaking summer heat waves and major winter storms where we had to use industrial space heaters to keep the excavated dirt from freezing in the screens. All the common concerns of spending most of your day outdoors apply—from avoiding the local poisonous flora and fauna to taking preventative steps against sunburn, heat stroke, dehydration, hypothermia, pesky insects, and the occasional falling tree limb. One of my coworkers was knocked out by an acorn while surveying the woods around Dulles Airport in Virginia. Through it all, the opportunity to travel, to experience different cultures, to develop a deep sense of camaraderie with fellow crew members, to work outside in the fresh air, and to be on the frontline of archaeological discovery outweigh any temporary discomfort I've encountered over the years.

The soundtrack of my first archaeological experience was the tuba-driven bass of Banda music that oompahed from the open windows of the rebar-and-cement block-constructed houses of Xaltocan, Mexico, punctuated by the gobble of domestic turkeys, braying of a hobbled donkey, occasional snarls from a pack of dogs that roamed the village streets, and the chatter of neighborhood kids who made it part of their daily rounds to see what the archaeologists were finding in their backyards. Xaltocan is a small village in central Mexico, a man-made island of sand in the middle of an expansive salt flat, the dried bed of former Lake Xaltocan. The entire village is a stratified archaeological site built up over thousands of years of human occupation. By the end of my first field season, I was five feet down excavating microlayers from a dwelling floor where an Aztec woman may have prepared meals for her family with obsidian blades and grinding stones, or wove cotton textiles with ceramic spindle whorls to pay as tribute to the ancient capital of Tenochtitlan.

After graduating from college, I moved to Philadelphia and landed my first job as a professional archaeologist working on a potter's field that served as a cemetery for a late nineteenth-century almshouse and a burial ground for cadaver remains from one of the first medical teaching facilities in the city. Since then, I've worked on projects that have mainly focused on Native American sites encapsulated in flood deposits on the major waterways of Pennsylvania, including the Ohio, Susquehanna, and Delaware River drainages.

No matter where a project takes me, as a field archaeologist it's my job to observe and document pockets of intact and disturbed human activity as I dig or survey—one archaeofact at a time. This is a term one of my college professors used to describe the process of constructing the archaeological record from small pieces of data collected in the field. Put together, these clues can then be used to describe the bigger who, what, where, when, why, and how of a site. Comparing archaeofacts from several sites of the same time period and cultural affinity can then describe a more complex trend or pattern. The picture grows larger and larger, but it all begins with the systematic documentation of archaeofacts.

The value of an archaeofact is based entirely on the evidence used to support it, and in the world of archaeology, context can make or break the importance of any individual find. An archaeofact is not just an object or a type of soil, it is the detailed description of the relationship of the specific object or soil to its physical location on a site. An object found in a mixed or disturbed context, such as a plow zone or rodent burrow, does not tell us as much as an arrowhead or refuse pit found in intact or undisturbed soil. Likewise, if I had excavated a large area without carefully documenting and mapping the different deposited layers of soil; the origin, shape, and contents of pits, hearths, and post molds; and the exact location of artifacts, I would have destroyed the site's context. The research potential of undocumented archaeological material is just as limited as an arrowhead found in a rodent burrow.

I've had technical training in the methodology of archaeological excavation and in many different academic fields in order to understand what I am observing as I dig. I continue to learn and adjust to the particular challenges presented by each new project. Although it may seem tedious at times, understanding how and why documentation is important makes the effort worthwhile. You don't find a complete projectile point or a reconstructable pottery vessel everyday, but when you do, you value it as an archaeofact, not just as an object. Its story is much deeper than simply identifying an object's shape and the material from which it was made. Through its context, it can tell the story of the people who used it, their life, their actions, and potentially what the object meant to them. It is an insight into human history and, in some instances, a direct ancestral link to the past.

We all have a rich cultural history, whether or not it was recorded in books. It's my job to document leftover pockets of unrecorded history wherever they are found for future generations. The opportunities to work outdoors, to travel, and to make archaeological discoveries, one archaeofact at a time, are some of the many perks of my job.

Historic Preservation, Contract Archaeology, Compliance Archaeology, Applied Archaeology = Archaeology for the People

Archaeological sites are important. They are important as scientific data to analyze the past and predict the future. They are significant as evidence of a heritage that has no written history and assist in balancing biased historic records with objective cultural data. Following World War II, the United States experienced a period of intensive construction and infrastructure development. The interstate highway system, hydroelectric and flood control dams, and urban renewal projects caused the widespread destruction of archaeological sites. In 1966, the National Historic Preservation Act passed by Congress established a process for the consideration of archaeological resources prior to the beginning of federal construction projects. It also created the National Register of Historic Places.

The National Historic Preservation Act and subsequent legislation required federal agencies to identify historic resources—buildings, structures, archaeological sites, and objects—that may be affected by projects and to determine which of these are eligible for the National Register of Historic Places. There is much confusion about the purpose of the National Register. Although the name sounds important, the National Register is simply a planning tool for federal agencies to assist their staffs in designing and developing projects. It is a list of resources that require consideration prior to federally funded or licensed activities that may adversely affect them. Resources are eligible if they meet one of four criteria. Archaeological sites are generally eligible under Criterion D—they increase our understanding of past cultural behavior.

For those sites that are listed or eligible for listing, the federal agency is required to consider alternative designs to avoid impacting the eligible resources. The National Register does not prevent the destruction of archaeological sites; the law only requires the consideration of alternative designs. For locations that cannot be avoided, their destruction is usually mitigated through an archaeological excavation that recovers the most significant data from the site.

Until the passage of these preservation laws, universities and museums conducted most of the archaeological research in the United States. Gradually, after 1966, with the passage of similar state legislation, government agencies became the main sponsors of archaeological research. Currently, well more than 90 percent of all research in the country is conducted in preparation for state and federal construction projects. Some agencies have their own archaeologists, but they usually hire private consultants to do the actual work. The work is divided into three phases: finding sites or site survey is called Phase I survey; determining the eligibility of sites for the National Register of Historic Places is known as Phase II survey; and mitigating the destruction of a site and recovering the significant data is referred to as Phase III investigation.

The Pennsylvania Department of Transportation (PennDOT) needed to widen U.S. Route 11/15 along the Susquehanna River to increase safety and reduce fatalities caused by vehicular accidents. The existing road could be widened on either side of the right-of-way. Archaeological surveys were conducted for all of the alternatives and many archaeological sites deemed to be potentially eligible for the National Register were identified. PennDOT designed the new road to avoid most of these sites. For sites that could not be avoided, a data recovery excavation was conducted to retrieve the most significant information. Usually a sufficient sample of data (artifacts and features) can be recovered with less than 50 percent of the site being archaeologically excavated and the rest of the site destroyed during construction. The artifacts were analyzed and a report was produced. The artifacts are in the collections of The State Museum of Pennsylvania, Harrisburg, administered by the Pennsylvania Historical and Museum Commission, so they can be used by future researchers or placed on exhibit.

About two hundred of these investigations (Phase I, II, and III surveys) are conducted each year in Pennsylvania, and they result in some type of written archaeological report. The sites are being excavated because they contain data significant to our understanding of past cultural behavior. These excavations cost many thousands of dollars and they contain critical archaeological information. Because subsequent reports are written in lofty technical terms, produced in limited quantities, and hard to find, they are referred to as "gray literature." The irony of this process is that, although these projects are being financed by tax dollars, it may require many years for the citizens to receive the benefits of the research. And so what have we learned? One of the main purposes of this publication is to make this information available to the public.

When Are Archaeological Sites Eligible for the National Register of Historic Places?
Douglas W. McLearen, Chief, Division of Archaeology and Protection, Bureau for Historic Preservation, PHMC

The National Register of Historic Places, which is kept by the Department of the Interior, U.S. National Park Service (NPS), is described by the agency as "the official list of districts, sites, buildings, structures, and objects significant in American history, architecture, archeology, engineering, and culture. National Register properties have significance to the prehistory or history of their community, State, or the Nation."

Although the National Register is a list of significant properties, it is also a management tool. Under federal regulations that implement Section 106 of the National Historic Preservation Act, federal agencies are obligated to consider whether projects they fund, permit, or license will adversely affect any sites, buildings, districts, structures, and objects that are listed, or eligible for listing, in the National Register. The tool for evaluation for these properties is the set of National Register criteria. For a property to be eligible for the National Register, it must meet one or more of these criteria: association with an event or a pattern of events important in American prehistory or history; association with specific individuals who are considered important in our nation's past; importance for architecture, engineering, or artistic merit; and possess potential to yield important information. Under Criterion D, the property must provide information that is important to our understanding of American prehistory or history. In short, the criteria are event, person, design or construction, and information potential.

Information/data potential is the criterion by which most archaeological sites are judged—but this evaluation can't be made in a vacuum. To have information potential, a site must be able to help answer a set of questions asked of the data.

The site data may have potential to indicate whether the people who lived there did so on a permanent basis or only during certain seasons. A site with poorly dated key artifacts (so-called "diagnostic" artifacts) also contains carbonized wood and other organic material with good potential for radiocarbon dating that could confirm or better establish the time frame of these artifacts. These organic artifacts may also contribute to our understanding of the foods that were being eaten.

In order to have potential to answer questions posed, the site also must have "integrity." In other words, the site's physical conditions must not be so badly disturbed that the material remains have been moved about (or even partly removed) to the point that the patterns and associations once present cannot be identified and interpreted.

One example of a prehistoric site with good integrity would be one in which there are separated artifact clusters of the same time period, but the artifact types appear to have been used for different purposes from one cluster to another. For instance, one cluster may contain pottery and grinding stones indicating food preparation, while another may contain incomplete stone tools and lots of waste flakes from working the stone. A study of the patterns formed by these distinct artifact groups can establish how people used different parts of the site and what their work areas and community patterns looked like.

A site may possess what archaeologists refer to as *features.* These can include pits, cellars, hearths and cooking areas, evidence of structures, and so forth. What makes these features a valuable part of the data set is that they usually represent fixed points in time, without the mixing of unrelated materials from different time frames.

A site may be *stratified,* meaning that it has deposits of earlier time periods sealed off beneath later ones. In such cases, each layer can be analyzed independent of the overlying and underlying one. A study of a stratified site can help establish how the site use may have changed over time and how artifact styles, forms, and materials changed as well. This independent analysis by time period can only be successful if there is stratification and separation as opposed to deposits that have become collapsed and mixed so that the time periods cannot be pulled apart and observed separately.

The National Register is a management tool—a list of important sites that should not be destroyed without some consideration by federal agencies. Listing an archaeological site in the National Register does not guarantee the site will be protected or that federal agencies will be forced to redesign projects. Listing means that a federal agency will consider redesigning a project and they usually recover a sample of the significant data prior to destroying all or part of the site. The National Historic Preservation Act outlines a process for the management of archaeological sites, but it does not determine the outcome of this process.

Douglas W. McLearen

Chapter 2
Pennsylvania Prehistory

Environmental Episodes for Pennsylvania

EPISODES	¹⁴C yr BP	CLIMATIC CONDITIONS
Woodfordian substage of the Wisconsin glaciation	23,000	Beginning of last major glacial advance
Last Glacial Maximum	21,000	Lowest temperature/highest precipitation
LAST GLACIAL	16,500	
Bølling	12,600	Rapid warming
Older Dryas	12,000	Cold
Allerød	11,400	Warming
Younger Dryas	10,950	Sudden cold and dry
HOLOCENE		
Pre-Boreal	10,150	Sudden warming
Boreal	9200	Warm and dry
Atlantic	8490	Warm and moist
Sub-Boreal	5060	Principally warm and dry
Sub-Atlantic	2760	Warm and moist
Medieval Warming	1050 BP (AD 900)	Warm and moist
Little Ice Age	550 BP–150 BP (AD 1300–1800)	Cold and wet

Native American cultures developed in what is now Pennsylvania more than sixteen thousand years ago with their ancestors migrating to the New World during the Ice Age, or the Pleistocene epoch. By 1492, the ultimate test for Native Americans was coping with the sudden appearance of a culture totally unlike any they had ever encountered—Europeans. During the eighteenth century, most Native Americans in Pennsylvania were forced to relocate because of the overwhelming intrusion of Europeans. Between the period of the arrival and the dispersal of Native Americans, there is a fascinating story of an incredible variety of cultural developments and responses to changes in the natural and cultural environments. Much can be learned from this compelling story.

Influenced by cultural ecology, archaeologists in the 1960s began to examine prehistoric cultures from an ecological perspective—human culture as part of the environmental system. Using an elaboration on a definition for culture developed by American anthropologist Leslie White (1900–1975) in 1959, Lewis Binford (1931–2011), an influ-

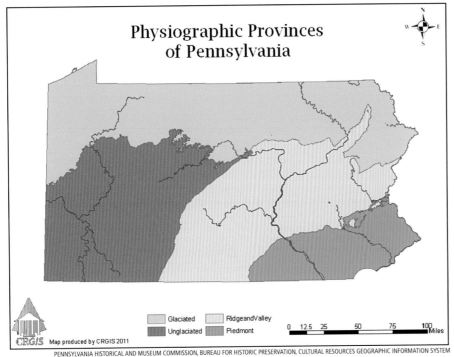

Physiographic Provinces of Pennsylvania

Glaciated
Unglaciated
RidgeandValley
Piedmont

0 12.5 25   50   75   100
                                Miles

Map produced by CRGIS 2011

PENNSYLVANIA HISTORICAL AND MUSEUM COMMISSION, BUREAU FOR HISTORIC PRESERVATION, CULTURAL RESOURCES GEOGRAPHIC INFORMATION SYSTEM

The four major physiographic zones in Pennsylvania are Piedmont, Ridge and Valley, Glaciated Appalachian Plateau, and Unglaciated Appalachian Plateau.

ential archaeologist, wrote, "Culture is an extra-somatic adaptive strategy that is employed in the integration of a society with its environment and with other cultural systems." Archaeologists of the 1960s viewed culture as an adaptive system and focused on the processes that affected this system. Technology, subsistence, demography, and ecology are major factors in the adaptive system and these can be documented and studied in the archaeological record. This was the beginning of processual archaeology that, with some modifications, continues to dominate the profession today. Archaeologists emphasize the process by which culture changes.

Archaeologists now describe cultural evolution as changes in the adaptive strategy or changes in the adaptive system. Changes in culture are described as responses to the natural and cultural environments. Artifacts, features, community patterns, and settlement patterns are the traits of a prehistoric culture. They are the material remains of the adaptive strategy. Cultures able to extract sufficient calories from the environment, educate the next generation, and reproduce sufficient offspring will be successful (or selected in a Darwinian sense).

Human culture is not only our adaptation to the natural environment but also to the cultural environment. Cultural evolution is not simply a gradual linear increase in cultural and technological complexity with man "pulling himself up by his own bootstraps." It is problem-solving at the societal level. It is a process of

people adapting and responding to changing natural environments, increasing human population density, and influences of adjacent cultures while developing new solutions to complex interpersonal relationships.

Human adaptation in Pennsylvania is extremely variable and diverse because of the complex and varied topography, environment, climate, natural resources, plants, and animals. Spring in Lancaster County is still late winter in Erie. Broad, flat, fertile floodplains of the Susquehanna Valley make farming much easier than in the narrow ravines of the Monongahela Valley. Even with modern technology, we can imagine the differences in cultural adaptations faced by the Native Americans. Pennsylvania archaeology is varied, complicated, and intriguing because of this diversity.

Lying on the southeastern border of New England, the eastern border of the Midwest, and the northern border of the South, Pennsylvania constitutes a unique physiographic, ecological, and prehistoric cultural crossroads. From east to west, the state ranges from the flat Atlantic Coastal Plain and the rolling Piedmont, through the numerous northeast-southwest trending valleys of the Ridge and Valley section, to the deeply eroded Appalachian Plateau of the Upper Ohio basin. Within these physiographic zones, Pennsylvania is divided into three major drainage basins. The Delaware River drains the eastern part of the state and leads to the Atlantic Ocean. The Susquehanna River begins in New York and drains all of central Pennsylvania into the Chesapeake Bay. The Allegheny, Monongahela, and Ohio Rivers lead into the center of the North American continent, the Mississippi River, and the Gulf of Mexico.

Human Biological Evolution

Human biological evolution began more than three million years ago in Africa. Only in the past thirty thousand years have humans dispersed far enough across Asia to have an opportunity to enter the New World. There is no evidence that the first people in

North America represent any form of earlier humans, such as Homo erectus or the Neanderthals. The Native Americans had to have been relatively recent arrivals to the New World because of the strong physical resemblance to the people of East Asia. The details are still being debated, but based on general appearance, similarities in language, blood types, teeth, and DNA, the evidence points to Asian origins.

Glaciation

Humans entered North America during a time when glaciers covered large regions of both North and South America. This is defined as the Pleistocene epoch and it is characterized by a series of glacial advances and retreats (warm and cold periods). A *glacier* is a huge mass of ice that grows and moves downhill by gravity with increases in snowfall. Glaciers are formed when temperature drops and precipitation increases so that more snow falls in winter than melts in summer. It requires less than a 10° decrease in temperature and less than a 10-inch increase in precipitation. At least eight times over the past two million years glaciers covered most of Canada, Northern Europe, Asia, and the major mountain ranges of the world. The ice over Hudson Bay in Canada twenty thousand years ago was nearly two miles thick; ice covering the South Pole measured nearly three miles thick. So much of the earth's water was locked up in ice that the sea level dropped hundreds of feet. When this occurred, the continents became larger as Great Britain connected with Europe, the Philippine Islands with Southeast Asia, and Siberia with Alaska.

Siberia is the East Asian landmass situated across the Bering Strait from Alaska (see map of possible entrance routes). Siberia thirty thousand years ago was a massive grassland similar to the Great Plains of the United States. Although it was cold, large numbers of bison, horse, musk ox, mammoth, mastodon (forms of woolly elephants), woolly rhinoceros, and caribou roamed the region. Because of their large size, these animals are termed *megafauna*. Along with these herbivores (plant-eating animals) came a variety of carnivores (meat-eating animals), such as arctic fox, short-faced bear, lion, saber-toothed tiger, and wolf. This was a hunter's paradise, even if they were only armed with spears. Once humans figured out how to live under these cold conditions, they spread throughout Siberia between twenty thousand and thirty thousand years ago.

Climatic Episodes

The changing environment of Pennsylvania is important to understanding how Native American cultures evolved over the past sixteen thousand years. The glacial environment had a huge effect on cultural evolution all over the world, but when the glaciers began to melt, modern conditions did not suddenly appear. The process took thousands of years and, as is true today, the environment continues to evolve and has acted as the stage on which human culture has evolved. Climatologists, geologists, paleontologists, and archaeologists have been able to reconstruct changes in the climate (temperature and precipitation), vegetation, and animal life in the Middle Atlantic region since the glaciers began melting and retreating northward. They have been able to identify eleven climatic episodes beginning with the maximum extent of the glaciers. The following is a brief overview of these episodes.

The Pleistocene was a time of cold and wet glacial advances alternating with warm glacial retreats. Temperatures during glacial advances were 10° to 20° Fahrenheit colder than at present and the interglacial phases were as warm as or warmer than at present. During glacial phases, the winters were longer, colder, and produced more snowfall than at present. High winter daily temperatures in Pennsylvania would have averaged in the teens and twenties and high summer daily temperatures would have averaged in the sixties and seventies.

The last glacial advance occurred during the Wisconsin glacial episode and the maximum movement south of the glaciers is referred to as the Last Glacial Maximum (LGM). This took place around twenty-one thousand years ago. After this period, there was a general warming followed by the rapid warming Bølling episode; followed by the Older Dryas cold period; followed by the Allerød warming. During this time glaciers melted north across the Saint Lawrence River. The warming periods allowed vegetation to spread to previously glaciated areas. Throughout this period of deglaciation, the megafauna (large-bodied animals weighing one hundred pounds or more) were becoming extinct. They were replaced with a cast of modern animals, species with which we are familiar. However, 10,950 years ago marks the beginning of the Younger Dryas climatic episode that represents a return to glacial conditions. There were many changes in climate during the Pleistocene but the Younger Dryas was different. It grew cold quickly—a drop of 10° possibly in forty years and it was dry rather than wet as in previous glacial episodes. The migration of animals and plants adapted to warmth from the south was dramatically reversed with the Younger Dryas.

It has recently been argued that the temperature reversal was caused by a flood of freshwater into the North Atlantic Ocean. After the glaciers retreated across the Saint Lawrence River, tremendous amounts of freshwater from the melting ice masses began to directly enter the North Atlantic. This disrupted the warm Gulf Stream and caused a sharp reversal in temperatures.

The end of the Younger Dryas occurred as quickly as it began. Technically, this was the end of the Pleistocene and the beginning of the Holocene epoch, but many archaeologists believe that it was simply an interglacial phase of the Pleistocene. It was followed by the Pre-Boreal and Boreal episodes, characterized by temperatures slightly higher than present and dry conditions. Although the temperatures changed quickly between the Younger Dryas and the Pre-Boreal, it required hundreds of years before the open, spruce-pine forest of the Younger Dryas became a closed pine-oak forest during the Pre-Boreal approximately nine thousand years ago. The Atlantic episode began at 8000 BP and represents the beginning of a long warming and wet trend. The forest was characterized as oak-hemlock. Up until this time, the cold air from the glaciers had prevented warm air in the Gulf of Mexico from moving north. Beginning about 6000 BP, however, there was evidence of cyclonic storms (hurricanes) in the form of thick flood deposits along the major rivers in Pennsylvania. The Atlantic episode lasted until 4500 BP, when the Sub-Boreal signaled a warm and dry episode. Reduced vegetation during this period allowed for greater runoff during storms and caused local flooding. This lasted about fifteen hundred years and was followed by a return to warm and wet conditions during the Sub-Atlantic episode.

This was followed by the Scandic episode, which was cool and moist, and then the Neo-Atlantic, also known as the Medieval warming period. The Pacific and Neo-Boreal were both cool, the former dry and the latter moist. The Neo-Boreal, also known as the Little Ice Age, lasted from 700 BP to 200 BP. During the Medieval warming episode, farmers in Europe had moved into the northern limits of farming. During the Little Ice Age in Europe (and Greenland) populations suffered and some areas were abandoned. Evidence exists that Native American populations also felt the effects of this cooling period.

Populating the New World

How and when Native Americans first entered the New World is hotly debated, but research is conclusive that humans inhabited North America 11,200 radiocarbon years ago and southern South America 10,700 years ago. This based on many radiocarbon dates and the distribution of distinctive artifacts. Since the first arrivals had no idea that they were leaving the Old World and entering the New World, we assume the process was gradual and a part of their existing cultural lifestyle. However, as Native Americans eventually moved farther into this unoccupied land they must have realized that there was no evidence of people (in the form of old campfires or lost tools) and this may have affected how they moved. The questions are: What was the migration route? When did they migrate? How quickly did they migrate?

The most likely scenario for humans moving into the New World is that they followed the large herd animals traveling across the connecting land between Siberia and Alaska called the Bering Strait Land Bridge. This is named after the stretch of water that separates these land masses today. As the glaciers grew during the last glaciation, sea level in the Bering Strait dropped more than three hundred feet, forming a land mass that stretched one thousand miles from north to south.

One can only imagine what it was like confronting a life-altering choice between maintaining the successful pattern of survival in Siberia or attempting something different and moving into a land that no one had previously inhabited. What motivated people to move from their homes in Siberia? Based on excavations of Siberian sites from this period, these people were doing well at hunting, fishing, and gathering a variety of wild plants. Did they leave Siberia because it was too crowded? Was it the availability of more food? Did the invention of a new technology allow them to have a better life in Alaska? Was it an argument with their neighbors, or simply a desire to explore a new land? To us, Siberia seems cold and desolate, but to the people who lived there twenty-five thousand years ago, it was home and a safe and familiar place to live.

Most archaeologists believe the movement was prompted by a combination of factors. Hunters and gatherers typically moved their home base when they believed (be it real or imagined) their land was becoming overcrowded. Frequently, after a family disagreement, one branch of a family relocated to a new territory. This was generally a slow process. However, in many ways, the environment in North America, especially south of the glaciers in the continental United

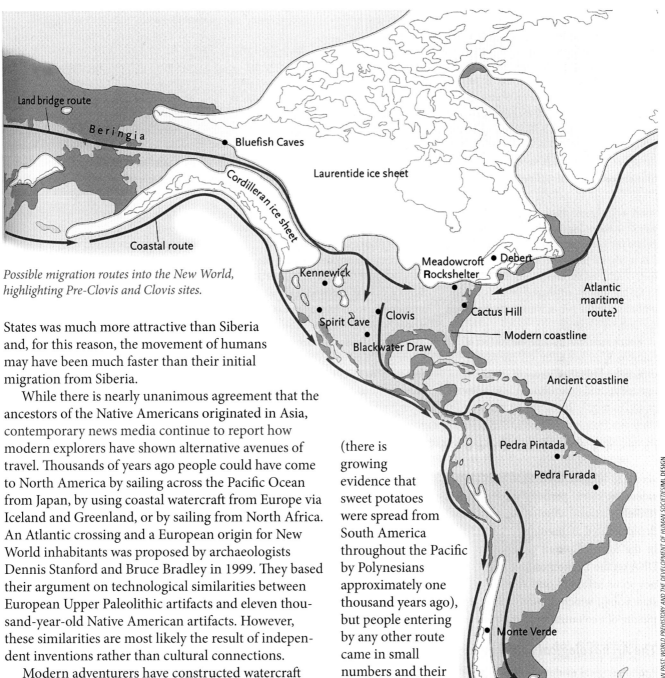

Possible migration routes into the New World, highlighting Pre-Clovis and Clovis sites.

States was much more attractive than Siberia and, for this reason, the movement of humans may have been much faster than their initial migration from Siberia.

While there is nearly unanimous agreement that the ancestors of the Native Americans originated in Asia, contemporary news media continue to report how modern explorers have shown alternative avenues of travel. Thousands of years ago people could have come to North America by sailing across the Pacific Ocean from Japan, by using coastal watercraft from Europe via Iceland and Greenland, or by sailing from North Africa. An Atlantic crossing and a European origin for New World inhabitants was proposed by archaeologists Dennis Stanford and Bruce Bradley in 1999. They based their argument on technological similarities between European Upper Paleolithic artifacts and eleven thousand-year-old Native American artifacts. However, these similarities are most likely the result of independent inventions rather than cultural connections.

Modern adventurers have constructed watercraft using prehistoric technology capable of these journeys, but they know where they are traveling, how long it will take, and how much food and water to carry. The original travelers would not only have needed to have this information, but also the ability to return to their homeland and persuade others to make the arduous journey. Even Christopher Columbus had a difficult time obtaining support for his voyages. Based on DNA, language, and dental patterns, Native Americans are most closely related to people from East Asia. We cannot be certain that people never entered the New World by any route other than the Bering Land Bridge (there is growing evidence that sweet potatoes were spread from South America throughout the Pacific by Polynesians approximately one thousand years ago), but people entering by any other route came in small numbers and their impact on the genetics and technology of the Native Americans was insignificant.

While many individuals debate which ocean was crossed to arrive in the New World, others are more concerned with when people arrived and which route they took from Alaska into the lower forty-eight states. During the Pleistocene, Canada was covered by two glaciers; the Cordilleran covered the Rocky Mountains in the West, and the Laurentide centered on Hudson Bay in the East. Once they moved from Siberia to Alaska, the first immigrants may have traveled east of the Rocky Mountains

Most archaeologists do not support the Atlantic Ocean crossing and European origin for Native Americans. "It's Iberia, not Siberia," wrote Dennis Stanford and Bruce Bradley in 2012.

through an ice-free corridor between the two glaciers. A second theory is that the first people entered by following the coasts of Alaska, British Columbia, and then the Pacific Northwest by boat. Watercraft constructed from logs, skin boats, or dugout canoes would have made travel along the rugged Northwest Coast easier than walking the shoreline on foot. The food supply would have been more diverse and abundant than far inland. Small bands of people would stand a better chance of dispersing into comfortable econiches along this route than those moving directly inland and through the ice-free corridor. Discoveries in 2011 on Santa Rosa Island off the coast of California support a coastal route. There are, however, problems with demonstrating either scenario.

The problem with the ice-free corridor route is that the ice did not begin to significantly melt and the corridor did not open until approximately thirteen thousand years ago. This did not give much time for the New World to be populated 11,200 years ago. Furthermore, during the warm part of the year, the ice-free corridor would have been filled with water from the melting glaciers. During the winter, it would have

been frozen and inhospitable. In addition, water would have washed away most campsites in this region. The coastal route is equally difficult to prove because the Pleistocene coastline is at least one hundred feet underwater due to melting glaciers causing a significant rise in sea level. Archaeologists are beginning to look underwater for sites, notably off the coast of Florida, and surveys have been encouraging. Although underwater archaeology is time-consuming and expensive, spectacular discoveries may be made in the near future.

The concept of Paleolithic people traveling in boats across the oceans or along the Northwest Coast implies a relatively sophisticated maritime technology and seems unlikely to some archaeologists. Waterlogged and preserved dugout canoes are the earliest hard evidence for water travel, but the oldest preserved dugouts discovered so far are less than twelve thousand years old. However, based on indirect information, boats must have existed long before this date. We know that humans reached the continent of Australia at least sixty thousand years ago. For this to be accomplished, they had to traverse sixty miles of open ocean. Even during the coldest times of the Pleistocene, when the sea level dropped hundreds of feet, Australia was never connected to mainland Asia and would have required somewhat sophisticated watercraft to reach it. Because of the rise of sea level, the most likely archaeological sites in which to locate these vessels are now deep beneath the ocean's waters.

Dating the first location of entry is also hotly debated. Archaeologists are not simply competing for rights of who has located and identified the oldest site. This is a significant anthropological issue and it represents a model on how humans occupy a new land and the rate of their migration. How quickly can this happen? Has the incredible variety of Native American cultures, languages, and DNA been created in twelve thousand, eighteen thousand, or even twenty-four thousand years?

Clovis First vs. Pre-Clovis

There are hundreds of well-dated sites in both North and South America documenting that humans had occupied both continents between 10,700 and 11,200 years ago. These people used a distinctive technology called Clovis. The main artifact is a Clovis-style fluted spearpoint. Some archaeologists argue that humans crossed the Bering Strait Land Bridge at about twelve thousand years ago and quickly occupied all of North and South American by 10,700 years ago, moving seven thousand miles from the central United States to the tip of South America in fifteen hundred years. This is called the Clovis First model and usually includes a provision called the "blitzkrieg overkill hypothesis" proposed by American paleobiologist Paul S. Martin (1928–2010). This theory proposes that the megafauna of the New World were not familiar with humans as predators and were quickly exterminated as humans migrated south. In fact, the justification for the rapid movement by humans across the continent is their search for food in the form of big game animals.

Other archaeologists believe this is much too rapid for human migration, especially considering humans needed to cross several significantly different environmental zones between Alaska and the tip of South America. These archaeologists argue humans entered much earlier at eighteen thousand or twenty-four thou-

ILLUSTRATION BY KIMBERLY L. STONE

The blitzkrieg overkill hypothesis. *The Clovis First model argues for the rapid movement of Paleoindian people, the rapid spread of fluted points, and the rapid extinction of the megafauna.*

The Meadowcroft Rockshelter is now open to the public.

MERCYHURST ARCHAEOLOGICAL INSTITUTE

sand years ago and slowly filled the New World. This is called the Pre-Clovis model. This group also does not support the "overkill hypothesis" and presents alternative data that supports environmental change as the cause for the extinction of the megafauna.

Pennsylvania has been at the center of this controversy since the 1970s with the excavation of Meadowcroft Rockshelter (36Wh297) in Washington County. This site dates to at least 16,250 years ago and contains artifacts similar to those found in Siberia dating to about the same time.

Approximately 20,000 years ago in Asia, Africa, and Europe, humans were using a distinctive stone tool technology called blade tools. This is an efficient use of raw material where a block of stone can be easily converted into tools without wasting much of the stone. It is widespread in Siberia, but surprisingly, it is not common in the New World during this time period. The interesting aspect of Meadowcroft Rockshelter is that some of the earliest tools are bladelike in their appearance. They have been interpreted as a blending of Old World technology with innovations developed in the New World. This type of technology is to be expected in a group of people who have been in the New World and separated from Asia for hundreds or thousands of years. They would have continued using these traditional technologies but added new techniques to adapt to a new environment.

Four significant sites have recently been discovered: Cactus Hill in Virginia (16,200 years old), Topper in South Carolina (16,000 years old), Monte Verde in Chile (12,500 years old), and Gault in Texas (13,500 years old). The Cactus Hill and Gault sites illustrate a combination of Old World and New World technologies. These obviously support the early dates of Meadowcroft Rockshelter and represent evidence of an early migration. Because there are

MERCYHURST ARCHAEOLOGICAL INSTITUTE

Excavation at Meadowcroft Rockshelter illustrating the complex stratigraphy. The bottom of this excavation unit was dated to 16,250 years ago.

many sites dating to the period from 11,200 to 10,500 years ago, it is hard to imagine that humans would have dispersed so quickly without a Pre-Clovis population in place. In fact, recent studies indicate the Clovis technology was invented in the southeastern United States, meaning that people (Pre-Clovis people) must have been here prior to Clovis. Most archaeologists have shifted to the Pre-Clovis model, but the debate continues unabated.

Artifacts excavated from the lower levels of Meadowcroft Rockshelter.

Paleolithic blade tools from the Old World dating to between 20,000 and 30,000 years ago are similar to artifacts excavated from Meadowcroft Rockshelter.

A Paleoindian Child's Narrative

Megan Jennifer Carr

TIME 17,000 YEARS AGO.

PLACE THE BERING STRAIT LAND BRIDGE.

CLIMATE 10° COLDER THAN PRESENT AND LESS RAIN AND SNOW THAN TODAY.

FLORA AND FAUNA A VAST GRASSLAND WITH LEAFY TREES ALONG THE RIVERS AND SMALL PATCHES OF SPRUCE ALONG THE RIDGES. MAMMOTH, MASTODON, BISON, HORSE, MUSK OX, WOOLLY RHINOCEROS, CARIBOU, ARCTIC FOX, SHORT-FACED BEAR, SABER-TOOTHED TIGER, WOLF, MOOSE, ELK, AND DEER ARE THE MOST COMMON BIG GAME ANIMALS.

DISTINCTIVE ARTIFACTS LEAF-SHAPED STONE SPEARS AND KNIVES, SCRAPERS, BONE AWLS, AND NEEDLES.

"Okay, is everyone comfortable?" Grandma settled down by the warm fire to tell the story of Little Lynx and her first trip to the New World.

"Oh my, it must have been back when my name was still Little Lynx," the wizened woman began. "I had lived with my family for fourteen winters. When I was born, I was wrapped in a blanket of lynx fur, and that's how I got my name Little Lynx. I lived with my mother, father, sister, two brothers, and grandmother."

"Just like you live with us, Grandma," one grandchild interrupted.

"Yes, that's right, just like I live with you."

"My brothers were older than I was, and my sister was younger," she continued. "I also lived with some of my uncles, aunts, and many cousins. We called our tribe The People and we were the greatest hunters that ever lived. We lived on a land where it was flat as the ice that forms on lakes in early winter. The flatness was only interrupted by a few stands of spruce trees. There were many lakes where we lived. The summers were hot and very short, but our winters were bitterly cold and terribly long.

"My father, uncles, and brothers were the hunters in our family. From early spring until the late fall, we would follow the great herds of mammoth, bison, caribou, and horses that migrated on the land bridge between our land and the mountains far to the east. No one ever traveled to the mountains because they were so cold and scary. We moved every few weeks as the herds of animals migrated. We didn't have many toys or things to play with because we had to carry everything from camp to camp. When I was not helping my mother, I played with my sister, brothers, and my cousins.

"During that winter, we set up our camp along the Bering Sea. In our winter camp we lived in big tents made from elephant hides and whale bones. The elephant hides were thick and helped keep the tent warm in those extremely cold winters. There weren't many trees, so we burned elephant and whale bone for fuel. It kept us warm and smelled better than wood.

"Around the camp, I helped my mother gather food like nuts, berries, and bird eggs. I even set traps for small animals like foxes and snowshoe hares. We also collected cattails and lily roots and speared fish in the nearby lakes and swamps. Mother made a game of it and it was fun. Sometimes, when my father and uncles hunted for caribou, they dressed to look like the animals wearing the skins and antlers. They could more easily get closer to spear and hunt game. My father told me that when he put on the antlers, he felt he could think like a caribou and be more successful. After they killed the caribou, or whatever the animal might have been, I helped my mother cut it up and carry the meat and skins back to our camp. After we had eaten all the delicious meat off the bones, I helped my mother make beautiful and wonderfully sewn clothing out of animal hides and skins. My mother was very good to me. She had stories for every occasion and I learned everything from her. I felt I was her favorite.

"I helped my mother by taking care of my little sister when she was busy with other things. And I helped my Aunt Brightstar by taking care of her two little boys, who were so extremely cute. I helped my brothers make spearpoints out of sharp rocks we found. In the summertime, our camp smelled bad, and flies came in because of all the elephant bones our house was made of. We would let our fires get smoky to keep the flies and the mosquitoes away. It helped a great deal.

"We had many dogs that were useful to my family and me. The dogs were good for carrying lots of big and heavy supplies for long distances. They were very playful, too. When there wasn't much going on, my brothers, sister, and cousins often had dogsled races. They were so much fun!

"Some of the dogs were mean, and the men kept them tied up unless we were traveling. My dad's favorite was Fang. He was the meanest. My mom told me when she was a girl, sometimes in the late winter, when the meat was all gone, they would eat the dogs. I suggested we eat Fang, but she said he was too old and tough.

"I remember one beautiful spring day, when I was looking for bird eggs with my mother and Aunt Brightstar. I shouted in a frustrated way, 'I can't find any bird eggs!'

"Then my mother said in an annoyed voice, 'Go look up on the rocks and try and find some there!' So I went up to the rocks to look for some eggs. I couldn't believe what I saw. It was a huge herd of mammoths! I wanted to get a closer look. I was so completely amazed to see a herd that big. I finally came out of the daze when I heard my mother and aunt yelling and screaming, 'Ahhhhhhhhhhhhhhhhhh! Ahhhhhhhhhhhhh! Oh my goodness! Shoo, go away!' When I turned around to see what they were screaming about, I could see that they were being chased by an ugly, mean-looking, red-eyed, deviled-faced saber-toothed tiger. As I was running away, it saw me and started chasing after me. That's when we split up. I was running one way and my mother and aunt were running in the opposite direction. I started to scream as loud as I possibly could, 'Ohhhhhhhhhh! Nooooo! Mommy, Mommy, help me!'

"My mother and aunt could not do anything about it because things were getting worse. The tiger must have scared the herd of mammoths, because it started a stampede and they were charging toward my mother and Aunt Brightstar. The rock I was standing on had a small, but tall enough, tree that the tiger couldn't climb. I shimmied up the tree to get away from that mean, drooling tiger. After the tiger ran away, chasing the mammoths, my mother and aunt were also gone. They were nowhere to be found. I walked in the direction of our camp, but I only found the trampled ground from the stampede. It was getting dark and I was getting really worried. Had my mother gotten caught in the stampede? Was the tiger still lurking? Where were she and my aunt? Then it began to snow real hard.

"I didn't have any flint to make a fire and could not find any wood to make it the hard way. I decided to just find a place to get out of the weather. I headed towards some tall rocks. I hesitated, but went ahead anyway, because it was not in the direction of our camp. As I turned the corner and got closer, I could smell people and, at first, I was scared. I slowed down and crept around the corner. To my surprise, a group of people was just setting up camp and starting a fire. Before I could think, there was a noise off to the side, and a huge man was staring at me. He was as surprised as I was because you don't see many strangers on the tundra. He started looking around and asked me where my tribe was, and how I got here. I told him, he smiled, and I felt better. 'I know your father,' he said. 'Let's get you some food and warmed up."

"I learned my aunt White Rabbit was his wife, and I felt much better. The bad side was they could not take me back to my tribe, and it was too dangerous for me to go back alone. It turned out that someone had an argument with one of my uncles and was afraid of meeting my people. After the argument, they decided that it was too crowded in Siberia, and they would move farther east where there did not seem to be any tribes. Now, the storm was getting worse. They needed to move to the mountains for shelter. I was sad about moving farther from my family, but excited that we were moving to a place in the east where there were mountains and valleys, a place where no hunters had ever seen or been to before.

"The first winter was rough, but in the spring the hunting was incredibly easy. We found a rock called obsidian that was very good for making spearpoints and knives. We spent all summer and fall in the hills where there were bison, horses, and elephants. We ate like lions. As the flies started to get bad, we decided to move back to the ocean where the breezes would keep them down. Just before winter, we moved back to the Bering Sea. What do you know? I found my mother and father there. Everyone was happy, and I told them about the new land I had seen when I was with my Aunt White Rabbit. I gave my brothers a big beautiful piece of obsidian, and we decided to move to the new land in the spring with my Aunt White Rabbit and her tribe. That is how we became the First People."

"That story was swell, Grandma!" said the granddaughter.

"Yes, that was a great story!" replied the younger brother.

"In memory of my adventure, I have kept a little piece of obsidian from my first trip to the new land." The children all gathered around to touch it.

"Well, little ones, it's getting late and you better head off to bed now. Maybe tomorrow night I could tell you about when I married your grandfather."

Chapter 3

The Paleoindian Period: 10,000 to 16,500 years ago

TIMELINE

Contact Period	1500 AD–1700 AD
Woodland Period	1500–2700 years ago
Transitional Period	2700–4300 years ago
Archaic Period	4300–10,000 years ago
Paleoindian Period	**10,000–16,500 years ago**
Late Paleoindian	**10,000–10,300 years ago**
Middle Paleoindian	**10,300–10,900 years ago**
Clovis	**10,900–11,200 years ago**
Pre-Clovis	**11,200–16,500 years ago**

Environment: Cold Pleistocene climate, spruce pine parkland, open in the north, more forested in the south. The climate gradually warmed but became very cold with the Younger Dryas episode. Megafauna were gradually becoming extinct and were completely replaced by modern animals by approximately eleven thousand years ago.

Making and using tools (typical artifacts and technology): The toolkit consisted of many standardized stone tool shapes such as endscrapers, sidescrapers, knives, wedges, and spokeshaves. There was a clear preference for high-quality stone such as cherts and jaspers. Tools were made using a distinctive technique. Fluted projectile points are the most distinctive artifacts.

What people ate (subsistence): Hunting a variety of large and small game and fishing probably provided at least 60 percent of the diet. In the northern part of the state there is evidence of the hunting of migratory caribou. In the southern part of the state, general foraging in the form of gathering seeds, nuts, berries, and roots and fishing were more common but hunting prevailed.

Where people lived (settlement patterns): Most of the sites were small and located in river valleys. Special trips were made to high-quality chert quarries to gather stone for toolmaking. Territories were large, ranging between one hundred and two hundred miles in diameter.

People living in groups (social organization and belief systems): People lived in highly mobile egalitarian bands, moving frequently and over long distances. The bands consisted of approximately fifteen to twenty-five individuals, possibly two bands for each of the major drainages, totaling 90 to 150 individuals for the state.

The fluted spearpoint is the most distinctive artifact of the Paleoindian Period.

Definition

The first period of human settlement in the New World is called Paleoindian ("Early Man"). It dates from 10,000 to at least 16,500 years ago. It began with the first people moving into the New World during the Pleistocene and it ended with changes in the environment and cultural adaptations to a more forested setting. It is divided into at least two periods: the Pre-Clovis, dating between 16,500 and 11,200 years ago, and the Paleoindian, dating between 11,200 and 10,000 years ago. The Pre-Clovis period is highly controversial and some archaeologists do not believe that humans were here prior to 11,200 years ago. The Paleoindian is further divided into Early, Middle, and Late periods, and these are defined by styles of fluted spearpoints. The hallmark of the period is the fluted projectile point along with a variety of small distinctive scraping tools and knifelike cutting tools. The Paleoindians were highly mobile and generally lived in small groups. In the western United States, they were hunting now-extinct animals such as mastodon, mammoth (forms of woolly elephants), bison, and horse, but there is little evidence for the hunting of extinct animals east of the Mississippi River and none in the northeastern United States. In Pennsylvania people practiced a foraging lifestyle, although hunting was more common than later times. Early in the Paleoindian period, they may have hunted caribou. There are several unusually significant archaeological sites from this period in Pennsylvania representing some of the oldest, largest, and best-dated Paleoindian sites in the eastern United States.

The Environment

During the Pre-Clovis phase of the Paleoindian period, glaciers covered northern Pennsylvania in an arc stretching from the Delaware Water Gap in the east to 9.3 miles north of Williamsport in central Pennsylvania and to 4.9 miles south of New Castle at its western end. Southern Pennsylvania was characterized by a patchwork of forests and open grassy environments with no modern analogues, or no place in the world that looks like the vegetation of Pennsylvania fifteen thousand years ago. The foods available to humans included mammoth, mastodon, musk-ox, horse, camel, giant sloth, peccary, moose, caribou, elk, small mammals, fish, roots, seeds, nuts, and berries. The glaciers began to melt about 16,500 years ago (see the Environmental Episodes chart in Chapter 2) but the melting was interrupted several times by cold periods. The Bølling and Allerød episodes generally represent warming periods allowing animals and vegetation to move into formerly glaciated regions. The intervening Older Dryas episode halted this process. The glaciers had retreated across the St. Lawrence River and into Canada by 12,600 years ago. Megafauna adapted to the cold gradually became extinct, replaced by a group of modern animals by eleven thousand years ago. The Younger Dryas began at 10,950 years and lasted until 10,100 years ago. During this time, the melting of the glaciers was halted and Pennsylvania was characterized by a cold, dry climate.

The vegetation of the Younger Dryas can be characterized as a spruce parkland, consisting of a forest of mostly spruce and pine trees but intermixed with open areas of low bushes and grassy meadows. Particularly in southern Pennsylvania and in the river valleys, there were also broad-leafed deciduous trees, such as hickory and oaks. These are nut-producing trees that humans can eat, but just as important, they attract small mammals and birds that humans can also eat and use for clothing. However, because of the cold, dry Younger Dryas episode, erosion was common and the vegetation was frequently changing. Erosion delayed the development of the climax forest, and the forests were filled with open spaces and small trees. Finally, since erosion rather than deposition was the general rule in river valleys, archaeological sites were more likely washed away than buried and protected.

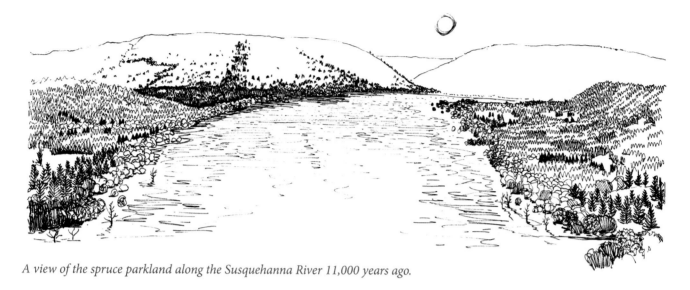

A view of the spruce parkland along the Susquehanna River 11,000 years ago.

Pre-Clovis in Pennsylvania

Based on the Meadowcroft Rockshelter, human population density during the Pre-Clovis period was very low. Family groups or bands moved frequently in search of a variety of foods. Because food was plentiful compared to the human population, special tools to exploit this environment were not needed, and no really distinctive tools have been identified for this period. Implements included flake tools for scraping, sawing, and drilling, some bladelike flakes, and multipurpose, leaf-shaped bifaces that served as knives and probably also as spearpoints. Because the Pre-Clovis technology was not distinctive and human population density was low, sites from this period are difficult to identify and are extremely rare. Meadowcroft Rockshelter is the only one found to date in Pennsylvania and one of only a handful in North America.

MERCYHURST ARCHAEOLOGICAL INSTITUTE

Tools recovered from the lowest levels of Meadowcroft Rockshelter.

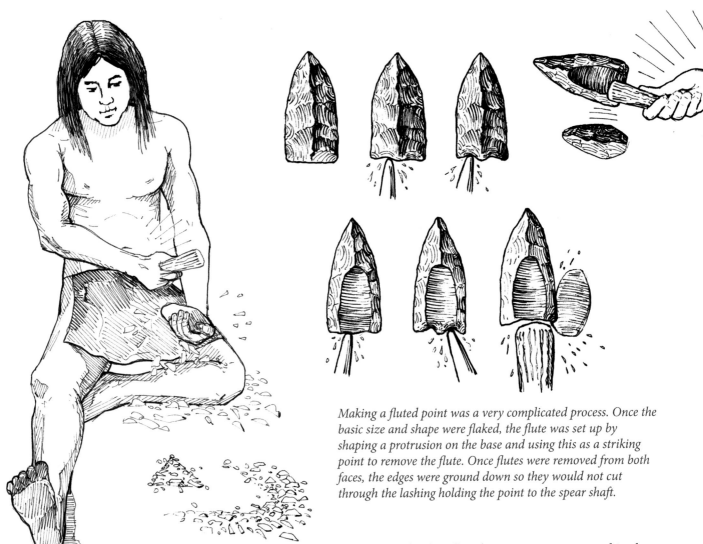

Making a fluted point was a very complicated process. Once the basic size and shape were flaked, the flute was set up by shaping a protrusion on the base and using this as a striking point to remove the flute. Once flutes were removed from both faces, the edges were ground down so they would not cut through the lashing holding the point to the spear shaft.

Making and Using Tools: Typical Artifacts and Technology

Approximately 11,200 years ago a new and distinctive spearpoint style was invented somewhere in North America. It is called a fluted point because of the flute or channel down the length of both sides of the spearpoint. The groove likely facilitated the hafting of the spearpoint to the spear shaft. Fluted points are extremely interesting for a variety of reasons. They are unique to the New World. Humans have been making stone spearpoints for at least 20,000 years, and in no place else were they fluted. They are relatively difficult to make and approximately 10 percent were broken in production. Why would the first visitors to the New World choose such a difficult and unique spearpoint form? Maybe just for this reason: it was unique and it distinguished them from everyone else.

Because the first fluted points were excavated in the American Southwest and are associated with old radiocarbon dates, it was believed that fluting was invented in this region. However, archaeologists have recently been looking more closely at the Southeast, particularly Alabama, Mississippi, and Florida. This is based on the large numbers of sites, the variety of fluted point styles, and a growing number of early radiocarbon dates. The earliest fluted point style is called Clovis, after a community in eastern New Mexico where these were first discovered, associated with mammoth bones. Clovis seems to be the most widespread style or type of fluted point extending throughout the West, the Southeast, and as far north as the Shawnee-Minisink site (36Mr43), near the confluence of the Delaware River and the Broadhead Creek in northeastern Pennsylvania's Monroe County. A recent review of radiocarbon dates places the Clovis type rather precisely between 11,100 BP and 10,800 BP. Interestingly, the "Clovis first" model credits this group with causing the extinction of the megafauna. However,

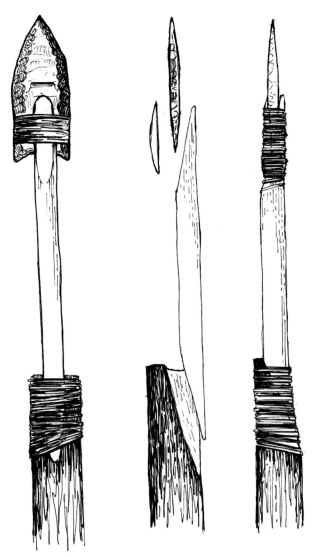

The fluted point was hafted to the spear shaft using a foreshaft frequently made of bone or ivory.

most of these large-bodied mammals, excluding elephants and bison, were extinct prior to Clovis and all megafauna were gone prior to the Younger Dryas. Contrary to popular belief, there is no evidence that Clovis or the megafauna became extinct because of a meteor or comet impact.

One of the explanations for Clovis being so widespread is that people with Clovis projectile points were able to move throughout North America during the warm Allerød episode. It was during the extreme cold of the Younger Dryas that people began settling in large regions, although some in the north continued to move long distances during their annual round. In the East, Clovis evolved into a variety of regional fluted point styles including Gainey, Debert, Barnes, Crowfield, and Holcombe. These have all been recovered in

Pennsylvania and it is assumed they date between 10,000 and 10,900 years ago. Although it is debated and there is no physical evidence, Paleoindians probably brought the *atlatl,* or spear thrower (see page 78), with them from Asia and used this device to propel fluted point-tipped spears to their prey.

Paleoindian sites are known for their variety of stone tools in standardized shapes, including different types of scraping tools, especially small triangular scrapers but also chopping, cutting, carving, drilling and sawing tools. Archaeologists believe many of these were used in butchering animals. Scrapers were used to clean hides for clothing and shelter. They were also used for shaping wood, bone, and antler for stone tool handles and other objects. Paleoindian toolkits do not include grinding tools for processing seeds and nuts or large woodworking tools such as axes, which are common in later years.

Compared to later groups, Paleoindian spearpoints, knives, and tools were made with rock that had a high silica content, such as cherts and jaspers. Silica is a hard glassy material that allows for highly controlled flaking. Even if the cherts were not of the best quality, they were chosen over argillite or metarhyolite, which were commonly used later. Using quality stone, Paleoindians were able to resharpen spearpoints and tools, using them for longer periods of time. In addition, the Paleoindian toolkit was made using a different flint knapping technique or process than was used during later periods. Paleoindians most frequently used large bifacial cores to make their tools. This type of core was multipurpose and used as a source of flakes (called tool blanks) that were converted into tools. With its sharp edges, a bifacial core could also be used as a large chopping tool for butchering animals and working wood. Paleoindians probably carried a variety of bifaces and flakes in a skin bag. The bifaces could be quickly converted into choppers, knives, or finished fluted points. The flake blanks could be quickly made into scrapers for hide or wood, wedges for splitting bone, or spokeshaves for making handles.

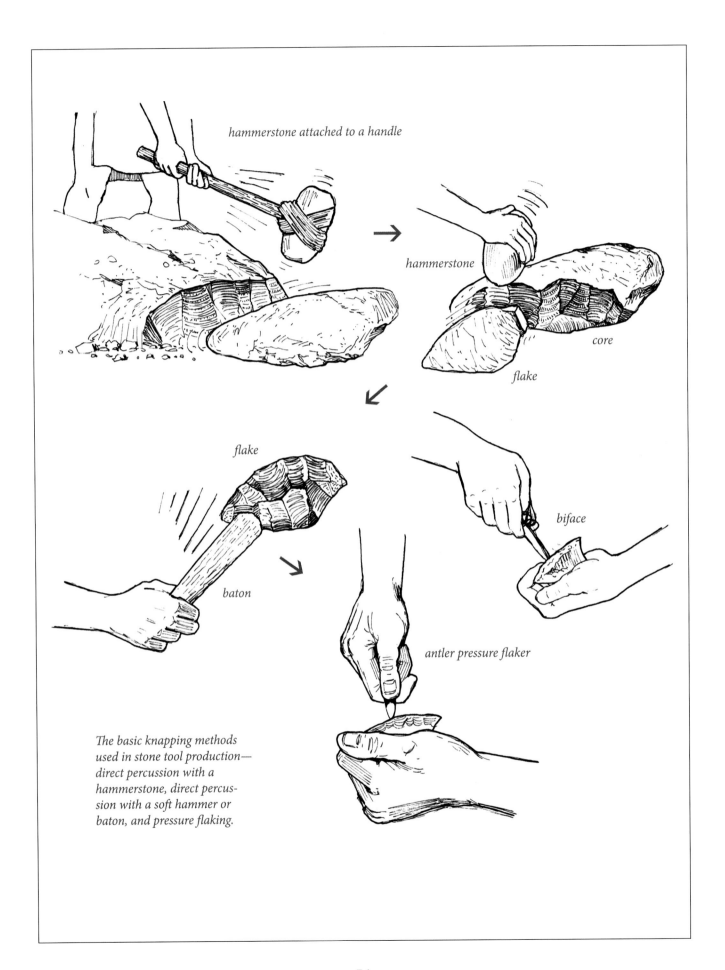

hammerstone attached to a handle

hammerstone

core

flake

flake

baton

biface

antler pressure flaker

The basic knapping methods used in stone tool production—direct percussion with a hammerstone, direct percussion with a soft hammer or baton, and pressure flaking.

How to Make Chipped Stone Tools

Making tools from stone dates to at least 2.6 million years ago. The earliest tools were very simple—basically rocks with sharp edges. They gave early humans an advantage on the African savanna that allowed them to survive and spread all over Africa and into Asia and cooler climates by 1.8 million years ago. By 15,000 years ago, stone tools had spread all over North and South America and they were found in many different sizes and shapes, seemingly for every purpose needed by humans.

There are two general trends that can be observed in stone tool technology. One, the tools became more specialized and two, techniques developed that were less wasteful of raw material. For early human groups, constantly on the move, it was important to maximize the amount of useable tools per pound of stone.

Making stone tools is analogous to whittling wood. It is a subtractive process. Pieces or chips or flakes are removed from a block of stone ending with a finished tool such as a knife or scraper or spearpoint. The process of removing flakes to produce a tool is called knapping or flint knapping. Not all types of rock can be flaked into shape. Stone tool makers need to be able to predict how a rock will break and most importantly control how it will break so that tools can be easily shaped. Good quality rock for making stone tools is also referred to as toolstone. It needs to be relatively hard, with a glasslike (cryptocrystaline) structure and homogeneous (not including impurities).

The block of stone to be chipped is called a *core* and the tool that does the chipping is called a *hammerstone*. The hammerstone is usually a round, river-worn rock of equal or greater hardness than the core. When properly struck along the edge of the core, a flake will pop off. The edges are usually very sharp and a flake can be used as a cutting tool without any modification. A large flake can be further reduced into a more specialized tool such as a scraper, saw, drill, knife, or spearpoint. Hammerstones usually produce large thick flakes and are not suitable for the detailed work necessary to make these tools. A soft hammer, made from antler or hard wood called a *baton* is used for this work. These produce thin flakes and are good at

converting thick hammerstone flakes into thin projectile points and knives. This is the tool that does most of the work in stone tool production. The final sharpening and shaping of a stone tool is done with an antler pressure flaker. This process involves literally pressing off a flake along the edge of a tool. These are usually less than 3/4 inch long and are only found on the edges of a tool. Pressure flaking is used in shaping the base of a spear point and forming the notches.

Unmodified flakes or flake tools only modified on one surface are called *unifaces*. Most stone tools such as scrapers fall into this category. Flakes that are modified on both surfaces are called *bifaces*. These take the form of knives, spearpoints, and "arrowheads." Producing a spearpoint requires skill and practice, but it was a very common activity in prehistoric times. A large quantity of small flakes is produced and these are called *waste flakes* or *debitage*. Archaeologists have found tight concentrations of waste flakes that are the result of one individual sitting on the ground and making a single spearpoint. These are called *chipping features* and contain hundreds of waste flakes. Since they all come from the same block of stone, archaeologists have been able to refit them back together (at least partially) like a three-dimensional jigsaw puzzle. This type of analysis has been very useful in understanding how tools were made.

Flakes and stone tools are the most common artifacts found on prehistoric sites in Pennsylvania, and in many cases they are the only artifacts recovered from the site. Up until the 1980s archaeologists focused on the tools and ignored the flakes. However, there was a renewed interest in flint knapping and archaeologists began experimenting with making stone tools. It was discovered that each of the basic tools used in flint knapping—hammerstones, batons, and pressure flakers—produces a distinctive flake shape. Archaeologists now regularly analyze these shapes to determine the kinds of knapping activities that were conducted at a site. They have been able to identify where projectile points are being made, where flake tools are made, and where stone tools are being resharpened. Using this information, they have been able to map different types of tool production areas across a site.

Clovis

Middle
Paleoindian

Late
Paleoindian

Clovis, Middle, and
Late fluted point types
from Pennsylvania.

a.
b.
c.
d.
e.
f.
g.
h.
i.
j.

Paleoindian stone tools
from the Wilhelm,
Wallis, and Shoop sites.
a. knife
b. wedge
c. wedge
d. fine cutting tools
e. concavity
f. side scraper
g. scraper plane
h.–j. end scrapers

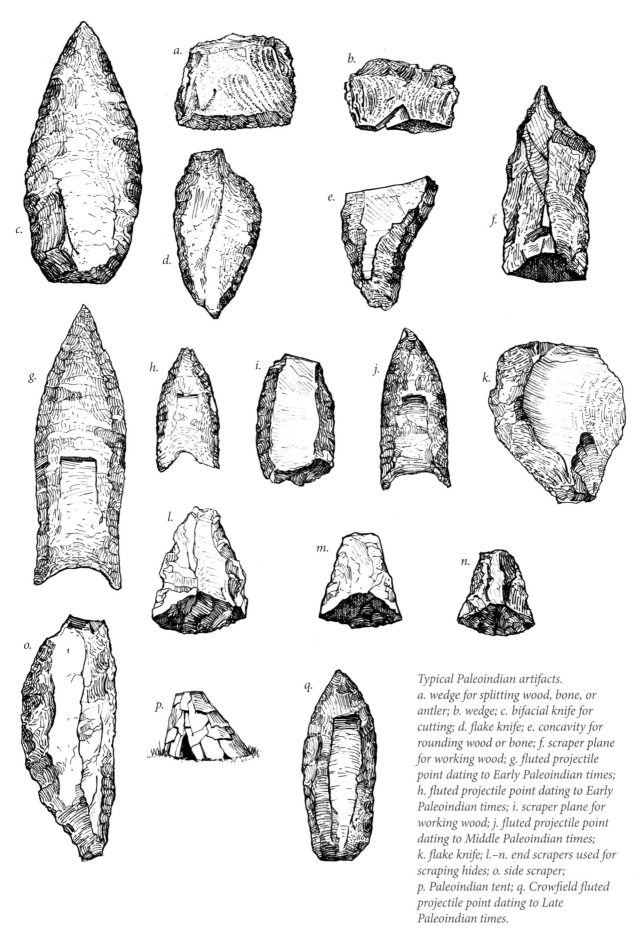

Typical Paleoindian artifacts.
a. wedge for splitting wood, bone, or antler; b. wedge; c. bifacial knife for cutting; d. flake knife; e. concavity for rounding wood or bone; f. scraper plane for working wood; g. fluted projectile point dating to Early Paleoindian times; h. fluted projectile point dating to Early Paleoindian times; i. scraper plane for working wood; j. fluted projectile point dating to Middle Paleoindian times; k. flake knife; l.–n. end scrapers used for scraping hides; o. side scraper; p. Paleoindian tent; q. Crowfield fluted projectile point dating to Late Paleoindian times.

What People Ate: Subsistence

Based on sites excavated in western North America, archaeologists long believed Paleoindians in Pennsylvania were highly mobile big game hunters. However, in the eastern United States, there has always been some debate concerning the Paleoindian diet. In the American West solid evidence confirms the people consumed mammoth, mastodon, bison, horse, camel, and giant sloth. In Florida, there is also a growing body of data indicating mammoth steaks were part of the Paleoindian subsistence pattern. It was assumed they also hunted a variety of smaller animals and ate a wide variety of plant foods, but a significant part of their diet was based on now-extinct animals. In the Northeast, there is no evidence that Paleoindians were hunting now-extinct megafauna. In fact, the East (north of Florida) does not contain much data to address the issue of diet.

The Shoop site (36Da20), located in upper Dauphin County approximately nine miles east of the Susquehanna River, was one of the first Paleoindian sites reported in the East and appeared to support the "big game hunting" hypothesis. It is the largest Paleoindian site in Pennsylvania and one of the largest in the eastern United States. It was first analyzed in 1952 by John Witthoft, who served as the Commonwealth's state archaeologist at the time. The site has yielded more than one thousand tools, including hundreds of scrapers and approximately ninety-two fluted spear-points. The stone used to make 98 percent of these tools is called Onondaga chert and its nearest source is western New York, 250 miles to the north. There are at least eleven concentrations of arti-facts at the Shoop site. Archaeologists believe each represents a separate visit between western New York and central Pennsylvania. No food remains have been found, but it is hard to attribute the large number of spearpoints on a ridge-top setting to anything other than hunting. Archaeologists have long specu-lated this site was probably situated on a caribou or elk migration route and was visited yearly by Paleoindians to hunt these animals.

The Shawnee-Minisink site, one of the few in the East to produce dietary remains, has changed the theory portraying the Paleoindians as big game hunters. A rare example of a deeply buried Paleoindian site in the East, it contained many tools, including more than one hundred scrapers but only two fluted points. Based on radiocarbon dating, these tools are 10,950 years old, a relatively early date for fluted spearpoints in the Northeast. The two fluted points excavated from this site appear to fit the Clovis style and that places the site within the Clovis period. Several cooking hearths were found and these contained a variety of carbonized

A sample of stone tools from the Shoop site. Top row, fluted points; middle row, end scrapers; bottom row, side scrapers.

seeds, including hawthorn, plum, and hickory, as well as fish remains. Unfortunately, the fish bone could not identify to the species. The occupants of this site seem to be generalized foragers rather than big game hunters. Compared to the Shoop site, there is no evidence in the form of large numbers of stone spearpoints for exten-sive hunting at Shawnee-Minisink. Further, 95 percent of the stone for making tools was a locally quarried chert most likely collected within two miles of the site. The remaining toolstone originated less than one hundred miles from the source, suggesting a territory much smaller than the Shoop site.

Caribou hunting.

ILLUSTRATION BY WILLIAM PARSONS

Fluted projectile points of the Clovis type from the Shawnee-Minisink site dating to 10,950 BP.

Where People Lived: Settlement Patterns

Paleoindian sites are rare, representing less than 5 percent of all archaeological sites recorded in the Pennsylvania Archaeological Site Survey (PASS) files. Of these sites, only about 5 percent have been analyzed to date. In terms of locations and compared to sites from later time periods, the majority of these are located along major streams and rivers and not in upland settings near spring headwaters. Most of these are small and consist of a few stone tools and usually only one fluted spearpoint. Most sites appear to represent small groups of families. Their small size, in terms of numbers of artifacts and square feet, suggests they were not frequently revisited. The Younger Dryas climatic episode was a time of constantly changing vegetation. A campsite that was good one year may not have any food the following year.

Paleoindian people moved their camps in a seasonal pattern, or "round," to the locations of predictable food resources, such as along the migration routes of caribou, waterfowl, or anadromous (spawning) fish. The seasonal round also included a number of plant food collecting sites, although archaeologists do not know much about them. Compared to later groups their seasonal round was quite sizable. They were probably collecting the most concentrated foods, especially those that did not require special processing. Their adaptation involved moving long

distances to easily exploitable resources. The Younger Dryas was a harsh time, but human populations were low and there was little competition between bands over the easily exploitable foods.

Animals congregated and plants produced edible roots, seeds, berries, and nuts during the spring and autumn months, possibly prompting several families to join together to collect these concentrated foods. During the summer, many plant and animal foods would be available but scattered throughout the valleys, and this would be a time when single-families would forage for these resources. During the winter, hunting would have been the main subsistence base. To reduce competition, this was also probably done in single-family groups. Finally, the seasonal round included stops at chert and jasper quarries to collect toolstone. In Virginia, Paleoindian quarry occupations are large and seem to represent meeting grounds for several family bands. These would have been places for important social and religious events. However, this type of site has yet to be found in Pennsylvania.

It would seem that the Shoop and Shawnee-Minisink sites represent different settlement patterns and Pennsylvania seems to be on the boundary between two different adaptations. However, when this issue is examined on a regional basis, these two sites seem to fit a pattern. The Shoop site is similar to sites in New

Spring

Summer

Winter

Fall

The Paleoindian settlement pattern focused on the major river valleys. In the fall, families grouped together to hunt caribou, moose, or elk. In the winter, they broke into small family groups and spent most of their time hunting. In the spring, the families joined together to fish and collect a variety of foods. In the summer, families broke into small groups to exploit a variety of plants and animals. Several times a year, small groups or entire families visited quarries to collect toolstone.

England and the Great Lakes. In these regions, there are several sites with many tools, large numbers of spearpoints, toolstone transported two hundred to three hundred miles from its source, and large sites consisting of multiple concentrations of artifacts possibly representing different family tents or individual campsites. In several cases, small samples of charred caribou bone have been found. It appears these sites represent highly mobile hunting groups. In contrast, the Shawnee-Minisink site is similar to sites to the south. These contain only a few spearpoints, and the majority of the toolstone is locally available. These southern bands occupied a territory of 75 to 150 miles and collected a variety of plants and animals. Contrary to the image of big game hunters, they were essentially generalized foragers.

As with all periods, settlement patterns—the ways people distribute themselves throughout the landscape in order to take advantage of the environment—change over time. It has been difficult to identify these changes during the Paleoindian period in Pennsylvania. However, in other areas, such as New England and Virginia, it seems the territories become smaller. Based on lithic sourcing, Late Paleoindian bands appear to have used more local toolstone and moved shorter distances.

The Paleoindian period is especially fascinating because there was a point in time that Pennsylvania was occupied by only one band of Paleoindians—a founding population. Because they were unfamiliar with available resources and were the first (due to no competition with other bands), they may have exploited the environment differently. They could have moved through the region quickly, seeking the best and most easily exploited resources in terms of food, stone for tools, reeds for baskets, and every other resource that was important. They may have moved to a central region, established a base camp, and sent out reconnaissance groups to find the easiest resources to gather. They may have been wasteful since there was so much for so few people. In the beginning they almost certainly would have missed certain resources. Archaeologists have speculated on this period of discovery, trying to identify sites that might represent this first founding band of Paleoindians. It is generally believed sites from this founding population should be different from other sites. Interestingly, the Shoop site stands out as a unique Paleoindian site in the region and could represent that first population.

People Living in Groups: Social Organization and Belief Systems

The Paleoindian period was an amazing time in Pennsylvania prehistory and a unique time in cultural evolution. Pennsylvania was sparsely populated by small families of foragers. There were probably never more than 150 people living in what is now the state at any one time. The climate had been evolving from Pleistocene conditions, and the mixture of plants and animals was very different from what it is today. The human groups were small, probably fewer than twenty-five individuals, and they most likely traveled for months without meeting other families. Based on what archaeologists know of other foraging cultures living in small groups, the bands living in Pennsylvania (and the Middle Atlantic region) were probably related. They shared uncles, aunts, and cousins, and there was little conflict between bands. When they met at a pre-arranged location, it was probably a time of celebration. The Thunderbird site in northern Virginia and the Plenge site in New Jersey and possibly the Shoop site may represent these large communal camps. Groups of fifty to one hundred people may have come together to visit and share stories of what had happened since the last time they met. These meetings would also include religious ceremonies to rejuvenate their beliefs. Because each band consisted of mainly close relatives and their spouses, meeting other bands was a time for finding a mate and marriage ceremonies.

The end of the Paleoindian period corresponds to the end of the Younger Dryas episode. This occurred rather suddenly with temperatures rising significantly and precipitation reaching modern levels within one hundred years. Other than a change in projectile point types, Paleoindian artifacts and settlement patterns are remarkably similar to Early Archaic artifacts and settlement patterns. It is interesting that the most significant environmental change in the past forty thousand years occurred ten thousand years ago and the change in the archaeological record is not nearly as great. Although the environment changed significantly, it seems that the general adaptive strategy for exploiting the environment used by Native Americans in the Middle Atlantic region did not change as significantly. By all accounts, in the Middle Atlantic region—at least during the Early Archaic period—the Paleoindians are the genetic ancestors of these people.

The Paleoindian period presents an exciting opportunity for the anthropological study of low-density populations adapting to what appears to be relatively abundant conditions—if for no other reason than there was no competition for food other than from members of one's own group. This period documents how people occupied a new land and developed cultural traditions that lasted for thousands of years. Today's archaeologists are beginning to understand Paleoindian technology and diet, but have much to learn about their social organization and religious beliefs.

Paleoindian Research in Pennsylvania

Based on the presence of fluted spearpoints or radiocarbon dates from this period, as of August 2011, there were 304 Paleoindian sites recorded in the Pennsylvania Archaeological Site Survey (PASS) files. The main evidence for the Paleoindian occupation was a single fluted point at each of these sites. There were probably more artifacts, but they were not particularly distinctive and could not be distinguished from the artifacts of other time periods. Fewer than fifteen sites have been specifically analyzed. Most of the artifacts were found close to the surface and are mixed with artifacts from later cultures. There are only four stratified Paleoindian sites in Pennsylvania: the Shawnee-Minisink site (36Mr43), Monroe County; the Meadowcroft Rock Shelter site (36Wh297), Washington County; the Wallis site (36Pe16),

Perry County; and the Nesquehoning site (36Cr142), Carbon County. These sites are where the artifacts are buried and have not been disturbed since they were originally dropped more than ten thousand years ago.

Paleoindian Research in the Delaware Drainage Basin

Based on the presence of fluted spearpoints, there are only forty sites dating to the Paleoindian period recorded in the Delaware River Valley. Most of these sites are close to the Delaware River or one of its tributaries, such as the Lehigh and Schuylkill Rivers. Two sites, the Pocono Lake site (36Mr37) in Monroe County and the Poirier site (36Nm15) in Northampton County, contain a number of fluted points and many tools. However, the artifacts are the result of surface collecting and these sites have not been systematically excavated. Although many of the tools are made from local stone, both sites contain stone that was carried from eastern New York. These probably represent larger camps or places that contained a reliable food source and were visited on a seasonal basis for several years. These sites may be related to the Shoop site pattern of hunting and traveling considerable distances.

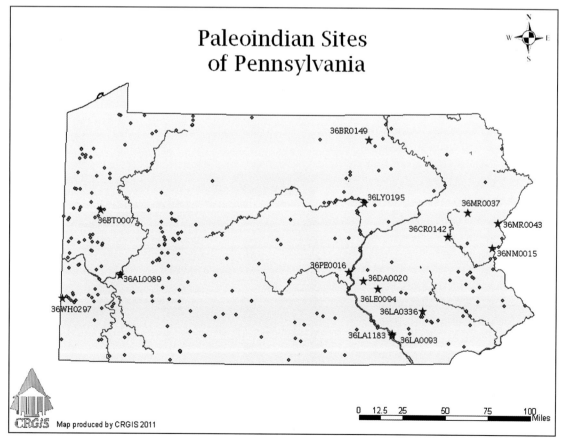

Map illustrating the distribution of Paleoindian sites in Pennsylvania.

PHOTO BY JOSEPH GINGERICH

Artifacts from the Shawnee-Minisink site used for cleaning and processing hides.

The Shawnee-Minisink site (36Mr43), near the Delaware Water Gap, represents the most significant excavation in the valley and has been listed in the National Register of Historic Places. Located on a terrace of the Delaware River, the site was discovered by an avocational archaeologist, Don Kline, who recognized the significance of deep test pits, careful excavation, and attention to the smallest of artifacts. In an early deep excavation, he found a tiny, thumbnail-size scraper typical of the Paleoindian time period. Although similar tools were uncovered later, he was convinced that the depth of the find suggested it was extremely early. Kline contacted Charles McNett, and a major excavation was initiated and conducted over several years by American University, Washington, D.C. Removing thousands of cubic feet of soil, archaeologists recorded the deepest stratified Paleoindian site in the valley.

American University's excavations produced spectacular results. The stratigraphy was good and the Paleoindian level was more than six feet deep, separated from later occupations by a layer of sand that prevented the mixing of artifacts. There were many tools, especially end scrapers, but also one Clovis fluted point. Some of the most interesting data came from two hearths. Paleoindian cooking features are extremely rare in the East and these contained the remains of a variety of seeds and fruits, but most significantly, fish remains. At a time when archaeologists believed Paleoindians were big game hunters, finding fish bones suggested a need for a major revision in thinking concerning the Paleoindian diet. The hearths produced several radiocarbon dates placing the site between 10,500 and 10,900 BP.

In 2004 Kline returned to the site and, with the assistance of students from Temple University, notably Joseph Gingerich, excavated several more three-meter units. These produced another fluted point, additional radiocarbon dates, and thousands of artifacts. The average of six radiocarbon dates from three hearths place the site at 10,950 years old, making it one of the oldest fluted point sites in the East. It is believed the Shawnee-Minisink served as a base of operations during the Paleoindian period in the upper Delaware Valley. Based on the variety of food remains found at this site and the use of local lithic sources, Shawnee-Minisink represents the typical foraging pattern for Paleoindian bands in Pennsylvania and to the south.

The most recently identified stratified Paleoindian site in Pennsylvania is the Nesquehoning site (36Cr142) located along the Lehigh River in Carbon County. The site was excavated by Temple University beginning in 2010. Although the stratigraphy is somewhat complicated, the occupations date from the Paleoindian through the Contact periods. The Paleoindian occupation is situated at least eight feet below the surface in the best stratified sections of the site; this occupation is situated just above the river cobbles. The Paleoindian component is represented by several occupations spanning hundreds of years. A radiocarbon date of 9940+50 years BP was associated with a Late Paleoindian occupation. The single projectile point is only fluted on one side and is similar to projectile points in the Great Lakes identified as the Crowfield type. The artifact density is relatively low. The site seems to represent a limited number of visits by nuclear family groups.

PHOTO BY DELL BECK

The Late Paleoindian Crowfield projectile point type from the Nesquehoning site dating to 10,340 ± 40 BP.

Paleoindian Research in the Susquehanna Drainage Basin

One hundred and thirteen Paleoindian sites have been recorded in the Susquehanna Valley, of which the Wallis site (36Pe16), located near Liverpool, Perry County, is the only stratified Paleoindian site excavated to date. This site was excavated by archaeologists working for the Pennsylvania Department of Transportation when U.S. Route 11/15 was redesigned in the late 1990s. This site contained two Paleoindian components: an earlier component was destroyed by a canal built in the 1840s and the later occupation was dated by radiocarbon to 9890+40 years ago and yielded a small collection of tools and a Late Paleoindian knife/projectile point. This artifact is only

The Late Paleoindian Crowfield projectile point type from the Wallis site dating to 9890 ± 40 BP.

A sample of fluted points from the Shoop site. Most of these have been resharpened many times.

fluted on one face and, like the artifact discovered at the Nesquehoning site (36Cr142), has been identified as a Crowfield type. The artifact assemblage is most similar to the Shawnee-Minisink assemblage and, although dating later in time, seems to represent a local foraging pattern. Unfortunately, much of the Paleoindian component was destroyed by the construction of the Pennsylvania Canal and the initial construction of U.S. Route 11/15. The sections that were preserved and excavated represent the bank of the Susquehanna River. The main living and working area was probably twenty feet to the west.

The most significant Paleoindian site in the Susquehanna Valley, the Shoop site (36Da20) in Dauphin County, returned approximately ninety-two fluted points, and thousands of tools, clustered in at least eleven concentrations scattered over an area of nearly forty acres. Most of the artifacts were made from Onondaga chert quarried from 250 miles to the north, near Buffalo, New York. As would be expected from a toolkit that has traveled this distance, the tools have been resharpened many times and are relatively small. The site is considered by many to be a major hunting camp used to hunt migratory animals such as elk or caribou. The site is listed in the National Register of Historic Places and has been nominated as a National Historic Landmark.

Unlike the Delaware Valley, there are several concentrations of Paleoindian sites located in Lycoming County, along the lower North Branch of the Susquehanna River, and in the lower Susquehanna Valley in Lancaster County. These may represent base camps where families clustered to gather seasonally available food resources. At least one of the sites in Lycoming County, the Warrior Spring site (36Ly195), contains many tools and artifacts made from Onondaga chert and could be related to the group that occupied the Shoop site.

A cluster of five sites is located along the Susquehanna River, south of Columbia in Lancaster County. These probably represent repeated visits by extended family groups. Their tools were made from local quartz but also from jasper that could have originated in Berks County or in the Shenandoah Valley, near Front Royal, Virginia. The lower Susquehanna Valley may have been the meeting area for two bands, one exploiting southeastern Pennsylvania and the other exploiting northern Virginia. A Paleoindian site in the upper Conestoga River drainage (36La336) was excavated and revealed tools and flakes of jasper. Because few tools were found, the site was interpreted as a special-purpose site, possibly related to hunting and the butchering of animals.

Paleoindian Research in the Upper Ohio Drainage Basin

To date, 151 Paleoindian sites have been recorded in the Ohio Valley of Pennsylvania. The most significant Paleoindian research conducted in this region was the excavation of Meadowcroft Rockshelter (36Wh297), conducted by the University of Pittsburgh, mainly in the 1970s. The site is located near the community of Avella, Washington County, and is open for visitation. The site is stratified to a depth of more than sixteen feet and contains thousands of well-preserved plant and animal remains. It dates to at least 16,250 years ago and represents one of the oldest sites in North America. The occupation occurred nearly five thousand years before the invention of Clovis fluted points. Meadowcroft was one of the first Pre-Clovis sites widely accepted as authentic by the archaeological community. The oldest remains consist of a small assemblage of scrapers and cutting tools. Some of these are made on elongated flakes called blades, and this is a technology similar to that being used in Siberia at the same time period. The single spearpoint, known as the Miller Lanceolate, is generally similar to a fluted point, but without flutes. This assemblage is especially significant because it appears to represent the ancestors to Paleoindian fluted point-using people.

MERCYHURST ARCHAEOLOGICAL INSTITUTE

The Pre-Clovis, Miller Lanceolate projectile point from Meadowcroft Rockshelter dates to at least 16,000 years ago.

The largest concentration of fluted point sites is located in the upper Allegheny Valley in an area that archaeologist Stan Lantz defines as the Upper Allegheny Paleoindian Corridor. These do not appear to be large sites in area or in numbers of tools. Two sites in the lower Allegheny and the Ohio drainages have been tested and, although the data is preliminary, they appear to represent nuclear family groups who foraged throughout large areas. The stone they used for making tools was frequently local but some originated as far away as Ohio or the Onondaga chert quarries of western New York State. Their annual movements or territory may have covered two hundred miles or more in search of food resources. They seem to be practicing a general foraging pattern similar to the lower Susquehanna Valley but using slightly larger territories. However, the true nature of their terms of diet and social organization, as is the case of most Paleoindian sites, is not known.

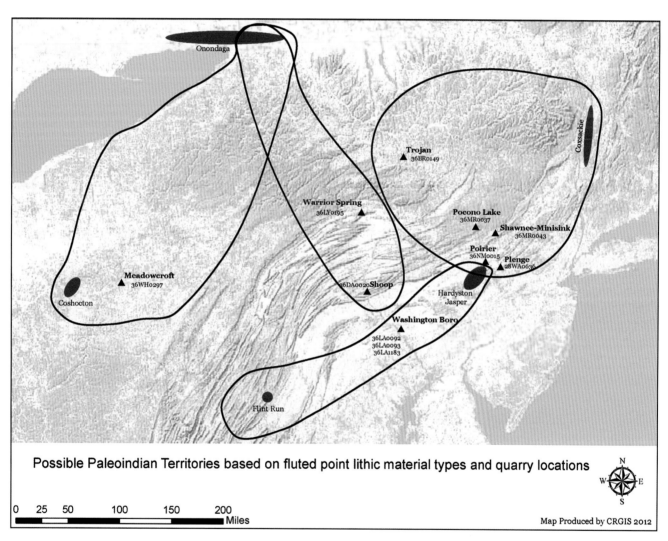

Map graphic of Front Royal, Lehigh County settlement pattern. Using lithic material sources used to make fluted points, several territories can be generally identified. These date to the Clovis period and the seasonal movements seemed to have involved over two hundred miles.

A Paleoindian's Narrative

My name is Clofolbuftem, and I am thirty years old. There are about one hundred men, women, and children in our tribe. We call ourselves The People. I live in a band with my cousins, aunts, and uncles. There are about fifteen of us. We only see the other groups a couple of times a year and some only once a year. I have a wife and two sons.

Many generations ago, our people came from the west and found this land. No one seemed to live here but every once in awhile, we would find a camp of the Old People. There are stories of our people meeting them and sometimes they were adopted and lived with The People. Eventually they disappeared but sometimes we still hear them in the forest. They can be helpful but usually they are mischievous. They scare away the elk or dull your knife.

Over time we divided into different bands and lived in different river valleys. In our land, the winters are long and cold but we are good hunters and we do well. Sometimes we run out of fresh meat. The summers are short and there is a lot to eat. We always tell each other that next year we will store more food but under summer conditions, it rots very quickly. In the winter, the cold keeps food from spoiling. In the warmer days we have to use smoking and drying to preserve the food. This takes a lot of time. This is work for the women and children while the men hunt.

In my wife's land to the south, it is a dense forest of evergreens and broad-leafed trees. The summers there are hot and there are many biting insects. We are lucky. Our land is a mixture of forest and open areas of small trees and shrubs. The forest is found along the rivers and at the base of the ridges. The open areas are on the ridgetops and in the flats. We find moose, elk, and berries in these open areas. We find deer, beaver, and bears in the trees. We have a favorite walnut tree and the swamps and ponds have many roots and young shoots that are delicious.

My favorite trees are the ones that lose their leaves late in the year. The cycles of these trees helps us know when to move to other camps. When the leaves first start to appear, it is time to look for small, tender plant shoots. These are

TIME 10,800 YEARS AGO.

PLACE THE SUSQUEHANNA RIVER VALLEY.

CLIMATE 15° COLDER THAN PRESENT AND LESS RAIN AND SNOW THAN TODAY.

FLORA AND FAUNA A SPRUCE PARKLAND WITH LEAFY TREES ALONG THE RIVERS, A SPRUCE AND PINE FOREST ALONG THE RIDGES AND OPEN MEADOWS ALONG THE RIDGE TOPS AND BROAD FLATS. MOOSE, ELK, AND DEER ARE THE MOST COMMON BIG GAME ANIMALS.

DISTINCTIVE ARTIFACTS FLUTED POINTS, END SCRAPERS, AND HIGH-QUALITY STONE FOR TOOL PRODUCTION.

much better than the dried, tough sticks we get in the wintertime. Digging in the near-frozen muck looking for cattail tubers is no fun. As the leaves cover the trees, we see birds, animals of all sizes, and more plants with flowers and berries. With our land filled with such different plants and animals, we have an easy life.

For most of the year, food is easy to find but firewood is another matter. It is best when we have enough firewood and enough food in the same place. Sometimes we have to carry wood for miles. I get irritated with my sons when they come back from a day in the forest and they do not bring any firewood. Even in the summertime, their mother needs it to cook, and the smoke helps to keep the flies away. Sometimes we just move our camp to where we find a pile of trees washed up along a streambank.

We live in shelters covered with animal hides, bark when we can find big-enough pieces, and pine branches. They are about twenty-five feet long. Our clothes are sewn from animal skins, and sometimes we make a poncho from reeds. In the summer, we wear a loincloth around our waists and a loose-fitting shirt. In warm weather we all take off our shirts, and the children frequently don't wear anything. We either go barefoot or we make sandals using reeds and thin strips of wood. In the winter we wear lined leather boots, pants, shirts, and long fur jackets with hoods. Our boots and pants need to be waterproof. The pants are sewn together with a bone needle and sinew or leather.

When I was young, we lived on the west side of where the big rivers come together. One year after a long hard winter, my father and his brothers had traveled to the east side of the river. They felt the hunting was better. It was decided that we would move for a while to the other side. My father was a little worried about this because he could remember that when he was a boy they had lived on the east side and after a long discussion, they had moved to the west side for the same reason.

We packed all of our belongings, our tools, sleeping furs to keep us warm, skins to cover our huts, and dried food. We packed some on the dogs and also hitched the dogs to small sleds. We walked for a long time to find a place to cross the river. The melting water from the snow filled the valley and made crossing very dangerous. We were very lucky to find a shallow area where the river was wide and filled with rocks. We had to unload the dogs, which meant that we made two trips. The water was running faster than I have ever seen. On the second trip, my poor old uncle fell and was washed downstream. My cousins tried to grab him, but the water was moving too fast. We were all very upset. He was just too old and weak for the journey. We spent two days searching the riverbank, and my oldest cousin even crossed back over the river to search the other side. We had no luck in finding my uncle.

That night, we decided to stop searching and stayed up late telling stories about him. He was a good father, a good husband, and he made the finest fluted spearpoints. He always used a stone that was colorful and easy to shape. Everyone wanted a fluted point made by my uncle. My aunt told the story about when they were very young and how he would help her collect bird eggs. Their parents thought it was a good match so they built a tent and moved in together. All of his life, he mostly did things with the other men but recently had begun to help her collect bird eggs again. Lately, his hand was stiff and nobody asked him to make spearpoints. He had not hunted in years and mostly helped his wife with their grandchildren. He was very knowledgeable. Elders are good for telling stories and maintaining the oral traditions of The People. We were all lucky that he had lived to be so old, but not too old that we had to carry him around.

The next day when I woke up I was very sick. I was sick for many days from the cold river water, but I was lucky my grand-father was with us. He is the shaman or healer for our band. He found the right plants and made a special tea to help me feel better. He is a very wise man who knows which plants are good for broken bones, the sickness of cold, and body sores. He told me once that the right plant is only part of the cure. You need to know which part to use, where to put it, and which song to sing for the best cure.

Some people thought it was a bad omen that my uncle drowned and I got sick. Maybe we were not welcome on this side of the river, maybe the animals moved back to the west side of the river while we told stories, and maybe I got sick because we stopped looking for my uncle. My grandfather said not to worry; his knowledge would drive the sickness from me. My father said to listen to my grandfather.

The shaman uses his skills only when needed. Most of his time is spent hunting with the rest of the men. In times of crisis and illness, he is the one everyone turns to—he always knows what to say and do. His mother was a shaman and he learned much from her but most of his knowledge comes from within.

In the winter, the men hunt and we eat a lot of meat. When it is warm we eat a lot of roots, seeds, and berries. It is odd,

but with each season, I get tired of the one food and can not wait until the spring thaw for tender roots mixed with our tough meat that has been frozen all winter, or the fall for fresh meat to be mixed with the roots, which are tough by then.

We spend most of our time along the big rivers. There is a lot to eat along the rivers, small animals to trap, water roots, and firewood is more plentiful. We move frequently. When the men kill a deer or small game, they bring it back to the camp. But when they kill a couple of elk, we frequently move to the kill rather than carry it all back to the main camp. After the meat is gone and all of the bones have been cracked to get the juicy marrow (a nutritious jellylike substance in bones), we sometimes move to another kill or back to the original river camp or to a new place that has lots of firewood. The old people spend most of their time at the base camp and they help the mothers with the children. The rest of us move along the rivers and streams hunting for meat or gathering for plants or just getting firewood; or the children just have adventures.

Our children are very dear to us and it is important that they grow up healthy and that they know how to behave. They learn by watching the adults. Once, in late winter, when I was about ten years old, we had visitors. The man was an old friend of my father's. They had traveled together when they were young men and had seen many different places. His family had not been able to find food for a while and they were visiting us for advice. We were eating and the man accidentally knocked my favorite wooden bowl and all its contents into the fire. He apologized but I started yelling at him and made a terrible scene. Everyone was upset, and I continued to complain that my food was ruined. I think I was just tired and hungry and angry that we had to share the last of our best elk meat with visitors. My father took me to the edge of the camp and told me to stay there until our visitors left.

The next day, my mother began to cry as soon as they were gone. "How could you shame us? What will our rela-tives think? Do we not know how to teach our children respect for others? No one will ever come visit us again!" My father agreed with her and added that we could never visit anyone for fear that they would treat us the same way. He explained how we must always be very polite to visitors. "They are frequently tired and hungry and they get the first pick at the meal. Isn't that the way we would like to be treated?" he asked. My aunt and uncle even came over and scolded me and said my father always spoiled me. I could see the shame that I had caused my parents and I felt awful. It is an embarrassment that I have never forgotten. Even today, my parents sometimes give me a little look or just a tap on my shoulder and remind me to behave correctly and make them proud. One time I saw my sister's husband slap his son. We would never think of doing that with our children. They learn by following our example. If we hit them, that means we are not being good parents.

Getting enough food is usually only a problem in the late winter. Getting firewood is always a problem. Watching out for predators is something we worry about daily. We are always watchful around the camp for cats that may steal the children. It does not happen often but when we visited my wife's family in the south, one of the little boys had been badly mauled by a cat but his grandmother was able to save him.

In the woods, these animals are a constant threat and all of us carry clubs and spears. If we hear wolves, we are especially worried. Sometimes a group of hunters will fight back and try to kill as many wolves as they can. My cousins collect their teeth and have made necklaces from them. We respect the animals of the forest but it is just not safe to let them roam too close to the camp.

In open areas when the men are hunting elk or the women are collecting berries, we need to be watchful for bears. Bears are like people and they are frequently in the same areas looking for the same foods. This is especially true when we go fishing. In the spring, there is always an argument among us as to whether we should go downriver to the waterfalls where the fish are easy to catch. But there are always bears doing the same thing. If we can find another family to join us, we usually go because there is safety in numbers. But, just as we find a safe spot along the river with lots of fish, a bear comes out of nowhere and then there is trouble. We have a saying "Sometimes you eat the bear and sometimes the bear eats you." Five summers ago, my cousin was killed and there was nothing we could do. She walked into an area where the bears were fishing; she got between a cub and its mother and she could not move away fast enough. We did not go back for several years but we are going to try again this year.

When I was first married, there were several years in a row where my cousins and I killed a bear. If we can corner young ones, once they are speared, a group of us can usually kill them. I have the bear claws to prove it. My aunt was angry with me and scoffed "What good did these claws do you when they stole my beautiful daughter?"

Our spearpoints are very special. They are a sign of The People. No one else can make them. Our spearpoints are fluted—they have a groove that starts on the base and continues up the face of the spear for about two inches. It is difficult to make and it took many hours of practice. I could make the blade easily enough but the fluting was the hard part and I kept breaking the blade in half. My father told me that I would not be a man until I could successfully flute four out of five blades. I went to my uncle and he showed me a trick on how to hold the blade so it would not break. He also showed me how to create a platform (a slight projection that makes it easier to hit) for the flute so that when it was struck with the elk hammer, I would get a perfect flute every time.

Our spears are made of several pieces—the fluted biface, two pieces of bone for the foreshaft, and a long, hard wooden spear shaft. We place the two pieces of bone in the flute of the blade and bind them together very tightly. This is the foreshaft and it is inserted in to a slot in the main shaft of the spear. Finding long straight pieces of hard wood is difficult so we protect the spear shaft by using a bone foreshaft.

Fluting is a gift from our spirits. A long time ago, huge beasts lived in our land. Some were so large, it was nearly impossible for The People to hunt them. The hunts were very exciting but dangerous. However, for a man to get married, he had to kill at least one of the great beasts. He always had the help of his cousins and brothers but most men only hunted them once in their entire lives. Many stories were told around the winter fires. Gradually, these animals began to disappear and The People began to worry. How would our sons get married if there were no huge beasts to kill to prove they are men and ready for marriage? One of our great hunters went into the woods for a long time to think about this problem. He spoke to the spirits and they confirmed his suspicions that the huge beasts were all dying. The hunter cried to the spirits "How will we prove ourselves to be men if these animals all die?" The spirits said that they would replace them with smaller animals that were not so dangerous and did not require so much work to hunt. The hunter was not satisfied. The spirits said, "We will give you a gift that only great hunters can use; this gift that will make you smarter and more skillful than any other hunters." The hunter brought the idea of fluting back to The People and since that time, it was the way boys proved themselves to be men and ready for marriage. (The real function of fluting remains unclear.)

The best stone for making spearpoints and knives is available in only a few places. It needs to be hard, with sharp edges when it is chipped into shape. Most importantly, we must be able to control and predict how it breaks. Our tools are important and they must be well made. In a pinch, I have made my spearpoints from poor-quality stone, but my brother laughed at me and reminded me that you can always tell the character of a hunter by the stone that he uses. I prefer jasper from along the Delaware River. It is a bright yellow and brown rock and it turns red if it is carefully heated in the fire. We need good-quality stone to make our tools and especially our fluted points.

We sharpen our tools many times and the better the stone, the more often the tools can be reused. When we are cleaning elk hides in the fall, we use many scrapers. The work is long and hard. My father taught me how to work stone but the first real job I had was making and sharpening scrapers for my mother as she cleaned elk hides. They start out three inches long but after a day of cleaning hides and frequent resharpening they are worn down to less than an inch.

In the spring, we make a trip to the jasper quarries about two weeks to the east. It is a great time because we meet our friends who live along the coast. They tell me that there is a huge ocean farther to the east that tastes salty. It is full of giant fish that sometimes walk out on the shore and are easily killed. That is something that I would like to see.

The men need really good stone for their spears and knives in the hunting camps. But, getting the right piece of wood for the spear shafts and knife handles and working it is more difficult than I thought. My father made it look so easy, but it is not. The wood must be very hard so it will not split, but that makes it very difficult to cut. Once the right cut is made and the knife is inserted, it has to be wrapped in sinew and held in place with glue from cooked animal parts. We use the knives so much that the handle must hold the blade very tightly. I can replace a broken stone knife or spear head in a few minutes but it will take me hours to make a new shaft or handle.

The women are less particular about the stones for breaking bones to get marrow, cracking nuts, and crushing the tough plants. They get these along the river. My wife makes a big deal about how hard she works. The women take the children, roam the woods picking up food and firewood, and bring it back to camp. How difficult is that? She is afraid of getting warts from a wild toad. Like that is worse than getting poked with caribou antlers because the spear head falls out of the shaft! I tease my wife and tell her how easy her life is. She is a good wife who is strong and works hard. She has given us two sons and a daughter. The girl was born in the winter. There was not much food and her spirit did not like it here, so she went back. My wife was very sad, but I promised her that we would be better prepared the next time and the baby would stay.

Most of the year, we spend our time in family groups. Sometimes, it gets lonely living with the same small group. When I was younger, I frequently wished I had more cousins. In the fall, we join other families to hunt elk and deer. This is a very exciting time. There are sometimes more than seventy-five of us. We need a big group to have a good drive to collect enough meat to last the winter. The big camps are lots of fun. We see old friends and relatives, we tell stories around the campfires, marriages are arranged, there is lots of trading and there is lots of dancing. We wear the elk skins when we dance. It makes the elk easier to hunt.

There is so much going on that it would be fun to live with a big group all of the time. The downside is that we quickly use all of the easy wood and then we need to walk long distances to find more. Once it snows, the wood is harder to find. The other problem with the fall camp is that with so many people, there are always arguments and sometimes fights. Young men fight over girlfriends, old

ILLUSTRATION BY NANCY BISHOP

men fight because they are too proud, and women get jealous that their husbands want a second wife or someone isn't sharing correctly. Some of the arguments are settled by singing contests or feats of strength. The singing contests can be very funny. My mother once sang a song about her brother's wife that compared her face to that of a moose. It was hilarious. But sometimes, the knives come out and someone gets hurt. After a month or so of this, the group thins out and we only get back together for special occasions.

By the time I was ready to be a hunter, I had been taught the ways of the animals. I had learned every part of the territory where the big rivers came together. I knew the best hunting spots and camps for 200 miles. My mother taught me about where to find roots and other plants to eat. My father and uncles taught me all about the forest and the meadows. The People do not travel to the ridgetops very often so my cousins and I would go exploring in these areas. Sometimes we would find new sources of rock for making stone tools. We are always on the lookout for the best stone for our tools.

My grandfather told me the story of how when he was a boy his family followed the caribou all year long, covering almost three hundred miles. They migrated north in the summer and south in the winter. Caribou live in large herds, much larger than elk, with hundreds of animals. Caribou do not usually migrate along the rivers because the biting flies are bad so they migrate higher up, along the ridges. But when they came down to cross the rivers that is a good place to trap them.

The families were bigger and they lived in large tents with twenty people per tent and fifty people living in the camp. In the summers, the families lived hundreds of miles to the north, near a huge lake. My grandfather was a young man at the time and he said the hunting was great. There was plenty of high-quality stone to make our fluted points and all of our other tools. But the northern camp was cold and snowy. Being close to the lake, it would begin to snow in early fall. Usually the grass was still green and my grandfather said that you would wake up one morning and there would be much snow on the ground. That is when it was time to move south. The People and the caribou would all move together. The caribou would move quickly to get away from the snow. Once they were out of the snowbelt, they would slow down and spend the rest of the fall moving to where the great rivers come together. Depending on the snowfall, that is where they would stay and they would divide into smaller groups.

For many years, my grandfather's family camped in the same area for the winter. It was many miles from the river but there were always caribou herds close by and the hunting was very good. In the fall they would come to this place before they moved down into the Great Valley for the winter. At this time my grandfather's band killed one hundred animals in a week. Red meat was hanging everywhere to dry. They used the hides to cover the tents and to make coats and boots. The meat that was not immediately eaten was dried and smoked. They made some tools from the bones, but most were split to get the marrow and a lot were burned in the fires for cooking and keeping warm. He said the biggest problem was firewood. The trees were small along the ridges so they were frequently carrying wood up from the river valleys. They also burned caribou dung. It did not smell as good as wood, but it kept them warm.

My grandfather said that when the first large bull was killed there would be a dance that evening. The hunters ate the bull's heart and liver because it gave them power. At the dance, they thanked the bull for allowing itself to be hunted and said how thankful they would be if all of the caribou would allow the men to hunt them. We do the same thing today.

His stories of hunting herds of caribou were exciting and the northern land was intriguing. But he said it was a lot of walking. Sometimes, they had to carry old people and new mothers had to work very hard at keeping up. Also some years, the caribou herd was small and harder to hunt. Worse yet, there were always wolves lurking around to steal from the humans or hunt the caribou. Over time, the families split up. They picked a good river valley and only hunted the caribou when they came through each year. Eventually, the caribou stopped coming this far south. No one knows why for sure but by that time, the People had settled into their own territories.

When I was young, I remember my grandparents talking about their lives. When my grandfather again told us the story about the biggest caribou he ever killed, this time my grandmother groaned and said, "All you had to do was kill it. The five children and I spent three days hauling it back to camp, removing the hide, slicing big chunks to cook over the fire, cutting some meat into strips to dry, cleaning the bones for your tools, and burying everything we weren't going to use to keep the bears away." My grandfather smiled back and said, "Sure tasted good after eating the roots and leaves you and the kids found!" For them it had been a long life and they had learned many things, but now it was almost done. For me, I was just realizing what I was facing.

Our lives are really quite good. Sometimes firewood is a problem, and sometimes it gets lonely but all in all, we live better than anyone around us.

Chapter 4
The Archaic Period: 4300 to 10,000 years ago

TIMELINE

Contact Period	1500 AD–1700 AD
Woodland Period	1500–2700 years ago
Transitional Period	2700–4300 years ago
Archaic Period	**4300–10,000 years ago**
Late Archaic	**4300–6000 years ago**
Middle Archaic	**6000–9000 years ago**
Early Archaic	**9000–10,000 years ago**

Environment: The Early Archaic period is characterized by a warm and dry climate and a dense spruce and pine forest. In the Middle Archaic period, the climate becomes warm and wet, with an oak and pine forest. During the Late Archaic period, the forest is dominated by oak and hemlock.

Making and using tools (typical artifacts and technology): The Early Archaic technology is similar to Paleoindian times but is characterized by corner-notched projectile points. By Middle Archaic times, bifurcate-based projectile points are being used, followed by stemmed and notched points; later ground and polished woodworking tools are added to the tool kit, the lithic technology changes, and local lithic sources are used. By Late Archaic times, grinding stones, grooved axes, notched netsinkers, bannerstones, rock-lined cooking hearths, and a variety of stemmed and notched projectile points are common.

What people ate (subsistence): Throughout this period a wide variety of plants and animals were exploited. By Late Archaic times, there seems to be an increasing emphasis on fishing and nut and seed collecting.

Where people lived (settlement patterns): The focus continues to be on floodplains during the Early Archaic, but during the Middle Archaic, sites are found throughout upland areas along small streams and at springheads. By Late Archaic times, upland sites are very common and sites in the floodplains increase in size.

People living in groups (social organization and belief systems): Families continue to be organized into egalitarian bands. Over time, the bands gradually became larger and less mobile. By the Late Archaic, there appears to be many regional bands. The Native American population in Pennsylvania by the Late Archaic period probably numbered in the thousands.

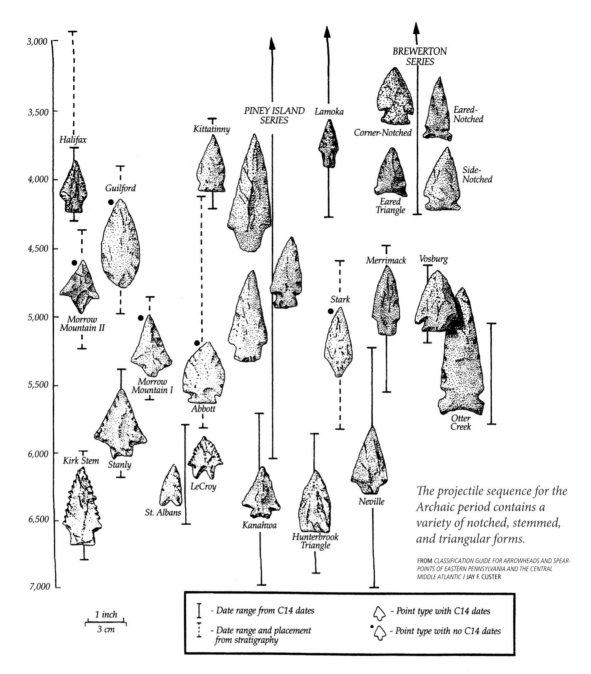

PINEY ISLAND SERIES

BREWERTON SERIES

Halifax

Kittatinny

Lamoka

Corner-Notched

Eared-Notched

Guilford

Eared Triangle

Side-Notched

Morrow Mountain II

Merrimack

Vosburg

Morrow Mountain I

Stark

Abbott

Kirk Stem

Stanly

Otter Creek

LeCroy

St. Albans

Kanahwa

Neville

The projectile sequence for the Archaic period contains a variety of notched, stemmed, and triangular forms.

Hunterbrook Triangle

FROM *CLASSIFICATION GUIDE FOR ARROWHEADS AND SPEAR-POINTS OF EASTERN PENNSYLVANIA AND THE CENTRAL MIDDLE ATLANTIC* / JAY F. CUSTER

1 inch / 3 cm

- Date range from C14 dates

- Date range and placement from stratigraphy

- Point type with C14 dates

- Point type with no C14 dates

Definition

The Archaic period represents an adaptation to a forest environment and involves a new set of tools. The period is divided into three subperiods—Early, Middle, and Late—based on changes in stone artifacts. Spearpoints are one of the most commonly preserved tools and they are found in many different corner-notched, side-notched, and stemmed forms. Throughout this period, a variety of woodworking, fishing, and nut and seed processing tools are added to the toolkit. Using these tools, Archaic peoples intensified and expanded their exploitation of the environment from floodplain settings to include many upland locations. They begin to exploit a wide variety of upland environments along smaller streams. In contrast to the Paleoindian period, the bands are less mobile, they do not cover large territories, and populations increase dramatically by the end of the period. In addition, bands begin to regionalize.

By the Late Archaic period, each of the major drainage basins is characterized by its own distinctive set of artifacts and probably its own culture. There may have been language differences between groups in the Susquehanna basin and the Ohio basin. This period represents 6000 years of human population growth and a diversification of tool technology. Some believe this represents the classic time of Native American forest adaptations. The Archaic period ends with the appearance of a new and very distinctive set of artifacts. These include broad-bladed spearpoints/knives aptly called broadspears.

A view of the Pre-Boreal closed coniferous forest along the Susquehanna River 9500 years ago.

The Environment

By 10,000 years ago, the climate had warmed. By all accounts, the Younger Dryas ended rather quickly and within one hundred years, temperatures nearly reached those of today. Animal populations were relatively modern and included most of the mammals, fish, birds, and other fauna of native origin that were here at the time of Columbus. The vegetation took much longer to evolve, however. Between 9000 and 10,000 years ago, the Pennsylvania forest was in a period of transition. This is the Pre-Boreal climatic episode. It began as a spruce-pine forest and ended as a pine-oak forest. The open forest of the Pleistocene was replaced by a denser spruce-pine forest similar to forests found in Canada today but different in that they had a greater variety of trees and shrubs. Deciduous trees, such as oak, hickory, chestnut, and maple were gradually spreading from the south, but these broadleaf trees did not replace the spruce-pine forest until after 9000 years ago. During the Pre-Boreal, food resources for humans in the form of roots, seeds, berries, and animals were concentrated in developing floodplains in the Susquehanna and Delaware drainages and around swamps and bogs in the Ohio drainage; however, overall this was a less plentiful environment than during Paleoindian times. A spruce-pine forest simply does not have the nuts, seeds, berries, roots, and bird and mammal populations that are found in a pine-oak or oak-chestnut forest.

During Paleoindian times, Pennsylvania rivers were very wide and rocky. They were not bordered by the broad, flat floodplains we see today. The rivers changed their courses frequently and Paleoindian sites that formed along these rivers were usually washed away. During the Early Archaic period, the rivers began to stabilize into one channel, and floodplains began to develop. Artifacts that were dropped by the Archaic inhabitants of these areas were covered by subsequent flood deposits. Imagine that the 12- or 15-foot-high floodplains of today were only 3 feet high 10,000 years ago. Archaeologists find that Early Archaic artifacts are frequently found in the deepest levels of these floodplains and only a couple of feet above the water table.

By 9000 years ago, the beginning of the Middle Archaic period, oaks and other nut-bearing trees became common throughout the region. The Pre-Boreal episode is followed by the Boreal episode, which is also warm and dry but characterized by a deciduous or broad-leafed forest. Beginning 8000 years ago, the Atlantic episode begins, and this is a period of warm and moist conditions approaching the current climate. Overall, the forest was richer in food resources, including walnuts, hickory nuts, butternuts, acorns, and a variety of seeds, roots, and berries. The birds and mammals that fed on these resources provided food for the rapidly increasing human population.

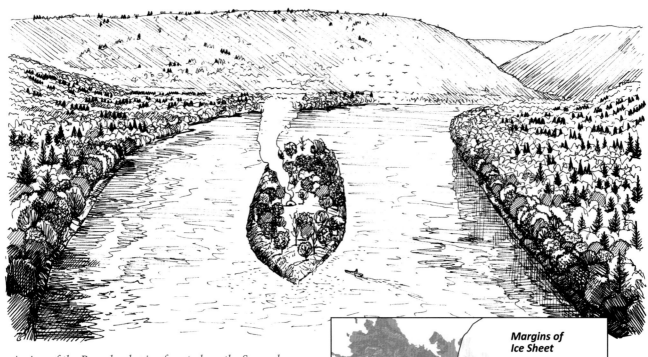

A view of the Boreal oak-pine forest along the Susquehanna River 6500 years ago.

Beginning about 6000 years ago, there was an interesting change in weather patterns. Although the glaciers had retreated well into Canada, they had continued to affect the weather of Pennsylvania. The presence of a huge mass of cold air (in the form of the glacier in Canada) prevented warm, moist air from moving out of the Gulf of Mexico. By 6000 years ago, the glaciers had sufficiently retreated north so that a new weather pattern developed. As a result, the Middle Atlantic region began to experience cyclonic storms (hurricanes) and drainage-wide flooding. These events are recorded at many archaeological sites as thick layers (several inches) of flood-deposited sands. Although the forests of Pennsylvania were constantly changing, between 4500 and 9000 years ago, the primary plants and animals were the same. Modest changes in climate resulted in shifts in the distribution of plants and animals, but the basic ecology was the same for over 4000 years. As Native Americans adopted agriculture and cleared forests, there were additional changes in the ecology, but many archaeologists consider the Archaic period as the classic adaptation to the primeval forest.

By 6000 years ago, the glaciers had sufficiently retreated to allow hurricanes to move into the Middle Atlantic region. These caused flooding and hastened the burial of archaeological sites.

FROM GENETIC STRATIGRAPHY: THE MODEL FOR SITE BURIAL AND ALLUVIAL SEQUENCES IN PENNSYLVANIA BY F. J VENTO

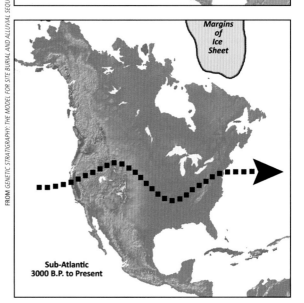

Margins of Ice Sheet

Atlantic
8000 to 4200 B.P.

Margins of Ice Sheet

Sub-Atlantic
3000 B.P. to Present

Making and Using Tools: Typical Artifacts and Technology

Paleoindian tools did not quickly become Archaic tools. In fact, the tool technology of the Early Archaic period was quite similar to the Paleoindian period. The main difference was that the spearpoints were notched rather than fluted. Charleston corner-notched, Kirk corner-notched, and Palmer are common Early Archaic projectile point types. In Pennsylvania, they are relatively broad and almost always serrated. As during the Paleoindian period, they are frequently made from chert or jasper, but metarhyolite and quartzite were added as preferred toolstone. Some archaeologists believe that the change in spearpoint shape was related to hunting with an atlatl in the dense forest of the Early Archaic period. The atlatl consists of

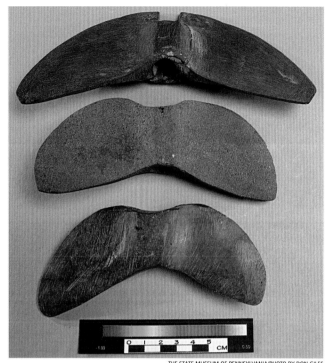

THE STATE MUSEUM OF PENNSYLVANIA/PHOTO BY DON GILES

Various styles of bannerstones found in Pennsylvania. Although most frequently interpreted as atlatl weights, their function is not well understood.

THE STATE MUSEUM OF PENNSYLVANIA/PHOTO BY DON GILES

Projectile points dating to the Early Archaic period from the Wallis, Treichler's Bridge, and Lewistown Narrows sites.

a wooden stick with a hook at one end to launch the spear. It served to lengthen the hunter's arm and increase the accuracy and speed of the throw. Notched spearpoints may have allowed for a more secure hafting mechanism that would withstand the greater speed of the atlatl. Wooden atlatls, however, are not preserved at archaeological sites, so we are not sure when they were being used. The stone weights that were sometimes placed on the end of the stick to increase its force are found at some Late Archaic sites, but prior to this time the evidence is conjectural.

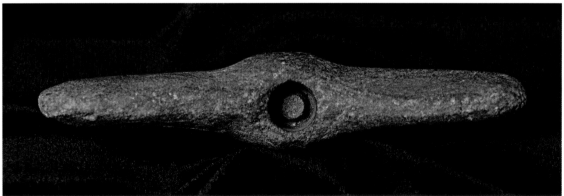

THE STATE MUSEUM OF PENNSYLVANIA/PHOTO BY DON GILES

A rare partially drilled bannerstone illustrates the use of a hollow reed and sand in the drilling process.

An atlatl consists of a piece of wood approximately two feet long with an antler hook on one end and an antler or bone grip handle on the other end. Sometimes a stone weight called a bannerstone was placed towards the end with the hook.

The Atlatl

The atlatl is a relatively simple device used to propel a spear farther and with more speed and accuracy than a hand-thrown spear. Although they come in a variety of shapes and sizes, a common form consists of a piece of wood, approximately 2 feet long, with an antler hook on one end and a grip handle on the other.

Also known as the spear-thrower, it seems to have been developed independently throughout the world. There are many names for it; "atlatl" is the Aztec term. They are at least 20,000 years old in Europe and probably much older than that. There are cave paintings in France that depict the atlatl in use. They were extensively used in Australia, where it is called the "woomera," possibly as early as 45,000 years ago. Atlatls are difficult to date, however, because they are mostly made out of wood and are rarely preserved at archaeological sites. Up until recently, they were still used in Mexico, Chili, Australia, Papua New Guinea, and by the Inuit (Eskimos). They may have migrated to the New World with Paleoindians when they crossed the Bering Land Bridge around 15,000 years ago.

A spear, or dart, thrown with an atlatl travels faster than if hand-thrown because the device acts as an extension of the throwing arm and provides more leverage; the atlatl's end moves faster than the hand holding it. The atlatl essentially increases the length of the thrower's arm, creating more power to propel the dart. In addition, the dart receives a much stronger parting thrust that results in a considerably longer trajectory. The darts resemble large arrows or thin spears, typically from 4 to 9 feet in length and 3/8 to 5/8 inch in diameter, and are designed to bend, allowing them to "spring" off the atlatl.

While the atlatl is capable of casting a dart well over 300 feet, it is most accurately used at distances of 60 feet or less. It is assumed that a few people armed with atlatls could bring down some of the biggest game animals of the Ice Age, such as the woolly mammoth. This would also be much safer than using handheld spears. While the advent of the bow and arrow initiated the decline of the atlatl in many cultures, in some cases, such as with the Aztecs and Inuits, the atlatl and bow were used at the same time. The Aztecs even used the atlatl with such skill that it was reportedly the only weapon that could pierce Spanish armor. The relative advantages of the bow over the atlatl are not well understood but some have speculated that the atlatl was a social equalizer. It required skill rather than upper-body strength and therefore could be used by women and children more effectively than a bow.

Since atlatls are rarely preserved in the archaeological record, their specific history is hard to determine. They were used in the Old World prior to humans migrating into the

New World; therefore, many archaeologists believe they were used by Paleoindians. Their appearance in Eastern North America is associated with the recovery of bannerstones from Archaic sites dating approximately 6000 years ago. A bannerstone is a stone weight that is attached to the atlatl. They are found in a variety of shapes, but in Pennsylvania, a bannerstone is typically flat and 4 to 6 inches wide, with a hole drilled longitudinally so that it can be fitted by sliding it down the shaft of the atlatl. It is usually highly polished and probably took considerable time to make. Typically it does not weigh more than a pound or two, but its function is ambiguous. None of the cultures that currently use atlatls use weights, and there is no recorded reference to them. The reason we think weights were used at all is because these artifacts have been found along with the antler hooks and handles of atlatls in gravesites. The function of the weight is also a matter of debate. Some archaeologists believe it acts as a counterweight, so that the thrower does not have to use as much force. Others think that it added stability. Still others contend that it muted the atlatl when thrown. The time and effort required to make these, and their aesthetic appearance, suggest some social or ceremonial value, but there does not yet seem to be consensus on this issue.

In eastern North American, it is generally believed that the bow and arrow replaced the atlatl at least by approximately 1000 years ago. At that time, projectile points get smaller and thinner and eventually all projectile points take on a triangular form. In dry caves, these have been found attached to arrow shafts.

In recent years, the atlatl has been resurrected for sports. There are meetings and events where people can throw darts with atlatls. Throws of almost 850 feet have been recorded. It has become particularly popular on college campuses using spears and atlatls built with both ancient and modern materials.

The real change in tools began during the Middle Archaic period. The beginning of the Middle Archaic is signaled by the appearance of bifurcate-based spearpoints. These points are distinguished by the central notch that is made in the base. They are found throughout the southeastern portion of the United States and the Ohio Valley, but generally only as far north as southern New England and Ontario, Canada. They seem to be associated with the spread of oak forests and may have provided some hunting advantage in this environment. This spearpoint style may have been made by a different people than those of the Paleoindian and Early Archaic periods and may represent a migration of people from the south.

Beginning around 8000 years ago, bifurcate-based projectile points were replaced with a variety of less distinctive short-stemmed points identified as Stanly, Neville, or Stark types. After 6500 years ago, side-notched forms such as Otter Creek and corner-notched forms such as Vosburg are found; however, there seem to be many different notched or stemmed forms that are found during this period. A distinctive series of projectile point types are not as obvious during the later Middle Archaic and the Late Archaic periods. Straight-stemmed and contracting-stemmed points are common during this time in the Piedmont and eastern Ridge and Valley regions of Pennsylvania, and these are known as Piedmont points. These are variously typed as Bare

There are a variety of bifurcate-based projectile point types found in Pennsylvania.

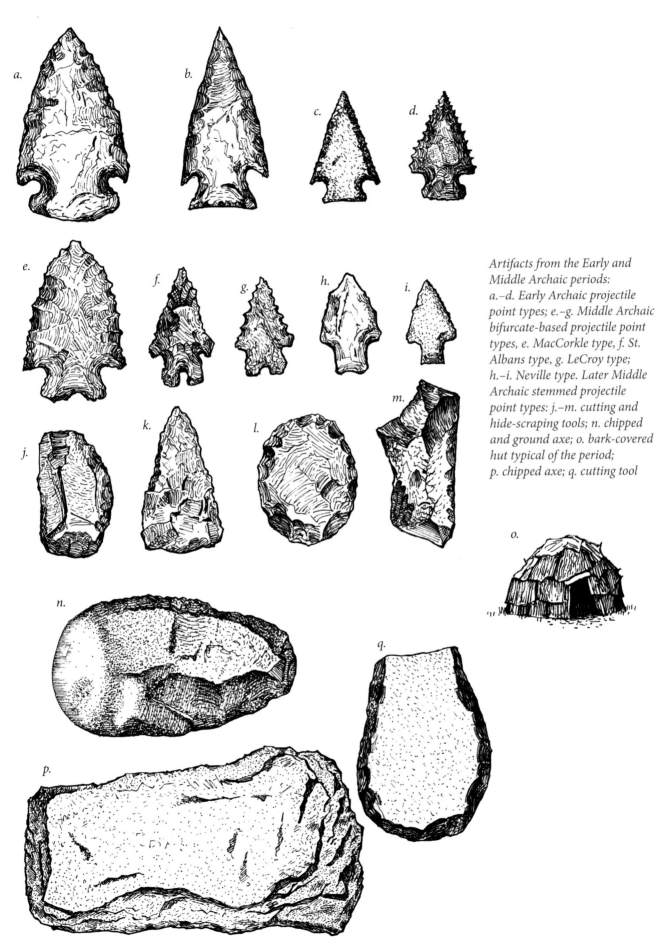

Artifacts from the Early and Middle Archaic periods: a.–d. Early Archaic projectile point types; e.–g. Middle Archaic bifurcate-based projectile point types, e. MacCorkle type, f. St. Albans type, g. LeCroy type; h.–i. Neville type. Later Middle Archaic stemmed projectile point types: j.–m. cutting and hide-scraping tools; n. chipped and ground axe; o. bark-covered hut typical of the period; p. chipped axe; q. cutting tool

Island, Lackawaxen, and Popular Island. Slightly broader, corner-notched and side-notched points are common on the Appalachian Plateau and these are called Laurentian. These are variously typed as Brewerton corner-notched, Brewerton side-notched, Brewerton-eared, and Lamoka; however, none of these are particularly diagnostic for a specific period and there is substantial regional overlap. Adding to the complexity, triangular projectile points are found throughout this time and all over the state. It is quite likely that several different styles of projectile points were being used by the same people at the same time. There may have been functional or social differences but the situation is not well understood. There has even been speculation that triangles in the Archaic period were indicative of the use of bow-and-arrow technological system.

The Paleoindian toolkit was characterized by a large number of stone tools in standardized shapes, such as end scrapers, side scrapers, knives, wedges, and spoke-shaves. These tools were frequently sharpened and used over and over again, until they could no longer be resharpened. The frequent sharpening necessitated that the Paleoindians use high-quality stone. This type of toolkit began to change slowly during the Early Archaic, and by the Middle Archaic, sharpening tools and the use of high-quality stone were no longer characteristic of this technology. Many tools were opportunistic; that is to say they were made for the activity at hand and discarded when the job was done.

Living in a hardwood forest with nut-bearing trees stimulated a huge change in the Archaic toolkit. By the Middle Archaic period, toolkits included a wide variety of woodworking tools. Woodworking tools included the full- and three-quarter-grooved stone axe and the adze. These were made using a new method of shaping stone. Similar to atlatl weights, axes were mainly made by pecking and grinding rather than chipping, the way spearpoints and knives were made. A different type of stone was used for these tools. Usually, it was heavier and denser in composition, such as greenstone basalt. Axes may have started out 1 foot long or more.

Although the general shape was accomplished by chipping, to achieve a smooth cutting surface the next step was to peck the axe into shape by repeatedly striking it with a stone hammer. The groove used to attach the axe to the handle was pecked into the rock in this fashion. When the pecking was finished, the axe had a very rough surface and was covered with small peck marks. The final process for smoothing the surface and sharpening the edge was to water-grind the axe on a hard

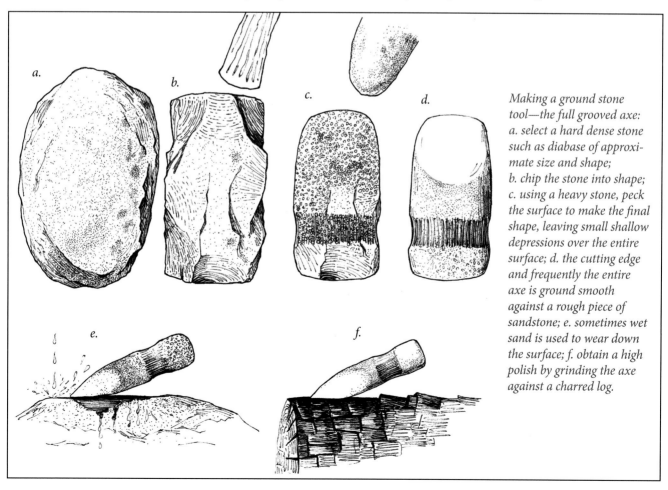

Making a ground stone tool—the full grooved axe: a. select a hard dense stone such as diabase of approximate size and shape; b. chip the stone into shape; c. using a heavy stone, peck the surface to make the final shape, leaving small shallow depressions over the entire surface; d. the cutting edge and frequently the entire axe is ground smooth against a rough piece of sandstone; e. sometimes wet sand is used to wear down the surface; f. obtain a high polish by grinding the axe against a charred log.

Chipped and ground stone tools used to exploit the hardwood forest of the Archaic period: a.–c. net sinkers; d. adze; e. gouge; f. axe; g. atlatl weight or bannerstone.

piece of coarse sandstone. This process was arduous and often took ten to twenty hours to complete. Most axes were ground smooth over their entire surface, but some were only ground smooth on their working edge. The bit end was maintained by simply grinding the edge whenever it became dull, similar to sharpening a steel axe today. In experiments with stone axes, a 6-inch-diameter tree could be cut down in less than thirty minutes.

Items made from bone: a. bone fishhook; b. bone for the cup-and-pin game; c. bone beads; d. bone awl for sewing.

Other implements in the Archaic toolkit consisted of notched flat stones that were used as weights for fishing nets. When organic preservation is good, bone fishhooks and harpoons also survive from this period. The presence of these artifacts confirms an increased dependence on fishing. In the Late Archaic period, a variety of stones used to pulverize seeds, nuts, and roots are found. Some of these were long and narrow, looking like a baker's rolling pin without handles. Most were simply unmodified, smooth river rocks, flat on one surface and rounded to fit the hand on the opposite surface. They all exhibit polishing on their used surface. An unusual nut-processing stone is called a pitted stone or a nutting stone. It is a relatively flat river rock, about 6 inches in diameter, with a small 1-inch (in diameter) depression in the middle of the flat surface. Sometimes this depression is found on opposite sides of the river rock, and these are called bipitted stones. They get their name from the belief that acorns, hickory nuts, or walnuts were placed in the depression and cracked open. Some archaeologists argue that there are much easier ways to open nuts than pecking a depression into a hard river rock and that pitted stones were used as anvils in the making of stone tools.

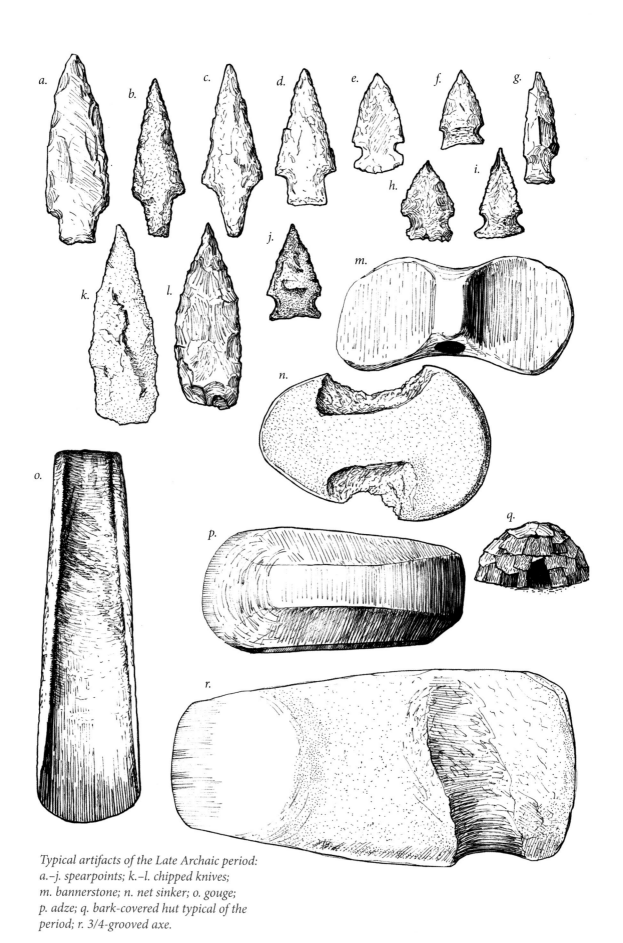

Typical artifacts of the Late Archaic period:
a.–j. spearpoints; k.–l. chipped knives;
m. bannerstone; n. net sinker; o. gouge;
p. adze; q. bark-covered hut typical of the
period; r. 3/4-grooved axe.

What People Ate: Subsistence

As was true for the Paleoindian period, very few food remains are preserved at Archaic sites and subsistence is inferred from tools and the potential foods available in the environment. It is assumed that people during the Archaic period were generalized foragers. They hunted, fished, and collected plant foods such as seeds, nuts, roots and berries. In the Ohio drainage basin there is evidence, in the form of large mounds of shell, that they also collected freshwater mussels. Overall, food resources were low in the spruce-pine forest of the Early Archaic period. Meat from elk, deer, beaver, and a variety of small mammals probably provided 50 percent of the calories. With the emergence of the oak forest during the Middle Archaic, it is assumed that plant foods became the dominant food source. It is simply easier to collect large quantities of seeds or nuts than it is to kill a deer.

In addition, plant foods usually preserve longer than animal foods. Middle Archaic populations were able to exploit these foods and recover sufficient calories to support their population without developing more specialized tools. By the Late Archaic, populations had significantly increased and technologies were developed that improved the efficiency of food gathering and

Nuts from deciduous trees such as hickory and butternut were important foods during the Archaic period.

processing. For example, humans developed a variety of tools for grinding roots, seeds, and nuts and they began fishing with nets to increase their harvest. Nets may also have been used to bring down migratory birds. We assume they had been opportunistically collecting these foods since Paleoindian times. By the Late Archaic, however, they were foraging for these foods on a scale requiring more efficient tools to increase their caloric intake. Finally, by the end of the Late Archaic, there is hard evidence in the form of charred nut shells and plant residues that an increased variety of plant foods, especially seeds, were being exploited.

Where People Lived: Settlement Patterns

Early Archaic bands exploited their environment in a similar manner as Paleoindians. They moved their camps frequently to be close to the food resources they needed. In the Delaware and Susquehanna drainages, Early Archaic sites are generally found in the river valleys (the same places as Paleoindian sites), but in the Ohio drainage, more sites are found in upland areas around swamps and bogs. They covered smaller territories than Paleoindian bands, but larger areas than later Archaic bands. Food resources, however, were not as plentiful as they were during Paleoindian times. Unlike the Paleoindian period Shoop site, archaeologists have not found any very large Early Archaic sites. People lived in small family bands of fifteen to twenty men, women, and children. The group changed in size depending on available resources. In the spring, the entire band may have exploited the fish migrations. In the summer, they may have split into smaller family groups to exploit a wide variety of floodplain or upland bog–related resources. In the fall, they regrouped to gather acorns or walnuts. But nut resources in the Pre-Boreal forest were not common and the band probably did not include more than twenty individuals. In the winter, they probably divided into small family groups and spent the winter hunting. Early Archaic people continued to prefer high-quality toolstone and part of their settlement pattern included regular trips to quarries. Metarhyolite and quartzite were added to their list of suitable materials. These were not as durable or workable as chert and jasper. In an environment with reduced food resources, people could no longer afford to make special trips to the chert and jasper quarries.

The human population gradually increased in size throughout the Archaic period, although Early Archaic populations were not much larger than the Paleoindian bands. There are 304 Paleoindian sites and only 344

Spring

Summer

Winter

Fall

The Early Archaic settlement pattern was similar to the Paleoindian annual cycle. However, they were living in a spruce-pine forest and food resources were reduced. In the fall, families grouped together to hunt large animals such as elk and deer. These camps were often in upland areas and around swamps and bogs. In the winter, they lived in small family groups and continued to emphasize hunting. In the spring, families joined together to fish and collect a variety of plant foods. In the summer, they broke into smaller groups to exploit a variety of plants and animals. There continued to be a preference for certain types of toolstone and the annual cycle included trips to quarries.

Spring

Summer

Winter

Fall

The Middle Archaic settlement pattern represents a change from previous times. Families were living in a pine-oak forest with many more food resources. Throughout the annual cycle they mostly lived in small family groups. In the spring, fishing in rivers was important along with collecting roots and seeds. In the summer, a variety of plants and animals were collected in floodplain areas. In the fall, nut collecting in upland areas was the main activity. In the winter, hunting in upland areas was the main focus.

Early Archaic sites recorded in the PASS files. Although the cause is debated, the slow increase in human population may be a result of the low productivity of the spruce-pine forest in Pennsylvania during the Early Archaic period. This type of forest has fewer edible plants and animals than the pine-oak forest to the south in Virginia or to the west in the Ohio drainage. There the forest was much more productive and Early Archaic populations were much larger.

By 9000 years ago, the pine-oak forest had covered most of Pennsylvania, resulting in a significant increase in food resources. Middle Archaic populations began practicing a very different lifestyle compared to Early Archaic peoples. The period from 8100 to 8900 years ago is associated with the use of bifurcate-based spearpoints and this may represent a migration of people from the south. This phase was the beginning of several trends in archaeological site distributions. For example, people began using a different type of stone tool technology and they no longer used the highest-quality tool stone. Chert, metarhyolite, argillite, quartz, and quartzite became the most commonly used lithic materials. It is inferred that this means that the seasonal round was smaller compared to previous times. In addition, they did not make special trips to quarries. They picked up whatever toolstone was available while they were foraging for food.

The number of sites—and the relative number of people it is assumed—more than triples at the beginning of the Middle Archaic period compared to the Early Archaic period. The increase is mainly in upland areas. There are more resources available in the uplands and people move to exploit these. The size of Middle Archaic bands appears to be different than Early Archaic or Late Archaic bands. The well-excavated, stratified sites of this period consist of small hearths with a few broken tools—likely representing nuclear families or small extended family activities. Rather than living in bands of fifteen to twenty individuals, these were smaller, possibly representing individual nuclear families. There may have been a few large base camps, but most of the year was spent in small family group settings. We do not understand why the common living group would be smaller, but it may have something to do with the plentiful environment combined with low human populations at this time.

By 6000 years ago, the beginning of the Late Archaic period, population density was increasing. Archaeological sites get very large and more sites are found in upland settings associated with small streams and springs. The obvious implication is that the foraging bands were larger. While Early and Middle Archaic groups were likely made up of nuclear families or extended families, Late Archaic bands may have included several extended families related by blood or marriage. The size and composition of the band changed throughout the course of the four seasons, based on the availability and diversity of food resources. For example, spring fishing camps may have included the entire band of fifty or more people. The nut-collecting camps in the fall were also occupied by large groups. In contrast, during the winter, the band may have split into microbands or perhaps nuclear family groups to better exploit sparse food resources.

Because of the growth in population density, the territories available to each band continued to shrink. As a result, bands had to develop new technologies and work harder to get more food from their territories by gathering a greater variety of food resources. The base camps are usually located in the valleys, but a wide variety of more specialized camps for hunting, seed gathering, and hickory nut collecting are usually found in upland settings along small streams. In fact, during the Late Archaic period, it seems as if they were using every possible food source in their foraging pattern.

Another trend in Archaic sites is the increasing presence and variety of features. These usually take the form of charcoal concentrations or fire-reddened earth with a scatter of rocks. Native Americans have been able to control fire since they first arrived in the New World, but Paleoindian hearths for cooking or heating are very rare. During the Archaic period, these become much more common and these assist archaeologists in the interpretation of archaeological sites. We assume that the hearth represents one of the main activity areas of a site and frequently focus our excavation efforts in these areas. During the Paleoindian period, people lived in small bands, moved frequently, and did not return to the same site on a regular basis. This partially explains why there are so few Paleoindian features. During the Archaic period, the bands eventually get larger, but more importantly, they returned to the same sites on a regular basis and used the hearth for longer periods of time. Therefore, they are more likely to be preserved in the archaeological record. Archaic hearths also contain fire-cracked rock, or FCR. This is rock that has been exposed to extreme heat, causing it to break into angular pieces. Native American cooking hearths during the Archaic frequently consisted of a layer of river rocks. These retained the heat better and also served as platforms for cooking. Over time, the rock cracks and breaks because of the repeated heating and cooling. These show up as concentrations of angular rock, 2 to 4 feet in diameter. By the Late Archaic, these FCR features get larger and FCR is a common artifact scattered across these sites.

Summer

The Late Archaic settlement pattern was similar to the Middle Archaic annual cycle but the bands were larger and changed size more frequently. In the spring, the families joined together to benefit from the fish migrations and collect a variety of plant foods such as roots and seeds. These camps were very busy and a variety of plant resources were also processed. In some cases, squash was planted. In the summer, families broke into small groups to exploit a wide variety of plants and animals in the floodplain and upland areas. In the fall families joined together to collect nuts and to hunt. In the winter, hunting in small family groups in upland areas was the emphasis.

Fall

Spring

Winter

89

People Living in Groups: Social Organization and Belief Systems

One of the most common stone tools found at archaeological sites of Pennsylvania are spearpoints. They are found in many shapes and sizes. Archaeologists have divided them into different categories based on similarities in shapes or what archaeologists call "types." In some regions and during some periods, spearpoints have very distinctive shapes and always date to the same period. Many of the periods used in this book can be defined by distinctive spearpoint styles. Many archaeologists assume that distinctive projectile point types represent a single culture. During some periods, the spearpoint can be a symbol of the group, just like distinctive clothing can represent a group within our culture. The fluted point of the Paleoindian period seems to fit this pattern. A specific culture shares ideas on how things should be made, so it is reasonable to conclude that the same is true about spearpoints. It has been assumed that every prehistoric band had their own style or type of spearpoint. Archaeologists used these types to date archaeological sites; however, as we shall see below, especially for the Late Archaic and Woodland periods, projectile point shapes are not usually representative of specific periods or cultures.

The Archaic period begins with a few large corner-notched styles and they seem to represent different regional bands of the same culture. Bifurcate points of the Middle Archaic period are found over a very large section of the eastern United States and last for nearly 900 years. They probably represent one culture or language group with many different regional bands. They may represent a migration of a new people. Between 4000 and 8000 years ago, however, there appears to be many different styles and they are no longer temporally diagnostic—that is to say, they cannot be used to accurately date sites or occupations.

Up through the bifurcate phase, spearpoint styles covered huge geographical regions such as the entire southeastern United States. The bifurcate spearpoint style is found from the Mississippi Valley to the Atlantic Coast and from Georgia to New York. After this time, spearpoint styles become regionalized, and archaeologists assume that Archaic bands began to take on a more local or regional style. The period after 8000 years ago is characterized by a variety of spearpoint styles, although few are distinctive in their shape, and they are difficult to identify as to their culture in the archaeological record. In fact, it is becoming increasingly clear that some spearpoints are no longer symbols of the group. During the Late Archaic particularly, it has been documented that groups were using several different shapes or styles of spearpoints at the same time. Archaeologists still use projectile point type names, however, to describe particular shapes.

The changes in the distribution, intensity, and specialization of campsites established during the Late Archaic period suggest a variety of changes in social processes. The seasonal movements become very structured. Groups were returning to the same locations for longer periods for the same reasons. The annual sites for fish migration, nut harvests, game hunting and butchering, and plant collecting and processing became predictable and established seasonal activities. Certain areas became known as the best locations for important resources during certain times of the year. As long as the human population density did not increase greatly, there were enough resources for everyone. From all indications, the people adjusted well to the changing environment by increasing tool specialization and adapting their seasonal round or cycle to exploit the best resources available to them. Competition for food and other material resources never became so great that warfare was necessary. Some believe that Late Archaic cultures are the epitome of foraging societies. They maximized their exploitation of a temperate climate forest environment without any extraordinary technological or social developments.

The places where Indians lived and collected foods would have inspired stories that explained the origins of hickory trees, fish migrations, deer, and quality stone for making spears and axes. These stories would become identified with the resources to the point that they were practically the same to Archaic Indians. Although we have very little evidence of religious beliefs for this period, Archaic people probably had concepts of supernatural beings and an afterlife. Foragers typically practice animism, in which plants, animals, rocks, and rivers have spirits and can be persuaded by reason. The forest is believed to be not only alive in a biological sense, but also in a spiritual sense.

The Middle and Late Archaic periods represent a 4000-year period of population growth and gradual intensification in cultural adaptations. The Archaic period is an interesting time of improving environmental conditions (mostly warming) resulting in a rich environment for humans to inhabit. Native American populations increased at least fivefold over the Paleoindian period. The population increase and the shrinking territories almost certainly resulted in changes in social organization. They may have begun

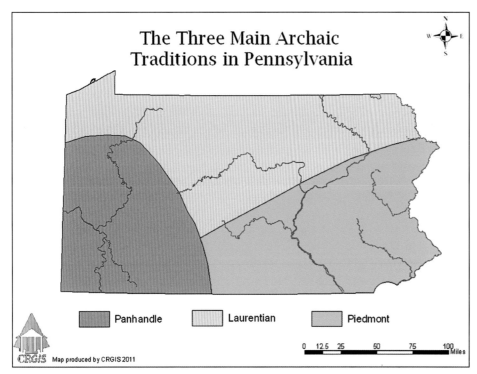

The Three Main Archaic Traditions in Pennsylvania

Panhandle   Laurentian   Piedmont

0 12.5 25   50   75   100 Miles

CRGIS   Map produced by CRGIS 2011

Distinctive projectile points define the Piedmont, Laurentian, and Panhandle Archaic traditions.

Kentucky. This is called the Panhandle Archaic, after the stretch of West Virginia that extends between Pennsylvania and Ohio. What is not known is whether these groups represented different tribes or language groups or whether they were simply selecting the most effective tools for use in different environments.

to organize themselves into *matrilineages*, descendants traced through women on the maternal side of the family, or more likely, *patrilineages*, descendants traced through men on the paternal side of the family. These types of family structures organize family groups so that they can more efficiently collect food resources. Unfortunately, the archaeological record does not reveal the specifics of social change during the Archaic period in Pennsylvania. In the Midwest, Great Lakes, and the South (or throughout the Mississippi Valley), however, there is evidence for significant social changes and the beginning of mound building and burial ceremonialism.

It may also have been a period of increasing group identification as related bands customized their adaptations to the specific environments in different regions of Pennsylvania. In the Piedmont and Great Valley regions, in the lower Susquehanna and Delaware Valleys, the projectile points from this period are generally long and narrow with contracting, straight, or expanding stems. These projectile points and associated tools are called the Piedmont Archaic. In the northern part of the state, the projectile points are generally wider and they are associated with a distinctive adze and a slate cutting tool called an ulu. This is called Laurentian and extends over a wide area of New York, New England, and Ontario. In the Ohio Valley, the projectile points and other tools share characteristics with Laurentian and the Archaic period in Ohio and

Archaic Period Research in Pennsylvania

The archaeological record of the Archaic period is fundamentally different from the Paleoindian period. First, there is a huge increase in the PASS database (more sites and more artifacts) during Archaic times. During the Early Archaic period, change is minimal, but there are three times as many Middle Archaic sites as during the Early Archaic, and the number nearly doubles again for Late Archaic sites. Late Archaic sites are larger, because they are visited by larger groups and are more frequently reoccupied. Second, Middle and Late Archaic sites are found on small streams, throughout the uplands, and in many different topographic and ecological settings. The people appear to be exploiting many different types of resources. By mapping the distribution of sites in different topographic settings at any point in time, archaeologists are able to describe how the environment was being exploited. When changes in this pattern occur, we assume that the adaptive strategy of people has changed. The different types of sites, in different topographic settings, along with differences in the toolkit, facilitate settlement pattern analysis for the Archaic period and we have a much more detailed picture of lifeways.

Third, and most significantly for archaeological research, many more Archaic period sites have been excavated and many of these are found in a stratified context. During the Pleistocene and the Paleoindian

91

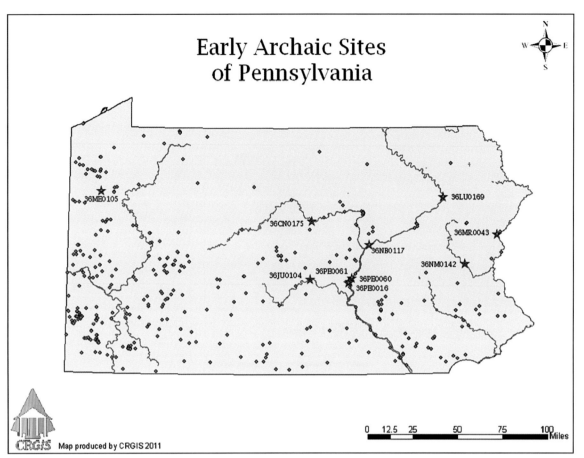

Early Archaic Sites
of Pennsylvania

36ME0105
36CN0175
36LU0169
36MR0043
36NB0117
36NM0142
36JU0104 36PE0061
36PE0060
36PE0016

0 12.5 25   50   75   100
Miles

CRGIS Map produced by CRGIS 2011

Map illustrating the distribution of Early Archaic sites in Pennsylvania.

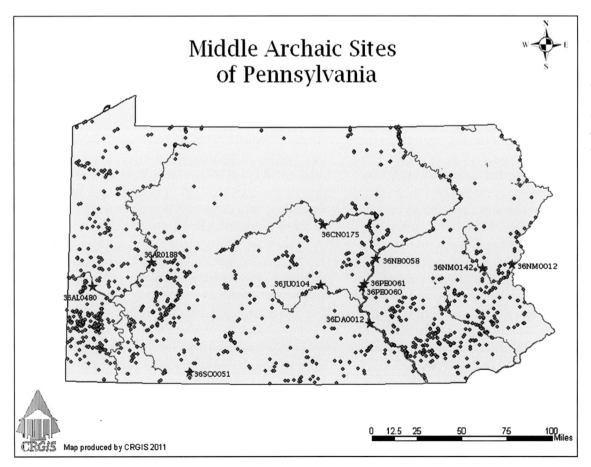

Middle Archaic Sites
of Pennsylvania

36CN0175
36NB0058
36AR0188
36NM0142 36NM0012
36JU0104 36PE0061
36PE0060
36AL0480
36DA0012
36SC0051

0 12.5 25   50   75   100
Miles

CRGIS Map produced by CRGIS 2011

Map illustrating the distribution of Middle Archaic sites in Pennsylvania.

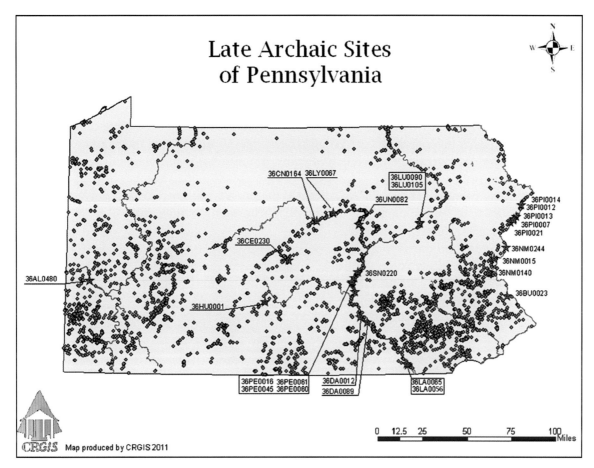

Late Archaic Sites of Pennsylvania

36CN0164 36LY0067
36LU0090
36LU0105
36UN0082
36PI0014
36PI0012
36PI0013
36PI0007
36PI0021
36CE0230
36NM0244
36NM0015
36NM0140
36AL0480
36SN0220
36BU0023
36HU0001
36PE0016 36PE0061
36PE0045 36PE0060
36DA0012
36DA0089
36LA0065
36LA0056

0 12.5 25 50 75 100 Miles

Map produced by CRGIS 2011

Map illustrating the distribution of Late Archaic sites in Pennsylvania.

period, erosion was the rule and floodplains were shallow. There was limited opportunity for Paleoindian artifacts to get buried by flood deposits. They were exposed on the ground surface and eventually mixed with later artifacts. The Archaic was a time of soil deposition, and floodplains were developing at a rapid pace. Thus, human occupations along the major rivers were buried, protected, and separated from the next visit to the site in a stratified setting, like a layer cake. Deeply stratified sites hold a detailed record of land utilization at a fixed location through time. This gives archaeologists the opportunity to examine one visit, or one culture, at a time and study how they changed through the years. At a stratified site, archaeologists can also examine artifacts and patterns of artifacts that have not moved since they were originally dropped thousands of years ago. This has resulted in a much more specific description and understanding of the Archaic period than the Paleoindian period.

Archaic Period Research in the Delaware Drainage Basin

The Delaware basin contains 130 sites in the PASS files from the Archaic period representing Early,

Middle, and Late Archaic time periods (population density increased as observed on maps). The Upper Delaware (the drainage north of Stroudsburg) is the most studied section of the basin. One of the first systematic investigations of this region was conducted by Max Schrabisch. He surveyed the Upper Delaware by boat in the early 1920s. The most intensive research, however, occurred in the 1960s and 1970s in preparation for the Tocks Island Dam project between Stroudsburg and Matamoras. The majority of these sites date to the Late Archaic period and later. The following descriptions of sites will be done by period—Early, Middle, and Late Archaic.

At the Shawnee-Minisink site (36Mr43) two Early Archaic layers were found situated 3 feet below the surface. The occupants used a greater variety of tools than during the Paleoindian period occupation at the same site, including scrapers, drills, gravers, knives, and axes.

During the Early Archaic period, Shawnee-Minisink probably served as a base camp for large, extended families that exploited a territory 50 to 75 miles in diameter. During the Middle Archaic, the groups visiting the site were smaller, possibly representing nuclear families, and the site was less frequently occupied.

In another large survey project, PennDOT commissioned a site survey prior to road development in the Marshall's Creek area of Monroe County. The survey found numerous sites used by prehistoric people to quarry chert for making stone tools. The chert is found in relatively thin layers in limestone. The quarries are small, very different from the jasper, metarhyolite, and argillite quarries. Rather than digging holes into the bedrock, these sites illustrate how the chert was pried out of the limestone beds. The most intensively used quarries were found surrounding swamps and lakes that would have contained a variety of food resources.

The Treichlers Bridge replacement project on the Lehigh River in Northampton County produced a deeply buried Early and Middle Archaic occupation. The excavation of the Treichlers Bridge site (36Nm142) recovered 20,000 artifacts, including at least five Early Archaic projectile points and twenty-three Middle Archaic bifurcate points. This is the largest single collection of bifurcate points from any stratified site in Pennsylvania. Unfortunately, these two components occupied the same land surface and were not stratigraphically separated by flood deposits. Although this factor severely limited the analysis, this site documents a repeatedly occupied camp during the bifurcate times.

Another deeply stratified site in the Middle Delaware Valley is the Sandts Eddy site (36Nm12), located just north of Easton. At this site, the earliest occupation dated to between 9300 and 9420 years ago. A bifurcate-based projectile point was associated with this date. This point type has been dated at other sites to Middle Archaic times, circa 8300 to 8900 years ago, so there is some debate concerning these dates. The occupation zone produced only a few artifacts and was

similar to the Middle Archaic occupation at Shawnee-Minisink, seemingly representing a nuclear family occupation. Most artifacts were related to stone-tool manufacturing, but the projectile point had evidence of use wear both as a spear and as a knife for butchering meat. A late Middle Archaic component dating between 7080 to 8450 years ago contained tools used for plant-food processing, carving bone or antler, and scraping fresh hides. The site was a base camp during the Middle Archaic period, but the small number of artifacts indicates that the site was occupied for only a short time and probably by nuclear family groups.

This bifurcate projectile point from the Sandts Eddy site was radiocarbon dated to between 9420 and 9300 BP.

The Upper Delaware Valley has produced an especially rich group of sites from the Late Archaic and is considered one of the best laboratories for the study of the Late Archaic through Late Woodland periods in the region. Dr. W. Fred Kinsey, of Franklin and Marshall

Early Archaic and bifurcate projectile points from the Treichlers Bridge site.

College conducted much of the work on the Pennsylvania side of the river. Late Archaic occupations are found buried on floodplains at the Zimmerman site (36Pi14), the Egypt Mills site (36Pi12), the Faucett site (36Pi13A), the Brodhead-Heller site (36Pi7), the Peters-Albrecht site (36Pi21), and the Driftstone site (36Nm244) excavated by Joe Blondino of Temple University. These sites were especially important in shedding light on the evolution of stone-tool technology, pottery technology, and diet between the Late Archaic and Late Woodland periods.

The excavation of stratified Late Archaic components also occurred at the Oberly Island site (36Nm140) in the Lehigh Valley and at the Lower Blacks Eddy site (36Bu23) in the lower Delaware Valley. Both of these sites seem to represent major base camps and are associated with large roasting features. Lower Black's Eddy is also associated with the argillite quarries in Bucks County. This outcrop was extensively used for tool stone beginning in the Middle Archaic period. This site was significant because it represented a base camp exploiting both the quarry and the riverine resources. The excavations at the Padula site (36Nm15) in Northampton County are a great example of a large upland, mainly Late Archaic site. This site produced thousands of artifacts, representing a base camp that was reoccupied throughout the Archaic.

For decades, archaeology in the Upper Delaware drainage focused on the floodplains. This resulted in a biased view of the region. In the 1990s, the National Park Service and private researchers began to examine upland areas, and a wide variety of sites were documented. Many of these were centered around upland swamps and bogs, typical of the Poconos. Some were very small and probably represent short-term camps occupied by just a few hunters.

Site survey and excavation projects have not been common in the Lower Delaware Valley or the Schuylkill Valley. The major survey conducted along the lower Schuylkill Valley was by Kingsley, Robertson, and Roberts (1990). This investigation located numerous small Archaic sites, but very few have been excavated; however, this survey report represents the best summary of the archaeology of the Schuylkill Valley.

Although not conducted in Pennsylvania, extensive excavations on the Delaware River near Trenton, New Jersey, have made very significant contributions to our understanding of the Archaic period. This group of sites is defined as the Abbott Farm Complex and the work was done in preparation for an interstate highway project. The sites were frequently stratified and date from Early Archaic through Late Woodland times. The location on the Delaware River is significant because of its association with large tidal marshes, which would have contained a wide variety of food resources. One of the most plentiful would have been migratory fish and the sites frequently document the exploitation of this resource.

The Middle Archaic occupations at Abbott Farm are mostly small, consisting of diminutive hearths and a few tools, probably representing nuclear family occupations. This is a pattern observed at other sites in the region for this period. It would seem that for most of the year, Middle Archaic people foraged in small family groups, possibly only joining with other families for annual ceremonies. Another interesting result of these excavations was the consistent finding of triangular projectile points, usually considered a trademark of the Late Woodland period, in sealed Middle and Late Archaic contexts. This clearly demonstrates their association with this period.

Late Archaic occupations at Abbott Farm are much larger and are characterized by large hearths and scatters of fire-cracked rock. It is felt that these represent large seasonal fishing camps. The fish were processed at these locations along with a variety of other food resources that were collected from the adjacent wetlands. Because of the abundance of resources, this location may have been occupied for at least part of the year by small groups; however, during the fish migration, bands from upstream, downstream, and coastal regions may have met at this location in groups of well over one hundred men, women, and children. These meetings would have been opportunities for trade on a large scale, exchanging resources from the Coastal Plain, Piedmont, Ridge and Valley, and even the Allegheny Plateau, similar to the regional trade fairs of today. Marriage and religious rejuvenation ceremonies would have been conducted at these sites. This concentration of activities was made possible by the concentration of food resources. The simple social organization of foraging bands may not have been sufficient to effectively manage resources on this scale and a more structured organization may have emerged. Charismatic leaders may have temporarily appeared during these meetings and exerted some control over resources. This is a level of unprecedented social complexity compared to earlier times and more interior regions, although this scenario is somewhat speculative at this point.

Archaic Period Research in the Susquehanna Drainage Basin

There are 225 recorded Archaic sites in the Susquehanna drainage basin. The majority of these sites are surface finds, but more than twenty stratified sites have been excavated as well. A detailed summary of three watersheds within the Susquehanna Valley has been published: the upper North Branch Susquehanna River, the upper Juniata River, and the middle West Branch of the Susquehanna River. This has provided insights into the evolution of Archaic cultures in the valley.

One of the most spectacular sites excavated in the Susquehanna basin was the Sheep Rock Shelter (36Hu1), located along the Raystown Branch of the Juniata River. A *rock shelter* is a rock overhang that provides protection from wind and precipitation. These were very commonly used in prehistoric times and have been termed "prehistoric motels." They may not always be located in areas containing food resources, but they are a safe haven in a storm. The Sheep Rock Shelter consists of a large rock face with a slight east-facing slope that protected an area about 30 feet wide and 15 feet deep. The sediments under the rock face were more than 12 feet deep and covered the evolution of Archaic and Woodland cultures in the region. Because the rock face protected the site from rain, it remained dry for thousands of years, resulting in the preservation of

organic remains. Parts of bark baskets, sandals, bone, antler, and wooden tools were recovered in the early 1960s prior to the site being flooded by construction of the Raystown Dam. These artifacts document the sophistication and complexity of Native American technology rarely found at open-air sites. Unfortunately, the stratigraphy of this site was incredibly complex and it is difficult to assign specific artifacts to specific periods. The site is currently covered by 125 feet of water.

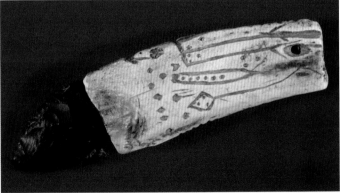

Organic artifacts from the Sheep Rock Shelter, rarely found at open-air sites. These document the sophistication and complexity of Native American technology. The bark basket is a type of container that was probably used as early as Paleoindian times. The handle with the stone knife blade was also probably very common in prehistory.

Excavation of the Sheep Rock Shelter.

The Kent-Hally site (36La56) on Bare Island and the Piney Island site (36La65), both located in the lower part of the valley, were some of the first stratified sites to be excavated on the main branch of the Susquehanna. These documented the variety of projectile points used over time during mainly the Late Archaic period. It was from sites like these that archaeologists developed projectile point types that they believed dated to specific periods and represented specific cultures. In fact, more recent studies of these excavations reveal that several different types were being used during the same period.

THE STATE MUSEUM OF PENNSYLVANIA/PHOTO BY DON GILES

Middle Archaic projectile points of the Nevelle type from the West Water Street site, Clinton County.

Over the past twenty years, several other significant stratified sites have been excavated in this valley. Stratified Early and Middle Archaic sites have been especially important in adding to our understanding of this period. The Central Builders site (36Nb117), near the confluence of the north and west branches of the Susquehanna River, was a relatively small excavation that produced deeply buried early occupations. It produced a metarhyolite corner-notched projectile point (typed as a Kirk corner-notched) and two large chert cores that were quarried locally. These were associated with a hearth that dated to 9165+210/-205 BP. The metarhyolite was carried 130 kilometers from its source in South Mountain near Gettysburg and demonstrates that Early Archaic bands were still moving over and occupying large territories.

The Conrail site (36Lu169), located at the mouth of the Lackawanna River, was excavated by the Frances Dorrance Chapter of the Society for Pennsylvania Archaeology. It produced stratified cultural deposits up to 27 feet deep covering the period from Early Archaic through Late Woodland times. The earliest carbon 14 date was 9070+50 BP and it was associated with a jasper corner-notched St. Charles point. The jasper originated at the Hardyston quarries west of Allentown. These quarries are located 80 miles to the south and are another example of the size of Early Archaic band territories.

Larger living surfaces were excavated at the West Water Street site (36Cn175) in Lock Haven. The Early Archaic component produced three projectile points

(Kirk corner-notched projectile points), tools, and a hearth with a date of 9430 BP. This appears to be a small base camp exploiting a territory less than 50 miles in diameter. This site also produced several Middle Archaic occupations resulting in the recovery of more than forty stemmed projectile points typed as Neville projectile points; however, archaeologist Jay Custer felt that these artifacts were the result of numerous visits by nuclear family-sized groups and not large extended families as were the Early Archaic occupations.

The Route 322 project in the Lewistown Narrows along the Juniata River surveyed a number of small sites. Water gaps and wind gaps through the ridges seem to have been favorite temporary sites throughout the prehistoric period. Site number 36Ju104 produced both Early and Middle Archaic occupations. These all seem to represent temporary occupations, but the site was also used to quarry a low-grade toolstone. The Mykut Rockshelter (36Hu143) was excavated as part of a PennDOT road improvement project and produced artifacts dating from Archaic through Late Woodland times. It is situated in a gap on Terrace Mountain connecting Little Valley with the Raystown Valley. As a rock shelter, it was already an attractive campsite, but its location on a path between two valleys made it an even more advantageous campsite. It was first used during late Middle Archaic times as a deer-hunting and hide-processing camp.

The Raker 1 (36Nb58) site in Northumberland County along the Susquehanna River was a small excavation conducted by PennDOT as part of a road-improvement project. The site was occupied several times during the Archaic period. Although limited by the boundaries of the construction area, the excavation revealed a series of small camps. Interestingly, during the period between 5000 and 6000 years ago, small storage or processing features were discovered that were about 3 feet deep. Their exact function is not known, but features of this size are very rare from this period in Pennsylvania. It has been proposed that this was a winter camp and seeds or nuts were being stored in these pits while food resources were scarce.

Several sites in the Liverpool area (36Pe16, 36Pe60 and 36Pe61) of the central Susquehanna Valley were excavated in the late 1990s during the widening of U.S. Route 11/15. These produced both Early Archaic and Middle Archaic living floors. The Early Archaic components contained jasper artifacts from eastern Pennsylvania demonstrating that people were continuing to use and occupy large territories. Based on the microscopic analysis of stone tools, common activities included the processing of meat, hides, and antler. The quantity and variety of artifacts suggest a base camp, but the excavations were concentrated along the river side of these occupations. The center of the occupation was destroyed by construction of the nineteenth-century Pennsylvania Canal and later U.S. Route 15.

On City Island (36Da12), in Harrisburg on the Susquehanna River, a Middle Archaic fire pit produced a date of 8730+130 B.P. The small collection of artifacts, including a bifurcate projectile point, probably represents a hunting camp. This site also revealed a large Late Archaic base camp consisting of a wide variety of tools and numerous cooking hearths. One of the more sensational finds was a grouping (or artifact cache) of seven axe and adze blanks that were found piled on top of one another. The numerous artifacts and cooking hearths from the Late Archaic occupation document a large and repeatedly occupied base camp from this period dating to around 4000 years ago.

The Calver Island site (36Da89), situated just downriver from City Island also produced a series of living floors from the Late Archaic, Transitional, and Early Woodland periods. This site, along with 36Sn220 and Gerty's Notch (36Pe45) on the main branch, 36Un82 and Canfield Island (36Ly67) on the West Branch, and Skvarek (36Lu132), Gould Island (36Lu105), and Jacobs (36Lu90) on the North Branch, have been

Microwear Analysis — Christopher A. Bergman, PhD

CHRISTOPHER A. BERGMAN

Christopher Bergman, Principal Archaeologist, URS Corporation.

It is well known that some kinds of artifacts made and used by prehistoric peoples are rarely preserved on archaeological sites. This includes objects made of fragile materials like wood, fiber, or leather, but also harder materials such as animal bones, teeth, or antlers. Frequently, the only evidence available for study consists of artifacts made of very hard materials like stone. In fact, tools made of chert, jasper, and other rocks are often the only artifacts preserved and available for archaeologists to study.

Prehistoric archaeologists analyze stone tools in many ways, including the raw materials selected for their manufacture, the ways the tools are made, and the way they are used. These studies all aim at understanding behavior in the past, a primary goal of archaeology. We know that prehistoric people selected certain kinds of stones for some purposes, but not others. For example, obsidian, a naturally occurring volcanic glass, is ideal for making spearpoints or arrowheads, but it is too brittle to make an axe for cutting down trees. We also know that different techniques were used to make tools. Stone axes made of tough igneous and metamorphic rocks are often shaped by pecking with a stone hammer, which pulverizes the surface of the stone into shape. The edge of the axe is usually finished by grinding and polishing on a sandstone slab.

In the past, educated guesswork was used to understand how prehistoric tools were used; therefore, an object with a sharp tip, as well as a base for fixing the tool to a shaft, was assumed to function as a spearpoint or arrowhead. Beyond this mere speculation, however, the manner in which stone tools were used remained somewhat of a mystery. A relatively new scientific technique focusing on microscopic traces of damage and wear on stone tools called *microwear*, or *use wear*, has made it possible for archaeologists to precisely determine the function of prehistoric artifacts. The underlying premise of the technique is based on the fact that tools employed for different purposes and for working different materials will display different types of microscopic damage. The wear appearing at the edge of a scraper used to remove the hair and flesh from a deer hide is visibly distinct from that of a drill used to bore holes in stone.

Since no living person has observed how prehistoric people used their tools, how do archaeologists know that working different materials causes distinctive use wear traces? The answer is through experimentation. By making replicas of prehistoric tools and using them in a variety of ways, archaeologists can characterize the resulting use wear. The wear traces on replica tools, both visible and microscopic, can be compared with that observed on prehistoric stone tools. Obviously, similar types of wear on both experimental copies and ancient artifacts provides an important clue as to how the prehistoric tools were used.

In our experiment illustrated in the photograph, a stone drill bit is used to bore a hole in limestone. The drill bit is

Bergman experimenting with a stone drill to replicate microscopic wear patterns to interpret archaeological specimens.

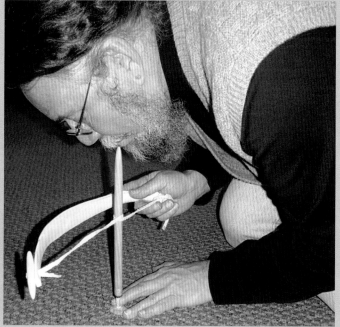

CHRISTOPHER A. BERGMAN

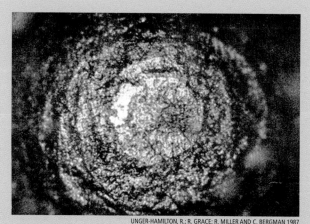

UNGER-HAMILTON, R.; R. GRACE; R. MILLER AND C. BERGMAN 1987

Microscopic wear patterns—striations and polish—on a stone drill tip.

mounted in a wooden shaft that is rapidly rotated using a bow consisting of a curved caribou rib and rawhide string. Such tools, not surprisingly, are called "bow drills" and are commonly used by modern hunter-gatherers like the Inuit peoples of the Arctic.

Perhaps the first lesson learned in this experiment is that a stone-tipped drill is very effective and performs in a manner similar to the metal drills we use today. Looking closely at the tip through a high-powered microscope shows that the use wear is characterized by lines called striations and glossy areas called polish. The striations, which look like scratches on the surface of the tool, provide information on the motions (directions of use) applied to the tool during use. Slicing motions, such as would be the case with a knife, typically align the striations in a direction parallel to the cutting edge. In this case, however, we see the striations form circular lines around the tip of the tool. These clearly suggest it was used in a rotational manner. The bright areas of polish indicate that the drill contacted a hard material like stone, resulting in the tip being smoothed and flattened as the tool was rotated.

The systematic analysis of wear patterns on stone tools has identified scraping, cutting, sawing, and drilling actions resulting from butchery, hide processing, and preparation of wooden and leather artifacts, as well as the creation of decorative ornaments in bone and antler among many other activities. This has greatly increased our ability to interpret human behavior, allowing for a detailed picture of life during prehistoric times.

A Middle Archaic bifurcate-based projectile point radiocarbon dated to 8730+130 BP from the City Island site.

Late Archaic projectile points from the City Island site.

A photo of a cache of axe and adze blanks from the City Island site insitu *and in the lab (right).*

instrumental in documenting the evolution of this important period. They have all illustrated how Late Archaic populations were increasing and how they were developing a wide variety of technologies to intensify their exploitation of the environment. One of the more interesting sites found on a small stream rather than the main river was the Jack's Mill site (36Ce230) located near State College. This site was situated near a large spring and was occupied throughout the Middle and Late Archaic periods. Several hearths and small pits were discovered from the Late Archaic. These contained the remains of a wide variety of seeds and nuts including acorns, walnuts, hickory nuts, and butternuts. This site documents the diversity of food resources used by Late Archaic cultures.

Archaic Period Research in the Upper Ohio Drainage Basin

There are approximately 160 Archaic sites recorded in the Allegheny, Monongahela, and Ohio drainage basins. Unfortunately, few have been excavated. Sites on slopes, saddles, and ridgetops are common, indicating that the foraging bands utilized a wider variety of environments and resources compared to Paleoindian times.

One of the few deeply buried locations is the Leetsdale site (36Al480) in Allegheny County just downriver from Pittsburgh on the Ohio River. It was excavated by the Army Corps of Engineers as part of a construction site for a replacement navigation dam. This site documented Middle Archaic through Woodland cultural developments. It is very important because it is one of the few stratified sites in the valley to include this time span. The Archaic occupations all seem to represent small multipurpose camps. The artifacts are different than those in the eastern part of the state, but the general changes in artifacts are similar to the patterns in the eastern part of the state.

The two oldest house patterns in Pennsylvania are found in this drainage basin. The Goddard site (36Me105) in Goddard State Park, Mercer County,

contained several fire features dating to the Early Archaic based on a radiocarbon date of 9180 BP. One of the fire features was surrounded by post molds and may represent a living structure with an interior hearth. A second set of post molds may represent a windbreak or a drying rack. This seems to represent a small campsite.

The Kinsinger Site (36So51) is on high ground overlooking Elklick Creek and was investigated by PennDOT as part of the Meyersdale Bypass project. This site revealed evidence of a Middle Archaic house with a central fire pit. Two deep features, identified as earth ovens, were also found. This site was interpreted as a base camp. Both this site and the Goddard site suggest people were living in small family groups during the Early and Middle Archaic periods.

The Brown site (36Ar188) was a stratified occupation along the Allegheny River. The main occupation was Middle Archaic in age, yielding a radiocarbon date of 6090+240 BP. It produced side-notched spearpoints and fragments of hickory and acorns. The Middle Archaic was a time when people were

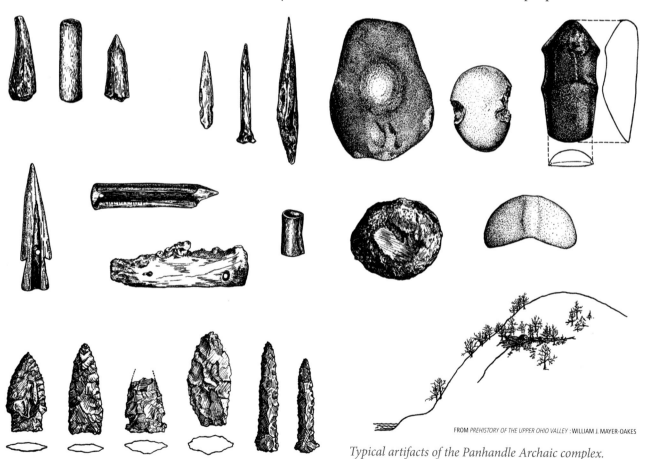

FROM *PREHISTORY OF THE UPPER OHIO VALLEY* : WILLIAM J. MAYER-OAKES

Typical artifacts of the Panhandle Archaic complex.

exploiting a wide variety of resources but did not seem to be using any specialized tools as were developed during the Late Archaic.

The Connoquenessing site (36Bv292) is located along a stream with the same name and over 5 miles from the main river valleys in the area. It produced a number of features, but was not stratified; however, an intensive analysis of projectile point types, lithic material types, and seventeen radiometric dates from eight features resulted in a determination that the main occupations were Late Archaic and Middle Woodland in age. Local cherts were the main source for the Late Archaic lithic artifacts. A variety of small and large mammals were processed during this occupation along with hickory, butternut, and black walnut. This site supports the hypothesis that Late Archaic peoples were exploiting a variety of food resources.

Mainly due to the lack of excavated stratified sites from the Upper Ohio Valley, the Archaic period has been difficult to define. Many nonstratified sites have been excavated, but a clear picture or a well-dated historical sequence has been elusive. Don Dragoo and William Mayer-Oakes of the Carnegie Museum researched this issue in the 1950s. They found characteristics in the region relating to the Laurentian Phase in New York and also to Archaic cultures in Ohio and Kentucky. It seems that initially during the Late Archaic, the Upper Ohio Valley was influenced by the Laurentian Tradition from New York. Later, influences from Kentucky and Ohio appear. Mayer-Oakes defined this as the Panhandle Archaic and it was identified by distinctive stemmed or lanceolate projectile points, the grooved adz, the crescent bannerstone, and the frequent location of the sites on high terraces associated with shell middens. The large mounds of freshwater mussels are significant because they contribute to the preservation of bone and antler not usually found at sites from this period. The shell middens from this period frequently contain a small number of burials. The Panhandle Archaic has a riverine focus and freshwater mussels seemed to be a regular part of peoples' diets. A large excavation was conducted in the 1990s on the East Steubenville site (46Br31) located just across the West Virginia state line along the Ohio River. Pits for steaming the mussels are a common feature at this site. Deer, catfish, nuts, berries, and seeds were also significant in the diet. The deer were butchered on-site, but the large pieces of meat were carried and eaten elsewhere. Research at this site has gone a long way to clarify the Archaic cultural developments of the region. Many more stratified sties need to be excavated from this region, however, to begin to understand this period.

A Middle Archaic Narrative

TIME 8400 YEARS AGO.

PLACE THE UPPER ALLEGHENY VALLEY.

CLIMATE SLIGHTLY WARMER THAN PRESENT.

FLORA AND FAUNA A MIXED OAK AND PINE FOREST—SIMILAR TO PENNSYLVANIA AT THE TIME OF COLUMBUS.

DISTINCTIVE ARTIFACTS BIFURCATE SPEAR-POINTS, ATLATL WEIGHTS, FULL GROOVED POLISHED AXES.

My name is Munxing. I am a forty-year-old man who has seen many changes. We live on the Clarion River of the Upper Ohio Valley. I have two daughters and a son. They are all grown and my daughters live with their husbands on the Conemough River to the south. My son, his wife, and his two daughters live with us. My brother and his family also live with us for most of the year. Our tribe is very large. We live on the Appalachian Plateau and our land extends across the upper parts of the Ohio, Susquehanna, and Delaware Valleys. There are hundreds of people in our tribe.

Our people came here many generations ago from the south. The people that lived here at that time were not doing very well and they were glad to share our ideas. They were very primitive and they mostly lived along the rivers. They did not know about all of the food that could be collected in the forest. We made their life easier and most were adopted into our tribe. My grandfather told me that they could still be found living in very small camps when he was a boy. I have never seen one but some people say they are descendants from the Old People, as we call them. They have a different look, with dark skin and small noses. There is a shaman in the next valley who claims he is a descendant of the Old People. He has dark skin and a small nose so maybe he is. He says his power and knowledge comes from his ancestors.

Our land is a good place to live. The summers are warm and the winters are snowy. We live in a large forest with many different types of trees. Having more trees means better cover for stalking game. There is more shelter from the heat and cold, more wood for building houses and shelters, and more wood for heating and cooking. There are many people but our forest contains many different foods. There are many animals for us to eat such as elk, deer, turkey, beaver, and bears. The streams are full of fish and the lakes are full of ducks and geese. There are also hickory nuts, butternuts, and walnuts. Sometimes we collect acorns but these are very bitter and a lot of trouble. They need to be soaked in water to remove the bitterness and we only collect them when we get desperate. Life is easy.

We make our tools using the materials around us such as stone, wood, bone, antler, animal teeth, mussel shells, and reeds for making baskets, sleeping mats, and sandals. The stone spearpoints and knives are the easiest. We use a black chert that we find in our land or we get cobbles out of the Allegheny River. It does not make much difference to us where we find the stone. I do not worry about my stone tools too much—they are easy to make.

Out of all of our stone tools, our spearpoints are the most special. They are a sign of The People. We put a special notch in the base so they do not come loose from the shaft. We make our spearpoints large, about 2 inches long. They are tightly secured to the spear shaft so they will not come loose once they have pierced the animal's hide. It is too much trouble to take them out so we sharpen them while they are still attached to the shaft. They eventually get small and then we throw them away.

Most people carry a knife with a wooden or antler handle. Usually the handle has a design carved or painted on it representing the person's guardian spirit. The handle lasts many years but the stone blade gets replaced every few months. Most of the time, when I need a scraper for hide cleaning or a saw for working wood, I just pick up a sharp piece of black chert that someone has dropped. There is plenty of it lying around and I just give it a toss when I'm done.

Men, women, and older children make and use stone tools. Some people are better than others but it is not an important skill in our culture. The important skill for women is making bags and clothing from furs. They also make boxes from wood and bark. We use a dye made from red or yellow ochre (a rock) to highlight the clothing with colors. Weaving mats, baskets, and sandals using reeds is an important skill mainly performed by men. We take great pride in our baskets. We color our baskets with the same paint used by the women. My father taught me this skill and I use the same designs as he used.

For hunting, we use the atlatl to throw our spears. The atlatl is a wonderful tool to make the spear go farther and penetrate the animal's body. It is a flat piece of wood, about 2 feet long with carvings on the handle and painted designs on the sides. Back in the old days, we had to get very close to the big animals and stab them to be sure to kill them. Of course we could throw the spear, but that did not always penetrate the thick hides. I prefer to stand back and use the atlatl. Even a wounded deer can kill a man with its antlers. My father made me my first atlatl and he painted the bear sign on the sides. He said this would make me wise in the forest. He also added a weight to my spear-thrower. He said it would strengthen my arm and make me more accurate in my throw. My cousins and I practiced with our atlatls until we could knock a crow from a tree at 20 yards.

There are many hardwood trees in the forest, such as oak and hickory. Our woodworking tools such as axes and adzes are very important. They need to be made from a hard stone. They are used every day and they are frequently sharpened. We use a greenstone from the south and we need to trade for it.

Men are important as leaders and as hunters. But if the truth be told, the women collect the most food. When I was young, I hunted every week. Now that I am older, I have other responsibilities. I spend a lot of time visiting other bands and we discuss important ceremonies. The early spring ceremony and the late fall ceremony are our most important ones and they take a lot of planning.

The women's main tool for getting food is the digging stick. My wife carries one all of the time. She digs tasty roots in the spring and knocks butternuts and hickory nuts from the trees in the fall. Birds and fish are also important. In the spring and fall when birds migrate, we have plenty of fresh food to eat. The trees and lakes are filled with birds. The children throw rocks into the trees and always kill a few birds. They also use nets to tangle up their wings and feet along the lakes. Sometimes there are so many fish in the river, all you need to do is walk in and pull them out. Our main camp is along the Allegheny River and only a few days' walk from all the other camps we use throughout the year. The spring and summer fishing camps, the fall hickory nut camp, and the winter camps are the biggest ones. We build shelters at each location because we will be there at least a month. Our tents are relatively small and hold only one family. They are covered with elm bark, furs at the entrance, and pine branches. Naturally, the tents at our winter camp are more substantial and sometimes we pile mud around the bottom to keep them warm. We go back to the same camps each year. We take the shelters down to keep them from being damaged by the weather. Once we have the correct-sized poles, they are easy to put up again.

Now that we are seeing other groups more frequently, we are trading more. As long as the situation is friendly, I like meeting strangers. Sometimes they have nicer stones for tools. Sometimes it is better fish. I am always on the lookout for greenstone for making axes. Trading is more than just exchanging items. We learn what other people are doing and how they make their tools. When there are lots of traders in the camp, it is interesting to see their different tattoos and hairstyles. Each band seems to have their own look. In our group, women have three tattooed lines over each eye. Their mothers put them there when they are ready for marriage. Men have an image of the first big animal they kill on their shoulders.

Once in the early spring, after a hard winter, I had argued with my wife and my brothers and decided to go by myself to the mountains. If I was lucky, I might be able to find a bear and we could talk about what was bothering me. But instead, I found a man from the Susquehanna Valley. I could tell where he was from by the tattooed lines on his forearm. He was lying in a rock shelter next to a dead black bear. He and his friend had been surprised by this bear. He was badly hurt. His legs and feet had been deeply clawed. His friend was also hurt but he was able to go for help. Before his friend left, they had eaten the bear's heart because they thought it would make them both strong. I helped him get more firewood. I shared some of my dried venison and he shared some of his dried fish. I stayed with him for several days. I offered to carry him back to our camp, but he wondered what would happen to the dead bear. I skinned the animal so he would have something to keep him warm in the evenings. I helped him make a necklace from the claws and the teeth. We talked a lot about bears, men, and our families. He was very proud that he and his friend had fought this bear and won. He offered me some of the meat, but it was not my bear so I declined.

ILLUSTRATION BY NANCY BISHOP

The man was young and he had demonstrated his bravery and cunning as a hunter. He will have the scars on his legs to prove it. While he is waiting for his friend, I would not be surprised if the spirit of the bear comes back and tells him the secrets of the forest. In the meantime, he has the bear's coat to keep him warm and the bear's flesh to feed him.

We had talked for several days. I had never spoken so long with someone who lived so far away. We had more snow, they had terrible floods. They hunted geese in the spring and fall longer then we did. He had an accent when he spoke, which I will always remember. They were different but we were cousins and, especially after this adventure, we would always be welcome in each other's camps. As I walked home, I realized that The People were a vast network of humans that cooperated with one another. I have my brothers and my children. We all have spouses and they connect us to other families. We share a language and other traditions that connect us with people in the next valley. I will probably never see this man again but knowing he is there makes my life easier. We have a very good life. Our forest is filled with food. My children are healthy. We are surrounded by friendly tribes. It is hard to imagine that it will ever change.

Chapter 5
The Transitional Period: 2700 to 4300 years ago

This period is also known as the Terminal Archaic; however, its definition and time range are somewhat controversial. Traditionally, the Archaic period is distinguished from the Woodland period by the introduction of fired-clay pottery. Based on radiocarbon testing, however, Archaic projectile points and the associated artifacts are dated with pottery. This makes the definition of the Woodland period based on a single artifact type problematic. Therefore, in this chapter, the Transitional period will be defined by a group of artifacts and features that reflect the broader cultural adaptation. The last phase of this adaptation includes fired-clay pottery.

T I M E L I N E

Contact Period	1500 AD–1700 AD
Woodland Period	1500 AD–2700 years ago
Transitional Period	**2700–4300 years ago**
Fishtail	**2700–3100 years ago**
Broadspear	**3100–4300 years ago**
Late Broadspear	**3100–3900 years ago**
Early Broadspear	**3900–4300 years ago**
Archaic Period	4300–10,000 years ago
Paleoindian Period	10,000–16,500 years ago
Pre-Clovis	11,200–16,500 years ago

Environment: This period generally corresponds to the Sub-Boreal climatic episode that is characterized as warm and dry. Reduced rainfall resulted in slightly fewer available food resources. There are indications that there were fluctuations in rainfall and periodic drying of wetlands, also resulting in less predictable resources. The end of this period corresponds to the beginning of the Sub-Atlantic climatic episode and a return to warm and moist conditions. Food resources increased and became more predictable.

Making and using tools (typical artifacts and technology): This period represents a significant change in chipped-stone tool technology compared to the Archaic period. There are significant changes in terms of the types of tools being made, the way they were made, and the stone used to make them. The hallmark of this period is the broadspear projectile point/knife. Other tools common during the Late Archaic period continue to be used, such as grinding stones, notched netsinkers, and stemmed projectile points.

Rock-lined cooking hearths become very common and very large. Another hallmark of the Transitional period is the use of soapstone or steatite cooking containers. In the Middle Atlantic region, ceramics first appear approximately 3200 years ago and briefly overlap in time with steatite bowls. The end of the period is characterized by fishtail projectile points, and these are made using the same technology as broadspears.

What people ate (subsistence): Throughout this period there is an increasing diversity of plant and animal foods being used. Significantly, domesticated squash appears and a variety of seed plants, such as little barley and chenopodium (lambs quarter), also seem to become important as food sources. The cultivation of squash, and possibly other plants, resulted in some sites being occupied throughout the growing season. Cultivation requires more work but was necessary to support the growing population.

Where people lived (settlement patterns): As with the Archaic period, sites are found in many different ecological settings in both upland and floodplain locales.

Generally, Transitional period floodplain sites seemed to be occupied by larger groups for longer periods of time. Jasper, argillite, and metarhyolite quarry sites became important. In addition, some sites seemed to have served as meeting places for macrobands.

People living in groups (social organization and belief systems): Bands continue to be egalitarian and gradually become larger and less mobile. The extensive trade involving jasper, argillite, metarhyolite, and steatite bowls; the caching of bifaces; and burial ceremonialism suggest increased social structure, although the exact nature of the bands' social organization is not clear. The regional bands that appeared in the Late Archaic seem to coalesce into drainage-wide groups that are united by trade and probably a variety of ceremonies. There may be locations along the fall line in both the Delaware and Susquehanna basins that served as meeting places for coastal bands and more interior bands. The social events held at these locations may have reached unprecedented levels of social complexity. The overall population continues to grow to high levels, numbering many thousands.

Definition

The Transitional period represents a response to the increasing population pressure building during the Archaic period. In addition, the beginning of the Transitional period corresponds to the warm and dry Sub-Boreal climate. This resulted in an overall reduction in food resources and a less predictable distribution of food resources. In response, this period exhibits a significant change in the toolkit, how stone tools were made, the stone used to make the tools, the introduction of portable cooking vessels into the archaeological record, the intensification of food-processing methods, extensive trade, a change in the organization of social groups, and probably burial ceremonialism.

It is defined by a distinctive set of broad-bladed knives and projectile points, known as broadspears. These were produced using distinctive knapping techniques and a limited set of lithic material types. Metarhyolite, jasper, and argillite quarries in Pennsylvania are the source of toolstone that is traded throughout the Middle Atlantic region. The broadspears are multipurpose implements and frequently reworked into distinctively shaped knives, scrapers, and drills. Carved stone bowls in steatite (soapstone) are the other distinctive artifact of this period. They represent the first portable cooking vessels found in the archaeo-

logical record. Sites from this period are found in the same diverse ecological settings as during the Late Archaic, but floodplain sites seem to represent larger and more sedentary groups. These large sites are characterized by extensive clusters of fire-cracked rock that are thought to represent intensive food-processing activities, such as roasting or stone boiling. The trade and the ceremonialism suggest that there were significant developments in social organization. Traditionally, this period ends with the appearance of the first fired-clay pottery in the Middle Atlantic region. Most of the characteristics of this period, however, continue in the succeeding Fishtail phase; therefore this phase will be included in the Transitional period. As archaeologists learn more about prehistory, it is becoming apparent that the terms used to reference different periods are arbitrary and do not represent the distinct cultural stages we once thought. During the Fishtail phase, fired-clay pottery appears and steatite bowls disappear by 3000 years ago. The shape of the diagnostic projectile point changes but otherwise all of the characteristics of the Transitional period continue until approximately 2700 years ago. At this time they are replaced by a diverse assemblage of pottery and tools and the preference for certain lithic types ends.

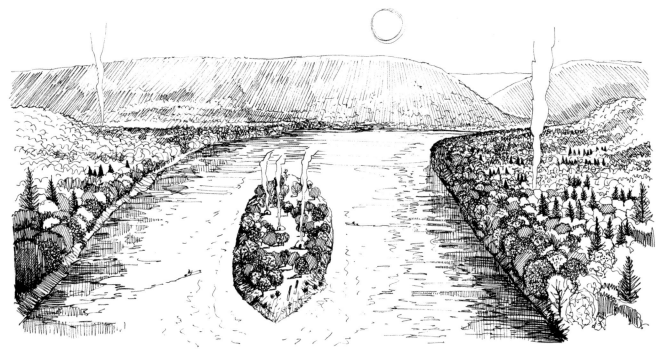

A view of the Sub-Boreal oak-hickory forest along the Susquehanna River 4000 years ago.

The term "Transitional" was first used by John Witthoft in 1953 when he defined this time as a transition between the foraging cultures of the Archaic period and the horticulture cultures of the Woodland period. We have since learned that this is an oversimplification. In addition, many archaeologists are not satisfied with the term "transitional," because they believe that all cultures are in transition. They recognize that this time represents a different adaptive strategy than the Late Archaic period, and the term "Terminal Archaic" is also frequently used. In this book, we are using Transitional because this period seems to be sufficiently different from the Late Archaic and Woodland periods to deserve its own period designation. Although it may not be the best term, it has been used for sixty years in archaeological literature, and in deference to John Witthoft (former State Archaeologist of Pennsylvania), we will continue to use the term within this publication.

The Environment

Beginning 8000 years ago, the Archaic period is characterized by a lengthy, warm, and moist climate called the Atlantic climatic episode. Approximately 4300 years ago marks the beginning of the Sub-Boreal climatic episode. This time is characterized as warm and dry. There would have been an overall reduction in food resources and the distribution of resources would have been less predictable. The vegetation begins as an oak and hemlock forest, but the hemlocks nearly disappear rather suddenly and are replaced by hickory trees. Although the drying environment may have been a factor, some paleobotanists believe that a disease or blight affected the hemlocks. The hemlock trees gradually return to the forests during the Woodland period. Some archaeologists believe the reduced rainfall caused an overall decrease in vegetation and that especially wetlands got smaller. The Sub-Atlantic episode begins approximately 3000 years ago and is characterized by a warm and wet climate. This period corresponds to the Fishtail phase. Vegetation would have increased in density under these conditions and wetlands would have increased in size.

It has been long recognized that Transitional period sites are associated with larger streams, suggesting that the smaller streams during the Sub-Boreal episode were not dependable for habitation sites; however, archaeologists debate over how dry the climate was and whether this had a significant effect on foraging techniques for getting food. Some believe that the effect was minor and reference pollen data that does not show any significant changes in vegetation (other than the replacement of hemlocks by hickory). Other archaeologists use increased rates of flooding to assert that there was a sufficient reduction in rainfall to reduce ground cover, resulting in more runoff, erosion, and flooding during heavy rains. The issue has not been resolved, but there are an increasing number of sites that support the increased flooding scenario.

Making and Using Tools: Typical Artifacts and Technology

In many ways, the Transitional period shares similarities in artifacts with the Late Archaic period. There was a continued use of a variety of woodworking and seed-grinding or nut-grinding stones. Net sinkers for fishing also continue to be used. But this period is distinguished from the Late Archaic by the addition of a new set of tools, a change in knapping techniques, and generally, a different strategy for exploiting the environment. The change in artifacts from the Paleoindian period to the Archaic period, even though it was associated with a rather sudden and spectacular climatic change, was gradual and required almost one thousand years to complete.

The change from the Late Archaic to the Transitional period required only several hundred years, and the change in tools was even more dramatic. The tools not only look different, but the broadspears were made using very different flint-knapping techniques compared to Late Archaic technology. These tools were frequently sharpened, similar to Paleoindian technology, and the broadspears were modified into scrapers and drills.

Plant Fiber and Wood Artifacts James M. Adovasio

Because of what some scholars call the "tyranny of preservation," only artifacts made of stone, or ceramics in later time periods, are usually preserved in archaeological sites in Pennsylvania. This, in turn, has led to a disproportionate emphasis on the importance of these so-called durable items in the lives of their prehistoric and historic makers. Conversely, objects made of plant fiber or wood are very rare in the archaeological record of Pennsylvania and most other states because the preservation of these items requires very special conditions. Specifically, the preservation of wood or plant fiber artifacts or objects of leather and other organic materials requires sites that are either very dry or continuously wet throughout their history. In

THE STATE MUSEUM OF PENNSYLVANIA/PHOTO BY DON GILES

James M. Adovasio, Mercyhurst Archaeological Institute

both cases, destructive microbial activity is curtailed because water is absent or, if present, contains salts, metals, or other chemicals that kill microbes. Both of these circumstances allow organic materials to last for long periods because they preclude the decay of such materials from microbial agents. Finally, if carbonized (that is, burnt to charcoal) plant fiber and wood artifacts may be preserved indefinitely even in sites subject to periodic moisture. Because of their rarity in Pennsylvania and nearby states, the importance of plant fiber or wood artifacts is often neglected or minimized.

In this regard, two facts are notable. First, where preservation of organic artifacts is very good, such as in dry caves or rock shelters or in bogs, plant fiber and wood artifacts are far more common than stone tools or ceramics. Second, in all types of living or recently living hunting and gathering societies from all known environments, plant fiber and wood tools make up 85 to 95 percent of the entire toolkit of these groups. Put most simply, when archaeologists recover only stone tools or pottery, they are missing most of what prehistoric Native Americans made or used in their daily lives.

Artifacts made of plant fiber or wood subsume a remarkably diverse array of objects. These notably include cordage in the form of string or thicker-gauge rope as well as cordage by-products like fishing or hunting nets and bags. Also included are baskets, in the form of containers, bags, or mats, and textiles such as clothing, floor coverings, and wall hangings. This diverse group of items may also contain sandals, cradles, and hats. Wooden tools are similarly produced in a great variety of shapes from pounders and

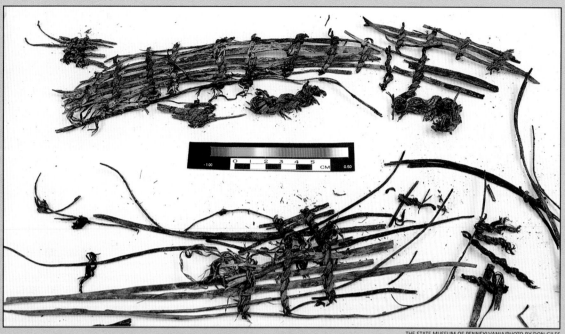

Basketry recovered from the Sheep Rock Shelter.

clubs to bows, spear and arrow shafts, tent pegs, and in conjunction with cordage, traps and snares.

All of these items were critical to the lifestyles of Pennsylvania Indians in all periods, but as noted above, they are seldom recovered from archaeological sites. At present, the oldest basketry or wood artifacts from the Commonwealth come from Meadowcroft Rockshelter in Washington County. At this remarkable site, which Indians visited periodically for more than 14,000 years, basketry and wooden tools have been found that are more than 12,000 years old. Indeed, a piece of what may have been a simple woven basketry container is the oldest such specimen in all of North America. Basketry and minute fragments of string, all carbonized, have been recovered from later levels in the site as well and were important to the site's generations of visitors throughout its long history. As in many other areas, baskets, string, and wooden tools were used to collect, transport, and process both plant and animal foods and were at least as important as stone in the daily lives of their makers. Additionally, because the manufacture of almost all types of plant fiber and wood artifacts is a highly standardized process, they are heavily influenced by local group customs and standards. As such, these items often inform us about things like tribal territories and may serve as population-specific ethnic signatures.

Moreover, unlike stone tools, which are often associated with male activities, the production of wood or plant fiber artifacts frequently reflects female labor and therefore provides us with insight into gender issues in the past.

In later periods, actual basketry and string specimens as well as wood artifacts have been recovered from Sheep Rock Shelter in central Pennsylvania. These items, unlike those from Meadowcroft and a few other sites, are not carbonized and illustrate the kind of perishable technology in use by Pennsylvanian Indians just prior to the arrival of Europeans.

Whenever they are found, artifacts of wood or plant fiber provide archaeologists with insights into past lifeways that are both unique and highly informative of their ancient makers. While perhaps not as exciting as flaked stone spearheads or groundstone axes, fragments of basketry, string, or similar items reflect the richness of prehistoric Pennsylvania Native American technology.

Suggested Reading

Adovasio, J. M.
2011 *Basketry Technology: A Guide to Identification and Analysis*. Left Coast Press, Walnut Creek, CA.

111

The projectile points of the Transitional period: bottom row left, stemmed point, and the right three are Lehigh broadspears; second row left, stemmed point, and the right three are Perkiomen broadspears; third row left, stemmed point, and the right four are Susquehanna broadspears; top row, Fishtail points.

The Transitional period can be divided into two phases: the Broadspear phase and the Fishtail phase. Broadspears are the hallmark of the Transitional period and are found in several styles or types in Pennsylvania. The development of broadspears is expressed all over the eastern United States. The earliest broadspears date to around 4300 years ago and are found in Virginia and the Carolinas. They are called Savanna River points and are very large. In the Middle Atlantic, the early broadspears are smaller and are called Koens-Crispin or Lehigh broadspears. These types are broad-bladed with stems that taper slightly. Beginning at 3900 years ago,

broadspears changed shape and are found in two expanding-stem varieties: the Susquehanna broadspear and the Perkiomen broadspear. The Susquehanna style has angular corners on the blade and is usually made from South Mountain metarhyolite from Adams and Franklin Counties. The Perkiomen style has rounded corners and a narrower base. It is usually made from jasper from Lehigh and Berks Counties. These are sometimes found at the same sites, but the Perkiomen type is most common in the Delaware drainage basin and the Susquehanna type is most common in the Susquehanna drainage basin.

The three main braodspear types: a.–c. metarhyolite Susquehanna broadspears; d.–e. jasper Perkiomen broadspears; f. chert Perkiomen broadspear; g. jasper Lehigh broadspear; h. diabase Koens-Crispin broadspear; i. jasper Lehigh broadspear.

Soon after the appearance of broadspears, there is a change in the lithic material that was being used to make them. The early broadspear types, such as Koens–Crispin or Snook Kill were made using a variety of lithic material types, such as chert, quartzite, argillite, metarhyolite, and jasper. Susquehanna and Perkiomen broadspears, however, were almost exclusively made using jasper, metarhyolite, or argillite. Initially, it was only the broadspears that were made using these toolstone types, but by 3400 years ago, 60 to 80 percent of all artifacts were made from these three lithic types. This is true for sites that are 200 miles from the source, suggesting an extensive trading system.

Archaeologists have long pondered how Transitional people acquired the raw material. Did they make regular trips to the quarry and dig it out of the ground themselves? Did they trade with the families who lived close to the quarry, or was the material traded through several groups? If it was the result of trade, it is not known what commodities were received in exchange for toolstone. The region around the jasper and metarhyolite quarries does not contain high frequencies of nonlocal material and sites in the region are not larger, suggesting the local bands were getting "rich" from the trade. Blanks for broadspear and Fishtail preforms found a hundred or two hundred miles from the quarries are in similar shapes. It seems that these standardized shapes were made at the quarry and traded from group to group with only a slight reduction in size until they were finally completed as broadspear or Fishtail forms. The specific nature of this system continues to be unclear.

Lithic Quarries

Native Americans were dependent on many different resources other than food and water. Also important were wood for fuel and construction, furs for clothing and shelter, reeds for baskets and mats, and shell, bone, and antler for tools and ornaments. In Woodland times, good clay sources were essential for pottery. At least as important as all of these was stone (lithic or toolstone) for tools. Wood, furs, reeds, and even clay sources were relatively common, but good-quality stone for tools

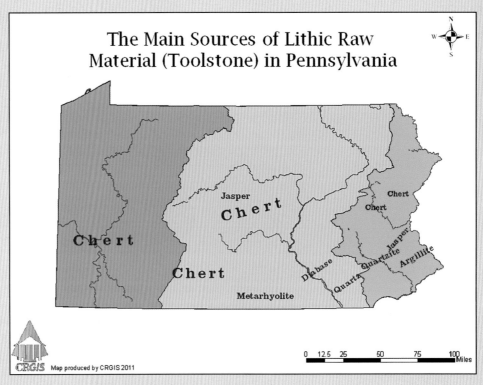

The location of the main toolstone sources in Pennsylvania.

was difficult to find and high-quality lithics were widely dispersed across the region.

To make stone tools requires a material that breaks in a predictable and controllable fashion. The rocks that were used in Pennsylvania have a *conchoidal fracture*, meaning they break like glass. The pieces that come off the rock are cone-shaped. The most commonly used toolstones in this region were chert, jasper, metarhyolite, quartzite, quartz, argillite, diabase, and chalcedony. Within Pennsylvania, chert, chalcedony, and jasper are sedimentary rocks, and the rest are metamorphic in origin.

Native Americans were expert geologists. They were always on the lookout for quality toolstone. Much of this could be collected in streams and rivers. Quartz and quartzite are found on the surface of ridgetops in the Commonwealth and also frequently end up in riverbeds. Many of the other lithic resources, however, had to be dug out of the ground. Over the past 11,000 years, these mining operations have created huge piles of broken and unfinished artifacts. Partially because of their size, prehistoric quarries have fascinated archaeologists, and they represent some of the earliest research in the Commonwealth.

The following is a brief overview of lithic quarries in Pennsylvania. Jasper is a multicolored sedimentary rock of various shades of red, brown, and yellow. It was used most extensively during the Paleoindian and Transitional periods. It is found close to the surface in two areas of Pennsylvania. The Hardyston jasper quarries in Berks and Lehigh Counties have some of the best toolstone in the Middle Atlantic region. There are also lesser-quality jasper outcrops in Centre County known as the Bald Eagle or Houserville quarries. Henry Chapman Mercer investigated the Hardyston quarries in the late nineteenth century, and Jim Hatch of Penn State University investigated both quarries in the 1990s. It is not clear whether the Centre County quarries were associated with extensive digging by Native Americans or if the material was simply gathered from the surface. In contrast, the Hardyston quarries represent the deepest prehistoric mining operations in the Commonwealth. Mercer reported shafts over 40 feet in depth and recent work has documented quarry pits 23 feet in depth. Prehistorically, there were approximately ten major jasper outcrops, with Vera Cruz and Macungie being some of the largest. Each of these was characterized by sixty to one hundred mining pits covering 6 to 10 acres. They were 40 feet deep and 100 feet across. Currently, the pits are relatively small depressions, at most 5 feet deep and 20 feet across.

114

These pits were created by repeated visits for over 11,000 years. At the Kings Quarry in Lehigh County, it was documented that the jasper was first used by Paleo indians, who probably simply collected material from the surface. During the Early Archaic Period, the surface material was probably exhausted and they began to dig. The jasper is found in large blocks within a layer of sandstone bedrock. The sandstone has decayed into soil and the miners used digging sticks and the shoulder blade bones of elk as shovels to excavate down and expose the large blocks. In some cases, the miners dug holes and backfilled adjacent older pits as they went. Throughout the Archaic Period, the quarry pit eventually took on the appearance of a large crater with steeply sloping sides, and it reached a depth of 23 feet and at least 80 feet across. By Middle Woodland times, the piles of dirt surrounding the pit began to wash in and slowly backfill the pit. The last pit excavated in the bottom of this crater was approximately 3 feet deep and 4 feet wide. It was evident that water-deposited sediments gradually filled this one in. By Late Woodland times, jasper was no longer the preferred lithic material in the region (except by the local tribes), and the pit filled in to a depth of about 12 feet. It is assumed that the pit was completely backfilled during historic farming.

Rhyolite, or more accurately metarhyolite, is a volcanic rock that was metamorphosed by a mountain-building episode about 300 million years ago. It was first commonly used during Early Archaic times and was most heavily used during the Transitional and Early Woodland periods. It is found in South Mountain in Adams and Franklin Counties and also in Maryland. It is not the same quality as jasper, but it is found in massive formations. The mining process was probably similar to that used for jasper but on a smaller scale. The pits are less than 10 feet deep and the documented examples illustrate that as one was being dug, the previous pit was frequently being backfilled.

The argillite quarries in Bucks County are found in the Lockatong Formation. This formation extends fifty miles into New Jersey and contains many quarries. The Pennsylvania quarries were first investigated by Mercer in the 1880s. Argillite is similar in quality to metarhyolite. This material was mined in a similar fashion as the metarhyolite, although the quarry pits seem to be smaller. This material witnessed its highest utilization during the Archaic, Transitional, and Early Woodland periods. Large amounts of this material were transported all over New Jersey, Delaware, and Maryland. Interestingly, in Pennsylvania, the Lockatong argillite is not found in high quantities in the Susquehanna basin.

Chert is one of the most common types of lithic materials used by Native Americans. It was used during all periods and is found across the state. It is black, dark blue, or dark green in color and varies greatly in quality. The best-quality material was transported over long distances, especially during Paleoindian times, but most chert was only used locally. There are a few large chert quarries similar in appearance to the metarhyolite quarries where Native Americans dug in the ground to extract the raw material. More frequently, it is found in layers, alternating with limestone and shale. This material is mined in a different fashion and usually does not result in the huge piles of waste material that are associated with jasper, metarhyolite, or argillite. The bedrock layers range up to a foot thick. The adjacent layers of rock have not decayed, as with jasper, and Native Americans did not have the technology to dig down through solid rock to retrieve the chert. Commonly, the miners looked for rock exposures. Using a combination of bone, wood, and antler picks and wedges, they pried the chert out of the layered bedrock. Usually, these outcrops are localized and are not character-ized by large piles of chipping debris commonly found at the jasper, metarhyolite, or argillite quarries.

Quartz and quartzite are found in large formations in several areas around the Commonwealth. These types vary greatly in quality and they are relatively difficult to work. These materials rarely moved over long distances and were primarily used locally. The outcrops in Berks, Lancaster, and York Counties are some of the most extensively used. These materials were recovered directly from the surface, and they do not seem to be associated with quarry pits. They are relatively hard and do not weather as quickly as other lithics and therefore are frequently found in streams and rivers as large cobbles.

Finally, steatite or soapstone was mined to make stone bowls during the Transitional period. Steatite is found in thick formations in southern Pennsylvania, particularly along the Chester County and Lancaster County border. The mining of steatite is very interesting because the bowls were partially carved at the quarries. They were carved upside down right in the bedrock. Once the outside was finished, the bowl was detached from the bedrock and the inside was carved out.

Prehistoric quarry sites are essentially large industrial sites. The quarries were probably treeless with little vegetation. The quarry pits were frequently filled with water and a clear line of sight; they were probably good hunting areas. As archaeolog-ical sites, they are difficult to excavate because they are usually not well stratified, or the stratigraphy is very complicated. They are extremely important, however, because they document a significant Native American industry.

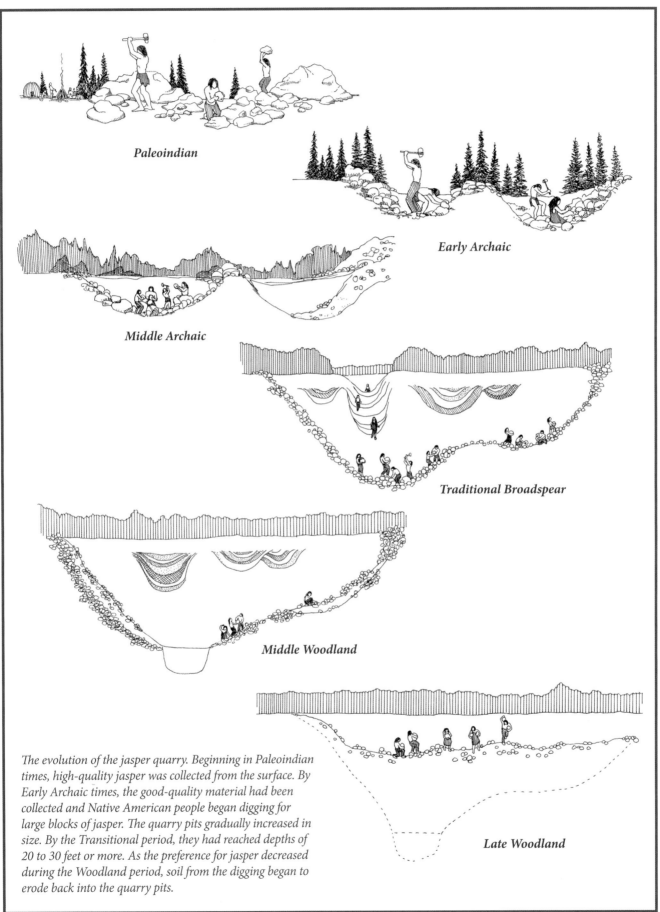

Paleoindian

Early Archaic

Middle Archaic

Traditional Broadspear

Middle Woodland

Late Woodland

The evolution of the jasper quarry. Beginning in Paleoindian times, high-quality jasper was collected from the surface. By Early Archaic times, the good-quality material had been collected and Native American people began digging for large blocks of jasper. The quarry pits gradually increased in size. By the Transitional period, they had reached depths of 20 to 30 feet or more. As the preference for jasper decreased during the Woodland period, soil from the digging began to erode back into the quarry pits.

The knapping techniques used during the Transitional period are fundamentally different than those used during the Middle and Late Archaic periods. The making of broadspears starts at the quarries. Blocks of metarhyolite or jasper were dug out of the ground, and large stone hammers were used to break them into flat flakes, a foot or more in diameter. These flakes were chipped into "blanks," or preforms, using large wooden or antler hammers. These "soft hammers," also known as batons, looked like small baseball bats and were 3 inches in diameter and 18 inches long. The large flake blank was bifacially thinned (chipped on both sides) to less than 3/8 inch thick and finished by notching the base. Broadspears started out their use-life with long and wide blades but were frequently reworked to be used as knives. This resulted in an asymmetrical shape (not the same on both sides), because one edge was more frequently sharpened than the other.

The archaeological specimens are usually less than 3 inches long. Many broadspears were sharpened into scrapers or drills that were hafted (attached) to handles in the same way that the spears and knives were hafted. The scrapers are distinctive and larger than the small

A very thin quarry blank and broadspear preform recovered near Selinsgrove, Northumberland County. The knapper who created these artifacts first struck a large but thin (1/2-inch) flake from a block of metarhyolite. This was followed by removing an equally large, but even thinner flake. The knapper began to make a large broadspear but for some reason stopped. Both of these pieces required great skill.

scrapers typically found during the Paleoindian period. The drills were used for putting holes in wood, bone, shell, and soft stone such as steatite. Some of the drills are very long—too long to have started out as broadspears. These were specifically made for this purpose, but their true function remains problematic. Fishtail points were made using the same techniques as broadspears, but they were less frequently reworked into scrapers or drills; however, the blade is frequently asymmetrical, suggesting it was multifunctional and used as a cutting tool.

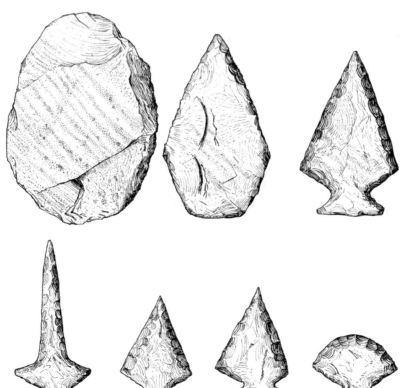

The hypothetical life cycle of a Susquehanna broadspear. A broadspear was a very flexible tool that could be reworked into a knife, drill, scraper, or spearpoint.

117

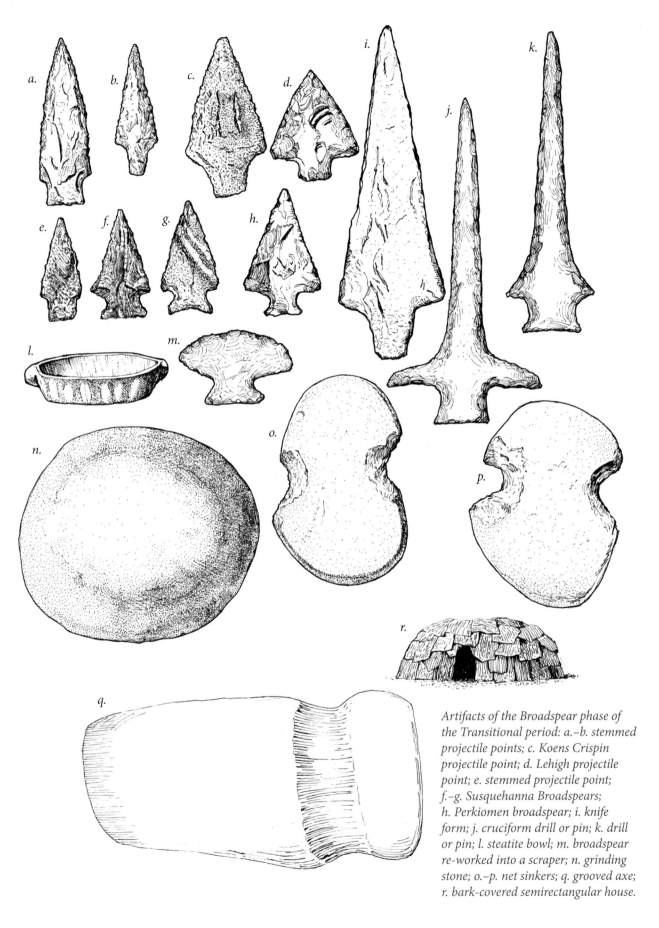

Artifacts of the Broadspear phase of the Transitional period: a.–b. stemmed projectile points; c. Koens Crispin projectile point; d. Lehigh projectile point; e. stemmed projectile point; f.–g. Susquehanna Broadspears; h. Perkiomen broadspear; i. knife form; j. cruciform drill or pin; k. drill or pin; l. steatite bowl; m. broadspear re-worked into a scraper; n. grinding stone; o.–p. net sinkers; q. grooved axe; r. bark-covered semirectangular house.

Broadspears are not the only spearpoint or biface type used during the Transitional period. The narrow-stemmed spearpoints (so-called Piedmont points) are also found with broadspears. Some archaeologists believe that broadspears were not used as spearpoints at all and always functioned as cutting, scraping, or drilling tools. They base this conclusion on edge-wear analyses, as well as practicality. They argue that the wide blades would not have had the penetrating power of the narrow blades of the Late Archaic spearpoints. The edge wear suggests that many broadspears were used for cutting soft materials, such as animal flesh, hides, and even wood. Archaeologists who believe broadspears were multipurpose knives argue that stemmed spearpoints that are sometimes found with broadspears are the only real spearpoints in the Transitional period toolkit. Other studies have shown, however, that they were just as frequently used as spear-points, so the function of broadspears continues to be debated. Interestingly, the stemmed projectile points are made from local toolstone and not the preferred tool-stone of the Transitional period—jasper, metarhyolite, or argillite.

The other distinctive artifact of the Transitional period is the carved soapstone or steatite bowl. These were the first portable and permanent cooking vessels to appear in the archaeological record of the north-eastern United States. We use the qualifying term "appear in the archaeological record," because bark baskets, skin bags, and wooden bowls had been used since Paleoindian times as cooking containers for boiling and steaming foods. These are rarely ever found at archaeological sites in the East because they decay very quickly.

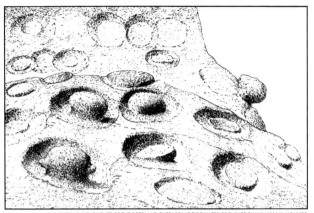

FROM *STONE IMPLEMENTS OF THE POTOMAC-CHESAPEAKE TIDEWATER PROVINCE* BY WILLIAM H. HOLMES

Holmes's drawing of the steatite quarries.

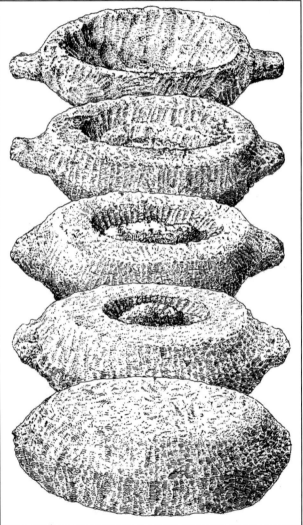

FROM *STONE IMPLEMENTS OF THE POTOMAC-CHESAPEAKE TIDEWATER PROVINCE* BY WILLIAM H. HOLMES

Once the general shape of the bowl was detached from the bedrock, the piece was turned over and the bowl was carved from the inside.

THE STATE MUSEUM OF PENNSYLVANIA/PHOTO BY DON GILES

A complete steatite bowl with two lugs (handles) found in Dauphin County.

Steatite is a very soft stone that contains talc. It is a metamorphic rock found near the border of Lancaster and Chester Counties and also in Maryland in what is known as the serpentine region. The layers of steatite are very thick, and the bowls were first carved upside down directly into the bedrock. Archaeologists have found stone gouges and picks along with incomplete bowls at the quarries, providing clues on how they were produced. Once the outside shape was complete, they were detached from the bedrock and the inside was carved out. They are found in round, oval, and rectangular shapes, with both rounded and flat bottoms. The larger specimens have handles or lugs on the ends. The edges or rims of the bowls are sometimes notched or incised, decorated with geometric designs such as triangles, rectangles, or squares. Small beads were also made with steatite to be used as artifacts of adornment. Steatite has been used commercially in historic times to make cooking grills. The extraction of steatite for this purpose has destroyed many Native American quarry sites.

Steatite bowls could be very heavy, but they were regularly transported a hundred miles or more, and it is assumed this was done by dugout canoe. Their function as cooking containers seems obvious, but the explanation is not that simple. There is evidence in the form of smoke-blackened exteriors and baked food on interiors that supports the interpretation that these bowls were the first portable cooking containers and the precursors to fired-clay pottery; however, there is great variation in the size of steatite vessels. While some steatite vessels resembled large cooking pots with flat bottoms, others were very small and impractical as food containers. So it is argued that steatite vessels probably served multiple functions. But what were these functions?

Why go to the trouble of carving a stone bowl and transporting it a great distance when it would only hold enough food for one person? There are also many vessels that lack heat markings entirely. Does this mean steatite vessels may have served a nonutilitarian (noncooking or nonstorage) purpose? Were they used for social or even ceremonial purposes? Steatite was probably an important trade item and it may have been important in the formation and maintenance of social networks. Such vessels may have been used as special dishes during important feasts. We know that when modern forager bands come together, they frequently hold "feasts" in celebration of marriages and childbirth or to reinvigorate belief systems. Steatite vessels may have been important ceremonial objects during these feasts. They may have been given as gifts to important individuals or they may have been part of a gift-exchange system between important individuals. We will probably never know the details, but the widespread use of small bowls suggests a social or ceremonial function. These artifacts along with broadspears and trade in toolstone suggest a very different social system than existed during the Archaic period.

Although steatite vessel fragments are found at many sites, they are rarely common at any one site. Whatever their function, they were probably considered very important commodities. They were so important that there are many examples of broken vessels being repaired by drilling holes in the two halves and lashing them back together. Since they could no longer hold water, these types of repairs also suggest these bowls were very special and had nonutilitarian uses.

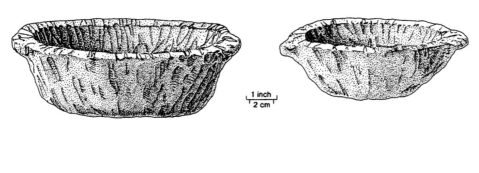

1 inch
2 cm

Various styles of steatite bowls.

JAY CUSTER/*PREHISTORIC CULTURES OF EASTERN PENNSYLVANIA*

THE PENNSYLVANIA DUGOUT CANOE PROJECT

The Pennsylvania Historical and Museum Commission (PHMC) has carved three dugout canoes from large trees since the 1990s. These have been made as part of public programs using replicated historic and prehistoric tools. The sight of people dressed in loincloths, with wood chips flying and fire, attracts a lot of attention, and these programs have been very popular with the public. The resulting dugouts have been included in a variety of presentations, most notably the annual Pennsylvania Farm Show. Although the publicity is good, these projects are examples of experimental archaeology. They are being conducted to aid in the interpretation of the archaeological record.

Dugout History

A *dugout canoe*—often known simply as a dugout—is a hollowed-out log used as a watercraft. It is typically made in a cycle of burning the log with a controlled fire and then scraping and chopping out the charred and softened wood with a variety of tools as diverse as shells, stone adzes, and wooden scrapers. The dugout is most likely the earliest form of constructed watercraft in the world, and European examples have been dated to nearly 10,000 years old. However, considering that Australia could only be settled by boat and it was occupied by humans at least 45,000 years ago, dugouts are at least that old. In both North America and South America, dugouts had been the main form of water travel since Native Americans arrived from Siberia more than 16,000 years ago. In the eastern United States, dugouts are preserved in the lakes and bogs of Florida, Louisiana, North Carolina, Tennessee, Ohio, and Pennsylvania, the oldest of which dates to more than 6000 BP.

This 1575 drawing by John White illustrates the steps in making a dugout canoe.

BROWN UNIVERSITY LIBRARY

Based on early descriptions of Native American vessels, including the well-known accounts of Captain Arthur Barlowe (1550–1620), an English explorer and protégé of Sir Walter Raleigh, and John White (1540/1550–1608), artist and governor of the "Lost Colony" of Roanoke, Virginia, archaeologists possess some idea of construction methods and variations in size and shape. Although both Barlowe and White described a process of burning and scraping logs with shells to fashion such canoes, they do not mention the use of stone axes or adzes. In Pennsylvania, less than twenty dugouts have been documented in bogs and lakes, primarily in the Poconos of northeastern Pennsylvania. It is believed that in pre-European times, many of the lakes in this region would have had at least one resident dugout for hunting, fishing, and gathering by Native Americans. Since their weight and bulkiness made them extremely difficult to transport over land, dugout canoes were probably not moved between lakes but most likely stored year-round at the lakes where they were made. Once taken out of water, they are prone to cracking and deterioration, and evidence exists that in the winter Native Americans may have filled their canoes with rocks and sunk them below the freeze line to escape being crushed by ice and to keep them from being damaged by repeated freezing and thawing.

Although many recognize the portable birchbark canoe as a Native American watercraft, this type of vessel was rarely used in Pennsylvania. Such canoes could be made only in regions to the north, where birch trees grew to a sufficient size to allow for their construction.

The Tools

PHMC archaeologists staged the most recent Pennsylvania Dugout Canoe Project in September 2005 as a public exhibition. One of their goals was to use tools of the type that would have been available to pre-European contact peoples of Pennsylvania. The archaeologists constructed one metarhyolite and four basalt adzes that they hafted to hardwood handles. Basalt is a hard, dense rock the Native Americans frequently used for woodworking tools. Project participants ground, shaped, and polished the basalt adzes. Grinding each one consumed eight hours. The early process was not without its drawbacks, though, and ultimately evolved into a routine of trial and error. For instance, the initial thin edges of the blades broke, requiring them to be increased in thickness. The most difficult aspect of constructing these tools was affixing the blades to the wooden handles. In their first attempts, archaeologists attached the blades to the bottom of forked branches, but the handle broke quickly and they moved the cutting surface to the top of the fork. This position worked well, but the tools loosened and had to be reattached. After some experimentation, the most successful method consisted of sinew, a tendonlike attachment, covered with rawhide and adhered with pine pitch. To expedite the experiment, at least one adze was reinforced with commercial twine.

Construction

For the dugout itself, the team began with a white pine log measuring approximately 20 feet that had been donated and delivered by the staff of Michaux State Forest. A storm had toppled the tree about seven months earlier. As a model for the watercraft's design, participants used a circa 1250 AD dugout from Mud Pond near Pleasant View Summit in eastern Luzerne County, now on exhibit at The State Museum of Pennsylvania in Harrisburg. This dugout was found by a group of boys in Mud Pond in 1935 and donated to the museum in 1968.

Archaeologists began work on the canoe by cutting and charring the ends of the log to bevel the bow and stern. This was followed by creating a channel down the top and length of the log through a repeated process of burning, chopping, and scraping the charred area. By the fifth day of burning, the log's side walls were sufficiently thinned so that the tops of these areas, the gunnels, were covered with clay before additional burnings to prevent additional charring. Each morning the team applied a layer of clay insulation to the gunnels and ignited a fire the length of the dugout, which they allowed to burn for two to four hours. They then removed the charred material by scraping the interior with beveled pieces of wood and stone

The adzes made by the archaeologists worked very well (left and below).

adzes. Scraping progressed slowly as workers removed less than 1 inch daily. Nearing completion, they rubbed the rough surface of the interior with sandstone to reduce splinters and increase comfort. For the final treatment, they applied pine tar mixed with hot wood ash as a sealant, after which they smoothed the coating by abrading it with fine wood chips and hand rubbing it with medium-coarse sand.

The entire process required seventeen days. On the final day, it was launched into the Susquehanna River for a 5-mile trip and has since been paddled in nearby lakes. The stone adzes worked very well. In fact, the project would have gone faster with more chopping using the adzes or more directed burning using fans. The burning facilitated the removal of wood, but the last firing also hardened and preserved it. The burning required a lot of time.

The adzes developed a distinctive set of wear patterns from the chopping on their edges. These were compared to prehistoric stone adzes in the collections of The State Museum of Pennsylvania. Interestingly, the wear patterns did not always match those on the experimental pieces and additional analysis will be necessary to determine their function.

The 2005 Pennsylvania Dugout Canoe Project enabled PHMC staff archaeologists to not only test theories and experiment with Native American construction techniques and tools, but it also educated and informed thousands of individuals, young and old, who watched it being made. Since then, it has been on exhibit many times, allowing archaeologists and volunteers to provide information on dugouts found in the East, describe their methodology, and illustrate the dramatic results—both the canoe and the prehistoric toolkit that was used to make it.

THE STATE MUSEUM OF PENNSYLVANIA/PHOTO BY DON GILES

Adzes being used to construct the dugout.

THE STATE MUSEUM OF PENNSYLVANIA/PHOTO BY DON GILES

The second phase of the Transitional period is called the Fishtail phase and fishtail points begin to replace broadspears around 3100 years ago. The Fishtail phase is distinguished by the use of narrow, expanding-stem projectile points. Fishtail-style projectile points are similar to Susquehanna broadspears, only narrower, and they document a continuation of this cultural tradition. In the Delaware basin, they are most frequently made in jasper, argillite, and chert. In the Susquehanna basin, the favorite toolstone is metarhyolite.

In Pennsylvania, they are found in two varieties, the Orient style and the Drybrook style. The Drybrook form is asymmetrical and slightly thicker than the Orient form; however, the two forms are found at the same sites and in the same levels, so the meaning of these two shapes is unclear. Fishtail projectile points are common and found throughout the Delaware and Susquehanna drainage basins. There is a continuation of the lithic trade system as well as the use of scrapers and drills. As with the Broadspear phase, however, other local lithic types continue to be used. Large fire-cracked rock features are frequently found at Fishtail sites. Net sinkers are common, and we assume fishing continued to be important. Fishtail projectile points are replaced by a variety of very different types beginning at approximately 2700 years ago.

During the transition between the Broadspear phase and the Fishtail phase, steatite bowls are replaced by fired-clay pottery. Pottery is found at these sites in low frequencies and is of a very poor quality. The first pottery was hand-molded, with small handles, flat bottoms, and plain surfaces. These are clearly ceramic copies of steatite bowls. Some of these pots were made on woven mats because the mat impressions are preserved on the bottoms of pots. Frequently, crushed soapstone bowls are used as temper in these earliest pots. Temper is a gritty substance, such as sand, crushed quartz, or other types of crushed rock, that is added to the clay to strengthen the pot during firing. This type of pottery in the Middle Atlantic region is called Marcy Creek or Seldon Island. Based on earlier dates for pottery to the south in North Carolina, South Carolina, and Georgia, we assume this technology was not invented in the Middle Atlantic region but was introduced by other peoples.

Vinette ware is another type of early pottery, but it had a rounded rather than a flat bottom. It is usually thick and made with large pieces of temper using coils of clay. These were welded (compressing the clay) together with a cord-wrapped paddle. The wrappings left impressions of the cordage, called cordmarks, on the outside and sometimes on the inside of the pot.

Projectile points of the Fishtail phase all in jasper.

The distinguishing characteristic of Vinette ware is that it is cordmarked on both the interior and the exterior surfaces. The cordmarking is oriented vertically on the outside and horizontally on the inside. Interestingly, cordmarked pots are found all over the world and are a characteristic of many early pottery traditions. The cordmarking has a functional aspect in that it increases the surface area of the pot and improves the thermodynamics (heating or energy production and distribution) of the vessel. This prevents it from cracking during the firing process and when it is used as a cooking utensil. The roughened surface also makes it easier to hold and less likely to slip out of one's hands and break.

Although fragile, clay pots probably represent a significant change in the processing and storage of food resources. Collecting the clay, forming the pot, and firing represent significant work and an equally assumed significant value.

Pottery was in use along the coast of the southeastern United States (Georgia) about 4500 years ago. Surprisingly, it spread very slowly. It reached Pennsylvania at approximately 3200 years ago. For about 200 years, both steatite and ceramic containers were being used. The obvious question is why did it take so long for the lighter and more flexible ceramic pots to replace the steatite bowls and why were both used at the same time?

123

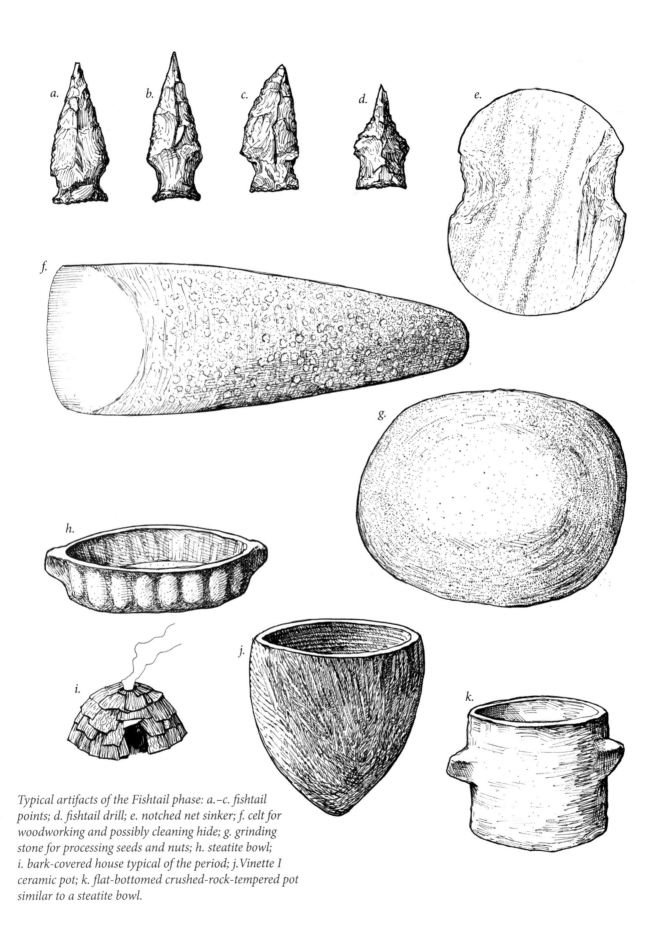

Typical artifacts of the Fishtail phase: a.–c. fishtail points; d. fishtail drill; e. notched net sinker; f. celt for woodworking and possibly cleaning hide; g. grinding stone for processing seeds and nuts; h. steatite bowl; i. bark-covered house typical of the period; j.Vinette I ceramic pot; k. flat-bottomed crushed-rock-tempered pot similar to a steatite bowl.

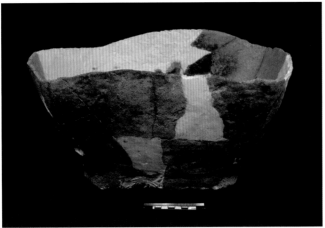

Steatite-tempered pottery is one of the earliest types of pottery found in Pennsylvania. The type name is Marcy Creek.

Ken Sassaman has proposed that steatite bowls may have remained important because this technology was controlled by men. Since steatite had to be transported long distances, it is assumed that men dominated such transportation. It remained favored by men even after the introduction of fired-clay pottery, which was primarily controlled by women. Steatite trade helped men to maintain their power, and so they may have been

Impressions of a cord-wrapped stick or paddle were made to increase the surface area of the pot and improve the heating characteristics of the vessel.

reluctant to adopt pottery. The shift from steatite bowls to ceramic pottery may signal a shift from an economy dominated by males to one dominated by females.

Pottery of the Transitional period from the Susquehanna and Delaware drainage basins: a. a flat-bottomed steatite-tempered pot similar to a steatite bowl; b. Marcy Creek pottery type—steatite tempered pottery; c. Vinette I variant—grit-tempered and exterior cord-marked; d. Vinette I pottery type—coarse-grit-tempered and interior/exterior cordmarked.

What People Ate: Subsistence

Based on artifacts and site locations, people of the Transitional period ate the same wide variety of foods that were consumed during Archaic times. Deer, elk, a variety of small mammals, fish, hickory nuts, walnuts, acorns, and a variety of seeds, roots, and berries were all part of their diet—seemingly everything edible in the forest. There were, however, two major differences from the Late Archaic period.

During the Transitional period, food was cooked differently than previous times. Floodplain sites in particular usually contain large quantities of fire-cracked rock (known to archaeologists as FCR). Late Archaic sites contain rock hearths, but Transitional period sites contain more hearths and much larger quantities of FCR. During the Transitional period, FCR features are commonly over 10 feet in diameter and 6 inches thick. Because these sites were usually along major rivers, archaeologists have long thought that the FCR features represent large fish-drying racks. Archaeologists have researched other explanations for FCR concentrations by experimenting with a variety of cooking techniques, using a variety of foods. Based on this research, these features could have been used to dry or roast other meats, shellfish, or nuts. Large quantities of these types of foods are frequently harvested on a seasonal basis.

Complicating the roasting interpretation, however, is that FCR features rarely contain fishbone, or any other type of bone, and frequently very little charcoal. An alternative to the roasting/drying explanation for these concentrations is that they result from a process called "stone boiling." This process begins with digging a hole in the ground or hollowing out a log and lining it with animal hide in order to seal it. Then it is filled with water. In a nearby fire, rocks would be heated. With the use of tongs, the heated rocks would be added to the water. Within half an hour, a soup of hickory nuts, seeds, and fish could be brought to a boil. Fish oil could also be rendered in this fashion. Another method involves filling the pit with heated rock and green leaves to construct an earth oven for steaming. Boiling and steaming foods preserves more calories than roasting foods over an open fire and represents a more efficient exploitation of the environment. These processes produce large quantities of FCR. In some cases, it appears as tight clusters or piles, as if it was dumped from a container. In other cases, the FCR is scattered over large areas of the living floors. These features represent a more efficient cooking process that resulted in more calories being extracted from these foods and the environment in general.

The second difference in subsistence patterns is probably more significant and has come to light as the result of improved archaeological methods. The preservation of organic materials and the reconstruction of prehistoric diets has long been a problem for archaeologists because food remains are rarely preserved at archaeological sites.

Beginning in the late 1990s, however, archaeology experienced a transformation in collecting techniques called the "paleoethnobotanical revolution." This is the regular and systematic use of field and laboratory methods that recover artifacts and organic remains representing subsistence patterns. The common use of flotation methods has resulted in the recovery of many small artifacts, especially food remains such as seeds and nut parts. In addition, archaeologists are now able to analyze the charred residue found on the inside of steatite bowls and early pottery. They have even been able to identify plant residues on grinding stones. The consistent application of these methods has revealed a more extensive use of plant foods than previously realized. Several new foods have been identified, including little barley and chenopodium (seed-producing plants). In the Mississippi Valley, these plants are part of what is

Chenopodium seeds became a more common component of the Transitional diet.

known as the Eastern Agricultural Complex. They were domesticated and grown in small gardens. It is debated as to whether they were domesticated in Pennsylvania during Transitional times, but they may have been cultivated rather than simply collected wild. Squash (gourds or pumpkins) has also been found at one Transitional period site in Pennsylvania. Squash is not native to Pennsylvania and was domesticated in the southwestern United States more than 5000 years ago. Initially, its main function may have been as containers because squashes retain their shape when dried. The remains found in Pennsylvania could be the result of trade, but the more common recovery of little barley and chenopodium suggests they were planted by local peoples. Although only a small start, it would seem that Transitional people may have been cultivating gardens.

Although Transitional period people were using as many different foods as Archaic period people, they were processing them more efficiently, and they probably added some domesticated foods. Maintaining a garden, however, requires more work than simply collecting wild seeds and nuts. In addition, some foods, such as acorns from white oaks (as compared to red oaks) contain tannin and require processing to remove this bitter-tasting substance. Transitional period people had begun the process of cultivation, but they were spending more hours at recovering calories from their environment. It is assumed by many archaeologists that the extra work was necessary to support a larger population.

Where People Lived: Settlement Patterns

When John Witthoft first defined the Transitional period, he characterized it as a "canoe traveling culture, exploiting fish, waterfowl and large game." Later, Fred Kinsey characterized this period as having a "riverine focus." Both men felt that the Transitional period culture was different from Late Archaic cultures and that one of its distinguishing factors was the preference for living in river valleys. After much research, it seems that sites from this period may be in slightly different locations, but they are exploiting the same ecological settings. They are both found along the valleys of the major rivers, in the uplands along small streams, and adjacent to swamps and bogs. The reduced rainfall during the Sub-Boreal caused some small streams to dry up in the summer and, generally, wetlands got smaller. Transitional period sites are found slightly

closer to water than previous periods but this is because water levels were lower, not because people were more interested in food resources near rivers and swamps. There are differences between the two periods, however. Transitional period sites along rivers are usually larger and contain more artifacts than Late Archaic sites. The sites along the large rivers appear to be base camps for macrobands or even meeting places for macrobands from adjacent territories.

As discussed above, another characteristic of Transitional period sites is that they contain many large FCR features. Through experimentation, we have learned that some of this is the result of steaming or boiling and some is the result of open fires used in cooking and roasting. Although the specific foods are debated, these sites represent large food-processing areas. Adding to this explanation, the large FCR features may be the remains of ceremonial feasts, where steatite vessels would have played an important role. In addition, some of the fire-cracked rock was probably used in sweat lodges, which were used during ceremonies and feasts. So, FCR may represent all of these methods of heating rock, along with the social implications. The scale of food processing and the possible social implications is not found at Late Archaic sites. On Transitional sites, it represents both a more intensive strategy for exploiting the environment and an increased level of social activity.

When excavating sites from this period, archaeologists frequently focus on the FCR features. This large concentration of artifacts and features is frequently interpreted as representing base camps, which were places occupied by large groups of people for several months; however, the FCR features, especially the scatters, could simply represent food-processing areas. The debris and smoke would have made them unpleasant as living areas. The food may actually have been consumed elsewhere on the site or at a different site altogether. If these are base camps, there should be evidence of houses and family hearths. Unfortunately, archaeologists have rarely excavated large areas beyond the FCR features, although when they did, evidence of houses has not been found, so it is unclear where large groups of people were actually living.

Based on the location of sites, the types of artifacts, and features found at these sites and our understanding of the environment, archaeologists have developed a hypothesis on the annual movements or settlement patterns of Transitional period peoples.

Summer

Fall

The Transitional period settlement pattern was similar to the Late Archaic annual cycle, but the camps involved more families who lived there for longer periods of time. The spring fish migration site was probably the largest. This site was probably a meeting place for several bands. Trading and ceremonies took place in this camp. Squash and seed plants of the Eastern Agricultural Complex may have been grown here. Small groups may have stayed at these locations throughout the summer to protect the gardens. In the summer, families broke into small groups to exploit a wide variety of plants and animals in the floodplain and upland areas. In the fall, families focused on collecting a variety of nuts but also hunted in the uplands. In the winter, hunting in small family groups in upland areas was the norm. This also may have been the time when groups went directly to the quarries to collect toolstone and/or steatite.

Spring

Winter

129

The largest sites are on floodplains, but there are also a large number of mostly smaller sites in a wide variety of upland topographic settings. The largest camp was probably associated with the spring fish migrations, such as shad, Atlantic sturgeon, or Atlantic salmon. These would have been busy places involving many families, possibly representing a macroband. The fish were caught with nets, traps, and spears. They were then processed by drying, roasting, and boiling. In addition, there are other foods, such as tubers and wild waterfowl, that were available in large numbers around wetlands. These sites were probably also the locations of feasts and special events such as marriages and naming and religious ceremonies.

In the summer, a variety of tubers, berries, seeds, mammals, birds, fish, and turtles were dispersed throughout the riverine and upland areas. After the fish migrations ended, the bands separated into family groups and lived in small camps. They spent the summer moving to these different food resources. At some of these camps, they may have cultivated squash, chenopodium, or little barley, especially when food resources were scarce. To protect the plants, these sites would have been occupied into the fall or until the crop was harvested. The early summer was also a time to collect reeds and cordage for baskets and mats. Some groups may have visited the lithic quarries to make steatite bowls or collect toolstone for broad-spears and fishtails. In the fall, walnuts, hickory nuts, acorns, and migratory waterfowl were concentrated in large numbers. Families joined into macrobands to exploit these resources. These camps were mostly in riverine areas, but nut-collecting camps could have been located in more upland areas. Foods were processed at these camps for the winter, a time of scarce resources. Sheltered upland sites may have been the location of winter camps. These were occupied by single family groups who mainly hunted and ate foods processed in the fall.

Finally, the fall lines on the Delaware and Susquehanna Rivers are areas where brackish water from the ocean meets freshwater from the interior. These are very special areas where there were very large quantities of food resources. The Transitional period sites at these locations are very large. Some archaeologists have speculated that these represent macroband meeting areas between coastal people and more interior people. Because of the quantity of food resources, these may have been occupied for many months of the year. These sites may have been areas where macrobands from different regions met and traded a wide variety of items—food, baskets, carvings, mats, ground and polished axes, and adzes—but lithics (jasper, argillite, metarhyolite, or quartzite) and steatite were certainly present. They may have resembled modern "trade fairs," with a wide variety of commodities being exchanged. A variety of ceremonies probably took place, but more importantly a different type of social organization may have appeared. Charismatic leaders or individuals with strong personalities may have emerged at these sites—individuals who actually had some control over the goods being exchanged.

People Living in Groups: Social Organization and Belief Systems

The lives of people who lived during the Transitional period were different from the lives of people who lived during the Late Archaic period in five major ways: they made and used tools differently, they processed their food differently, they were involved with regional trade systems, they were involved with burial ceremonialism, and they were probably organized into different types of family groups. Trade and burial ceremonialism certainly existed during Late Archaic times, but they are not commonly manifested in the archaeological record of Pennsylvania. Trade especially becomes more obvious in the record and seems to be extremely important for economic and probably social reasons. The exchange of stone was important for making tools; some types of stone were even traded over hundreds of miles. It is not clear, however, as to why extensive trade arose in only a few exclusive stone types: steatite, metarhyolite, argillite, and jasper. Perhaps these stone types were thought to be most advantageous for Transitional peoples' purposes, such as broadspears. Or it may be that these stones are all that remains of a trading system that included many other commodities. The exchange possibly included food, raw materials, or even people, although none of these are preserved in the archaeological record.

These stones may have been traded as parts of social networks. Perhaps trade relationships were established more for their symbolic importance than for what was actually traded. Trade indicates a dependence on neighboring families and it suggests that social networks were larger. The purpose of these connections may have been to increase security and establish alliances in case the groups ever needed help in the future. For example, some archaeologists believe that changes in the environment were occurring at this time, and these arrangements could represent a safety net or insurance policy that led to food sharing during difficult times.

It is probable that the nature of their social lives was also altered in significant ways with increased interregional contact. Burial ceremonialism appeared for the first time in the Middle Atlantic region, although it was not common in Pennsylvania, and it is assumed that there were significant changes in social organization. This is not to say this is the first time Native Americans buried their dead or conducted ceremonies at the gravesite. Native Americans have been disposing of their dead using rituals since they arrived in the New World. But this is the first time in the Middle Atlantic region that cremation burials are found with grave goods. The rise of burial practices may indicate different perceptions of relationships between family and nonfamily members, as well as changes in culture and worldview. There was now a need to remember deceased individuals as well as to prepare them for an afterlife. In addition, the grave goods that were part of the burial ceremony provide information about the status of the individual as well as the nature of trade. While this may be an explanation, it is difficult to interpret the specifics from the archaeological record.

There are Transitional period cremation burials in New York and New Jersey. In southern New Jersey, at the Savich Farm site, a cemetery has been found that contains cremated burials and grave goods in the form of atlatl weights and large numbers of broadspears of the Snook Kill type. Many of the artifacts have been burned and broken, likely during the cremation process. Finding broken artifacts in a grave sometimes means that the tools were ceremonially "killed," releasing the spirit of the tool to join the spirit of the deceased.

At least four Orient Fishtail cemeteries were uncovered on Long Island in New York. These were situated on hilltops at some distance from habitation sites. The cemeteries consisted of individual graves and large communal pits. The largest were 20 x 30 feet in size and 5 feet in depth. The majority of the interments were cremation burials, but some had been defleshed and only partially burned. Typically, each burial included a cache consisting of a fire-making kit, projectile points, one or more "killed" stone bowls, a hammerstone, and a celt or adze. In addition, knives, drills, pendants, gorgets, grooved axes, and bannerstones were also included. Red ochre, up to two bushels in volume, was recovered from some of these cemeteries. At least some of the cremations took place on-site. These must have been relatively spectacular ceremonial events in the lives of Transitional peoples. As described by William Ritchie (1969: 175), "use of large burial pits, associated, it would appear, with periodic and elaborate magical observances, probably under shamanistic direction . . .

included the addition of utensils of stone and clay to the grave offerings."

Although these types of cemeteries have not been recovered in Pennsylvania, the appearance of burial ceremonialism and extensive trade during the Transitional period suggests that there were changes in the way families were organized. Again, the specifics are unclear, but there were probably more rules on how specific relatives should be treated and maybe even who one should marry or where a couple lived after they were married.

In western Pennsylvania, the change from the Archaic period to the Transitional period was less dramatic. While such things as broadspears, FCR, and steatite were present, they were far less common than in the Susquehanna and Delaware drainages. This represents some early differences in cultural and social development between the two regions. Perhaps cultural traits did not spread as readily between the east and west because of the difficulty of travel, caused by a lack of connecting rivers. However, it is interesting that steatite bowl fragments found at the Leetsdale site (36Al480), located just west of Pittsburgh, originated in the steatite quarries of Lancaster County. Metarhyolite is also found in the Upper Allegheny valley more than 150 miles from the source at South Mountain. This again demonstrates the importance and extent of trade. FCR features are found, but broadspears and steatite bowls are less common in this region. The Archaic adaptation seems to have continued through the Transitional period with only a few of the distinctive artifacts from eastern Pennsylvania being included. Indeed, following the Transitional period, cultural evolution in the Ohio Valley of Pennsylvania is heavily influenced by developments to the west in what are now Ohio, Indiana, and Illinois.

For archaeologists, the Transitional period is an exciting but perplexing time in Native American cultural development. It appears to represent sudden and significant technological, economic, and social change. What was the function of broadspears and steatite bowls? Why was the use of local toolstone discontinued? Why was stone for toolmaking and other commodities traded over such large areas? Were the technological developments and trade a reaction to increased population that had been building up through the Archaic period? Was all of this the result of a slight change in temperature and precipitation, or had changes been building during the Late Archaic that are not visible in the archaeological record? Or was the Transitional period of eastern Pennsylvania being influenced by the significant developments in the Mississippi Valley? It is equally perplexing that, for the most part, the following Woodland period was also very different from the

Transitional period. The Transitional period appears to be different from any cultural developments before and after. In fact, some archaeologists believe that the Early Woodland period is more similar to the Late Archaic but with the addition of fired clay pottery. This lack of continuity in cultural evolution adds support to the idea that there was a brief environmental crisis, and the Transitional period was a reaction to that crisis. It is interesting that broadspears are replaced by fishtails at the end of the environmental change. Obviously, to explain all of these issues will require a great deal more research by archaeologists.

Transitional Period Research in Pennsylvania

There are more than 1,210 Transitional period sites recorded in the three major drainage basins of Pennsylvania. Because of the distinctive shapes and distinctive raw material of broadspears, sites from this period are more visible compared to other periods. Stemmed projectile points, however, were also used during this period and these can be easily confused with projectile points that date to the Late Archaic period, so there are certainly more sites from this period than just those counting broadspears. The sites are commonly found in stratified floodplains and over twenty of these have been excavated and reported.

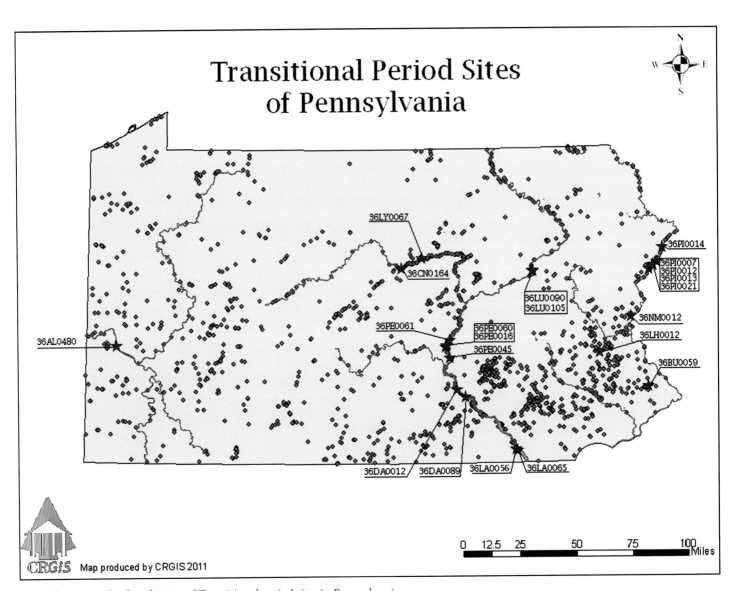

Map illustrating the distribution of Transitional period sites in Pennsylvania.

Transitional Period Research in the Delaware Drainage Basin

Approximately 281 Transitional period sites are recorded in the Delaware drainage basin. Many of these sites contain evidence for the intensive processing of food resources in the form of large roasting pits or stone boiling dumps or both. The Upper Delaware has witnessed the most excavation of sites from this period.

Transitional period occupations are found buried at many of the same sites as the Late Archaic period. In the Upper Delaware drainage basin, the Transitional period component at the Peters-Albrecht site (36Pi21), the Brodhead-Heller site (36Pi7), the Faucett site (36Pi13a), and the Zimmerman site (36Pi14) are found stratified above Late Archaic occupations. The Transitional period components all contained net weights, indicating that nets were used as an efficient method of catching large numbers of fish (or birds and other small animals). Steatite bowl fragments, including a large fragment of a bowl found at Zimmerman, were also found at these sites.

Perkiomen broadspears were the most common biface type, but Lehigh and Susquehanna types were also present. All of these sites contained large amounts of FCR, and these could be the result of roasting hearths, stone boiling dumps, or sweat lodges. At the Zimmerman site, tools such as drills, knives, and choppers were found with large hearths and associated with Susquehanna broadspears. The quantity and diversity of tools at these sites and the massive amounts of FCR suggest that they were base camps for macroband groups. The extensive work in the Upper Delaware basin in the 1960s and 1970s established basic stratigraphic relationships between Late Archaic and Transitional period occupations. In addition, these sites produced large artifacts and feature assemblages that continue to be used by researchers for comparative purposes.

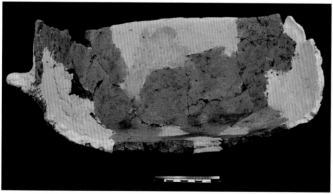

A large, partially reconstructed steatite bowl recovered from the Zimmerman site, Pike County.

The Transitional period occupations at the Sandts Eddy site (36Nm12) located in the lower Delaware drainage contained large amounts of jasper chipping debris. In contrast to the sites in the Upper Delaware Valley, no fire pits and only a few tools were found. This suggests that Sandts Eddy was probably a small camp for short-term hunting trips. Broadspears made from jasper and argillite are common in the lower Delaware. Bedrock sources for jasper are found in Lehigh and Berks Counties. Both finished and unfinished broadspears have been recovered at quarries such as the Kings Quarry (36Lh2) near Vera Cruz, Pennsylvania. Systematic excavations have not been conducted at the argillite quarries located along Gadis Run, Bucks County; however, extensive excavations were conducted at the Lower Black's Eddy site (36Bu23), situated on the Delaware River and adjacent to the outcrops. This site contained large FCR features and a huge amount of waste flakes from the production of Late Archaic and Transitional period tools. Although completely destroyed by looting, the Eel Skin Rock Shelter (36Bu59), located along Tohicken Creek, Bucks County, contained a large argillite workshop area for the production of Lehigh broadspears.

Transitional Period Research in the Susquehanna Drainage Basin

More than 750 Transitional period sites have been recorded for the Susquehanna River drainage basin, with more than fifteen of these being systematically excavated. Two of the earliest (1950s and 1960s) investigations took place at sites on Susquehanna River islands: the Kent-Hally site (36La56) on Bare Island and the Piney Island site (36La65). Both had layered sequences of Late Archaic and Transitional period occupations with stemmed spearpoints, broadspears, and steatite bowl fragments. Other artifacts recovered on the islands included drills, ground and polished tools such as axes and celts, and rough stone tools, such as mullers, pestles, and milling stones used for grinding nuts and seeds. The earliest, clearly nonutilitarian artifact ever recovered from Pennsylvania was radiometrically dated to 4300 BP. This is a round rock with eyes, nose, and mouth pecked into its surface. It may have been painted or adorned with feathers or antlers, but it is interesting that this early piece is associated with a time when social complexity was increasing. These early investigations were important in that they provided basic data on the nature of Transitional period artifact assemblages.

The earliest nonutilitarian or possibly ceremonial arti-fact from Pennsylvania. The image of a human face was pecked into a rounded rock. It is approximately 5 inches in diameter. It was recovered from Piney Island and dated to 4300 BP.

The excavation of a Transitional period hearth at the City Island site, Dauphin County. This feature contained a metarhyolite Susquehanna broadspear and was radiocarbon dated to 3250+90 BP.

Other sites excavated in this basin include the Jacobs (36Lu90) and Gould Island (36Lu105) sites on the North Branch of the Susquehanna River, the Memorial Park (36Cn164) and Canfield Island (36Ly67) sites on the West Branch of the Susquehanna River, and Wallis (36Pe16), Gerty's Notch (36Pe45), Pe60, and Pe61 sites on the main branch and the Mykut Rockshelter (36Hu143) on the Raystown Branch of the Juniata River. This database of systematic excavations has been very informative. They have demonstrated an extensive steatite trading network throughout the Susquehanna drainage basin where there are nine times as many sites with steatite compared to the Delaware drainage basin. The metarhyolite network has also been illuminated. Along the main branch of the Susquehanna River, metar-hyolite is found in large quantities as both finished tools

and debitage. In the upper part of the basin and along the smaller streams, it is mainly found as tools. This suggests that large blanks in the lower valley were being worked into tools to be traded in the upper valley. Finally, broad-spears recovered from the Mykut Rockshelter demon-strate that Transitional period people were also exploiting upland environments.

The City Island site (36Da12), located at Harrisburg, included a metarhyolite Lehigh broadspear, Susquehanna broadspears, and a small FCR feature dating to 3250+90 BP. More recent excavations on Calver Island (36Da89), located just below Harrisburg, recovered a large sample of artifacts from this period associated with a large number of fire pits, roasting pits, and scatters of FCR. Stemmed projectile points outnumbered broadspears, documenting that the latter

Broadspears and associated stemmed points from Calver Island.

were not the only spearpoints used during this period. In addition, Calver Island and the sites in the upper valley have been instrumental in adding to our understanding of the increasing importance of plant foods. The recovery of potentially domesticated foods such as squash, little barley, and chenopodium suggest that these were being cultivated. This represents a huge impact on Transitional period society. These sites indicate that islands were an important part of the Transitional period settlement system.

Transitional Period Research in the Ohio Drainage Basin

Only 179 Transitional period sites are recorded in the Ohio drainage basin. The small number of sites suggests that this period is not well represented or defined in the western part of the state. The Leetsdale site (36Al480) on the main branch of the Ohio River represents one of the largest Transitional period excavations. It contains steatite and broadspearlike implements that have been dated by radiocarbon methods to the Transitional period. Using rare-earth isotope analysis, the steatite has been sourced to outcrops near Christiana in Lancaster County. These finds are not exactly like the broadspear assemblages from the eastern part of the state. The broadspears are not as finely flaked. They are made with local lithic material instead of traded material, and the FCR features are diffused and scattered. This site is very interesting because it seems to represent the western Pennsylvania equivalent of the Transitional culture and one of the last times that cultures on both sides of the Alleghenies are closely related.

COURTESY OF THE U.S. ARMY CORPS OF ENGINEERS, PITTSBURGH DISTRICT

Transitional period projectile points from the Leetsdale site, Allegheny County, in the Upper Ohio drainage basin illustrating the differences with Transitional period points from the eastern part of the state.

The Siggins site (36Fo1) is another example of the Transitional period in the Ohio Valley. It is situated on a wide floodplain of the Upper Allegheny River in Forest County. It has produced artifacts from Early Archaic through Middle Woodland times. Of note here are Forest Notched points that were originally defined at this site by William Mayer-Oakes in 1955. Later, Richard George of the Carnegie Museum conducted additional analyses of this point type and defined it as an expanding-stemmed projectile point with "gracefully executed curving shoulders." This point type was radiocarbon dated at other sites to between approximately 2500 BP and 3100 BP and is similar in shape to the fishtail points of eastern Pennsylvania. Mayer-Oakes also recorded a large number of tubular fireclay pipes at Siggins and other Forest County sites. Fireclay is a soft, shalelike rock that is easily carved and was extensively used beginning as early as Late Archaic times. Mayer-Oakes reported a large number of tubular pipes from the region and some were unfinished. Traditionally, fireclay supposedly originates near Portsmouth, Ohio, but Mayer-Oakes speculated that there was a local source for this raw material.

Forest Notched projectile points, tubular pipes, and Half-Moon pottery are an interesting assemblage of artifacts, but their cultural context is not well known. They are clearly contemporary and related to the Fishtail Complex of eastern Pennsylvania and seemingly represent the local manifestation of this period in the Upper Ohio Valley. The dates for this

FROM *PREHISTORY OF THE UPPER OHIO VALLEY* BY WILLIAM MAYER-OAKES

Forest Notched projectile points from the Siggins site. These are similar in shape and date to the same time period as fishtail points.

complex of artifacts, however, overlap with the Adena Mound Builders (discussed in the next chapter) and Adena artifacts are sometimes found with Forest Notched points. The Fishtail Complex in eastern Pennsylvania is clearly a different culture/adaptation than the Adena Complex concentrated in Ohio and Indiana. Were Adena people using Forest Notched points? Is Adena a separate culture from the people who made Forest Notched points? Was there a local population who borrowed traits from both of these cultures? This is a very dynamic period in Native American prehistory and we may never understand the true relationship between these two groups.

A transitional Period Narrative

Time 3200 years ago.

Place The Delaware River above the Delaware Water Gap.

Climate Slightly warmer with slightly less rainfall than present.

Flora and fauna An oak-chestnut forest with animals similar to Pennsylvania at the time of Columbus.

Distinctive artifacts Broad-bladed spearpoints that were frequently used as knives and soapstone cooking bowls.

My name is Witbrodnokik, and I am a very old man. We walked 10 miles from our last camp on the other side of the river. I have made this trip every year of my life. I know every landmark and every place we stop for water and a quick rest, and this makes the walk go faster. I sense this is my last year. I only know of one person who has lived as long as I have.

We are traveling to the spring shad run site. I live with my son and his family. His son and daughter's families also live with us. There are about twenty-five of us in all. My wife died several years ago and I am too old to remarry.

Our people extend from the ocean in the east to the Ohio Valley in the west and from the spruce-pine forest far to the north to the warm red clay flatlands in the south. There are several different tribes over this region. We speak the same language, but we are not all friendly. Each river valley is occupied by a different family. The families move up and down the valleys as the seasons change. Sometimes the streams dry up and we must move even greater distances.

Although there are several different tribes, we are all united by one spirit. We have lived in this land since the beginning of time. We did not always live as we do now. Many generations ago, The People were suffering. The streams were drying up and the trees were not giving as many nuts. Sometimes the fish did not come up the rivers and sometimes the deer were gone from the mountains. It wasn't always bad, but it was unpredictable. Nobody could explain why nature seemed so chaotic and The People were afraid. Many felt it was being caused by forest spirits, so three men were sent into the forest to try to find an answer to the problem. These men were old, like me. They were brothers. They were not good hunters, they did not have big muscles, they were not good in council meetings, and they were not shaman. But they were excellent flint-knappers. At that time, making stone tools was not an honored craft among the people. Basketry was the special craft of men; anyone could make stone tools. But these three were the best anyone knew.

The men separated and each went to their favorite stone quarry: one to the jasper quarry, one to the argillite quarry, and one to the metarhyolite quarry. At each place, they found the same thing. A wolverine had taken control of the quarry and had gained much power. The wolverines were behind the disruption of the fish and geese migrations and the lack of hickory nuts, deer, turkey, and beaver. The wolverines were jealous of humans because they did not know how to make stone tools.

At each of the quarries, the brothers decided to challenge the wolverines to a contest. "If you will stop confusing the animals, the fish, and the nut trees, I will honor you by only using this quarry and whenever I visit, I will leave a magic tool that can do anything." The wolverines did not believe the brother, so they threw out a fish. The brother quickly made a large broad-bladed implement and he put it on a handle. Then he quickly scraped off the fish scales with the broad blade, cut out the entrails, and neatly sliced the fish into four neat pieces. "You can cut up a little fish, but what about a deer?" The brother quickly attached his knife blade onto a spear shaft and hit the deer, killing it immediately with his very large spear. Again, he used the broad blade to remove the dear hide, chop it into large pieces, and neatly slice it into fine steaks. Soon, he was cooking the steaks in the oil of his fine steatite pot. He even used the same blade as a saw to cut the deer antlers to use as handles. On each of the handles, he used the tip of the blade to carve the image of a wolverine.

The wolverines were getting angry and they took the brothers' favorite pots and broke them in half. Each brother quickly reshaped his blade into a drill; he drilled a hole in each half and tied the bowl back together. After this, he changed the blade again into a hide scraper and made the deer hide into a fine shirt for the wolverine. After all of this work, the blade was as good as new and the wolverine agreed that the brother was the smartest animal in the forest. The wolverines were not good at making stone tools, so the brothers promised they would leave a broadspear every time they visited the quarries.

Some say that is an old story, but since The People have been making broadspears, as they have become known, and offer donations to the wolverines, they are ready for any food or circumstance that confronts them.

I remember when I was twelve, I made my first broadspears. My father had given me a large, flat piece of jasper called a core, which he had made at the quarry. He also gave me a large elk antler hammer to work the jasper. I had been practicing on smaller pieces, but this was the first time I was allowed to practice on such a large piece. My mother and sisters knew this was a special time for me. I studied the core for a long time. My father had made me an excellent piece. I started by making blanks. These are broad, flat flakes about 6 inches long, 3 inches wide, and less than 1 inch thick. I used the antler hammer for this. Many of mine broke or were too thick, but I got about eight from the core before it was all broken up. The real test came when I started to chip the blanks into blades. I was much better at this, and I was able to convert six of the eight blanks into finished blades. My father and mother were very proud. My older sister laughed and said I would have been in big trouble if I had failed. My father reminded me to keep one for our next trip to the quarry, and we will leave it as a gift for the wolverines. Actually, I kept my second-favorite blade and gave it to my first son when he came of age.

My father also made me my first adze for making a dugout canoe, and I was very proud of it. The stone came from far to the south, and my father had traded his favorite knife handle to get it. It took him many hours to grind it into shape on a flat piece of fine-grained sandstone, but it was very smooth and sharp when he was finished. My brothers and I went to work making a dugout that we finished in a few days. We had many adventures in the dugout until one day it was washed away in a flood. Since then, I have made many dugouts and I have made adzes for each of my sons.

Finally, my father gave me my first steatite bowl. After I made my first broadspears, he gave me a bowl that was given to him by his father. It was very old and not very big. It had broken and been tied back together several times. There were little notches around the rim. My father said this bowl had witnessed many important decisions by the men of the tribe, and I should take good care of it. I was now allowed to sit with the men at the fall feast.

Before I got married, my father took me to the steatite quarries to make a bowl for myself and one for my future father-in-law. It was a long trip that took four days by dugout. The return trip was mostly upstream and it took six days. The steatite quarries are not like the jasper quarries. There are not any deep holes and the area is dotted with old campfires. There are hardly any trees left and there are many different types of plants that I have never seen before. The bowls were carved directly in the bedrock and the area was covered with partially finished bowls and broken bowls.

I could have worked the steatite with my jasper knife or the antler handle, but my father found me an old stone gouge with a handle. We spent a day exploring for a good spot. My father showed me how to start by carving the outside of the bowl directly on the bedrock. In theory, once the outside was roughly carved, this piece was chiseled off and the inside was completed. I broke my first two attempts, but we moved to a better spot and I roughed out two bowls in about three days. While I worked, my father worked on an antler handle and told me stories about why the quarry area was different and why men use steatite. On the way home, I finished smoothing out the insides and the lug handles at either end. When I got home, I put notches around the rim just like my grandfather had done.

That was many years ago and now we are on the way to the shad fishing spot. We stop at the jasper quarry, because we will need stone to process the shad and later to trade. The jasper quarry is about a two-day walk from our camp. It is a very exciting place, because you never know what you will find or who you will meet. For generations, our people have been digging holes into the ground to get the best and most brightly colored material for tools and for trading. The main pit is over 20 feet deep. Sometimes we wonder how deep we can dig until we reach the dark spirit world. You never know what might happen when you put such a large cut into the earth. Before going down, we always build a big fire and sing the quarry song before we begin our digging. Sometimes there will be a large boulder just waiting for us, and sometimes we need to dig a hole as deep as a man is tall. We sometimes meet the people from downriver and we all sing. When we are hunting and meet these people, they sometimes steal our game and there is a fight, but at the quarry, everyone is polite and respectful. The earth spirits do not like quarreling.

I quickly made fifteen blanks. I always remember how difficult this was when I was a boy. Some were brown. Some were yellow. Mainly I want good-quality material with no impurities that I can easily make into tools and also material that I can easily trade. I know some will be knives and others will be scrapers and drills. I need to have the right tool at the right time, but all I need is a few minutes to shape it from the blanks.

According to the legends, my people have been coming to the fishing place forever at this same time of year. This is the time when the river is filled with shad. We are very lucky to have so many fish, because there is so little other food. We have eaten the last of the dried venison and nuts from last fall. The ground is cold, so the plants are not growing and we cannot dig for roots.

My grandfather told me that his grandfather told him that his grandfather's father remembered stories of what this same place looked like in his day. When my people first came here, they saw many trees. They had to cut trees to make a clearing for their camp. The very young children walked only a short distance to pick up dead wood for the fire. The men walked into the river, speared many fish, and cooked them over small fires. The ones they didn't eat were dried on racks near the campfires. Some were boiled in deep pits for fish oil or to make fish cakes. They fished for several weeks until the fish stopped coming in large numbers. Later, they moved a short distance away from the fishing camp to hunt deer and squirrels and to gather the emerging shoots and green plants.

Things are different now. Many families come at the same time to work together to prepare for catching, boiling, and drying the fish. If all the bands worked alone at their own camps, they could not get as many fish as everyone working together at one large camp. It also takes a lot of cooperation to maintain the fish traps and the huge nets. I was excited to see so many people working. We share stories with people we have not seen since last year.

I remember how difficult it was to bring many cobbles out of the river to stack onto the banks. We were only small boys, but we carried heavy stones for three days. The young men placed the stakes in the river to guide the fish to where others would spear them. I was too young to collect wood, because it was so far away. I couldn't see any trees along the entire floodplain. Men and women walked for several hours to bring big logs for the huge fires. Some logs were longer than me standing on my father's shoulders. I was not strong enough to split the logs, but I remember the sounds of the green sticks banging against the stone wedges. The stacks of wood were huge, but they would all be gone before we departed.

In addition to the firewood, we put many posts into the ground near the pile of cobbles. Each post was about the length of a man from the next. These were for the drying racks. We were lucky when posts would be left from the year before. Other times these were burned or rotten and had to be replaced. We usually had to find ten longer, thinner posts for our tents. We carried the hide covering from the last camp.

We rolled the logs onto the cobbles and then stacked more cobbles onto the pile of wood. I remember the huge fires and the hot stones. During the early winter, we were never warm enough, but now we are very hot. Even though it was very cold at night, we had our small tents to block the wind and the heat from the stones to keep us warm. The men took turns standing in the cold water to spear fish all day. They tossed the fish onto the banks, where the women picked them up and made a slit with their broad blades to remove the entrails. They ran long cords made from grapevines into the fish's mouth and out one gill. They carried the strings to the wooden racks. With eight big fish to a string, they tied the ends to the strong support posts and went to the riverbank for more fish. The old men pushed hot stones from the hearth with long poles under the strings of fish. The children picked up the cool stones under the drying racks and tossed them back onto the hearth to heat again.

Some of the fish were eaten immediately, but the dried ones were packed into baskets. We also made soups in hide bags. We start by digging a hole in the ground and we line it with a large elk skin. The hole is filled with about 5 gallons of water. The women put the smaller fish in the water. They got the water boiling by dropping in hot stones that are heated in an adjacent fire. Many hot stones were needed to keep the water hot enough to cook the soup. Everyone liked the hot soup on a cold day, especially the men spearing the fish in the cold water. All of this requires a lot of wood.

In the fall, we do the same thing with hickory and butternuts. We crack the nutshells with nutting stones and dump the shells and nutmeat into boiling water. As the nutmeat heats, nut oil floats to the top, and it is skimmed off and placed in bags or steatite pots

At the feasts, the fish soup or nut cakes are heated and served in the steatite bowls. Each man has several bowls for serving and cooking. Depending on a man's status, he has more and a larger variety of bowls. Important men who organize the feasts usually have several very large cooking pots that are used to serve everyone food.

Families from all around the region gather in the late fall for a grand meeting and feast. We usually meet on a large island in the territory of the most important family. Everyone brings items to trade. And everyone brings their best food. The families exchange gifts of bone beads, painted porcupine quills, bear claws, eagle talons, stone bifaces, stone bowls, colorful baskets, and fancy bird feathers. The host family supplies a lot of food.

The first few days of the feast are spent setting up the camp. As new families arrive, each is welcomed with gifts and great discussion. When all have arrived, the men begin meeting to discuss the events of the past year. How was the fishing? How big were the elk? Do we need to make repairs at the quarry? Which streams had dried up during the summer? Had any of the hickory or butternut trees died? Were the children healthy? Were there any problems with marriages? Were the families getting along and sharing properly? These discussions are very important. During these discussions, the men eat and drink from steatite bowls. The bowls are special and help the men think. Each man brought several. Sometimes bowls are exchanged between relatives. Sometimes old men give their favorite pot to their son or another close relative. The fact that these have been handed down for generations makes them very powerful.

ILLUSTRATION BY NANCY BISHOP

Towards the end, these discussions become more spiritual. Have we cremated our ancestors properly? Is everyone behaving correctly? Have any families insulted the spirits? Is there some way to get the spirits to send more fish or more hickory nuts? How deep can we dig at the jasper quarry until something bad happens? These are important questions because there can be dire consequences.

The headman of the host family is admired for his knowledge, for his ability to organize the group for fishing and feasts, but most of all for his generosity. The headman is chosen by the families. He can not order people around. He is an organizer and he functions based on group consensus. Sometimes the families disagree and they move away. Usually everyone goes along with his ideas. It is a hard job. When a headman gets too old, he frequently passes on his title to his oldest son. But usually, within a month or two, the families may choose someone else.

The first leader I can remember was from the Lower Delaware band. He was a great speaker, a great hunter, and very generous. He always helped families in need. His son was not so generous, and we began having our feasts with the Middle Delaware Valley band. This caused problems for a while, but eventually everyone got over it. This is where the families have met for most of my life. This was a good family, with a good headman. Several families had trouble during the late summer and he was very generous in allowing them to live with his band for several weeks.

Lately, we have been having problems with the bands to the south. They have begun to ask for more in exchange for our gifts of dried fish and hickory nuts. My father always traded a large basket of fish and a basket of hickory nuts for a generous pile of bifaces. Now the pile is getting smaller and we don't think they are being good neighbors. We will discuss this at the fall meeting.

When my father died in the late winter, he was temporarily buried near our camp. We placed his atlatl and best spears in the ground with him. The following fall, we dug him up and carried his bones and tools to the great feast. At the end of the feast, we cremated his body and those of several other old men who had died that year. The atlatl and the supply of spearspoints are broken and burned along with a large elk antler, so that they will also be sent to the afterworld. As the smoke rose from his funeral fire, we knew his spirit was traveling to the afterworld and we sang. We were sad when he died, but now we are happy that he was starting a new life. His ashes and the broken atlatl and spearpoints were wrapped in a reed mat and buried together in the cemetery with the rest of our ancestors. Not everyone is buried in cemeteries. Some families take their relatives home and bury them in secret places. Of course, women and children are cremated at their home camp.

I wonder what the future will hold for my children. We work hard and we usually have enough food to last through the winter, but sometimes we do not. There has not been a great drought for many years. We worry about another one, but all of the families are doing well. Some families have stopped making the special broad-spears. They say that they don't need them anymore and the little spears are just as good. Also, the trade for toolstone is not going as well. Fewer families show up from the south with toolstone to trade and fewer of our families meet them. But I am glad we are still holding our fall feast and that all of the families still attend. It is important that the men meet and eat and drink from our steatite bowls. The bowls are strong and represent generations of men discussing the events of the past year and events of the future.

Chapter 6

The Woodland Period: 2700 years ago to 1550 AD, Part 1

The Early and Middle Woodland Periods: 1100 to 2700 years ago

The Woodland period, spanning 2700 years ago to 1550 AD, represents an explosion of data compared to earlier periods, especially in its later phase; therefore, it will be presented in two chapters. This chapter will describe the Early and Middle Woodland periods. Chapter 7 will describe the Late Woodland period in the eastern part of the state and what is known as the Late Prehistoric period in the Upper Ohio drainage basin. The archaeology is so different in the Upper Ohio that archaeologists even use different terminology to describe it.

Archaeologists are able to define many more subdivisions or cultures within this period and this is largely because of the widespread and common presence of fired-clay pottery in the archaeological record. This technology allows for a great deal of variation in designs and shapes. Many styles have been identified by archaeologists, and these have been used to define a large number of different pottery types, phases, or archaeological cultures. Archaeologists do not agree on what this all means, but in terms of the archaeology of Pennsylvania, it is clear that the Early and Middle Woodland cultures of the Upper Ohio drainage are very different from the Delaware and Susquehanna drainages. The cultures of the Early and Middle Woodland periods in these latter drainages are poorly understood, but the two periods seem to share a number of artifact types and will be treated together in this chapter. The cultures of the Early and Middle Woodland periods of the Upper Ohio basin are reasonably well known, at least in terms of artifacts, and will be described separately from the eastern two drainage basins.

To provide a better context for understanding the events of the Woodland period, we will begin this chapter with an overview of the period as a whole.

TIMELINE

Contact Period	1500 AD–1700 AD
Woodland Period	**2700 years ago–1500 AD**
Late Woodland/Late Prehistoric	**1100 years ago–1550 AD**
Middle Woodland	**1100–2100 years ago**
Early Woodland	**2100–2700 years ago**
Transitional Period	2700–4300 years ago
Archaic Period	4300–10,000 years ago
Paleoindian Period	10,000–16,500 years ago
Pre-Clovis	11,200–16,500 years ago

Environment: The Woodland period is generally warm and wet but with a few cold periods. The vegetation can be characterized as an oak-chestnut and hemlock forest. The repeated use and probably intentional burning of floodplain areas during the Late Woodland resulted in these settings frequently being covered by meadows or small trees.

Making and using tools (typical artifacts and technology): The major change in this period is the extensive use of fired-clay ceramics. Pottery becomes thinner and better made as the period progresses, with a variety of shapes and more elaborate designs. There are a few distinctive projectile points from this period, but a wide variety of stemmed and notched forms are found. Although the bow and arrow was probably used during the Archaic period, the widespread appearance of triangular points in the Late Woodland period demonstrates the preference for this technology over handheld or atlatl-propelled spears. Grinding stones to process plant foods are common and several different forms develop. For a variety of reasons, bone, antler, and shell artifacts are more regularly preserved. These materials were used to make harpoons, awls for sewing, and burnishers for hide working, but also as nonutilitarian items, such as beads, combs, and other forms of adornment. Although rare, axes, adzes, spearpoints, pressure flakers, and beads made of copper have been recovered from Pennsylvania sites. This material may have originated in the copper deposits of Michigan or elsewhere.

What people ate (subsistence): A wide variety of mammals, fish, and birds are exploited; however, there is an increasing dependence on plant foods. During the Early and Middle Woodland periods, elements of the Eastern Agricultural Complex (little barley, knotweed, and chenopodium) are used. During the Late Woodland period, people become dependent on domesticated plants, such as corn, beans, and squash.

Where people lived (settlement patterns): The location of Early and Middle Woodland sites is poorly documented. It is believed that there were a few small base camps in floodplain areas and numerous small camps in a variety of upland ecological settings exploiting a wide range of food resources. During the Late Woodland period, agricultural sites are on floodplains in the Susquehanna and Delaware drainage basins, but sites in the Upper Ohio basin are usually on ridgetops. These large villages are also associated with a wide variety of special-purpose camps. Throughout the Woodland period, features such as hearths and in-ground food processing and storage pits become more common.

People living in groups (social organization and belief systems): The Woodland period is a very dynamic time in Native American cultural evolution. The society evolves from foraging egalitarian bands to sedentary tribal organizations focused on farming. Unfortunately, there are few well-excavated sites from the Early and Middle Woodland periods and therefore the early part of this process is not well documented. The Native American population in Pennsylvania by the end of the Woodland period was 9000 to 10,000 people. In the Ohio and Susquehanna Valleys, families were concentrated in villages containing hundreds of people.

Definition

The Woodland period dates between 2700 years ago and 1550 AD and the hallmark is ceramics. This period is characterized by a slow and increasingly complex pottery technology and more elaborate pottery designs. The projectile points vary in shape with the majority not being very distinctive or diagnostic until the Late Woodland period, when triangular-shaped arrowheads became the dominant form. The period is characterized by gradually increased focus on a limited range of plant foods and eventually dependence on domesticated crops, such as corn, beans, and squash. During the Archaic period, as Native American populations grew in size, they intensified their exploitation of animal foods, especially fish and a variety of nuts. This adaptive strategy had limits in terms of the quantity of food it could produce. During the Woodland period, Native Americans intensified their exploitation of plant foods, and some archaeologists believe they focused their attention on an increasingly limited range of plants that could be easily collected in large quantities, initially seed plants and finally corn, beans, and squash.

The population continues to increase, although the evidence for this during the Early and Middle Woodland is unclear. The archaeological evidence for houses and other types of structures becomes more common. All evidence suggests that populations become more sedentary. Eventually, year-round hamlets (smaller than a village) are occupied and in the Susquehanna and Ohio drainage basins, permanent villages develop. The village sites are characterized by a variety of storage pit features, family hearths, earth ovens, burials, and post molds, representing a variety of structures such as houses, storage structures, drying racks, and windbreaks. The period ends with the appearance of large numbers of Europeans and the introduction of European technology and diseases. The latter issue led to rapid and significant changes in Native American cultures.

As discussed in the introduction to our overview of prehistory, Pennsylvania lies at the crossroads of several different environmental and cultural zones. As expected, this diversity had an effect on cultural development. Throughout prehistory, the Susquehanna and Delaware drainage basins always shared characteristics and were influenced by cultures to the south or north, whereas western Pennsylvania was influenced by cultures in the Ohio and Mississippi basins.

Beginning with the Woodland period, the cultural history of these two regions becomes very different, and archaeologists use seperate terms to describe the different cultures. As long as everyone was practicing a foraging lifestyle, these influences were not a problem, and we could use the same temporal terminology (such as Paleoindian and Archaic) to characterize all of Pennsylvania. By 2700 years ago, however, the Upper Ohio basin begins to follow a different evolutionary path—one that includes early farming, a continental trading system, and a more structured social and political system.

The Woodland period is subdivided into Early, Middle, and Late periods; however, significant differences in cultural developments begin between the major drainage basins. The Ohio basin is especially different from the Delaware and Susquehanna basins, and the former will be treated separately in this publication. The Early and Middle periods in the Delaware and Susquehanna are poorly understood and will be treated as a single unit in Chapter 6. As explained in the previous section, we are taking an unconventional approach. In this publication, the Early Woodland period does not begin with the appearance of fired-clay pottery as is the traditional approach. The first ceramics are found with the Fishtail phase, and we are including that phase with the Transitional period. In the Delaware and Susquehanna drainages, the Early Woodland begins with the Meadowood and Hellgrammite phases.

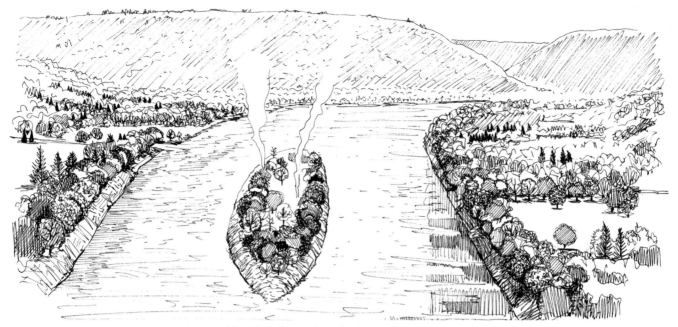

A view of the Sub-Atlantic oak-hickory and hemlock forest along the Susquehanna River 2,000 years ago.

Early and Middle Woodland Periods of the Susquehanna and Delaware Drainage Basins: 1100 to 2700 years ago

Environment: The Early and Middle Woodland periods are generally warm and wet but with a cold period in the middle. The vegetation can be characterized as an oak-chestnut forest.

Making and using tools (typical artifacts and technology): Compared to the Transitional period, there are many changes in the way stone tools are made. Lithic preferences are no longer as strong as they were. Distinctive projectile points include the Meadowood, Hellgrammite, and Fox Creek types. These are found, however, with a variety of stemmed and notched shapes. Grinding stones in the form of pestles and pitted stones become more common. Pottery becomes thinner and improves in quality. During Early Woodland times it is conical, or bag-shaped, and cordmarked. By Middle Woodland times, cordmarking continues, but netmarked, dentate-stamped, wiped, and fabric-impressed designs are also found.

What people ate (subsistence): People are eating the same types of plants and animals that were consumed during the Transitional period, with two differences: Fire-cracked rock was generally not part of food processing, and it is believed that people were increasingly cultivating plants such as squash, little barley, knotweed, and chenopodium. By Middle Woodland times, at least squash and possibly all four plants were domesticated; however, we have very little dietary evidence from this period.

Where people lived (settlement patterns): There are very few large sites from this period and people seem to be living in small family groups. Sites are found in many ecological settings but concentrated in riverine environments. In the spring, small gardens are planted and a small group of people probably live near the gardens into the late summer when the seeds are harvested. Most of the population, however, is spread out in small groups, exploiting a wide variety of resources. In the winter, they may move from the floodplains to more sheltered upland settings, including rock shelters.

People living in groups (social organization and belief systems): This is a poorly documented time in Pennsylvania prehistory. There may have been thousands of people living here in small family homesteads tending gardens, but the archaeological data does not support this or any other scenario. Assuming that the shapes of projectile points and pottery designs have social meaning, the variety of projectile point types and especially the variety of pottery types suggests a variety of social groups representing different families or maybe tribes. Evidence to discuss social organization, however, is lacking. It is assumed that families were organized into egalitarian bands, although these may have been evolving into a tribal organization.

Definition

The Early Woodland period is defined in this publication as those artifact assemblages that do not contain artifacts of the Fishtail phase and date after approximately 2700 BP. Some archaeologists like to characterize the Early and Middle Woodland periods as a return to the Late Archaic lifestyle, but with the addition of pottery. This is an oversimplification, but many of the artifacts appear more similar to Late Archaic toolkits than to Transitional artifact assemblages. The pottery improves in quality, and by Middle Woodland times, the rims are frequently decorated. Broadspears and fishtail projectile points are replaced by a wide variety of projectile point types, notably Meadowood, Hellgrammite, and Fox Creek forms. Fire-cracked rock features gradually disappear. During the Meadowood phase, lithics are part of a trading system and burial ceremonialism continues. After this phase, however, local lithics dominate stone tools, and burial ceremonialism is no longer evident in the archaeological record of the Susquehanna and Delaware drainage basins.

Ceramics are the most distinctive artifact type of the Early and Middle Woodland periods, but initially they are uncommon and poorly made. The poor quality results in low preservation and reduced visibility in the archaeological record. There seem to be a variety of projectile points associated with this period, but few are distinctive. This adds to the difficulty of identifying sites. Few sites have been excavated, but those that have been are characterized by an increase in subsurface features such as hearths and storage and food processing pits. This suggests a need to store food to support larger populations, and this was especially important over the winter months. The increase in features and the pottery suggest a reduction in mobility and an increase in a sedentary population. The sites appear smaller than Transitional period sites, although the database is very limited. Based on pottery types throughout the Susquehanna and Delaware drainage basins, there seem to be several different social groups. The specific nature and relationship of these groups is unclear; however, they all seem to be living in small family groups (with a few exceptions) and generally focusing on plant foods (also with a few exceptions). The Middle Woodland period ends with the appearance of well-made pottery and what appear to be horticultural hamlets and eventually large villages in the Susquehanna and Ohio drainage basins.

The Environment

The Early Woodland period begins with a warm, moist climate similar to the Late Archaic and today's climate. This is the Sub-Atlantic climatic episode (1800–3000 BP). These conditions stabilized floodplain environments by reducing the frequency of floods, although large floods from hurricanes continued. The Sub-Atlantic episode was followed by the Scandic episode (1000–1800 BP), which was characterized by cool and wet conditions. These conditions resulted in slightly less evaporation and more runoff during heavy rains and an increase in flooding. During both of these episodes, most of Pennsylvania was covered with an oak-chestnut deciduous forest, with an abundant variety of foods for humans. Preferred floodplain settlements were so frequently used by Native Americans that the locations were covered by meadows or small trees, rather than climax (fully mature) forests.

Making and Using Tools: Typical Artifacts and Technology

Pottery is the hallmark of the Early and Middle Woodland periods, and traditionally along with a few projectile point types, it is the single artifact that distinguishes the Early Woodland from the Transitional period. As with other period distinctions (the Paleoindian through the Early Archaic), archaeologists are learning that the changes in artifact forms were not as abrupt as originally thought.

Pottery at Early Woodland sites is scarce. It is more common than steatite at Transitional sites, but it is not a plentiful artifact. Early pottery contains large pieces of temper and it is frequently poorly fired. It is very *friable*, meaning that it crumbles easily and it is usually found in small pieces. But the addition of pottery, especially with designs, to the archaeological record significantly changes archaeological interpretation. Archaeologists assign names to regional pottery styles and assume that they originate with distinct cultural or ethnic groups. As groups traveled to new camps and interacted with other people, designs were shared and variations on existing types occurred.

Clay pottery is considered to be a very flexible medium. It is easily shaped, and cultural norms or designs are easily imprinted or transferred to it. Unlike stone tool technology, mistakes are easily corrected and therefore archaeologists feel it is a very good reflection of cultural norms or rules. Archaeologists are able to more specifically define cultural differences, we think,

145

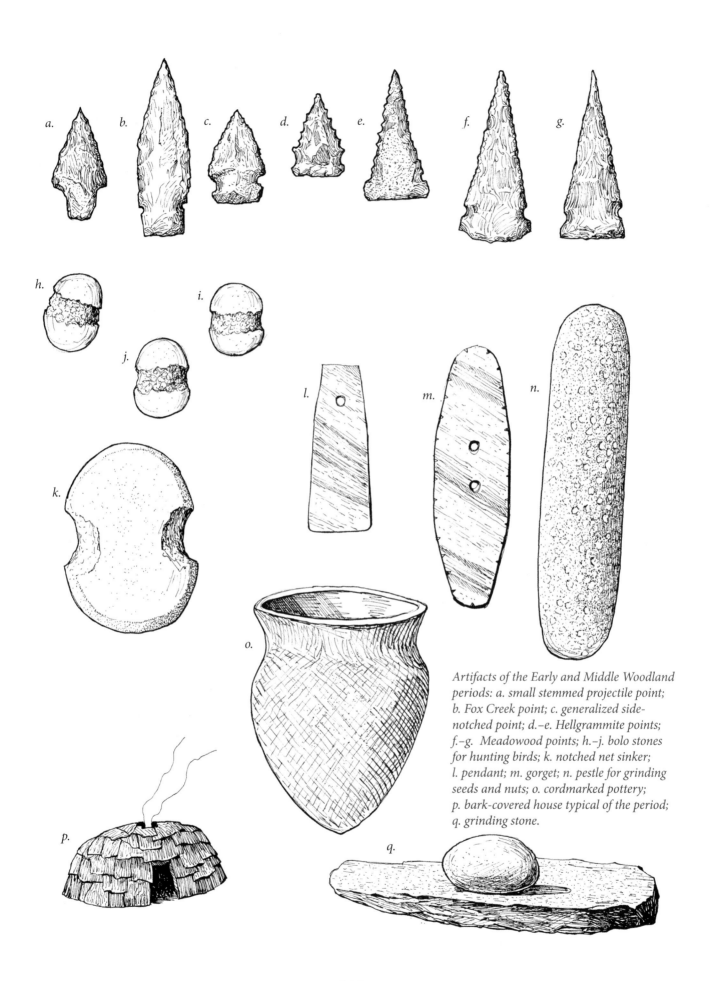

Artifacts of the Early and Middle Woodland periods: a. small stemmed projectile point; b. Fox Creek point; c. generalized side-notched point; d.–e. Hellgrammite points; f.–g. Meadowood points; h.–j. bolo stones for hunting birds; k. notched net sinker; l. pendant; m. gorget; n. pestle for grinding seeds and nuts; o. cordmarked pottery; p. bark-covered house typical of the period; q. grinding stone.

and associate pottery styles with different cultures. This means that the Woodland period can be characterized by many more cultures or other types of social groups compared to earlier periods without pottery. This is reflected in the discussion below where we shift from discussing groups of artifacts by broad periods to the discussion of archaeological cultures. Typically, archaeologists use the terms "complex" or "phase," rather than "culture," but we will use all three. The downside of depending on pottery is that Early and Middle Woodland sites without pottery are difficult to identify and are probably very underrepresented in the archaeological record. For example, it is less likely that ceramic containers would be brought to a short-term hunting camp and therefore very few of these are documented for this period.

How to Make Pottery James T. Herbstritt, The State Museum of Pennsylvania

The earliest fired-clay pottery, dating to more than 10,000 years ago, was found on the island of Japan. The use of pottery by Native Americans in eastern North America, however, began much later, around 4500 years ago during the Late Archaic period. Examples were found on the coast of Georgia, but the craft would not disperse from that area for several hundred years after 4500 BP.

Archaeological sites in the Delaware River and Susquehanna River basins produced some of the earliest pottery in the Middle Atlantic region, dating to about 3200 years ago. It overlaps in time with carved steatite bowls for about 200 years. This pottery was tempered with steatite that could well represent the broken bowls. Temper is a kind of binding filler used to hold the clay together and to keep the pot from shrinking and cracking as it dries in the sun and is fired. The rock temper is then mixed with the wet clay dug from a source located in a nearby riverbank. The mixture of wet clay and rock is hand-molded into thick, flat-bottomed pots that look more like a box than a pot.

A later form of steatite-tempered pottery had a rounded base with an outer surface that the potter roughened on the clay by using a wooden paddle wrapped with twisted cord. The rough surface that remained on the pottery after firing made it easier to hold the piece securely in hand. This technique, called *cordmarking*, remained the principal form of marking pottery surfaces for the next 2000 years. Nets and twined fabrics wrapped around wooden paddles served the same function and appeared during Middle Woodland times.

Hand-molded pots were followed by coiled pots. This technology required skill to gradually build up the pot by coiling, or flattening out, rolled lengths of clay and placing them on top of one another. Later methods involved molding the clay upward between a cord-wrapped paddle and a smooth, palm-sized stone. The stone acted as an anvil and helped support the wall of the pot as it was built with the paddle. The potter may have used a basket or similar object as a support for

A rare, cord-marked, rocker-stamped late Middle Woodland vessel (Conrail site, 36Lu58). This is an example of the variety of surface decorations developed during the Middle Woodland.

THE STATE MUSEUM OF PENNSYLVANIA/PHOTO BY DON GILES
RECONSTRUCTION BY JAMES HERBSTRITT

forming the base and then adding more clay to the sides until the desired shape of the pot was achieved. This method of hand building also required much skill and special care to prevent the pot from collapsing on itself from the weight of wet unstable clay.

At the beginning of the Late Woodland period, the slab-and-anvil technique came into use. The potter formed the clay into wide slabs, shaped much like fish fillets, and joined the slabs end to end, forming the shape of the pot. Additional layers were placed on top of the first and so on until the pot was completely shaped.

In addition to cordmarking pots, Late Woodland potters added designs on and near the rim with a small pointed tool made of wood, shell, bone, or stone. Designs were typically done in repeated geometric shapes by incising, dragging, or carefully stamping the pointed tool over the pot's surface. The Iroquois typically used triangular-shaped patterns that they in-filled with oblique, vertical, or horizontal lines. Such patterns placed on the collars and necks of pots were often quite elaborate. Sometimes these patterns extended onto other areas on the pot, thereby making a larger design. Although some tribes to the south also used incising, a more popular method for decorating pots in that region involved an array of simple stamped cord patterns. The rim was typically decorated by pressing a twined cord, a twig from a tree, or a bone modified from the wing of a bird on the top of the pot. The wet clay was allowed to dry thoroughly for a week.

Now all that remained was to fire the pot. Firing a pot made it hard and more durable around the campfire. Firing was accomplished, according to modern experimental studies, by stacking burning wood around the pot for several hours. Once the wood ashes were completely cold, the pot was finished, durable, and ready for use.

As native cultures entered the Contact period, handmade pottery became a thing of the past and was rarely made by the Native Americans of Pennsylvania. By the late 1600s, clay pots were replaced by metal kettles that were much more durable.

Cordmarking on an Late Woodland pot. An analysis of these markings allows archaeologists to understand the way cordage was made and used.

Native American pottery techniques: a. Hand modeled, with wide slabs of clay and small pieces of rock temper added for the construction of the pot; b. Coil modeled, paddle-and-anvil method, with small pieces of rock, sand, or shell temper added to clay for construction of the pot; c. Fillet modeled, with narrow slabs of clay—slabs first stacked inside a basket mold to form the base followed by additional slabs for the body, neck, and rim, and then slabs welded together using the paddle-and-anvil method; d. Firing method, with pots first dried and then fired upside down.

Initially, the pots were plain or covered with cordmarking but without formal designs other than a few notches in the rim. By Middle Woodland times, geometric designs (straight or diagonal lines around the rim or a series of triangles filled with lines) appear on pots of this region. The artists may have been copying painted designs from baskets. These designs probably had significant meanings representing myths and legends common in their society, but we can only imagine.

The most distinctive phase of the Early Woodland period is the Meadowood complex. This follows the Fishtail phase in the Upper Delaware River and the North Branch and West Branch of the Susquehanna River, but it is less frequently found south of Harrisburg. In the lower Susquehanna drainage, the distinctive projectile points from this period are thick, side-notched points called Hellgrammites, but this manifestation is not well known.

THE STATE MUSEUM OF PENNSYLVANIA/PHOTO BY DON GILES

Early Woodland Hellgrammite projectile points from the lower Susquehanna drainage basin.

It may represent a different cultural group, but sites from this period are not well documented. Hellgrammite points are also found in the Lower Delaware drainage basin, but it is clear that throughout both drainage basins there is a variety of projectile points and pottery types being used contemporaneously. Whether these represent different tribes or simply different family groups (most likely) is not known.

The Meadowood complex is characterized by distinctive side-notched projectile points that are thin, with small notches and a straight base. The pottery is usually an interior and exterior cordmarked type defined as Vinette I. This pottery type, however, can also be found with other projectile point types, which complicates the definition of this complex. The distinc-

THE STATE MUSEUM OF PENNSYLVANIA/PHOTO BY DON GILES

Early Woodland Meadowood points in Onondaga chert from the Susquehanna drainage basin

tive projectile points are rarely made from jasper or metarhyolite and are most frequently made from Onondaga chert mined in western New York. The frequent use of this chert type suggests a trading system. As during the Transitional period, large caches of Onondaga chert in the form of incomplete Meadowood bifaces have been found as part of the trade network. Meadowood sites are rarely associated with large fire-cracked rock features, which suggests a change in the subsistence pattern. What this change means continues to be the subject of debate.

The Meadowood complex is found mainly in the northern Middle Atlantic region, although isolated occurrences can be found throughout the region and into the Great Lakes area. This complex is especially well documented in New York. In coastal New York, it is associated with burial ceremonialism in the form of cremation burials and grave goods (artifacts placed in the grave). The Meadowood burials contain preforms for projectile points, gorgets, and pendants covered with red ochre, a powered iron ore pigment. Gorgets and pendants are highly polished flat rectangular artifacts with one hole (a pendant) or two holes (a gorget) drilled through them. It has been debated whether these were purely decorative or had some more practical function. Some archaeologists believe that the gorgets functioned as atlatl weights. Cremation burials, pendants, and gorgets are rarely found with Hellgrammite projectile points.

Interestingly, gorgets, pendants, and beads were also made from native copper. It has long been thought that the copper originated in the Keewanaw Peninsula of Michigan, but local sources in eastern Pennsylvania and New Jersey have also been discovered. It is a relatively soft material and was cold-pounded (using a minimal

THE STATE MUSEUM OF PENNSYLVANIA/PHOTO BY DON GILES

Pendants and gorgets dating to the Early and Middle Woodland period.

amount of heat) into flat sheets using stone hammers. The sheets were made into beads or combined in layers to form small adzes, axes, and even spearpoints. Generally, utilitarian items such as axes and adzes date to Late Archaic times and ornaments date to Early Woodland times. These artifacts have been found on Adena sites in the Upper Ohio basin and, although rare, in both the Susquehanna and Delaware drainage basins. What appears to be an Adena site has been found in New Jersey on the Delaware River. These artifacts may represent trade or some other type of interaction with these sites.

Red ochre is an iron-rich rock that can be crushed and mixed with animal fat or plant juice to produce paint. It can also be made from an iron-rich yellow rock called limonite. This substance could have been used to paint wooden objects and reed baskets, but archaeologists frequently find it in burials as powdery stains. It is believed that the mourners covered the cremated body with red paint (possibly a symbol of life) and because it is inorganic it is preserved on the remains. Evidence for Early Woodland burial ceremonialism is common in New York. Although it is rare in Pennsylvania, two Meadowood cachcs believed to be associated with cremation burials were discovered in the Susquehanna drainage basin. One was recovered near Halifax, just north of Harrisburg, and contained more than ninety Meadowood blades. Interestingly, this cache also included one Hellgrammite point, indicating the contemporaneity of these two phases. A second cache in York County contained a tubular smoking pipe and a birdstone. Like gorgets, the function of birdstones is debated, but it has been suggested that they also may have functioned as atlatl weights.

In Pennsylvania, it is not clear what "Meadowood" represents. The artifacts are very distinctive, so their distribution can be mapped, but very few habitation sites have been systematically excavated. In coastal New York, it seems to represent a culture. In Pennsylvania,

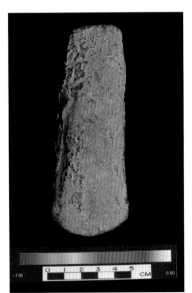

BRYAN FATTA/PHOTO BY DON GILES

DARRELL KLAWITTER/PHOTO BY DON GILES

A very rare copper axe from Dauphin County. These are found at Adena sites and may represent some type of Adena presence in the Susquehanna basin.

A very rare copper adze from Northampton County. These are found at Adena sites and may represent some type of Adena presence in the Delaware basin.

150

A birdstone and blocked-end tubular pipe made of serpentine, similar to those found at the Oscar Leibhart site, York County.

for the most part, the sites seem to be isolated and surrounded by people who were not involved in the trade or burial ceremonialism of the Meadowood phenomenon. Meadowood blades and gorgets may, in fact, be ceremonial "add-on" artifacts that are sometimes found with Early Woodland cultural materials but are not representative of any particular regional culture. They may be a symbol of religious significance that is shared by several different cultural groups like the Christian cross, Jewish star, or Islamic crescent moon and star.

After the Meadowood and Hellgrammite phases, there are a variety of poorly defined archaeological complexes, such as the Bushkill complex, dating to the early Middle Woodland. These are associated with

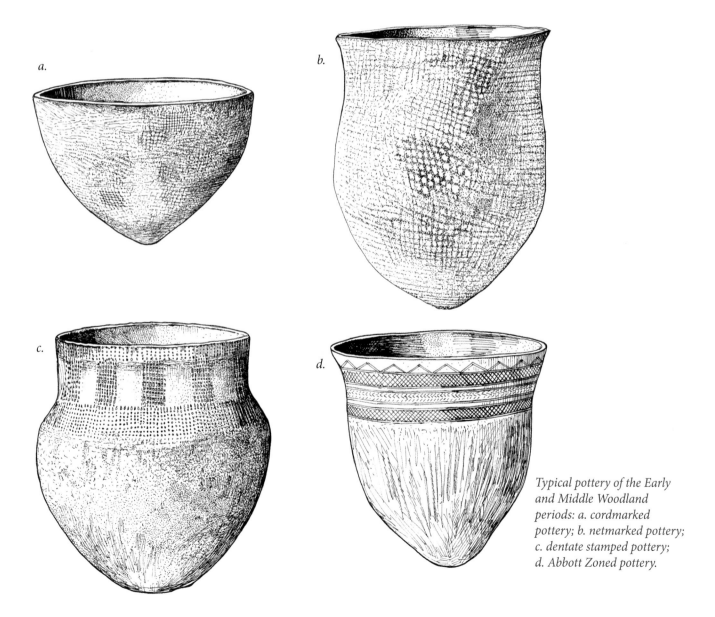

Typical pottery of the Early and Middle Woodland periods: a. cordmarked pottery; b. netmarked pottery; c. dentate stamped pottery; d. Abbott Zoned pottery.

151

Two examples of netmarked pottery from the Middle Woodland period.

small stemmed projectile points and exterior cord-marked pottery. Plant-processing grinding stones are common. The Middle Woodland period begins about 2000 years ago. This time is defined by improvements in pottery technology and an increase in the frequency of pottery use. Although some pots have very distinctive designs, most are generally undecorated and frequently net-impressed instead of cordmarked. Pit features, suggesting more permanent occupations, are more common and larger, but house patterns are rare and the size of habitation sites is unknown.

The lanceolate Fox Creek point is the most distinctive projectile point type from this period, but a variety of shapes are used, including notched and stemmed shapes. Many of these are not distinctive and not helpful in dating sites. Argillite and metarhyolite seem to be part of a trading system associated with the Fox Creek phase and this is especially true in the lower parts of the drainage basins. During this time, however, many stone tools are made from local materials and other stemmed shapes are also being used. The functional change in artifact assemblages appears in the form of a greater use of plant-processing tools, including grinding stones for processing flour from seeds and nuts.

The Abbott Farm complex is based on work conducted at a group of sites in New Jersey along the middle Delaware River near Trenton. Several large sites from Early and Middle Woodland times were excavated, and these seem to be different from any other occupation in eastern Pennsylvania. The artifact assemblage includes large numbers (hundreds) of argillite Fox Creek bifaces. Included with these are both grit-tempered and shell-tempered pottery with elaborate designs. Although there were not any large FCR features, archaeologists believe the large numbers of bifaces were used to process fish during the spring migrations. Remains of sturgeon, along with deer, bear, and beaver were found in refuse pits. The association of both grit-tempered and shell-tempered (oyster shell from the Atlantic coast) ceramics is unusual. Archaeologists believe that this represents the annual movements of both coastal and interior people meeting at this large base camp. In addition, the pottery is very unusual because of its complex designs. Contemporary pottery in the Delaware and Susquehanna drainages exhibits very simple designs or no designs at all. Pottery types, such as Abbott Incised Zoned, Abbott Zoned Net-Impressed, and Abbott Zoned Dentate, are unique for the region but are believed to have local origins that are not the result of outside influences.

What People Ate: Subsistence

This period is poorly understood, but the data leads archaeologists to believe that plant foods continue to increase in importance in the diet. Some of these, such as knotweed, little barley, and chenopodium, produce large quantities of seeds and were domesticated in surrounding areas. To protect the gardens, habitation sites would have been occupied for longer periods. This process has been generally documented in other states, but there is not a lot of data to support this in Pennsylvania.

Where People Lived: Settlement Patterns

As discussed above, the database for the Early and Middle Woodland periods is very poor. Meadowood sites are not common and decrease in frequency in the lower Susquehanna drainage basin. In addition, there do not seem to be enough Meadowood sites to support the estimated population numbers, so there must be other types of sites not recognized from this period. After the Meadowood phase, there have been very few sites that have been systematically excavated. Sites with Fox Creek points are the most common in the PASS files. A few stratified sites have been excavated in the Delaware basin and these have been interpreted as small camps. A number of rock shelters have been excavated in the lower Delaware basin that contained Early and Middle Woodland pottery. In the Susquehanna drainage basin, when the stratified sites on the floodplains are excavated, the Middle Woodland period is frequently missing or the occupations are small and transient. Because the artifacts from this period are not very distinctive, archaeologists have hypothesized that many upland sites, especially base camps are being missed. In contrast, some archaeologists have argued that Native Americans abandoned the region entirely during this time. The nagging questions are, Where did they go? and Why did they leave? It would seem that they were not living in base camps on the floodplains; most archaeologists assume that they were in the uplands somewhere.

The use and production of pottery, which is difficult to transport, suggests fewer base camp movements and more permanent settlements. Early Woodland bands probably continued to move on a seasonal basis, but base camps in favorable environments, such as high-fertility soils, may have been occupied from spring until fall. It is assumed that the bands were cultivating plants and maintaining small gardens that needed to be protected from grazing animals. From these base camps, work groups may have been sent out to harvest wild plant foods such as seeds, roots, or nuts; hunt deer, waterfowl, and other game; and fish. During the winter, families may have moved to the more sheltered uplands and especially to rock shelters. Other than the base camp where the gardens were located, Early and Middle Woodland people spent much of the year in small family camps exploit-ing dispersed resources. This settlement pattern is in contrast to the Archaic period strategy, where the entire band moved to the resource.

People Living in Groups: Social Organization and Belief Systems

As bands became more sedentary, the social organization probably changed, but there is so little data that the specifics are unknown. The burial ceremonialism and trade of the Early Woodland period suggests a more structured social organization. One can imagine large groups maintaining their identity with shared religious beliefs and trade; however, there are probably groups that are contemporary with the Meadowood complex (such as the Hellgrammite phase) who did not participate in the ceremonies or the trade. Did these cultures have a less structured social organization? Based on the present interpretation, they seem to have lived in loosely organized and small egalitarian bands. The variety of pottery and projectile point types suggest a variety of social groups. They all may have been one culture or they may represent different cultures, or simply different family groups. This is probably one of the least understood periods in Native American cultural development in Pennsylvania.

Although little is known about the Middle Woodland period, this was probably a very interesting time in Pennsylvania prehistory. People became more settled and had begun planting and cultivating wild seed plants. Middle Woodland sites are generally small and seem to represent one or two families. Although they were more settled, they were not living in large camps. This is an interesting contrast to the Late Woodland period.

Considering what we know about the Late Woodland period, the Early and Middle Woodland periods were probably very dynamic, with significant technological, social, and religious developments. Unfortunately, our understanding of these developments is very poor. Now

Summer

The Early and Middle Woodland settlement pattern was different from the Transitional period annual cycle. The family groups seem to be small and widely dispersed. In the spring, they focused on fishing but also planting crops of the Eastern Agricultural Complex. A small group of individuals probably stayed at this camp to protect the gardens all summer and into the fall. In the summer, small family groups moved throughout the floodplain and the uplands to collect a variety of foods. These resources may have been brought back to the garden camps on the floodplain. In the fall, nut collecting was

Fall

Spring

the emphasis and these may also have been brought back to the floodplain camp for processing and storage. Along the fall line, such as at the Abbott Farm Complex, large fishing camps would have been used. In the winter, small hunting camps in upland areas would have been occupied. Rock shelters would have been frequently used throughout the year.

Winter

that cultivation of crops was becoming more important, the role of males and females within Native American societies was changing. Women gained a more significant voice in decision making. By European contact, we know that many groups were organized into patrilineal or matrilineal clans. These gender-defined groups had their beginnings during the Early and Middle Woodland period.

The Early and Middle Woodland of the Upper Ohio Drainage Basin

For most of the Archaic period, the archaeology of the Ohio drainage basin in Ohio, Kentucky, Indiana, Illinois, and Tennessee has always been very different from the Susquehanna and Delaware drainage basins in Pennsylvania. It represents a very different culture area. The archaeology of the Ohio drainage basin in western Pennsylvania has reflected these differences but shared many similarities with the cultures of eastern Pennsylvania. This begins to change during the Transitional period, and by the Early Woodland period, cultural developments in western Pennsylvania began to follow a very different adaptive strategy. These include the use of burial mounds, elaborate burial ceremonies, a very extensive trade system, ceramics, and the early use of domesticated plants. Behind these developments was a very different social and political system that is not found in eastern Pennsylvania. In addition, contrary to eastern Pennsylvania, the Early Woodland period in the Upper Ohio drainage is defined on the basis of fired-clay pottery and specific pottery types.

The very first Early Woodland cultural adaptations in the Upper Ohio drainage basin, however, are similar to the adaptations in eastern Pennsylvania. The Meadowood phase extends south from its homeland in New York into northwestern Pennsylvania. It is identified by Meadowood points and Vinette I pottery and dates between 2500 and 3000 years ago. In the southwestern part of the state, the Half-Moon phase is the first Early Woodland culture and it is identified by Half-Moon cordmarked ceramics. This pottery is thick–walled and flat-bottomed, with medium to large pieces of temper and sometimes lug handles. As is the case in eastern Pennsylvania, this pottery type seems to be imitating steatite bowls. There are a variety of projectile points associated with this pottery type, including Stubenville Stemmed and Adena Ovate Base. There were no burial mounds associated with this phase and basically this is a continuation of the Archaic adapta-

tion, but now it includes pottery. People continued to hunt and fish, but intensified their use of wild plant foods. They gathered hickory nuts, walnuts, and acorns. There is good evidence they gathered seeds from chenopodium and ground them into flour. They also cultivated squash and tobacco. Squash was used as both food and containers. This plant was not natural to Pennsylvania and is believed to have been domesticated in Mexico and gradually transported to northeastern North America.

Adena Interaction Sphere

A new set of artifacts from 2500 years ago appear in the Upper Ohio drainage marking the Cresap phase. This is also known as Adena and is part of a regional development that extended from the upper Mississippi Valley to the upper Ohio Valley and into western New York. Adena is not a single culture. It is a ceremonial and trading system that is defined by a distinctive group of artifacts, houses, feature types, hamlets, and mound centers. In some areas of Ohio and Illinois, all of these traits are found together and seem to represent a regional culture. In other areas, such as Delaware or New Jersey, there are single isolated sites that seem like outposts, colonies, or missionary posts. In the Upper Ohio drainage basin of western Pennsylvania, there seems to be a mixture of Adena traits and those of the local population. The people who were using Half-Moon pottery became involved with the Adena ceremonial and trading system.

Adena people lived in oval or rectangular houses clustered in small hamlets. Sites are most frequently located on floodplains and terraces of rivers and large streams. Adena is best known for burial ceremonialism. The burial mounds are made of earth and typically constructed on promontories away from the hamlets. Each mound began as an individual burial. The burial was simple and mostly utilitarian items were added as grave goods. Typical artifacts include drills, scrapers, stone axes and adzes, copper beads (probably from Michigan or less likely from local sources), shells, gorgets, and tubular pipes. The bodies were frequently painted with red or yellow ochre. Over time, other individuals were added to the mound. Some of these were cremation burials and in some cases the body was defleshed prior to burial. With each of these additional burials, the mound grew in size. During Late Adena, the burials became much more elaborate with log chambers, trophy skulls, effigy pipes, and engraved stone tablets. It is believed that the groups in

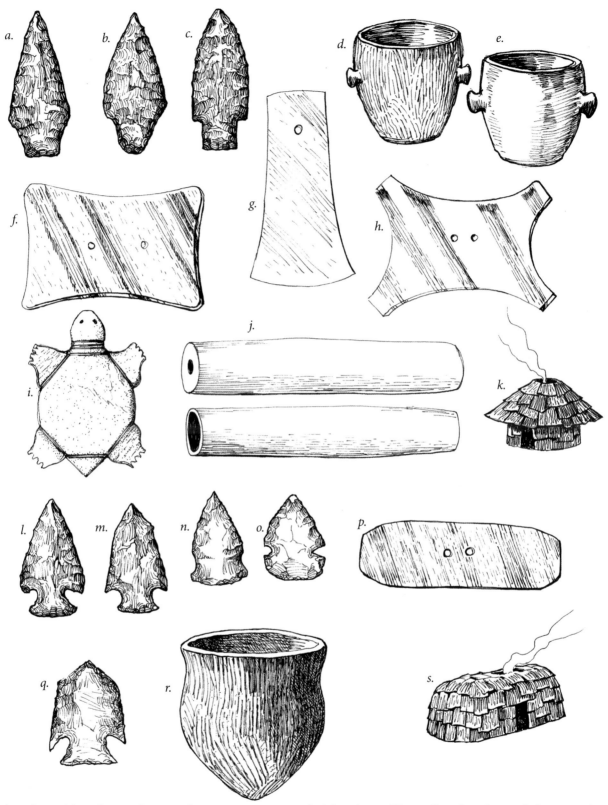

Typical artifacts of the Adena and Hopewell cultures: a. and c. Cresap spearpoints; b. Robbins spearpoint; d. Adena Half-Moon cordmarked pottery; e. Adena plain pottery; f. and h. quadriconcave gorget; g. bell-shaped pendant; i. turtle effigy tablet; j. blocked-end tubular pipes;

k. Adena house. Hopewell artifacts: l. Murphy's stemmed spearpoint; m. Snyder's corner-notched spearpoint; n. Manker stemmmed point; o. Raccoon side-notched point; p. rectangular gorget; q. Jacks Reef corner-notched point; r. Watson cordmarked pottery; s. Hopewell house.

Summer

The Cresap phase (Adena) settlement pattern was centered around a small hamlet of up to five houses. This site was occupied for many years. It was the location of gardens for squash, tobacco, and crops of the Eastern Agricultural Complex. From this base camp, small work parties went out to hunt, fish, and gather a variety of other plant foods in floodplain and upland environments. Groups of hamlets may have shared burial mound sites.

Fall

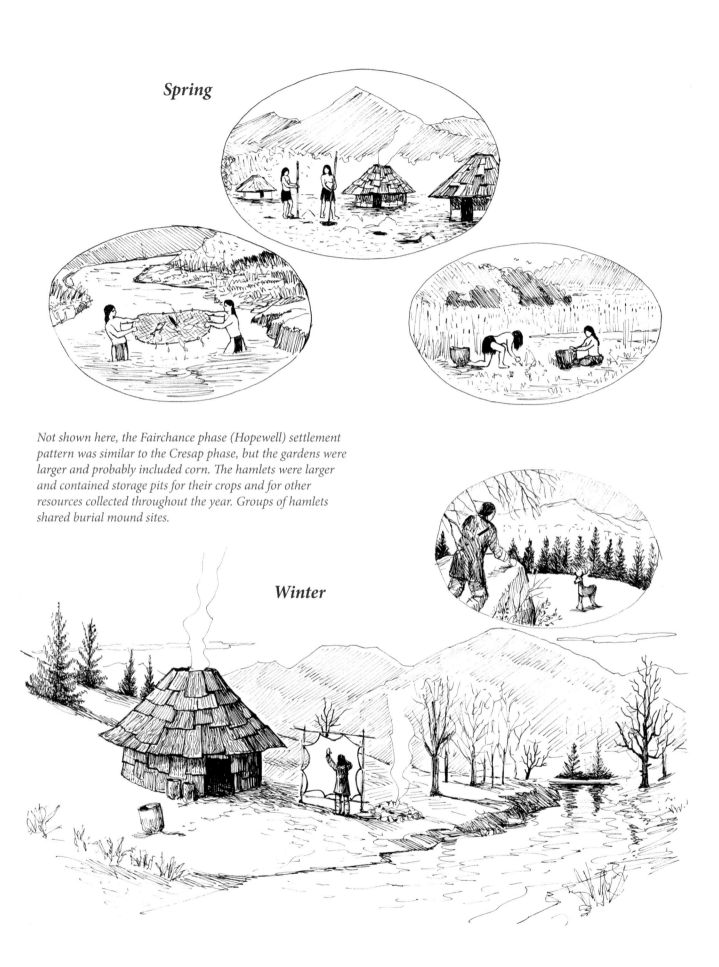

Spring

Not shown here, the Fairchance phase (Hopewell) settlement pattern was similar to the Cresap phase, but the gardens were larger and probably included corn. The hamlets were larger and contained storage pits for their crops and for other resources collected throughout the year. Groups of hamlets shared burial mound sites.

Winter

Pennsylvania lived in small egalitarian bands. The individuals buried in these mounds were simply of high status, influential men within their bands. In anthropological terms, they are sometimes called "big men." They earned this recognition through their accomplishments within their society. They were not kings or royalty. Their status was not passed on to their descendants, although there are a few child burials found in the mounds during Late Adena times.

The Cresap phase is Pennsylvania's own distinctive version of Adena. The most common projectile point form continues to be the Adena Ovate Based point, but notched and stemmed points are also found. These are frequently made from a high-quality chert mined in central Ohio that is aptly named Flint Ridge. This material is mined using a similar process as the jasper quarries in Lehigh County, but the pits are significantly larger and the entire outcrop covers hundreds of acres. Half-Moon Cordmarked pottery along with a plain version, McKees Rocks Plain, are the typical pottery types. Other common artifacts are blocked-end tubular pipes, reel-shaped gorgets, copper gorgets, and engraved stone tablets.

Approximately fifteen mounds have been identified in Pennsylvania from this period. They range in size from 2 to 16 feet high and 60 to 200 feet in diameter. The central tomb was frequently lined with log or bark and may have consisted of a crematory basin. The majority of artifacts were placed with this individual. Lesser individuals were added later and were placed in crematory basins or less complex tombs around the central burial crypt. Habitation sites have rarely been excavated but include oval or rectangular houses with central hearths, earth ovens, and features that possibly served as storage pits. Based on food remains from these sites, Cresap people continued to exploit a wide variety of plants and animals. Squash and tobacco were cultivated and probably chenopodium and knotweed. People were living in small hamlets with up to five houses. The hamlet was the location of small gardens and served as a base of operations for the exploitation of a wide variety of foods, both in floodplain and upland environments. Groups of hamlets may have shared burial mound sites, but the specifics of the relationship between mounds and habitation sites are unclear.

The Cresap phase represents a similar adaptation that was taking place in eastern Pennsylvania, but the social organization was much more structured and there was a greater dependence on gardening. When families live in permanent hamlets year-round, they require more rules on how to behave to maintain social order. In eastern Pennsylvania, we have speculated on the possible presence of important individuals who may have had special influence in the trade systems. In the Upper Ohio drainage, these individuals existed and they were placed in elaborate tombs with a sample of their important trade items. One explanation for the differences between the two regions is that human population densities were greater in the Upper Ohio drainage basin; more food needed to be extracted from the environment and more social structure was necessary to organize labor to extract the necessary calories.

Hopewell Interaction Sphere

In the Ohio Valley of Indiana, Illinois, and Ohio, an expansive trade network developed during the Middle Woodland period, which archaeologists call the Hopewell Interaction Sphere. The network extended from the Gulf of Mexico to Yellowstone National Park to the Delaware Bay. Trade items included marine shells, ocean turtle shells, and shark and alligator teeth from the Atlantic and Florida coasts; copper and silver from the Great Lakes region; and obsidian, a volcanic glass from the western United States. Hopewell mounds were larger and frequently contained many more burials than Adena mounds. Ceremonial artifacts, especially those from long-distance trade, were placed in the burials of high-ranking individuals. The trade network was associated with a pattern of burial ceremonialism and mound and effigy mound complexes that existed throughout the Upper Ohio drainage basin. Effigy mounds did not contain burials but rather were in geometric shapes and frequently surrounded burial mounds. Hopewell people in Ohio, Indiana, and Illinois were true horticulturists, growing corn, squash, chenopodium, knotweed, and little barley and living in settled hamlets.

The presence and nature of Hopewell culture in western Pennsylvania has always been unclear. The effigy and burial mound complexes and the extensive trade do not seem to exist in Pennsylvania at the same intensified level as in Ohio and Indiana. At best, Pennsylvania is on the eastern fringe of the Hopewell Interaction Sphere. Was this a blending of Hopewell traits with the local native populations? Or is it mainly the local natives acquiring a few intrusive Hopewell trade objects? The answer to these questions has not been determined.

Hopewell in western Pennsylvania is identified as the Fairchance phase; the distinctive artifacts are the Snyders Corner Notched point and Watson Ware pottery. This pottery type is limestone-tempered and mostly cordmarked, but also plain and sometimes with incised lines. Other projectile point types are found, including stemmed and side-notched forms. Only a few mound and habitation sites have been excavated. They contain oval to rectangular houses with multiple hearths and storage pits. The food remains suggest that they had a similar diet as the Cresap phase, but maize was probably added.

The distribution of grave goods in the mounds suggests that the social organization was different from Adena. Some individuals were buried in elaborate stone-lined crypts with log coverings and large quantities of trade goods. In some cases, infants were given special treatment, suggesting that a family was important rather than individuals or charismatic leaders. In northwestern Pennsylvania, there is a group of mound sites that are part of the Hopewell Interaction Sphere called Squawkie Hill. Interestingly, these mounds do not contain individuals with large quantities of traded grave goods and there are no infants who received special treatment. Therefore, these seem to represent an egalitarian tribal society. Clearly, the interaction of the Hopewell influence with local populations took on several different forms.

Hopewell in western Pennsylvania likely ended approximately 1600 years ago. The period after Hopewell in southwestern Pennsylvania is termed the Watson Farm phase (1100 to 1600 BP) and is poorly known. Many of the artifact types such as Watson Ware pottery continue. The projectile points include notched and stemmed forms. The bow and arrow is in widespread use during this period. Other artifacts such as humped-back knives and preforms for making projectile points are common. These people lived in hamlets, but at least one village has been excavated. The village contained numerous hearths and post molds. Although other houses were probably present, only one was identified. This consisted of a roof-supporting central post surrounded by post molds encircling an area 30 feet in diameter. Based on the variety of plant and animal remains found in the village and the substantial house construction, this village was probably occupied year-round for several years. Although the data is scant, it is assumed that subsistence was similar to the Fairchance phase. It probably included maize, but remains of this plant are not common. Burial mounds were made in the Watson Farm phase. They include stone crypts, but grave goods are rare, suggesting there was a return to an egalitarian society.

In summary, Middle Woodland times and the effects of the Hopewell Interaction Sphere on local populations are not well understood. Some Pennsylvania groups seem to be very involved with Hopewell, but most do not. Groups seem to be more sedentary, living in hamlets of five houses or less, but some were living in villages. Growing plant foods is probably becoming more important, but the data is scant. Social organization seems to be growing more complex, with people probably living in tribes, but additional field work is required to determine the specific social characteristics of these groups.

Early and Middle Woodland Period Research in Pennsylvania

There are 1169 Early Woodland and only 542 Middle Woodland sites recorded in the PASS files. This is a reduced number of sites covering a longer period of time than the preceding Transitional period. The Middle Woodland period numbers are especially low. This apparent decrease in site numbers for this period is also found in surrounding states to the north and south, although not in the Ohio Valley. Some archaeologists believe that this represents an actual drop in human population because of migrations out of the region. Other archaeologists believe that the projectile points and pottery from this period (used to identify sites) are not very distinctive. The sites exist, but we do not recognize them as easily as sites from other periods.

Early and Middle Woodland Research in the Delaware Drainage Basin

There are 190 Early Woodland and only 44 Middle Woodland sites recorded in the Delaware drainage basin. The Meadowood occupation at the Faucett site (36Pi13A) contained gorgets, pendants, and caches of unused tools that probably had decorative or ceremonial value. It is difficult to identify Early and Middle Woodland sites because the artifacts, other than a few distinctive projectile point types (Meadowood, Hellgrammite, Fox Creek) or pottery types (Vinette I, Brodhead net marked), are not particularly distinctive. Radiocarbon dating is the most definitive method, but unfortunately few sites have been dated. Most sites seem to be small, but in the Lower Schuylkill basin, the Indian Point site (36Ch53) revealed the remains of

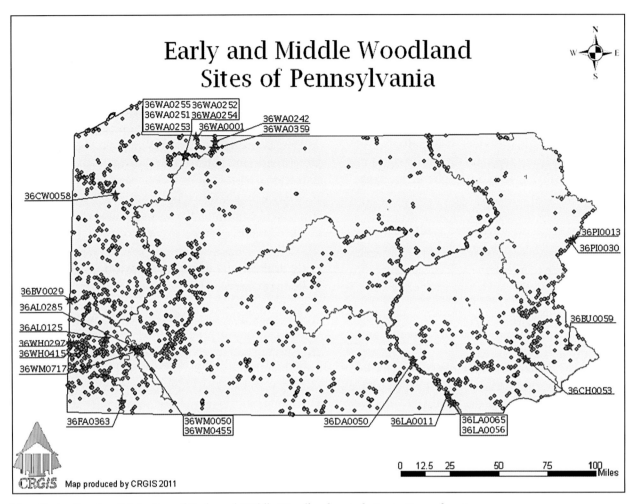

Early and Middle Woodland
Sites of Pennsylvania

36WA0255 36WA0252
36WA0251 36WA0254
36WA0253 36WA0001

36WA0242
36WA0359

36CW0058

36PI0013
36PI0030

36BV0029
36AL0285
36AL0125
36WH0297
36WH0415
36WM0717

36BU0059

36CH0053

36FA0363

36WM0050
36WM0455

36DA0050

36LA0011

36LA0065
36LA0056

0   12.5   25   50   75   100
Miles

Map produced by CRGIS 2011

Map illustrating the distribution of Early and Middle Woodland period sites in Pennsylvania.

a semisubterranean house, numerous hearths, and storage or refuse pits, representing a base camp. Therefore the sites exist, but more need to be investigated to understand their true nature.

The Middle Woodland in the Upper Delaware is defined as the Bushkill complex. Excavations at the Faucett (36Pi13A) and the Brodhead (36Pi30) sites revealed a variety of artifacts, pottery, and projectile point types, but no fire pits. The pottery was impressed on the outer surface with nets or fabric, and a large section of a netmarked pottery was found at the Brodhead site. At Faucett, a circular pattern of post molds indicated the presence of a Middle Woodland house. Interestingly, several groups of bola stones were found at the Faucett site. These are baseball-sized river cobbles, with a groove pecked around the middle. It is assumed that these were used for hunting waterfowl along the river.

Although not excavated in Pennsylvania, the Williamson site in the Middle Delaware valley on the New Jersey side has produced a large stratified Early

Woodland occupation. It is well dated and contains a variety of Early Woodland pottery and projectile point types, including the Hellgrammite type. It is believed the site served as a base camp for groups that were exploiting the adjacent floodplain. The site may have been occupied from spring until early winter and served as a base of operations. Work groups may have conducted periodic forays into upland regions to exploit a variety of resources. In the winter, the group would have dispersed into sheltered regions in the uplands. Many rock shelters in southeastern Pennsylvania, including the Eel Skin rock shelter (36Bu59), contain Early and Middle Woodland pottery and these may have functioned as the winter camps.

Also in New Jersey, the Abbott Farm Complex of sites produced extensive evidence of Early and Middle Woodland occupations. These are similar to the Transitional period and contain large FCR features. They seemingly represent large sites that were seasonally occupied by large bands exploiting a wide variety of floodplain resources.

Early and Middle Woodland Research in the Susquehanna Drainage Basin

There are 432 Early Woodland and only 100 Middle Woodland sites recorded in the Susquehanna drainage basin. Early and Middle Woodland occupations have been recovered at sites on Piney Island (36La65), Bare Island (36La56), and Three Mile Island (36Da50). The Three Mile Island site seems to represent a Middle Woodland base camp. Interestingly, this occupation produced a small collection of Flint Ridge chert blades, suggesting this site was involved with the Hopewell trade system. There are several rock shelters in the region, including the Erb Rock Shelter (36La11), that also contain Early and Middle Woodland occupations. Very few have been systematically excavated, however, and this is one of the most poorly understood periods of prehistory in this region.

Early and Middle Woodland Research in the Ohio Drainage Basin

There are 543 Early Woodland and 396 Middle Woodland sites recorded in the Upper Ohio drainage basin. These periods are well known relative to other regions of Pennsylvania. They also seem to be part of a different cultural tradition than the rest of the state—a tradition more related to cultures located farther west in the Ohio drainage basin. The people are more sedentary and settlements become more permanent. People began using pottery and were on the fringes of the trade networks that developed in the Ohio basin. In Pennsylvania, there are a number of habitation sites and burial mounds that have been excavated.

The Grays Landing site (36Fa363) and Mayview Bend site (36Al125) represent small habitations associated with the Half-Moon phase. These contained storage pits and suggest that these sites were being occupied for relatively long periods of time. The Ohioview site (36Bv9) contained a pottery kiln, a relatively rare find, also suggesting that Early Woodland populations were becoming more sedentary. Although the Meadowcroft Rockshelter is best known for its Pre-Clovis occupation, it also produced an Early Woodland hunting camp. Most importantly, the Meadowcroft field methods incorporated the extensive use of flotation for the recovery of food remains such as seeds and nuts. Squash remains were recovered from this occupation dating to between 2800 and 3000 years ago. Chenopodium, knotweed, and maygrass were also found in the levels containing Half-Moon pottery. This demonstrates that Early Woodland people were using domesticated plants and cultivating small gardens.

The Mayview Bend and Georgetown (36Bv29) sites represent Cresap phase habitations. They produced a variety of features but no houses. The Thorpe site (36Al285) produced five houses dating to this phase. These were oval to rectangular, with a single post supporting the roof, and measured 6 to 45 feet in diameter. But most sites from this phase are burial mounds. Excavations at Riverview Mound (36Wh29) produced mica, copper awls, and other exotic materials, indicating trade with Adena and Hopewell people in the Ohio Valley. The Anderson Mound (36Al96), in the borough of Oakmont, Allegheny County, is an interesting combination of Adena and Hopewell traits. It was 34 feet in diameter and contained the remains of two or possibly three individuals. They were cremated in place, although their legs were less burned, suggesting they were farther from the heat. The grave offerings included projectile points, cupstones, bolo stones, a banner stone, copper beads, and sandstone pipes. Most of the material was local, but some came from Ohio or western New York. The site has not been accurately dated, but the projectile points suggest that it dates to Late Adena times or to the Hopewell complex. It seems to be a local expression of a trading and ceremonial complex that was centered in the Ohio Valley.

A number of sites demonstrating more local traditions also have been excavated. Sites in the Monongahela basin are generally camps rather than hamlets or small villages such as those found farther down the Ohio Valley. For example, thirteen Early Woodland sites were identified in the Meyersdale Bypass survey in the Casselman River Valley. All were interpreted as short-term camps. No long-term camps or hamlets were found.

A number of Early and Middle Woodland sites have been investigated along the Youghiogheny River. One site excavated as part of a Consolidated Gas Transmission Corporation pipeline construction project revealed a variety of features, including fire pits, large roasting pits, storage pits, and evidence of posts, suggesting that houses were present. Radiocarbon dates indicated occupations during both the Early and Middle Woodland periods. A flat-bottom pot was found along with over 200 pieces of pottery.

The Billy #3 site (36Wm717) is situated on an upland flat overlooking Sewickley Creek and represents a major Fairchance phase hamlet. The site produced a pattern of post molds, indicating a rectangular house, along with a fire pit, a storage pit, and an earth oven. The age of the site was determined on the basis of its pottery, which is characteristic of the Middle Woodland period. Hickory and walnut shells, blackberry, raspberry, and one squash rind were found, representing a sample of the diet. A burial mound (36Wm50) that had been heavily disturbed was located 60 miles to the northeast of the hamlet. Excavation revealed a disturbed stone crypt with fragments of a human skull and six teeth.

The Watson Farm phase was radiocarbon dated at the Backstrum #3 (36Wm455) and Avella Mound (36Wh415) sites. The stone crypt tomb construction and cremation burials of the Avella Mound are typical of this phase. The lack of grave goods with most of the burials demonstrates the decline of burial ceremonialism during this phase.

The Squawkie Hill phase is represented by several mounds in northwestern Pennsylvania, notably Nelson (36Cw58), Sugar Run (36Wa359), Irvine (36Wa251-255), Cornplanter (36Wa242), and Corydon (36Wa1). The Sugar Run site contained at least three stone-lined crypts and these were each surrounded by a cobble pavement. It is believed that the cobbles were arranged in the shape of

The Sugar Run mound during excavation, illustrating the extensive cobble pavement.

a raptorial bird on one side of the burials and in the shape of a celt on the other side. Cobble pavements and other elaborate designs may have been present at other mound sites, but many were looted prior to professional excavations.

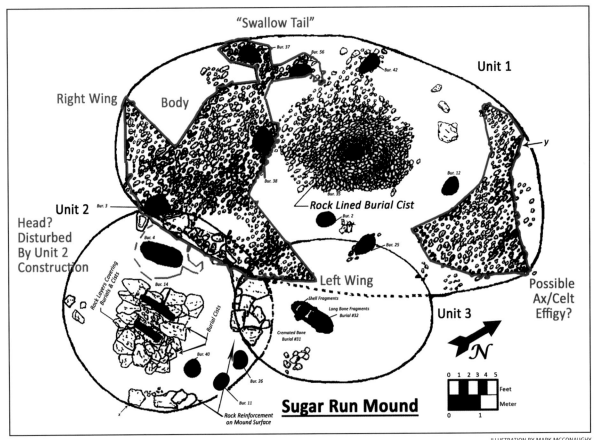

A reconstruction of the cobble pavement at the Sugar Run mound. It is believed that the cobbles were arranged in the shape of a raptorial bird on one side of the burials and in the shape of a celt on the other side.

An Early and Middle Woodland Narrative

TIME 2000 YEARS AGO.

PLACE THE MIDDLE SUSQUEHANNA VALLEY.

CLIMATE SLIGHTLY WARMER WITH MORE RAIN THAN PRESENT.

FLORA AND FAUNA A MIXED OAK, HEMLOCK, AND CHESTNUT FOREST—SIMILAR TO PENNSYLVANIA AT THE TIME OF COLUMBUS.

DISTINCTIVE ARTIFACTS POTTERY.

My name is Netmordelalk. I'm a sixty-year-old woman and have a story to tell. I have five children—three girls and two boys. My husband died many years ago. I live with my oldest son, his wife, and their oldest son's family. We live on the Juniata River. My tribe is scattered throughout the Juniata and Upper Susquehanna Valleys in small farmsteads of a few houses. There are over 500 people, although we rarely get together in one place. My family band is about thirty people, but it frequently changes. The men often travel and my children and grandchildren frequently visit me.

The Juniata Valley is a wonderful place to live. We collect many different kinds of food. Each season there is something different and we are always very busy. Our year is scheduled based on the foods we eat. Everyone probably works four or five hours every day. We have a main camp along the river. From this camp, we move to our seasonal camps. In the late summer and fall, when seeds and nuts are ripening, we move to harvest them. During the spring, we spend most of our time fishing and collecting ducks and duck eggs along the river. We usually start in the spring by moving from our winter camp and joining up with several other family bands for the big fish migration. The river is full of fish and is a resource we can't ignore. The men spend the early spring repairing the nets and setting them up in the water. We women set up the camp and collect firewood. I usually plant a garden with squash, knotweed, and goosefoot. The fish are dumped from the nets into baskets. We put them into large clay pots of boiling water. We skim off the oil that floats to the surface and put it into storage pots. Some of the fish are dried over fires and others, of course, are eaten right away. It is a good time and everyone is happy to have plenty of fresh food after the long winter.

We meet our friends and relatives who we have not visited all winter. We all say goodbye to people who have died over the winter and make a fuss over the new babies. For about three weeks, we stay together and then we divide up into family bands and return to our homes.

Throughout the summer, we continue to hunt, fish, and gather a wide variety of plants from along the river. The women are particularly good at finding tasty roots for making wonderful stews and leaves for hot teas. The young men and boys paddle the river in their dugouts, spearing fish and snaring ducks with their bolas. The bola is an interesting weapon that consists of three stones tied together on 3-foot cords. They swing it over their heads and throw the spinning rocks at a flock of geese. They usually hit at least one and sometimes more.

Men and women have different responsibilities in our tribe. The men hunt and fish. They cut trees to make the houses. They make tools, such as axes, spears, and knives. My husband spent a lot of time making his knife handle, but not much time making spearpoints. We use many different types of rock to make our tools, and some are much better than others. I wondered why we did not spend more time looking for better toolstones. I asked my husband about this and he told me it was too much trouble to go to the quarries or to negotiate a trade. He said that spears needed to have a stone tip and the stone needed a stem to attach it to the wooden shaft. There were many ways to shape the stone point and especially the stem. He made his stem square, but it could be tapered or notched. He quickly showed me how to do it. My mother had shown me how to sharpen my knife. I practiced making knife blades when I was younger, but I never made any spearpoints. Flint knapping is a skill that only a few people take seriously. Everyone uses stone tools. Everyone can sharpen and make stone tools. But there are much more important things to do than make them pretty.

During the summer, the young people frequently go visiting for a week or more. When we visit relatives, we always bring gifts of food, baskets, or stone for tools. When we return home, we bring many gifts and lots of news. There is a real mixing of the family bands at this

time. I remember the fun times we would have in the summer when I was a young girl. A group of teenage boys and girls would get a couple of dugouts and just go visiting up and down the river. We slept on the islands or we stayed with relatives in the other family bands. One of our favorite places was a large rock shelter just upstream from where the Raystown Branch joins the Juniata. This place was always dry and out of the wind. Rock shelters are great places to get out of the weather. They are like ready-made houses. Everyone uses them. There is always a central hearth and sometimes a small supply of wood. This one is especially good because you can canoe right to it and see anyone else who may come along. When we travel overland between the major rivers, we frequently schedule our campsites based on the rock shelters.

The fall is the busiest time. Everyone helps to gather the seeds, nuts, pawpaws, and berries that are ripening. Some are ground into flour, some are dried, and some are boiled for their oil. Hickory nuts, butternuts, goosefoot, and sunflower seeds are our main foods, but we collect many others to add flavor and for added nutri-

tion. This is also the time we collect the gourds and seeds from our gardens. Planting the gardens and protecting the plants all summer takes a lot of time and is hard work. But in late winter, the basket of seeds that we store are sometimes all the food that is left for my family. Lately, it seems that we depend on these more each year.

I stand by my mortar and pestle all day grinding the nuts into flour. My mortar consists of a hollowed log standing on end and my pestle is a long pole. The women work in groups so that they can watch the babies. From September until the middle of November, we work all day long. The returning ducks also provide a lot of tasty food, and if I am not grinding nuts, I am pulling feathers out of geese. This is a hard time for the young mothers, because they must work and care for their babies at the same time. I have always tried to help my daughters and granddaughters, just as my mother did for me. Everyone is very tired from working all fall. Sometimes there have been quarrels or fights. By the end of November, there is much feasting and dancing. As the family bands return home, all is forgiven.

Each family band has its own territory, but we always share if someone asks. A problem arises when someone is

COURTESY OF TRAUB DESIGN ASSOCIATES, INC. COPYRIGHT 2000/ILLUSTRATION BY DAN BRIDY

over the body of the pot. It doesn't slip out of your hands as easily as a smooth surface and the textured surface helps to evenly distribute the heat so the food is less likely to burn.

Our pottery is rounded on the bottom with a slightly flaring rim. The round bottom is easier to make than a flat bottom and stronger. They are also easier to set up on the uneven surface of our rock hearths. We make different sizes for cooking or storage but they are all the same basic shape.

Once the pot has been shaped, I like to put designs in the soft clay along the rim. After the designs are made, the pots are allowed to dry for several days. Once they are dried, we set them upside down and build a fire over top of them that lasts for several hours. Now they are hard and can hold water.

Everyone knows my designs. My daughters and grand-daughters have experimented with different styles, but we pretty much stick with the same. They are a symbol of our family and they are a reflection of our land. When I look around our summer camps, the pots are all very similar; they represent our family. At the fall camp, there are many pots representing many families and different regions. Some of them are very interesting but we never copy them. Why would you make images of the land of other families?

Pottery is interesting because our traditions tell us that we did not always have clay pots. In the old days, we had pots made out of stone, and they were made by the men rather than the women. That sounds crazy and they must have been terribly heavy. Around the campfire, my grand-mother told the story of how pottery was brought to The People. Many years ago, a man married a woman who lived many days journey to the south. She had clay pots. At first he thought these were interesting, but later he complained that food cooked in clay pots was not as good as food cooked in stone bowls. Once when his friends were visiting, in a rage he smashed all of her clay pots. He said that men must eat and drink from stone bowls and she was not allowed to make any more clay pots. But she was a very crafty women and she cast a spell on her husband. Whenever he went hunting, the animals ran away. Whenever he went fishing, he fell into the river. The food from his favorite stone bowl always tasted horrible. One day, the men went on a trip to trade with their neigh-bors to get more stone bowls. While they were gone, the woman made more pots. She showed the other women how to make pottery. They quickly realized that these

not respectful and does not ask. They steal our fish or ducks or butternuts. Our main camp consists of four or five large round houses. There are usually large baskets of food hanging from poles or trees. Frequently there are skins being stretched and cleaned. There is always a fire cooking something. In the summer, the fire is outside, and in the winter, the fire is inside. In the summer, we frequently sleep outside in hammocks. We do not create much garbage and our dogs eat almost everything that we don't want. We move our main camp once we have used up all of the nearby firewood. Sometimes it gets flooded and some-times we just move.

In the late summer, I help my daughters and grand-daughters make pottery. We need pots for cooking and storing food during the fall harvest. We collect the clay from a nearby stream and mix it with small pieces of crushed quartz rock. The rock is called temper and it strengthens the pot while it is being fired and when it is used for cooking. The clay is rolled into long strips and these are coiled together to shape the pot. The coils are pressed together using a small wooden paddle wrapped in netting material. The net leaves a cross-hatched design were much more convenient. They were lighter and each family could have many pots for cooking, storage, and carrying water. But they were afraid their husbands would just break them again.

Sure enough, when the men returned, there was a terrible argument. Fortunately, a wise old man had been watching all of this and suggested a compromise. He said, "Why don't you make your containers using both clay and stone?" Nobody liked this idea but it was a compromise and they agreed to try. They crushed up the stone bowls and mixed them with the clay. Many of the women thought this was a stupid idea that would not work. The men were equally upset about breaking up some of their stone bowls. In fact, they found out quickly that the pots were stronger and did not break as frequently while they were being fired. They also seemed to heat better when they were used for cooking. Everyone agreed that the food tasted great.

This is how The People first got pottery and why we add rock (temper) to our clay. When my grandmother first told us this story, she added that the men were probably getting tired of traveling to the steatite quarries, carving their bowls at the quarry, and dealing with crooked traders. Also, the feasting was getting to be more trouble than it was worth. The women and young men had stopped coming to the feasts because they were too busy with the nut harvest. The men probably realized that it was better to let the women work than feasting with old men. My grandmother was very intelligent.

Our families have always lived along the Juniata River. Many days journey to the north there lives another tribe. They speak a different language. My husband traded with them sometimes and learned to speak their language. The meetings are usually peaceful, but they are different from us. They got their names from the things that they brought to trade. We call them the Shell People, because they bring us large shells from the ocean. We know that the groups closest to the source get the most, keep the best, and trade the rest. Everybody along the trade line does the same. That is what we do. Nobody gets our fresh deer meat and berries with beaver fat, except my brothers, my husband's family, and other very close relatives in nearby groups. We have to pretend that we are giving our best and getting their best, but everyone knows better. The flavor of bear grease is not even close to that of beaver fat. Things have been like this forever and will continue.

Our land is starting to get crowded. We are a strong and healthy people, but I am worried that there are so many mouths to feed. The nuts are my favorite food, but they are harder to process than the seeds we get from along the marsh. We knock down the trees and bushes around the goosefoot and sunflower plants, so that there will be more seed plants, but I am worried that we will need to do something else to generate more food.

Our world is changing. My children and grandchildren need to be intelligent in the decisions they will need to make. Our neighbors to the west and south live in large towns and they grow their own food, but they spend long hours in their fields. They also spend much of their time worrying about dead ancestors and are always fighting each other. If we are going to survive, we will need to pick the good characteristics of these people and not the bad ones.

Chapter 7
The Woodland Period: 2700 years ago to 1550 AD, Part II

The Late Prehistoric and Late Woodland Periods: 1100 years ago to 1550 AD

The archaeological differences between the eastern and western drainage basins become particularly strong during late prehistory. First, Late Prehistoric and Late Woodland pottery designs are a much more sensitive medium for dating archaeological sites and identifying cultural differences than earlier pottery styles or other distinctive artifacts, such as projectile points. Therefore, these times are understood in greater detail than previous periods. It is clear that the pottery of the Upper Ohio basin in Pennsylvania is related to pottery styles found in cultures in Ohio and West Virginia rather than regions east of the Appalachian Mountains. Second, during these times, there is much better organic preservation. We have a relatively good picture of the Native American diet, bone and antler artifacts, and human biological characteristics as exhibited through burials. Again, the western Pennsylvania artifact assemblages demonstrate strong ties to the Ohio basin. Third, features and house types are more common and become distinctive for each of the drainage basins. Based on these differences, in the following discussion, the Upper Ohio will be treated separately and this time is termed the Late Prehistoric period. The Susquehanna and Delaware drainages share many traits, and in these drainage basins this time is termed the Late Woodland period.

TIMELINE

Contact Period	1500 AD–1700 AD
Woodland Period	2700 years ago–1500 AD
Late Woodland/Late Prehistoric	**1100 years ago–1550 AD**
Middle Woodland	1100–2100 years ago
Early Woodland	2100–2700 years ago
Transitional Period	2700–4300 years ago
Archaic Period	4300–10,000 years ago
Paleoindian Period	10,000–16,500 years ago

Environment: The Late Prehistoric and Late Woodland periods are generally warm and wet with a significant cold period, the "Little Ice Age," at the end. This cold event did not bring glaciers back to Pennsylvania, but it decreased the predictability of food resources, shortened the growing season, and affected Native American farming. The vegetation can be characterized as an oak, chestnut, and hemlock forest. The frequent use of floodplain areas for farming resulted in much of this area being open or in various stages of regrowth.

Making and using tools (typical artifacts and technology): Well-made pottery and triangular arrowpoints are the hallmark of this period. The pottery exhibits relatively elaborate designs, allowing archaeologists to identify various cultural groups. Agriculture is reflected in a variety of grinding stones, including pestles, mullers, and pitted stones. Bone and antler artifacts are more frequently preserved. These were used to make harpoons, fishhooks, awls, needles, hoes, and a variety of ornaments.

What people ate (subsistence): Corn, beans, and squash, "the three sisters," represent the main food source by the end of this period. Farming began in Middle Woodland times, however, in small gardens focusing on sunflowers, squash, and seed plants, such as chenopodium, knotweed, and little barley. These gardens increased in size, and corn was added to this existing subsistence system. Beans were the last of the three sisters to be added. Eventually, corn became the dominant food source and may have comprised up to 75 percent of the diet. Slash-and-burn agriculture became the main farming technique in many areas. A variety of other wild plants, mammals, fish and shellfish made up the rest of the diet.

Where people lived (settlement patterns): The focus continues to be on floodplains that contain the most fertile soil for simple farming. Specialized collecting sites are found throughout upland areas along small streams and at springheads. Village sites increase in size and are found in floodplains in the Susquehanna basin and on hilltops in the Upper Ohio basin. Hamlets are the norm in the Delaware basin. These year-round occupations are characterized by a variety of storage pit features, family hearths, earth ovens, burials, and post molds representing a variety of structures, such as houses, storage structures, drying racks, and windbreaks. Village sites can measure over 10 acres in size, containing scores of houses, and serve as a base of operations to exploit other resources. Population was frequently dispersed. As soil fertility decreased, village sites were moved every ten to twenty years. Sites from this period are the most commonly represented ones in the PASS files. This demonstrates that Late Prehistoric/Late Woodland people exploited a wide variety of ecological settings but were also very mobile.

People living in groups (social organization and belief systems): In the Susquehanna and Upper Ohio drainages, family groups evolved from living in small, relatively sedentary hamlets to living in large villages containing hundreds of people. These villages, however, were rarely full, and special work groups moved out of the villages to exploit a wide variety of resources. Villages were frequently surrounded by a wooden stockade and it is assumed that small-scale conflicts were common. In contrast, in the Delaware basin, agriculture was practiced in dispersed farmsteads consisting of a few families. The social organization evolved into a tribal organization during this time.

Tribes were organized by families who frequently traced their lineage through male or female ancestors. These larger and less flexible groups, compared to band organization, were necessary in order to organize labor to clear and maintain fields and to harvest and store crops. Some villages have special structures for community and ceremonial activities. Burials are more frequently preserved. They are found individually within the village or in small cemeteries outside of the village.

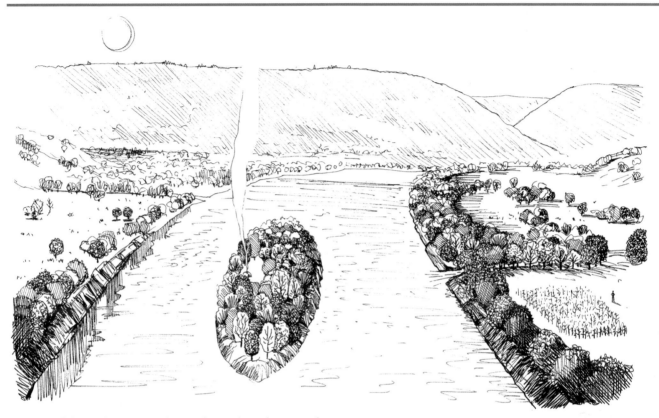

A view of the Little Ice Age oak-pine forest along the Susquehanna River 600 years ago.

Definition

The Late Woodland and Late Prehistoric periods are defined by well-made pottery; the widespread use of the bow and arrow; the adoption of slash-and-burn farming, focusing on corn, beans, and squash; village life; tribal social organization; and warfare. Using pottery designs, archaeologists believe that they can identify distinct cultures across the region and trace cultural change through time. Population levels reached the point at which families could survive only by growing their own food. Native Americans in the Mississippi Valley had been growing their own food for a thousand years prior to this time. The idea of agriculture and specific crops migrated to Pennsylvania from this region. Farming in each of the drainage basins of Pennsylvania took on a slightly different form. Therefore, they will be treated separately in the discussion below.

The Environment

The environment of the Late Woodland and Late Prehistoric periods begins as warm and moist during the Neo-Atlantic episode (1000-1400 BP) and changes to cool and dry during the Pacific episode (700-1000 BP). It ends during the Neo-Boreal episode (700 BP-1850 AD), known as the Little Ice Age. The favorable conditions of the Neo-Atlantic allowed for a greater dependence on agriculture and its final spread into the Upper Ohio basin, Ontario, New England, and eventually the river basins of eastern Pennsylvania. Agricultural hamlets and villages spread and increased in number throughout this region. In contrast, the Little Ice Age had deleterious effects all over the world and witnessed a retreat of agricultural peoples into warmer climates. Native American populations were affected by this climate and site distributions in the Upper Ohio basin were adjusted during this time. Interestingly, changes in the eastern part of the state are not as apparent.

The Late Prehistoric Period in the Upper Ohio Drainage Basin

Definition

During the Middle Woodland Period and continuing after the Hopewell influence, farming hamlets are found in the Upper Ohio basin of Pennsylvania. Their cultural affiliation and level of tribal organization, however, is unclear. By 950 years ago, these small communities have merged to form large farming villages containing hundreds of people in what archaeologists call the Monongahela culture. This culture is identified by distinctive pottery styles, house shapes, and a variety of personal ornaments. The Monongahela culture is found in the lower Allegheny basin, throughout the Monongahela basin, and on the Somerset Plateau. The people of the Monongahela culture grew corn, beans, and squash. They also relied on hunting and gathering wild foods, including shellfish.

The Middle and Upper Allegheny basin and the Lake Erie Plain were also occupied by farming villages during late prehistory. Based on pottery designs, these people are not part of the Monongahela culture. Many of these sites were also stockaded and contained hundreds of residents. Some of the more northern groups, such as the Meade Island Complex, were related to the Fort Ancient culture of Ohio. Others made pottery similar to the Iroquoian groups of Ontario and New York. The villages in the Middle Allegheny are similar to those in the Monongahela, but it is believed to be a different culture. The relationship between these groups, however, is unclear.

Making and Using Tools: Typical Artifacts and Technology

A diverse material culture is generally associated with Monongahela sites, including ornaments acquired through trade. The pottery is well made with simple designs around the rim. The bow and arrow replaced the spear as the standard hunting tool. Triangular-shaped stone arrowheads are common, along with large quantities of broken pottery and freshwater mollusk shells. Bone fishhooks, bone awls for sewing, and chipped stone hoes are also found on these sites. In addition, a wide variety of ornamental artifacts are found at Monongahela village sites, including bone beads, carved bone and teeth, and drilled bear, elk and other mammal teeth used as pendants and necklaces. Pendants were carved of shells from the Atlantic coast and demonstrate active trade with that region. Cannel coal (a type of soft coal that burns brightly) was carved

into pendants shaped like diamonds, triangles, claws, animal teeth, and disks. Stone and clay smoking pipes are also common. The clay pipes are small, elbow-shaped artifacts, sometimes with decorated bowls. Rarely are the bowls in the shape of animals. Although Indians probably have been playing games since they arrived in the New World, early evidence is found at Monongahela sites in the form of stone discoidals, or "chunkey stones." These are circular ground and polished stones that were probably rolled along the ground in some type of outdoor game.

Examples of Monongahela pottery. It is relatively plain compared to contemporary types in the Susquehanna and Delaware drainages.

Mainly based on pottery styles, Monongahela is divided into early, middle, and late phases. Early Monongahela pottery is smooth-surfaced and mainly shell-tempered. The Drew phase is defined by artifacts recovered from the Drew site (36Al62), and is related to pottery styles to the west in the Lower Ohio drainage basin. Moving east to the Somerset Plateau, the pottery is more frequently limestone-tempered and shares similarities with pottery styles in the Potomac drainage basin. Middle Monongahela is called the Campbell Farm phase, based on artifacts recovered from the Campbell Farm site (36Fa26), and is characterized by cordmarked pottery and includes shallow bowls or dishes. Late Monongahela sites contain a few European trade goods,

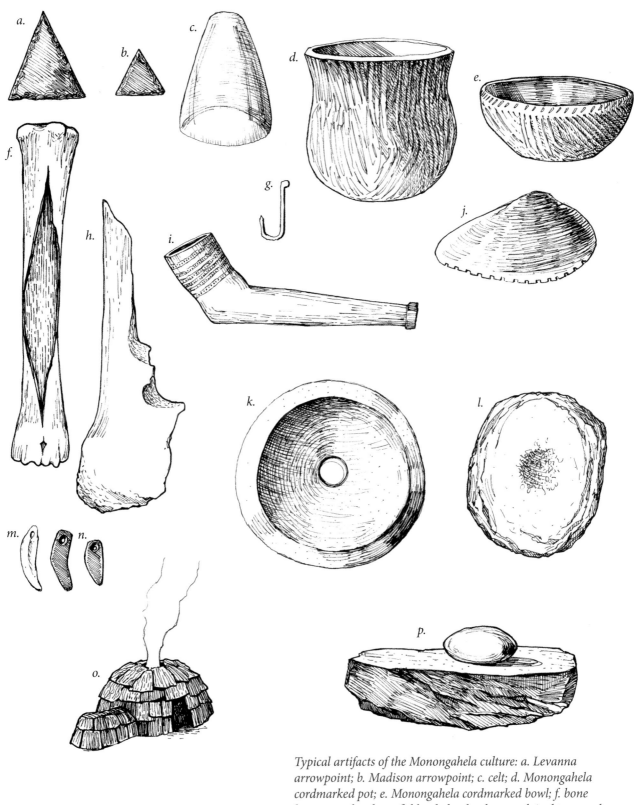

Typical artifacts of the Monongahela culture: a. Levanna arrowpoint; b. Madison arrowpoint; c. celt; d. Monongahela cordmarked pot; e. Monongahela cordmarked bowl; f. bone beamer tool; g. bone fishhook; h. ulna bone awl; i. obtuse angle clay pipe; j. serrated mussel shell tool; k. stone discoidal, or "chunkey stones"; l. anvil stone; m. drilled canine tooth; n. drilled cannel coal tooth or claw pendants; o. Monongahela wigwam; p. muller and slab grinding stone.

initially copper and brass items and later iron tools and glass beads. There is no evidence, however, that Europeans ever visited these sites.

In the Middle Allegheny drainage basin there are a number of sites where the pottery suggests something different from Monongahela. Ken Burkett has been the energy behind the excavation of four village sites (Fishbasket 36Ar134 and Fishbasket North 36Cl93 Locus 1, Locus 2, and Locus 3) that he defines as the Fishbasket Complex. These sites are located along Redbank Creek bordering Clarion and Armstrong Counties. The pottery is mainly limestone-tempered and the pots are elongated and globular in shape. The necks are slightly constricted and the rims are straight or slightly flaring. The rim and neck are usually smooth and the body retains light cordmarking. The decoration consists of cordwrapped stick impressions, punctations, or light incising on the rim or neck. An interesting characteristic on some vessels are handlelike straps. Pottery sherds are very common on these sites, but triangular

Archaeological specimens of the three sisters—from left to right, corn, beans and squash. These were the main foods of the Late Prehistoric period.

arrowpoints, drills, knives, and spokeshaves are also common. Notched netsinkers, siltstone hoes, smoking pipes, pendants, and stone and clay beads are also common. Similar pottery and stone tools were found at other sites in the area such as the Kimmel Mine sites 36Ar121 and 36Ar221. Radiometric dating of these sites ranges between 630 and 910 BP.

What People Ate: Subsistence

The Monongahela culture, the Fishbasket Complex, and the other cultures in the Upper Allegheny were dependent on slash-and-burn agriculture, focusing on corn, beans, and squash. The diet also included a wide variety of other foods, including mammals, migratory birds, fish, shellfish, and a variety of wild plant foods. Adults, especially males, had opportunities to travel and had access to a greater variety of foods. Unfortunately, children spent most of their time in the village where a high corn diet resulted in anemia. The Little Ice Age had an effect on Late Prehistoric subsistence patterns. To offset the unpredictability of this climate, the Monongahela people spread out into many different ecological zones where they collected a wide variety of foods. Although they depended on corn, they had other backup foods to survive an early frost. Most groups in the Upper Ohio also had in ground storage (semisubterranean) structures to preserve food for the winter.

PHOTO BY KENNETH BURKETT

Pottery from the Fishbasket site is similar to Monongahela pottery.

Slash-and-Burn Agriculture

The Monongahela, Shenks Ferry, and Susquehannock tribes practiced a type of farming called *slash-and-burn*, or *swidden*, agriculture. The actual planting and weeding of the crops was done with a simple wooden digging stick. They did not use fertilizers or any type of plow, so there was no mixing of the soil to kill weeds or introduce nutrients back into the soil. The soil fertility and crop yields, therefore, decreased quickly. Within five to ten years, the fields needed to be moved. Developing new fields in a primeval forest using only stone axes and fire to remove the vegetation was no small task. Several years prior to the actual move, the lower bark was removed from the larger trees and they died within two seasons. This is called *girdling*. When all of the trees were dead, the limbs were piled up around the trees and this was set on fire. The charcoal that remains is good for the soil and new crops are planted. Eventually all the fields within a reasonable walking distance, or about 2 miles, from the village were used. In advance of this point, the families were scouting locations for a new village. The new village needed to contain high-fertility soils, water, and enough small trees to provide saplings for new houses. It also needed to be easily defended. Several families were probably sent to the new location a year before the move to prepare the site. Fields were made ready at the new site, and the entire village would probably move in the fall after the harvest. People who practiced slash-and-burn agriculture were always in the process of preparing new fields and planning the location for a new village.

Where People Lived: Settlement Patterns

The Monongahela settlement pattern included a variety of small campsites, hamlets consisting of one or two houses, and large circular villages. On a seasonal basis, some families moved from the villages to the hamlets to be closer to important resources. During the fall harvest of crops, the main village would be completely occupied. This was a busy time bringing in the crops, getting them processed, and storing them for the winter. It was also the time for major ceremonies. During the fall and early winter, hunting expeditions were organized for elk, deer, and bear. This is the time when their furs were in the best condition for making clothing. The spring was another busy time of getting the fields ready for planting. But there are a variety of other foods available at this time, so the hamlets would have continued to be occupied. The summer was a time when resources were available in diverse ecological settings. This was when many families moved from the main village to the hamlets and other specialized camps. The villages, hamlets, and specialized camps were part of a seasonal round used to exploit the environment.

Initially Monongahela sites were situated on floodplains, but by 750 years ago, they were more often found on upland saddles (a low part of a ridgeline) between hilltops. There have been several explanations proposed for this move. The upland locations are more easily defended, and there is evidence that warfare or feuding may have increased at this time. Possibly there was a desire to conserve the floodplains by placing the villages on the ridgetops. Finally, the growing season was shortened by the Little Ice Age. It has been hypothesized that the hilltops had more frost-free days and therefore a longer growing season. Choosing a topographic setting with longer growing seasons is a good strategy for agricultural success. These theoretical correlations between topography, temperature, and the Little Ice Age are not universally accepted by the archaeological community.

Finally, during Middle and Late Monongahela times, villages were situated on ridges dividing major drainage basins. This allowed access to a variety of resources. It also allowed a village to control access to these resources. Regular conflict with outside groups or other Monongahela villages seems to have been a characteristic of this time. Slash-and-burn farmers frequently compete for land because they are constantly changing their fields. In the hilly environment of western Pennsylvania, competition for other resources may also have been a factor in the conflicts between groups.

The settlement pattern in the Middle and Upper Allegheny basin is not as well known. The Fishbasket Complex and the related sites are all on floodplains and near fords in the adjacent rivers that connected major trails. It is assumed that the villages followed a similar pattern of people moving out to small camps in the summer and returning for the fall harvest.

Summer

The Monongahela settlement pattern focused on a centralized agricultural village. The villages frequently contained over a hundred individuals, although people spent much of their time away from the village involved in other activities. They practiced slash-and-burn agriculture and were frequently clearing

Fall

Spring

new fields. Small, temporary hunting and fishing camps were established at a variety of locations within the territory of the village. Warfare with other villages was probably common and males were frequently absent from the village.

Winter

People Living in Groups: Social Organization and Belief Systems

The Monongahela people lived in small circular houses, suggesting they were occupied by nuclear families of five to seven people. The post mold patterns of some Early and Middle Monongahela houses are outsloping with a large center post, indicating that the walls were outsloping, probably with a steeply pitched roof and prominent overhanging eaves. This pattern is similar to classic Early Adena houses in Ohio and may have had a wattle-and-daub (clay over woven thatch) finish. Not all houses were constructed this way, however. Many were dome-shaped with a bark covering.

The houses were arranged in a semicircle or circle around a central plaza. Closely related families may have lived in adjacent houses. The large villages seemed to be planned. The central plaza was devoid of artifacts and was probably swept clean on a regular basis. Some villages contain a hearth in the center of the plaza that played a role in a variety of social and ceremonial activities. A distinctive structure type is the post-enclosed feature. This is a roofed, semisubterranean, teardrop-shaped structure about 3 feet wide and 6 feet long. Historically, these first appear during the Drew phase as freestanding structures, but later, during the Campbell Farm phase, they are freestanding or attached to houses. In a plan view these structures appear like petals on a flower. Some houses have two petals or more. Their function is unclear. They may have been used for storage or for processing foods like a smokehouse. These become most common during Late Monongahela times and the Little Ice Age, when resources may have been less predictable.

Monongahela villages were surrounded by a wooden stockade, suggesting that there may have been feuding among villages. At several villages, broken and burned human bone and complete skeletons have been found with embedded arrowpoints. This certainly documents some level of violence. The stockades frequently had small posts, however, and do not seem to be a significant deterrent in keeping enemies out. Some archaeologists believe these were simply a mechanism to keep animals out of the village.

Villages range in size from five to eighty-five houses, encompassing about 7 acres, with more than 500 residents. By 1450 AD, some villages consisted of multiple house rings. By 1500 AD, one or more of the houses

A reconstructed Monongahela village illustrating the structures attached to the houses.

contained multiple semisubterranean attachments that are known as "petal houses." Archaeologists have mapped and analyzed these structures in detail, but their specific function continues to be debated. Some archaeologists believe that houses with one or two petals represent resources controlled by single families. The move to multiple petal houses represents the shift to communal control of resources (although the specific resource is unknown). Another theory is that the centrally located petal houses correspond to the growth of the fur trade with the Europeans and these structures were somehow used to store or process furs. These houses were also probably used for council and ceremonial meetings.

Monongahela village sites are common in the Monongahela basin and the Somerset Plateau and seem to represent the highest population densities for prehistoric Pennsylvania. Many of these sites were occupied at least twice. This complicates the equation for calculating population numbers. Archaeologists have speculated on the reasons for the multiple occupations. For one, people had no chemical fertilizers and they needed to move their villages every few years as the soil became depleted. Western Pennsylvania is very hilly and there is not a lot of land that is flat and associated with a good water source. This type of farming meant that good village locations were hard to find and therefore were reused as soon as the soil fertility returned. It seems to have been a common practice to reoccupy sites that had been previously cleared and where the trees had not grown very large.

Another explanation for the frequent reoccupation is that the earlier occupation is usually small and may represent the group who was sent to prepare the new village. This group may have lived in the new location, clearing the fields, cutting saplings for the new houses, and planting the first crops.

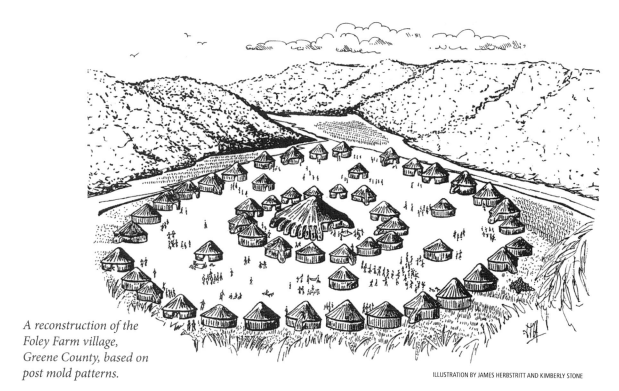

A reconstruction of the Foley Farm village, Greene County, based on post mold patterns.

ILLUSTRATION BY JAMES HERBSTRITT AND KIMBERLY STONE

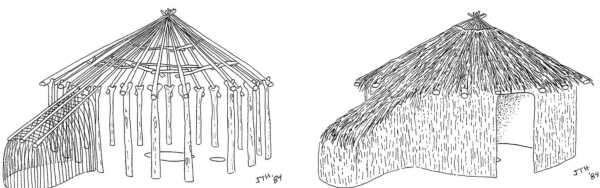

A reconstruction of the standard Foley Farm family dwelling with a single appendage that probably served as a storage structure.

ILLUSTRATION BY JAMES HERBSTRITT

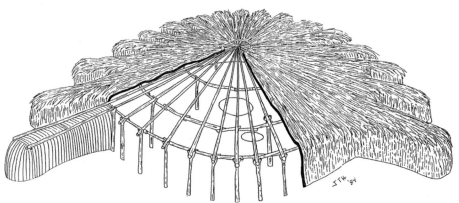

ILLUSTRATION BY JAMES HERBSTRITT

A reconstruction of the Foley Farm petal structure based on the actual post mold pattern.

During early Monongahela times, individual adult burials were arranged in a flexed position. Bodies were placed in shallow graves between the ring of houses and the stockade. Sometimes large flat rocks lined and capped the grave, forming a cryptlike enclosure. Grave goods are not common but included shells, bone awls, beads, and pottery. Child burials are found inside the houses and frequently under the hearths. A single flat rock is frequently laid on top of them. It is speculated that children were buried in houses so that they could be reborn to females within the household. Burial practices changed, however, during Late Monongahela times and adult burials are absent. Although only found at four sites, groups of adults numbering from four to twenty-four individuals have been found buried in houses. The houses were slightly larger than the average house within the village and some archaeologists call these "charnel houses." This practice is common in groups that traced their heritage through their male ancestors, indicating the Monongahela may have practiced a patrilineal social organization. This concept, however, is not accepted by most archaeologists.

The Monongahela were dispersed by 1635 AD and much of the region was unoccupied at the time of European contact. The demise of the Monongahela is somewhat of a mystery. Glass beads are found at the latest villages, so the Monongahela culture was in contact with Europeans but probably only through Native American middlemen. We have no written accounts of Europeans ever meeting these people, and there is no direct evidence of catastrophic warfare among Monongahela villages. As elsewhere in the New World, European diseases likely decimated these people prior to their ever meeting the Europeans. Those that survived took up residency with other tribes.

Stockaded villages with small, round houses arranged in a circular pattern are also a characteristic of the Fishbasket complex. This archaeological complex is found in the Middle Allegheny Valley and was identified by Kenneth Burkett. He and a group of volunteers meticulously excavated several villages in close proximity to one another. Based on pottery designs and a few other characteristics these people are different from the Monongahela culture but the relationship between the two is unclear. The Fishbasket culture used freestanding, post-enclosed storage structures but not petal houses. Large storage pits nearly 4 feet in diameter and 3 feet deep were concentrated along the edges of the plaza. The Fishbasket North Locus 1 site had eighteen of these and some were lined with a clay plaster and included large

flat stones on the bottom that served as a basement pavement. It is believed that these were communal storage pits shared by the entire community.

The Fishbasket complex also seemed to use the plaza area for community activities. Two of the sites had a large circular house situated on the edge of the plaza (not aligned with the domestic ring of houses) without a central hearth or storage features characteristic of the other houses. Adjacent to the structure was a large post, 15 inches in diameter, surrounded by small pits. Many of these contained entire pots. This is a relatively unique feature and it is believed that these were all part of a community ceremony.

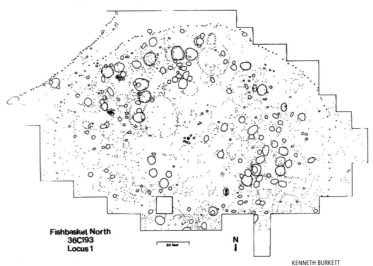

Fishbasket North
36Cl93
Locus 1

N

KENNETH BURKETT

The post mold pattern at the Fishbasket North Locus 1 site, illustrating the stockade, ring of houses, storage pits, and the open plaza. The houses have been rebuilt several times and therefore the post mold patterns are not always clearly visible.

KENNETH BURKETT

A freestanding, post-enclosed structure during excavation. This common storage structure found in villages from this period is semi-subterranean in construction but its aboveground shape is unclear.

180

Late Prehistoric Sites
of Pennsylvania

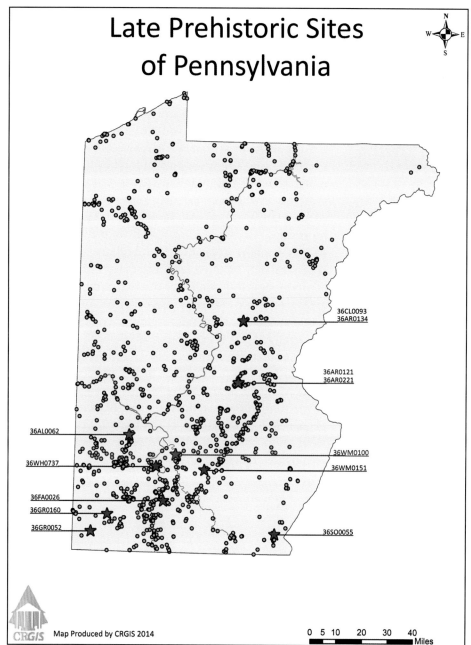

Map illustrating the distribution of sites in the Late Prehistoric period.

Map Produced by CRGIS 2014

0 5 10   20   30   40
Miles

seven Monongahela village sites were investigated, in addition to fourteen hamlets and campsites. One of the larger and most significant excavations was the Gnagey No. 3 site (36So55). The site consisted of two villages at the same location. The earlier had five houses with central hearths in a circular pattern around a central plaza. The second village had five houses, along with a large number of cooking hearths and roasting pits. A stockade surrounded both villages. This work was important in gathering data on subsistence and settlement patterns. The excavators were able to document how the same sites were used several times, sometimes as hamlets and sometimes as large villages.

Late Prehistoric Research in the Upper Ohio Drainage Basin

Over 870 sites dating to the Late Prehistoric period have been recorded in the Upper Ohio drainage basin. This is more than any other period in prehistory and represents the highest site density of all three drainage basins. We assume that human population has been constantly increasing, so the increase is not surprising. The excavated sites include many large villages, along with a few smaller hamlets and special-purpose camps.

In the 1990s, the Meyersdale Bypass Project, conducted by the Pennsylvania Department of Transportation, excavated a large number of Monongahela sites along the Casselman River. In this river basin alone,

Excavations at the Mon City site (36Wh737) indicated the specific contribution of wild plant foods to the agricultural produce. Four types of animals provided most of the meat: deer, wild turkey, turtles, and fish. In addition, burned bones of many smaller animals, such as squirrel, rodents, and snake, have been found.

The first sites to clearly demonstrate the appearance of a central petal house were the Throckmorton (36Gr160) and the Foley Farm (36Gr52) sites in Greene County. These date to 1550 AD and each has a central structure with numerous semisubterranean attachments. At least three other petal houses have been partially excavated.

The Sony site (36Wm151) is the largest excavated Monongahela site. The stockade enclosed more than 7 acres. It contained at least fifty-eight houses in two

181

Excavation of the Foley Farm central petal house, Greene County.

concentric rings. The inner circle clustered around two petal houses. This site also contained a charnel house with at least twenty-four burials. This was an exceptionally large village and probably represents the merging of several villages. They may have joined together to exploit the resources of the adjacent Jacob's Swamp or for protection.

The Consol site (36Wm100) was excavated by the Westmoreland County Archaeological Society of the Society for Pennsylvania Archaeology. The more-than-ten-year project was directed by Robert Oshnock. He made sure that all of the artifacts were processed on an annual basis along with producing a detailed report documenting the chapter's efforts. Oshnock is another outstanding example of a nonprofessional archaeologist doing a professional-level job. The following description of the site is a good example of Monongahela villages and was written by Oshnock.

The Consol site is located on high hilltop saddle 1.2 miles from the Youghiogheny River. It is a multicomponent site with both an early Drew phase Monongahela village component and a later Middle Monongahela village component. Both components are encircled by stockades that overlap each other by approximately 33 to 66 feet. The Early Monongahela component is the smaller of the two occupations and measures 138 x 164 feet in size. It is surrounded by a single stockade and contains eleven round houses that are arranged just inside the stockade wall. This village dates to the thirteenth century or approximately 1200 to 1250 AD. Features such as hearths and storage or processing pits associated with this occupation extend to the south and west, outside the stockade. A small plaza occupies the center of the Early Monongahela village and this was likely used as a communal activity area by the villagers.

Consol Site
36Wm100

Westmoreland County
Sewickley Twp.

Map of the Consol site villages. The early Drew phase Monongahela village is on the right and the Middle Monongahela village is on the left.

ROBERT OSHNOCK

The Middle Monongahela village is the larger of the two. It is generally oval in shape, measuring 253 x 368 feet in size. There are two concentric stockades surrounding the village. These stockade lines are a consistent 10 to 13 feet apart and encircle thirty-five round houses. Evidence has been found indicating three partial smaller and likely earlier stockade lines inside this larger village. The houses are arranged in an oval-shaped pattern. A 98-to-115-foot-diameter plaza occupies the center of the village and it appears to be devoid of features or evidence of any other type of activities.

Based on radiometric dating, this village was occupied sometime during the fifteenth century from approximately 1400 to 1440 AD. The purpose of the double stockade erected around this village, compared to the single stockade surrounding the earlier village, is likely related to climate change. The radiocarbon dates reported from the Middle Monongahela village correspond with the onset of the Little Ice Age. During this climatic episode, summer temperatures were slightly cooler than present thereby reducing crop yields. Following this scenario, maize and other cultigens would not have been able to produce sufficient yields to allow the villagers to survive over the starvation months of January through March. Therefore, one solution would have been the construction of a double stockade to protect stored food supplies from outside raiding parties who also suffered from dwindling winter stores.

The entrance to the Middle Monongahela village consisted of a zigzag passageway through the double stockade line. Bastion towers were situated on both sides of the entrance. These towers may have served as guard posts or as sentinel platforms and were used during times when the village was under siege. A good flowing spring is located 265 feet due south of this entrance. Even today, it flows copiously during summer droughts. A lesser-quality spring is located north of the village but is not associated with an entranceway. These springs were probably one of the principal reasons that the Early Monongahela and Middle Monongahela settlements were built at this location.

The Late Woodland Period in the Susquehanna and Delaware Drainage Basins

Definition

The Late Woodland period in the Susquehanna and Delaware drainage basins begins approximately 1000 years ago. The Middle Woodland emphasis on collecting seed plants culminates in gardening and eventually farming. It is a period of relatively rapid economic and social changes. Technologically, it is defined by well-made pottery, decorated with incised lines on the rim and neck. The bow and arrow replaces spears, and triangular points become very common on archaeological sites of this period. Initially, farming is conducted while living in small hamlets. In the Susquehanna basin, these occupations get larger and eventually stockaded villages form. Slash-and-burn farming becomes the main subsistence pattern in the Susquehanna basin, but a variety of wild animals and plants were also exploited. It was during this time that a change from egalitarian bands to an egalitarian tribal social organization took place. In the Delaware basin, hamlets continued to be used. Gardening, rather than slash-and-burn farming, may have been more common. There is some debate whether these groups developed into a tribal social organization.

In the Susquehanna basin, Clemson Island is the first Late Woodland culture and this is followed by the Shenks Ferry culture. Clemson Island dates between 700 and 1200 years ago and Shenks Ferry dates between 550 and 800 years ago. These seem to represent two different cultures, although their relationship is not clear. Clemson Island seems to be related to cultures to the north. Both seem to emerge from local Middle Woodland people who were living in small groups and growing a variety of seed plants, while continuing to collect a wide variety of animal and plant foods. In the Delaware basin, a similar process was probably taking place but the picture is less clear. The main pottery styles are Owasco, Overpeck, and Chance. It is not known whether these represent separate cultures or tribes. It is believed that Minguannan, Munsee, and Lenape pottery types are later in time and that they were the ancestors of the historic Lenape (Delaware) Indians. The Late Woodland period ends in these river basins about 1550 AD with European contact and the influx of European trade goods, diseases, and conflict.

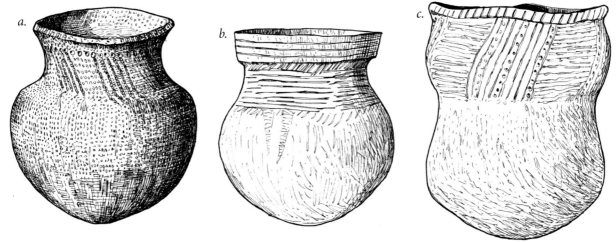

The Late Woodland period in the Susquehanna Valley is characterized by a variety of pottery types and designs: a. Clemson Island pottery; b. Early Shenks Ferry pottery (Shenks Ferry Incised); c. Late Shenks Ferry pottery (Funk Incised).

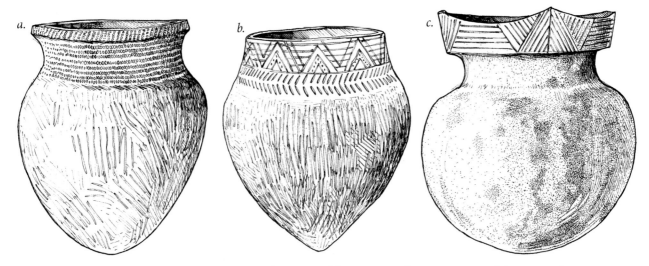

The Late Woodland period in the Delaware Valley is characterized by a variety of pottery types and designs: a. Owasco pottery; b. Overpeck pottery; c. Chance pottery.

An example of Overpeck pottery. This style is thought to represent the Delaware tribe.

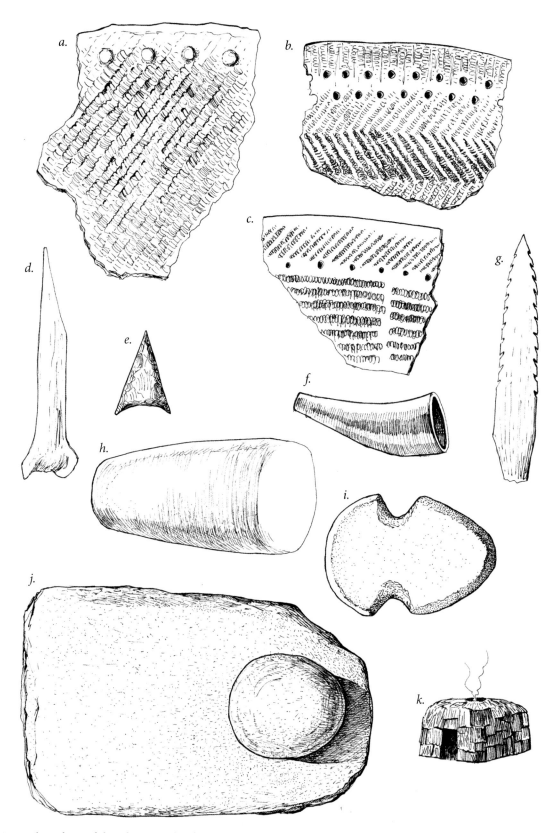

Typical artifacts of the Clemson Island phase: a.–c. Clemson Island punctate pottery; d. bone awl used in sewing; e. triangular projectile point used on an arrow; f. smoking pipe; g. harpoon tip used on a spear; h. polished celt used in woodworking or the skinning of animals; i. chipped net sinker; j. grinding stone on grinding slab; k. bark-covered semirectangular house.

Making and Using Tools: Typical Artifacts and Technology

Well-made pottery and triangular-shaped arrow-points are the hallmarks of the Late Woodland period. Pottery technology during this time was improving. Clemson Island pottery, named after the Clemson Island site (36Da1), is decorated with punctates, small round holes made with a hollow bone or reed, and cordmarked decorations in linear patterns on the rim. Later decorations were characterized by incised line patterns around the rim and neck. The lines formed a series of squares, rectangles, and triangles that became more elaborate over time. Clay smoking pipes were common. They were largely undecorated, but the bowl of some pipes is in the form of an animal. The bow and arrow replaced the atlatl, and the arrowpoint tips are all triangular in form. There is some evidence that the stone tips became smaller with time, but otherwise there is little variation in their shape throughout the region. Triangular "arrowheads" are very common on sites from this period. A variety of grinding stones, some very large, are used for processing corn and other plant foods. Late Woodland base camps were occupied for years at a time and contain a variety of cooking, storage, and processing/trash features. These features help to preserve organic artifacts. Bone and antler artifacts are common and include bone hide-

THE STATE MUSEUM OF PENNSYLVANIA/PHOTO BY DON GILES

Examples of Clemson Island punctuate pottery (the small holes are called punctuates).

scraping tools, bone awls for piercing hides to make clothes, barbed harpoons for hunting and fishing, and elk scapula hoes for farming. There are also a wide variety of bone beads and pendants, bear-claw and beartooth necklaces, shell beads, and a variety of carved (stone) animal effigy pipes.

Building a Wikiwah   Robert Winters

To build a wigwam or, more properly in the Shawnee language, a wikiwah, you need a supply of straight, limber saplings 1 to 3 inches in diameter and as long as possible. Hardwood saplings from second-growth forests or American river cane bamboo will work well. Level ground should be selected for placement of the wikiwah. The ground should be cleared of brush, weeds, and rocks, and the sod should be removed. A circle up to 18 feet should be scribed on the cleared, level ground by placing a pin in the center and using a sharpened stake with a string 6 to 9 feet long attached to the center pin to scribe the circle. This will be the boundary of the structure.

Next, select eight of the longest, heaviest saplings to be used as the main support poles. Using the rising sun

Robert Winters   PHOTO BY JUDY HAWTHORN

as a starting point, mark the four cardinal directions on the scribed circle. Cut a straight stick 16 to 18 inches in length. At each of the four cardinal points lay the story stick with the cardinal point at the middle of the stick. At the ends of the stick at each point, mark east, north, west, and south. Make a few stout stakes of dry wood about 12 inches in length and sharpen the ends. At the eight marks of the story stick pound a stake into the ground at least 8 to 10 inches in depth. Wiggle the stake and withdraw it. The resulting holes will be filled with the eight long sapling poles.

Sharpen the thicker ends of these poles and jab them into the eight holes. Bend the north/south set of poles first into a dome and lash them together with rope or cord using the story stick to maintain the proper width between the two poles. The height should be 8 feet. Next do the same with the east/west set of poles. Traditionally the east will serve as the entrance to the wikiwah.

Next, take the pounding stakes and make holes for additional upright poles around the scribed circle. These should be about a meter apart and have an opposite on the reverse arc of the circle. These will be added to the main supports for strength. Lash them in place, being careful to leave an open square or space about 18 inches in the top of the wikiwah dome. This is the smoke hole. Now the upright framework is finished.

Next, lash smaller, more limber poles to the upright frame. These are the horizontal stiffeners and will be circular, running around the framework to again add strength to the structure. There are usually three circles, the first commencing about 18 inches up from ground level and stopping on either side of the east doorway. The next will be 18 inches higher and go all the way around the outside over the east-facing entrance, thereby forming the upper limit of the door. A wikiwah is always entered in a stooped posture unless the individual is a juvenile.

Now the covering will be applied. Bark sheets, leather hides, bundles of long grass or weeds, and branches all can be used. Sheets of beechwood, tulip poplar, and smooth-bark hickory were preferred. Bunch grass, poor grass, sage grass, or orchard grass gathered into bundles and applied like shingles also make good coverings. Leather hides are terrific. For the modern wikiwah, canvas is the best bet.

If using bark or grass bundles, start at the ground level and lash the sheets or bundles to the first circular stiffener. Attach the next series of sheets or bundles to the second circular stiffener. Be sure to overlap them with the first series by at least one-third of the length (4 to 6 inches). Repeat this sequence for the next series until all the framework is covered except the smoke hole and the door. The lashing of the upper series can be done from the inside.

If using leather or canvas covering, peg down one side at the perimeter of the structure and then draw the covering tightly across the structure and peg down the other side. Repeat this process until the entire structure is covered, except the smoke hole and east door. The door will require a separate movable covering of heavy material. A hide fur, heavy blanket, or large plank is optimal.

A fire pit should be constructed or dug at the location of the center pin, directly under the smoke hole. If all needed materials are on hand at the beginning of construction a 19-foot-diameter wikiwah 8 feet high will take two people four hours to erect.

ILLUSTRATION BY JOHN KUCERA, FROM THE ARCHAEOLOGY EXHIBIT AT THE STATE MUSEUM OF PENNSYLVANIA

What People Ate: Subsistence

In the Susquehanna basin, people evolved from small-scale gardening to slash-and-burn farming of corn, beans, and squash. Population levels were high and a more intensive form of gathering food was necessary to support these populations. In the Delaware basin, a less intensive form of farming was practiced, but corn, beans and squash were the main crops. In both areas a variety of mammals, migratory birds, fish, shellfish, and wild plants were also exploited.

Where People Lived: Settlement Patterns

Clemson Island habitation sites usually contain one or two semirectangular houses of a size that would hold a small extended family. These sites are called homesteads and were probably shared by close relatives such as two sisters or two brothers. They are usually associated with large cylindrical storage pits. It is assumed they were storing corn or sunflowers, although the evidence is problematic. These sites were usually not stockaded, and they illustrate how the population was dispersed into widely spaced homesteads, rather than the concentrated villages of the Monongahela. Clemson Island homesteads stretch from Lock Haven (36Cn175) on the West Branch Susquehanna River to Wilkes Barre (36Lu39) on the North Branch Susquehanna River to Clarks Ferry (36Da126) on the Susquehanna River and all along the Juniata River. In addition to homestead sites, there are also many small sites in upland settings that represent short-term camps for fishing, hunting, or plant food gathering activities.

Clemson Island families exploited their environment in a similar fashion as Hopewell but without the extensive trade, high-status individuals, and ceremonial activities. The homestead was the location of large gardens and served as a base of operations for the gathering of a variety of wild animal and plant foods. The settlement pattern involved food preparation and processing activities at the homestead and gathering activities at a variety of ecological settings within a ten- to twenty-mile radius. During the spring, corn, squash, and perhaps chenopodium, knotweed, and little barley were planted at the homestead. There are a variety of other plant foods that would have been available at this time and fishing was also important. Families from several homesteads may have joined together for the spring fish migration.

In the summer, the elderly and infants probably stayed at the homestead while everyone else exploited a variety of resources scattered along the rivers and around wetlands. In the fall, the homestead was a very busy place of harvesting, processing, and crop storing. In the winter, the families subsisted on the stored food with periodic hunting trips into the uplands.

Clemson Island people buried their dead in burial mounds. The mounds are usually located along major rivers but not always. It does not seem that they were associated with individual hamlets but rather served hamlets within a large region of 10 to 20 miles in diameter. The excavated mound sites contain large numbers of individuals and seemingly represent all adults. The deceased may have been added to the mound soon after death or annually. Ceremonies were likely conducted in the fall after the harvest. This may have been a time when all the families from the homesteads within 10 to 20 miles of a mound joined together for a large burial ceremony. This also would have been an opportunity for trading news, exchanging gifts, and meeting potential marriage partners.

Beginning approximately 800 years ago, Shenks Ferry pottery appears in the Susquehanna basin. Although few sites have been excavated, the sites appear to consist of homesteads and villages. Family homesteads join into hamlets of five or fewer houses and by 600 years ago, some of these were surrounded by stockades. By 1500 AD, the Shenks Ferry people were living in villages surrounded by a wooden stockade, covering 4 acres and including as many as sixty nuclear family–sized houses. Fields planted with corn, beans, and squash surrounded the villages. Villages were moved approximately every decade as the soils were depleted of nutrients. The settlement pattern for Shenks Ferry was relatively simple. The village primarily served as a place to grow crops and as a base of operations from which work groups went out to exploit a variety of resources. As with the Monongahela villages, during the spring and fall, the villagers would have been very busy preparing the fields and harvesting the crops. Late fall would have been a time for large ceremonies. In the winter, hunting parties left the village and in the summer many people were out of the village collecting a wide variety of seeds, nuts, roots, and berries.

Habitation sites in the Delaware basin are different from those in the Susquehanna basin. Here the pattern mainly involves small, seasonal camps and a base camp for farming. Corn, beans, and squash have been identi-

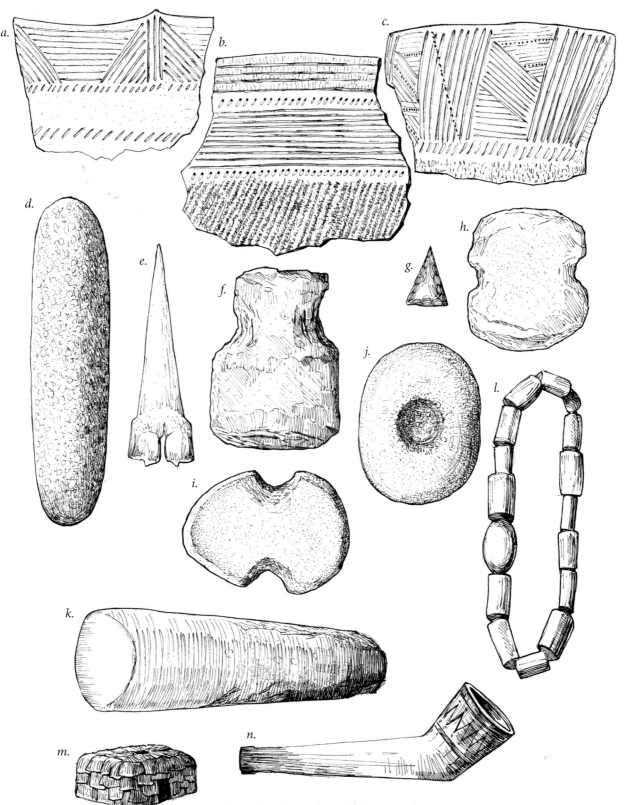

Typical artifacts of the Shenks Ferry phase: a. Lancaster Incised pottery; b. Shenks Ferry Incised pottery; c. Funk Incised pottery; d. stone pestle for grinding seeds, nuts, and corn; e. bone awl for sewing; f. stone hoe; g. triangular stone arrowpoint; h. chipped net sinker; i. notched net sinker; j. pitted stone used for grinding seeds and nuts; k. polished stone celt for woodworking or skinning hides; l. bone bead necklace; m. bark-covered semirectangular house; n. decorated smoking pipe.

The major Shenks Ferry pottery types, from left to right: Early Shenks Ferry (Shenks Ferry Incised), Middle Shenks Ferry (Lancaster Incised), and Late Shenks Ferry (Funk Incised).

fied on many sites, so it is clear that these crops were being cultivated. Very few Late Woodland houses have been excavated, however, and the nature of the farming base camp or homestead is unclear. Late-summer and early-fall hunting-and-gathering camps have been identified on floodplains. These sites frequently include large refuse pits (some 7 feet deep) containing charred seeds from domesticated plants, freshwater mollusk shells, and deer bones. Winter camps are thought to have been located in sheltered areas off of the floodplain. The settlement pattern is poorly understood but seems to have involved small family groups that maintained gardens but moved to exploit a variety of resources mainly on the floodplain.

Storage or processing pit commonly found on Late Woodland sites. Although frequently termed "trash pits" by archaeologists, these were not originally dug to dispose of trash but they were frequently back-filled with trash and dirt.

People Living in Groups: Social Organization and Belief Systems

The social, political, and religious interpretation of Clemson Island people is made more interesting by the fact that they constructed burial mounds. Less than half a dozen have been located and most are situated on the floodplains of the Susquehanna and Juniata Rivers. The Hopewell burial mounds of the Middle Woodland period in the Ohio basin are associated with elaborate trade items suggesting individuals of high status. The mounds of the Clemson Island culture are very different. They contain large numbers of individuals, seemingly a large sample of the adult population and few, if any, grave goods. This was an egalitarian tribal society and the burial mound was simply the place where the dead were buried. Although the population appears to have been dispersed, people must have joined into larger groups to bury their dead and to construct and maintain the mounds. They must have had a social organization and communication system that allowed for regular gatherings, although the mechanisms for this are still invisible in the archaeological record. These gatherings, however, may have been used to organize the clearing of fields or the exploitation of annual fish migrations. Admittedly, there is no archaeological evidence for either of these activities, but these are the kinds of things that have been observed with modern farming societies.

There is a better understanding of later Shenks Ferry culture and social organization. Houses in these villages were organized around a central plaza, sometimes in two concentric rings. As with Monongahela villages, the plaza contains few artifacts and was probably swept

An Alternative View of Late Woodland Villages   Roger Moeller

Not all archaeologists interpret the so-called Late Woodland villages as large-scale farming sites inhabited by hundreds of year-round residents. The classic interpretation of these villages is that they were central home bases for farmers who also hunted and fished in the surrounding area. Seasonal and special-resource camps extend to the boundaries of the territory commonly thought to be about 20 miles in diameter. Each camp is no more than a 10-mile, or a half-day, walk from the home base. The home base was occupied by the women, children, and seniors who tended the fields, maintained the households, and kept the home fires burning. The stronger, younger people occupied short-term, seasonal, special-purpose satellite camps and sent the fruits of their labors to the home base.

What these depictions fail to show is that the inhabitants of the satellite camps were rarely back at the home base for very long. The home base need only have been fully occupied by all members of the band when they returned for seasonal festivals. They were kept busy procuring, processing, and transporting the products from the satellite camps; moving to the next camp in the seasonal round; protecting themselves and the home base from potentially belligerent outsiders; and clearing land for horticulture.

Imagine a series of circles 20 miles in diameter spread across the length and breadth of Pennsylvania. At the center of each is the home base village. At the boundaries of each village are overlapping resource-rich areas being accessed (sometimes simultaneously) by people from different villages. As long as there is enough for everyone, there are no problems. The people will share and exchange ideas, ceramic and projectile point styles, food, and so on. These resources will return to the home village and to the next appropriate seasonal camp. In one year, the people from a single village could be sharing ideas and implements that originated 60 miles away. In ten years, the same styles could have traveled completely across the state. This is a more likely scenario than having one group settle at a series of villages spanning 600 miles in a decade. We must remember that we are looking at the movement of not one band per season, but of scores across the region simultaneously.

Despite the oft-heard mantra that Native Americans did not have the concept of land ownership, I still believe they had a strong belief in their right to use particular tracts

PHOTO BY JUDY MOELLER

Roger Moeller

through time. They had spent a lifetime learning the topography and timing of the seasonal resources. They likely returned to the same camps as long as the resources were still productive.

I see a decline in the yield of domesticated crops and a depletion of firewood as the primary reasons for abandoning the home-base village. A village has to control seven times the area needed to produce its annual supply of maize. Without replenishing the soil nutrients, the yield in three years is too low to support the village and is not worth the effort. Within twenty-one years, they will be back to the same tract that might have regained enough nutrients to be productive for two years. The problem is that the firewood will be depleted faster.

If the typical village lasted no more than twenty years and had to be moved no more than 20 miles, causing a shift in its catchment, and the Late Woodland period spanned a thousand years, then one village had to be moved fifty times and nearly 1000 miles. This is several times the width of Pennsylvania. In addition, we are talking scores of villages doing the same thing. Given the fact that not all tracts of land are appropriate for villages, then reoccupation of tracts once having villages is inevitable. As a purely practical matter, siting a new village no more than 10 miles from the previous one allows scavenging wood used in house and stockade construction for another use, if only as firewood.

clean. Sometimes the plaza contained a large circular structure that was likely used for community activities and ceremonies. Unlike the central houses of the Monongahela, there is little evidence of food processing or storage with these structures. Burials were scattered throughout the village, although often situated between the outer ring of houses and the stockade. The stockades suggest that there may have been feuding between villages, but villages were also probably being threatened by outsiders to the region. Based on the house size and our knowledge of small farming cultures in South America and the Pacific Islands, Shenks Ferry families may have been patrilineal in their social organization.

Although farming was practiced in the Delaware basin, it appears to have been less important than hunting and gathering. The use of domesticated crops appears to have begun relatively late in this region and to have had little effect on the native lifestyle. The reason for the late adoption of horticulture is not clear, but it is notable that farming requires more effort than gathering wild foods. Because wild plant foods were abundant relative to population density, there may have been little reason to make the change to intensive farming.

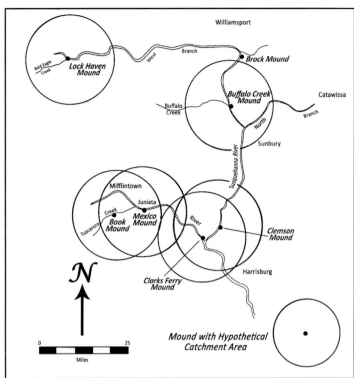

FROM *PHASE III DATA RECOVERY, SHERMANS CREEK SITE (36PE2), PERRY COUNTY, PENNSYLVANIA* 1995 BY R. M. STEWART

Map of major Clemson Island sites, highlighting the burial mounds. The mounds probably served the villages that were within a ten-to-fifteen-mile radius.

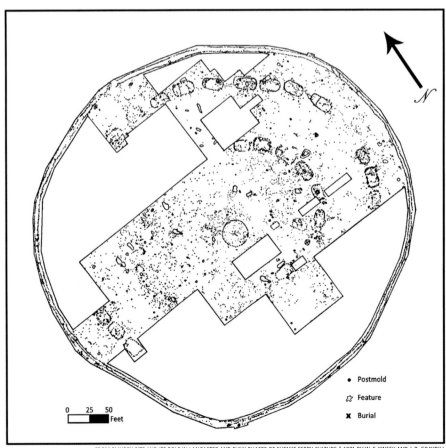

• Postmold
✿ Feature
✕ Burial

FROM "MURRY SITE AND ITS ROLE IN LANCASTER AND FUNK PHASES OF SHENKS FERRY CULTURE." 1971 BY W. F. KINSEY AND J. R. GRAYBILL

This is an interesting adaptive strategy compared to the strategy used by contemporary families in the Susquehanna and Upper Ohio basins. They were eating similar foods but they did not live in villages and they did not seem to have a unifying factor such as trade, burial ceremonialism, or even warfare with outside groups.

The Late Woodland complexes of the Delaware basin are identified by pottery styles termed Munsee, Minguannan, and Overpeck. We assume they represent different bands of the Lenape tribe. The Munsee style exhibits characteristics similar to those of Late Woodland populations in

Post mold and feature pattern at the Murry site. Shenks Ferry villages were planned and some consisted of two concentric rings of round houses with a central house for public or ceremonial use.

what is now eastern New York, while the Minguannan style is more similar to styles in Maryland. Based on historical accounts, the Lenape were matrilineal, and their houses were occupied by a group of sisters, female cousins, and their families. Although they had a social organization similar to the Iroquois, they spoke an Algonquian dialect. They supposedly lived in different house types depending on the season. Multifamily longhouses, occupied during the winter, were over 100 feet long. Groups were smaller and more mobile in the summer, often living in small houses near agricultural fields. However, this description is based on historic accounts and not on archaeology, where the evidence for any house type is very rare for the region.

The Late Woodland period is a time of social and economic change. In central and western Pennsylvania, Native Americans became dependent on agriculture and were more settled. They first moved into scattered homesteads, then larger collections of houses, and finally stockaded villages. Warfare or feuding between villages seems to be widespread by 1500 AD. In the Delaware Valley, agriculture is less intensive, and long-term settlements are less common. With the arrival of Europeans and a competition for their goods, warfare and disease began the destruction of Native American populations. Each of the tribes in Pennsylvania seems to have had a different experience with the Europeans, but in the end, their cultures were essentially destroyed.

Late Woodland Research in the Susquehanna and Delaware Drainage Basins

There are over 1,563 sites recorded for the Late Woodland period in the Susquehanna and Delaware basins in Pennsylvania. This is a greater density of sites than any other time in prehistory. We assume that human population was constantly increasing, so the large number of sites is not surprising. The pottery and triangular arrowheads from this time are very distinctive, which makes this period easy to identify in the archaeological record. The one problem in using these artifacts is that triangular projectile points were also made during the Archaic period; therefore, when using the PASS file database, it should be remembered that Late Woodland sites recorded on the basis of triangular arrowpoints may be incorrectly classified for this period.

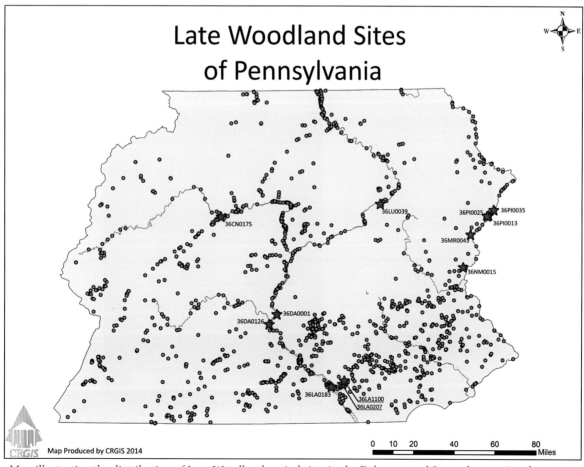

Map illustrating the distribution of Late Woodland period sites in the Delaware and Susquehanna river basins.

193

Late Woodland Research in the Delaware River Basin

In all, 497 Late Woodland period sites are recorded in the Delaware drainage basin. Although most are located along the Delaware River, there is an increase in the number of sites in the uplands and along streams such as the Lackawaxen, Lehigh, and Schuylkill Rivers. These sites likely represent seasonal camps related to hamlets on the main river.

The most extensive archaeological fieldwork took place in the upper Delaware basin in Pike and Monroe Counties. Late Woodland sites in this region are famous for their unusually large numbers of pit features, mainly used for food processing, storage, and trash disposal. As early as 1972, it was estimated that over three thousand pits had been excavated in the region. At the Kutay site (36Pi25), numerous pits over 4 feet deep were found full of freshwater mussel shells. Interestingly, stone mussel shell openers were frequently found with these features. Obviously, this food became more important during the Late Woodland period. Pit features in the upper Delaware are also noted for their lack of artifacts, therefore their functions cannot always be determined. Many were likely used for short-term food storage or food processing, and their contents were removed prior to the peoples' departure to a winter camp.

At the Faucett site (36Pa13a), also located in Pike County, a hair comb carved from deer antler was found. It was decorated with an oval human face. The comb was found with two rims of a pottery style from the New York coastal plain, indicating that trade was taking place between the two regions.

The Padula site (36Nm15), located along the Delaware River, Northampton County, produced tools specifically for hunting, as well as tools with evidence of use for butchering, hide preparation, and cutting and sawing of bone. The function of these tools was determined through a microscopic analysis of the scratches and polishing that occurs on stone tools when they are used. The tools were found around a hearth. The site was interpreted as a camp for hunting parties and was probably a common type of site in the Delaware drainage. Although small, these types of special-function sites complete the story of the Late Woodland adaptation in the Delaware drainage basin.

While there is little information on house types in the region, circular houses have been found in association with pottery characteristic of the early part of the Late Woodland period. A later Late Woodland occupation at the Shawnee-Minisink site (36Mr43) revealed evidence of a longhouse that was likely occupied by related family

PHOTO COURTESY OF W. FRED KINSEY

Deep processing/storage pits excavated at the Kutay site (36Pi25).

PHOTO COURTESY OF W. FRED KINSEY

Cross-section of processing/storage pit from the Kutay site (36Pi25).

PHOTO COURTESY OF W. FRED KINSEY

Mussel shell openers made of argillaceous shale found in the bottom of processing/storage pits at the Kutay site (36Pi25). They are well worn on the tip.

groups. Longhouses from this period also have been found at the Lee's Terrace site (36Pi35), Pike County, in the upper Delaware Valley and at sites on the New Jersey side of the Delaware River. These seem to represent individual houses and not villages. They probably represent the winter house of the Delaware tribe.

Late Woodland Research in the Susquehanna Drainage Basin

Approximately 1,139 Late Woodland period archaeological sites have been identified in the Susquehanna basin. Late Woodland cultural succession is better known in the lower Susquehanna basin than practically anywhere else in the state. Clemson Island sites are probably the most common and widespread Late Woodland type of the period. Sites from this time have been excavated from Lock Haven to Clarks Ferry.

The subsequent Shenks Ferry culture is also common. Many of these sites have been tested and large portions of three large villages have been excavated. One of the earliest excavations of a stockaded village was the Murry site (36La183), a 4-acre village along the Susquehanna River that dated to about 550 years ago. The excavations revealed evidence of fifty-two houses, indicating that the village population was

between three hundred and five hundred people. The houses were laid out in two concentric rings surrounding a large, central structure believed to be communal or ceremonial. There is little evidence for the rebuilding of houses, although at least one house was burned in place. In addition, there were not many features filled with artifacts and dietary remains. Although not the typical pattern of internment, a mass burial of sixteen or seventeen individuals was uncovered from that site. This may represent a catastrophic incident involving warfare or disease.

More recent excavations at the Slackwater site (36La207), located in the Conestoga River drainage near Millersville, Lancaster County, produced later radiocarbon dates, but a much less organized village plan. The Commonwealth's Archaeology Program excavated a Late Woodland village at the Quaker Hills Quarry site (36La1100) near Millersville between 2002 and 2007. This site is similar to the village plan at the Murry site. It is slightly larger than the Murry site and dates later in time to about 1525 AD. The Quaker Hills Quarry site is the largest Shenks Ferry village ever excavated. The excavation recovered large quantities of artifacts and dietary information, and the post mold pattern revealed many rebuilding episodes. It is believed this village was occupied for twenty years or more.

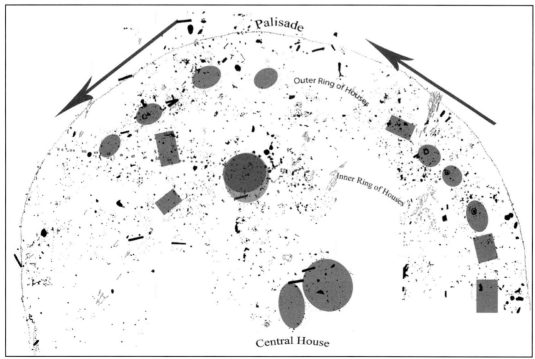

Post mold and feature pattern at the Quaker Hills Quarry site. The house ring and central structure are highlighted. The mass of post molds makes it difficult to define house patterns at this site. This is the result of a longer occupation and the frequent rebuilding of houses compared to the Murry site plan.

A Late Prehistoric Narrative

Time 600 years ago.

Place The Monongahela River Valley.

Climate The "Little Ice Age"—five degrees cooler and more rainfall than present.

Flora and fauna A mixed oak, hemlock, and chestnut forest similar to Pennsylvania at the time of Columbus.

Distinctive artifacts Triagular arrowpoints and well-made pottery.

My grandfather's name was the same as mine, Faymonset. I live with my two wives and three children—two girls and one boy. We are expecting another and I hope it is a boy.

We have lived in our land since the beginning of time. We can tell because there is evidence of old villages everywhere. Our land is an interesting mixture of cornfields, old cornfields grown up in weeds, old camps that are overgrown with saplings, floodplains where the trees are big but not full-grown, and uplands where the trees have never been cut. The overgrown fields and villages are great for hunting deer and turkeys. There are also well-worn paths that take us to our fields and other villages. There are wider paths that take us to the villages of other tribes or even to the ocean, far to the east. Traders use these paths and they bring us many different types of shells that we use as jewelry.

Our home is a village of 350 people on a narrow ridge above the Monongahela River. We are farmers and we grow most (75 percent) of our food. My wives work in the fields growing corn, beans, squash, and sunflowers. The rest comes from hunting, fishing, and collecting roots, nuts, seeds, and berries. From the spring until the fall, my wives are very busy planting, weeding, harvesting, and processing the plants for storage. Their main tools are a digging stick and a grinding stone. They also make very good pottery. We have pots of different sizes and shapes, depending on the need. There are storage pots, cooking pots, and serving bowls. They put designs along the rims that represent our clan.

When I was a teenager, I helped in the fields and around the village but now I hunt, fish, and talk with the men of the village. My main hunting tool is the bow and arrow, but I also use a spear, a knife, and a celt (a small polished stone axe). Our arrows have a painted design near the fletching that represents our clan. The stone point is small and triangular in shape. It does not need to be very large since it is shot from a bow. I am pretty good with my bow and I have shot many bears, elk, turkeys, deer, geese, and beavers. I even shot a catfish once, but we usually catch them with a net or a hook and line. We also use a small barbed harpoon for fishing from a dugout. Some men use a blowgun for hunting in the fields. Boys especially hunt birds and small animals while they are supposed to be guarding the fields.

Our village consists of two concentric rings of small, round houses surrounding a large open plaza. Our houses are about 17 feet in diameter and are built by forming a structure of posts and covering it with bark and branches. Inside each house are sleeping platforms, like bunk beds, because sleeping on the cold ground is very uncomfortable. There is a hearth in the center of our house with a small smoke hole in the roof. We all sleep together – usually my wives, myself, and our babies on one side of the fire and the older children on the other side of the fire. Fires are kept burning in the hearths inside the houses to add a little warmth, some light, and to keep out the rodents. Most of our food is stored in the house. Some is hung from the roof and some is stored in small attachments to our houses. These closet-like attachments are dug about 2 feet into the ground. We mound dirt over the outside of the attachment and the food is kept at a constant temperature. Since I have two wives, we have two storage closets. These are good in the summer because they keep the food fresh and they are good in the winter because they keep the food from freezing.

My house is next to my father's house, and my brother's house is on the other side of his. There are clusters of houses representing different families all around the village. There is a family on the opposite side of the plaza that just moved from another village. They had an argument with their neighbors and they moved here to live with the man's uncle to avoid trouble. They are members of the Turtle Clan, like us, so they are good people.

The plaza is used for ceremonies, holding feasts, dancing, and greeting visitors. There is a post in the middle of the plaza. The post holds our trophies. As our village has gotten larger, we have built a house in the middle to hold our important council meetings. The plaza is also used as a work area and as a play area for the children. So one day we can have a very solemn ceremony and the next day, children will be running and laughing.

We are constantly threatened by enemy tribes and the village is surrounded by a stockade or wall made from posts driven into the ground. The posts are several feet taller than a man and we weave branches between the posts so that only very small animals can crawl through. While the stockade could not protect us against a determined assault from our enemies, it serves as a first line of defense. It also serves to keep wild animals from foraging inside the village. Smaller camps for getting food and other resources are scattered around our territory. They are usually less than a day's walk from the main village, but in different directions. Nuts, deer, fish, bear, berries, roots, seeds, and many other foods from different seasons come into the main village. We also have camps where we collect stone for tools, reeds for baskets, and clay for pottery. Groups of men frequently go out hunting or fishing and are gone for many days. Young, unmarried men are frequently gone for weeks. Groups of women also go out collecting but usually only for a couple of days. Because we travel more, men eat more meat than women and children. Usually in the summer, the village is only half-occupied.

Our winters are cold and snowy. Most of the time is spent staying warm and collecting wood. We live off of our stored food. Sometimes men go out hunting and everyone is pleased when they bring back fresh meat. By the early spring, the people are anxious to get out of their houses. If we are lucky, at this time of the year, the river will be churning with fish and the sky will be black with passenger pigeons. There are many different ways to catch them, but the most productive is with nets and everyone joins in. As long as food is plentiful, it is a fun time. After this, the women and children begin the long, hard process of planting. Once the seeds are into the ground, they go back to the fields daily to remove the other plants trying to grow with the crops. Sometimes we eat the other plants if they have not grown too big and tough. Birds and deer are always trying to eat the seeds and young plants. The older children try to kill them for food. If they fail, at least they have scared them away from the gardens.

In the fall comes the harvest and we are all very busy. We worry a lot just before the harvest. What if the snow and cold comes too early? Will we have a good crop? Once we collect all the food, can we preserve enough to last the winter?

The beans and the sunflowers are the first to ripen. These are collected in baskets and then spread out on mats to dry. The beans are added to soups. The sunflowers are crushed for oil. It is very tasty poured over roasted corn. In the winter, the women rub it on their arms and legs to moisten their skin.

Harvesting the corn is the big job. The women and children spend days collecting it in baskets and bags. They pull back the husks to reveal the golden kernels. The husks are braided to make transporting the corn from the field easier. Our people prefer to dry the corn to make it hard and less likely to rot over the long winter. When the time comes, we can easily remove the dry kernels from the cob. The women grind the corn on stone slabs and cook it in soup and bread. The dry husks are used to line our moccasins. The cobs make a very flavorful smoke to preserve meat from animals killed in the winter. The squash is collected last. Some is cut up for soup. The larger gourds are allowed to dry and are used as containers or spoons.

If we are lucky, large quantities of hickory nuts, butternut, and black walnut are also processed. The crushed nuts are placed into ceramic pots filled with water. The boiling water makes the nutmeat and oil come to the surface, where it can be skimmed off. The nutshells sink to the bottom. The skimmed nutmeat and oil is stored in another pot. This is repeated time after time.

Fish caught in the river are split from the head nearly to the tail. They dry quickly on racks placed in the hot sun. We used to build large fires to dry them when we came here in the spring. Now there is not enough wood to do that. We had to change the time of year we come to this place. There are not as many fish this time of year, but we have so many more people to collect a greater variety of food to make up for the shortage of fish. Some years we also collect large quantities of freshwater mussels. They are not very nutritious but they are better than nothing.

Growing tobacco is a man's job and most men have a plant or two next to their houses. We each have special ways of taking care of our plants. Tobacco is a taboo for women and children and they are not allowed to touch these plants. We hang the leaves to dry in our communal house in the center of the village. Tobacco is smoked on special occasions, such as during ceremonies and when we have visitors. Sometimes, it is simply crushed between the fingers and allowed to blow into the wind as an offering to the spirits.

All the plants, mussels, and other foods are each processed in their own special way. We learned a long time ago that this is the most important time of year. If we do not store a lot of food now, we will not survive the winter. Harvesting the food is one chore, and processing it before it can spoil is a second chore, but we still have to protect it from animals, get it to the main camp for the winter, and store it properly. We can avoid so much of the natural decay with proper processing, but we must always be very careful.

The processing produces a large quantity of garbage. This attracts flies, bears, and raccoons. Flies cannot be avoided. They are everywhere, but they do not eat much. Bears and raccoons are a much bigger threat, because they can eat so much, so quickly. We are always anxious to get the food back to the main camp where it is more protected.

Early in the winter we hunt deer. The men go out in large groups and it is fun. We killed many deer this year and we had to make more racks to hold all the meat. The women spend days slicing the meat into thin strips to dry on the racks. Bear meat is also very good, but not as abundant. I really like the bear grease added to almost any food. The pottery holds the bear grease better than the old baskets we used to make.

Our soil is not very good for growing crops. After about five harvests, the crop production from a field is so low that we change fields. Actually, we begin to prepare new fields several seasons before we need them. The process starts with the clan leaders choosing a new area. The men and boys are sent out to begin the clearing. It starts by removing the bark from the bottom of the tree trunks. This is a process called girdling and it takes about a year for the trees to die. Men clear the big trees and open the forest with large stone axes. The smaller trees and branches from the bigger ones can be used for firewood. The women and older children collect them. The biggest ones are too large to cut for the hearths and are burned in the fields. The ash is good for the soil

Eventually, we have used all of the fields within two hours walk of the village. Firewood becomes scarce and after fifteen or twenty years, the village gets pretty smelly and dirty. The women complain and the people get depressed. Moving the village is a very important and complicated decision. The leaders talk about it for a long time. We consider several important factors such as finding fertile soil, abundant water, good fishing, wood for cooking, wood for building, places that stay warm into the fall, and most importantly, protection. The process starts a couple of years prior to actually moving the houses and the people. We visit several potential sites. Eventually, a new site is chosen and men are sent to the new place and they begin by girdling the trees. The second year, they cut the small trees and stack them for houses and the stockade. At this time, a few young people begin moving to the new site to protect our future home. The third year, we begin the move by planting the fields and building the houses. Eventually, the entire village moves. That last year, maintaining two villages, is the hardest because everyone works long days and we are maintaining fields at both villages.

Ideally, in another fifteen or twenty seasons, we can move back to a spot adjacent to the same village. Old villages are great for cornfields because of all of the dark organic soil that has accumulated. The other advantage of moving back to an old village is that it is covered with small trees that can be used for building houses and the stockade. However, sometimes spirits have occupied an old village or it is too close to a neighboring camp, and then we need to find a new spot altogether. Our life is a continuous cycle of moving our fields around our village, clearing fields for a new village, and moving to our new village.

One winter, food was in short supply and many people got sick after eating moldy corn. Our baby boy died during this time. He was buried in our house so his spirit would feel comfortable and return someday. One old man thought the corn might have gotten wet and rotted, even though it was hanging under the thick mat of reeds covering the roof. The shaman was convinced that a neighboring tribe had sent an evil spirit. He might have been correct. A group of hunters had brought in an old woman found wandering in the forest. Nobody knew who she was or where she came from. She spoke a language none of us understood. She must have brought the evil spirit that made everyone sick. None of our own people would cause this sickness among their family and friends.

The shaman said that he could perform a healing ceremony. His young assistants were sent into the forest to collect the necessary items to make the potion. Only each young man knew what he was to collect and not what anyone else was to find. Each brought his part of the potion to the shaman, who spent awhile mixing the ingredients. We brought the stranger to the shaman. Although she was kicking and screaming, four men held her down in the plaza. The shaman prepared a vile-smelling paste to spread on her face and lips and told her to drink the water in the turtle shell cup. She drank it just to get the taste off her lips. As she drank it, she calmed. Soon she was smiling and wishing us well in our own language. Our shaman is very knowledgeable and powerful.

ILLUSTRATION BY NANCY BISHOP

Our tribe is divided into several villages and they range in size from 30 to 80 families (150 to 400 people). Our village is mostly made up of the Turtle clan. Other villages are the Bear, Herring, Snake, Elk, Beaver, Owl, and Wolf clans. But each of the villages contains a mixture. A man must marry outside of his clan and his children are members of their father's clan. My wives are from the Bear clan. They wear a single bear claw on a string around their necks. They have four scars on their legs from the ceremony of when they became eligible for marriage. Sometimes they go back to the Bear clan village for ceremonies but mostly it is to visit their mother and other relatives.

I am known as a good hunter but also as a leader in war and peace. These are qualities that have allowed me to support my two wives. My cousins think that two wives must be very nice, but it is a big responsibility and extra work. I have extra help in the fields and preparing food and making clothing, but I also have extra mouths to feed. I am lucky because my wives are sisters and they generally get along with each other. Men who don't marry sisters frequently experience a lot of arguing.

Our village leaders decide which fields to clear and when to do it, and whether the village needs to be cleaned, and when to move the village. We also deal with bad behavior by our relatives and clan members. The clan leaders from all of the villages meet at least once a year and always in the late fall. We discuss important issues such as the corn harvest, fishing, the size of the deer herd, relations with other villages, and raiding parties.

We have a good life, but this is a hard land to farm. The soil is rocky and the bottomland frequently floods. In the days of my grandfather, they had a crisis. The winters started to get colder and the first frost started coming earlier and freezing our crops just as they were beginning to ripen. This is always something that we worry about but it started to happen every fall. The people talked about this a lot. Corn is the only way we can support our tribe. No matter what we did we could not get it to grow faster. My grandfather figured out that not all places were affected by the first frost. Some places stayed warm and did not freeze as early. We moved our fields to these warm zones and our crops were saved. Eventually we moved our villages to these new areas. It took a lot of work. I have watched in my lifetime how our villages have moved and we have changed where we live. I am proud that we have solved this problem but it means that there is less land that can be farmed. This has caused trouble with other villages but especially with our enemies.

Our people are good and honorable. We are respectful of strangers from other tribes and we do not steal. Sometimes the young men get excited and there are fights with the men from other villages. They fight over hunting rights, they fight over insults, they fight over women, and they fight to prove their bravery. These are usually small issues and if serious injuries occur, they are usually easily settled by the elders. Our more serious problem is the neighboring tribes, especially the Stinking Sparrow tribe to the east. They are dirty, without manners, and they have high squeaky voices. They steal and they cheat at trading. They have killed some of my relatives. Each time they kill one of ours, we must take revenge or our relative's spirit would not be happy. They are slowly taking our land and our power. Our elders have met with them many times but they cannot control their young men and the attacks continue. I have watched this for many years. Our only choice is to fight back.

When I was a young boy, my father was often called away to go on raiding parties. We were very proud of him but we were worried that he would be injured or worse. Some boys lost their fathers and the entire village mourned. The clan organized the funeral. They helped the family bury the man in the forest. When I was a young teenager, my father began taking me along on the raids. An enemy village was getting ready to move their fields into our territory. On my first adventure, we spent the fall setting fire to small camps and shooting arrows at the men in the fields. When we encountered their warriors we would shoot our arrows, but since we were outnumbered, we usually quickly retreated. If their group was small, we would chase them with our spears and clubs. When a warrior kills an enemy, he gains strength; if he actually touches an enemy, he gains much more power. The most power comes from killing an enemy in hand-to-hand combat and eating his heart. I was sure that some of my arrows had hit the enemy and when I got home, I felt great strength.

The following spring, when we made plans to harass their camps, I was anxious to prove myself as a warrior in hand-to-hand combat. I was very excited and I knew my father was proud of me. However, he warned me that the enemy might have their own plans. In the early spring we left with more than thirty warriors. Sure enough, the enemy had spies in the forest and they knew we were coming. They met us on the main trail with at least 100 warriors. It was a spectacular battle. Arrows were flying everywhere. We stayed in a grove of trees while the enemy tried to get at us. We shot our arrows all day. I could see that they were cowards and not very good shots. Several times, I ran out in the open and yelled insults at them. They would yell back and shoot many arrows. I was hit in the arm so that the point stuck out the other side but that did not stop me. I continued to run out and taunt them and show them that I was not hurt. By the end of the day several men on both sides had been hit. We were hoping the enemy would die. The enemy would gain much power by capturing our wounded, so I was made responsible for taking them home. After nightfall, we retreated back the way we came. My father stayed behind to guard our retreat. He told me to make sure that everyone got home safely. If I needed to stop, I was to move well off the main trail but not to stop at the Wolf Run Rockshelter because the enemy also knew of this hideout. It was hard traveling at night but the moon was bright and we knew the path.

My father and his warriors caught up with us the next day. He said they had ambushed the enemy as they had tried to follow him. He saw several killed and he was sure we were all safe. When we got back to our camp, we were welcomed as heroes. I wore a bandage on my arm for a week to show off my wound. That is the way the fighting has gone for many years.

Back in the old days we only had twenty families to feed. Now we have sixty families (300 people) and there are four more villages each with forty families (200 people) in the four directions only forty miles away. We need the plants to survive, but it is a daily struggle. We worry that we have enough food. We do not have enough room to move around. The crops do not grow well after three harvests in one field, so we move to another field, then another, and another. By the time we return to the first field, the crops only grow well for two harvests. All the villages face the same problem. Soon we will run out of land to grow plants. What will we eat then? Where are the new territories to move to? On top of it all, our enemies are killing us. They say they attack us because we have killed their relatives. But they started the killing and besides, I think they just want our land.

A Late Woodland Native American Woman Narrative

Judith A. Hawthorn, Retired, Cedar Cliff High School

> **TIME** 500 YEARS AGO.
>
> **PLACE** THE LOWER SUSQUEHANNA RIVER VALLEY.
>
> **CLIMATE** THE "LITTLE ICE AGE"—FIVE DEGREES COOLER AND MORE RAINFALL THAN PRESENT.
>
> **FLORA AND FAUNA** A MIXED OAK, HEMLOCK, AND CHESTNUT FOREST SIMILAR TO PENNSYLVANIA AT THE TIME OF COLUMBUS.
>
> **DISTINCTIVE ARTIFACTS** TRIANGULAR ARROWPOINTS AND WELL-MADE POTTERY WITH INCISED LINES AROUND THE RIM.

My name is Pakshimo (Sunset). I live in a long-house in our village with my husband, my mother, and grandmother. I have lived for a short time compared to these other two women. My husband is strong and brave and has contributed greatly to our tribe. He is a great hunter and a good son, who is well respected by our people. He belongs to the Bear clan and I belong to the Deer clan. Although his main duties are to his clan, he has been a good advisor to the Deer clan. I have bore four children with him; the eldest is our son, Kennapayasho (Rain Crow). My brother is the leader of our tribe. He is teaching my son to hunt and defend our tribe against invaders. Someday soon, our son will hunt deer and bear and contribute to our village the way his father and uncles have. My son is obedient to his uncles, who have taught him well.

Our longhouse is large and houses many families. My sister shares a fire with my family, and we often share stories while stirring the pot of food for our families. She has two children but is younger than me. My children are older, except for our babies, who were born one month apart. Many stories are told of children coming into the world, and our mother often tells us of the spirits that are within us.

My days begin early with preparations to feed my family. My infant girl child is hungry and cries as she awakens. She presses herself to my breast and eats until she is satisfied and contented. It is early and the sun is rising over the land to bring about a beautiful, cool morning. I look out of our longhouse to see the dew on the grassland. I think about the day before me and the tasks to be done. My children would wake soon and be hungry, so it is time to start my day.

The morning of this beautiful day was like any other morning for a woman in our clan. There are daily chores that are required, and I have started them after the baby has been fed. The first chore is to feed the fire and fill our cooking pot so that we can all eat. The children are hungry. My oldest daughter, Wabethey (Swan), is twelve years old and she helps. She cleans the berries that she had picked the day before and mixes nuts with the berries. I carry water from the stream for a tea brew, which all will enjoy. My daughter enjoys the games we play when gathering berries, and she pretends to be me when helping to feed all of us. She gives each person a portion that she feels they will eat and often takes care to give her great-grandmother the soft berries and fruits because her teeth are worn. She helps to take care of her great-grandmother, who is frail from a lifetime of caring for her family. My sister and I get the fire going and pour some cornmeal into the stew, which is constantly changing depending on the season. In the spring, we always have fish. In the fall, we have venison and by the end of winter, we have eaten all of the corn and we eat anything we can get our hands on.

My oldest boy, Kennapayasho, is coming of age. My heart is proud yet sad. He seems very young and yet his uncles have taught him to hunt and fish and defend our community in his short life. He is fourteen years old, and when the sun strikes his face, he looks like his uncles, who are brave and strong. His skin is still smooth, and his face has no lines. Yet his look is thoughtful, and he is concerned about his role in our clan. They have taught him to be proud of our people and learn the skills and tell the stories of our tribe. His brother and sisters are younger and are learning their roles in our village as well. The grandmothers are making a beautiful cloth for Kennapayasho to wear when we celebrate his coming of age.

After our meal, I strap my baby to my chest and take the younger children towards the water for gathering food and reeds. The children and I have fun while we do important work. It is not far from our village and we must walk for a short time to get to a good spot along the stream. The children love the water and explore the plants and animals that live nearby while we talk about the sky, rocks, and tree spirits around us. The spirits have blessed us with abundance this year as the grass and plants are green, lush, and full. My mother and grandmother stay in the village and continue to make baskets out of the reeds we have gathered over the past few weeks. They will be useful when gathering food for the winter.

As we travel through woods and down towards a stream, my oldest daughter Wabethey selects berries from bushes near the stream and searches for fish swimming in a nearby pool. We make a game of picking berries and gathering food. Wabethey throws a berry into the stream to see if the fish are hungry. One jumps up and she runs back to me quickly, laughing about the fright she had when the fish's spirit came through the water towards her.

On this day, Wabethey asks to find food on the other side of the ridge outside of our village. She pleads with me to let her go over the ridge and hunt for nuts. She tells me that the berries and nuts will be more abundant. She is mad at her sister and does not want her along. She says she knows the forest better than her older brother and can find more berries than any man. I detect some jealousy and remember when I thought I was better in the woods than my brothers. As I got older, I realized that the forest is for men and the village is for women. I think she is beginning to feel like a young woman. I know she feels that she is older than the two smaller children and wishes to help more as she gets older, so I have let her go. She will grow soon enough and it is good for me to let her feel responsible for her family. I warn her of dangers over the ridge like snakes, bears, panthers, and bobcats. I tell her to keep a watchful eye for these animals. I also warn her about straying too far from our trails, reminding her to be back to the village before the sun goes behind the trees. Wabethey is excited and assures me that she will do as I have taught her. She walks towards the ridge and waves her hand to all of us as we walk in the other direction back to the village. My daughter is growing too fast and within a short time will take a husband.

When we return to the village my sisters scurry to greet us and help us with our bundles of nuts, berries, reeds, and firewood. Whenever we leave the village we always bring back firewood. We have been in this village since just after my son was born and have cut down all of the small trees around the village. Now we must walk awhile to find wood for our fires. The corn does not grow as tall as it did a couple of years ago. The elders are talking about moving to a new place.

My mother mixes some of the nuts and berries together and adds some honey as a treat for the children. My thoughts drift to Wabethey on her adventure. I pray the forest spirits protect her and bring her safely back to the village.

Wabethey follows the stream over the ridge and walks for about an hour to find an abundance of nuts and berries that have not been picked before. She follows the stream and gathers more reeds for her grandmothers to make baskets. Soon her basket is full and Wabethey sits down by a tree to rest. She eats her fill from her large basket and drinks water from the stream. As the sun starts to fall, Wabethey feels tired from her day of work and falls asleep beside the tree. She is awakened suddenly by crackling branches. She is startled awake and finds that the sun is no longer high in the sky. She is frightened and jumps up to make her way towards home, but suddenly, she stops short in her tracks.

As the sun starts to set in the sky I step out of our longhouse and look towards the ridge hoping to see Wabethey. I am concerned about my daughter and have mentioned this to my mother. She assures me that most children don't have the same expectations as their parents. Children often test themselves at that age, thinking that they can push themselves beyond their limits while in the woods. Some do not survive, but those who do feel stronger about themselves. When I was young I thought I knew everything about the woods. Now, as a mother, I know more about the longhouse. They assure me she will be returning soon. They remind me of times when I was a child, and left them to worry about where I might be outside our village.

The sun has set and Wabethey has not returned. I am worried that something has happened. Maybe Wabethey lost her way, twisted her ankle, or worse, a bear or mountain lion has attacked her. My mother calls the longhouse together and small groups form to hunt for Wabethey.

Each starts off towards the ridge, being careful to cover the ground close to the stream. All members take part in the search except for the older women who take care of the babies. The loss of a child is cause for alarm and all members of the longhouse use all of their knowledge of the land to search for Wabethey. As the longhouse spreads out to search, darkness spreads over the land. Each leader carries fire to light the way and signals are agreed upon so all will know when the search ends, or regrouping must take place. I go with the group to the streambed where the children had played earlier. I start up the ridge where I last saw Wabethey wave to us. My heart is pounding. My brother and husband follow me to the place where I last saw Wabethey. As we get to the top of the ridge, we stop to look down the other side. The sun has set now, and it is very dark but a light is far off near the streambed. My brother gives the signal. We expect to hear the response in return, but we don't. Instead the light starts to come towards us. We become afraid that we have met someone who is not friendly in our range. As the light comes closer, a familiar voice cries out hesitatingly. It is Wabethey! But who is with her? She comes close, and the light is soon bright enough to see a young man with her. He is not from our village but has brought our daughter back to us.

We learn that the boy is from a clan that lives four days distance from our village. He is of the Bear clan and is remembered from a ceremony of our clans in the spring of the year. His name is Macatay Peshee (Black Panther). He is older than our son. We are fortunate that he found our daughter and brought her to us. He has been in the woods for two days with many more to go. He is on his quest to find his vision spirit, a ritual our son will also do in two more winters. Macatay Peshee is a serious young boy, who will be a man when he returns to his village. Upon his return, he will recount his quest to his tribe. They will have a great celebration of his manhood. He will be able to marry then and live with his family. We wish him well and are again thankful to our creator for returning our daughter to us.

My brother sends a signal to the others from our house. We return to the longhouse, happy that the creator has helped us. Wabethey has had an adventure she will remember for her life. Each adventure is a lesson, and for our daughter, it is one of limits. Knowing how far to travel within the light of day will be the lesson for our daughter.

Chapter 8
The Contact Period: 1550 AD to 1750 AD

Chronology

Because of the frequent use of historic records and the ineffectiveness of radiometric dating using charcoal less than 300 years old, all dates referenced in this chapter will use the modern calendar.

An image of a Susquehannock Indian taken from John Smith's map of 1612. Based on the early date, this is probably a reasonably accurate depiction of Native American clothing.

JOHN SMITH'S MAP OF 1612

T I M E L I N E

Contact Period	**1550 AD–1750 AD**
Woodland Period	2700 years ago–1500 AD
Late Woodland/Late Prehistoric	1100 years ago–1550 AD
Middle Woodland	1100–2100 years ago
Early Woodland	2100–2700 years ago
Transitional Period	2700–4300 years ago
Archaic Period	4300–10,000 years ago
Paleoindian Period	10,000–16,500 years ago

Environment

The Contact period corresponds to the cool and wet "Little Ice Age." Winters are harsh. The vegetation consists of an oak-chestnut and hemlock forest. Similar to the Late Woodland period, floodplains are the location of villages and farm fields and are frequently open in various stages of regrowth.

Making and Using Tools: Typical Artifacts and Technology

This period documents the evolution of Native American technology to European technology. Most Native American tools and ornaments are replaced with European goods within the first 100 years of contact. At the beginning of this period, Late Woodland people are using clay pottery, stone tools, and a variety of bone and antler tools and ornaments. Very small quantities of brass, probably traded from fishermen along the Atlantic coast, appear at archaeological sites in Pennsylvania in the early 1500s; however, it is not until after 1575 that trade items become common on Native American sites in Pennsylvania. Utilitarian items such as iron axes, knives, and hoes are the first items to be traded, but brass ornaments and glass beads are also in demand. Earthenware jugs and flintlock guns begin to appear by the 1630s. Brass kettles are part of the exchange system, but they are rare during the early period, because they are usually cut up to make ornaments and arrowheads. Native Americans prefer to cook in ceramic pots rather than metal kettles. Needless to say, a wide variety of blankets and cloth for clothing are also part of this system, but these materials do not preserve in the archaeological record of Pennsylvania. Entire kettles become common on Native American sites by 1640, along with wine bottles, kaolin pipes, and tin-glazed earthenware. Finally, by 1675, nearly all Native American material goods are partially or completely European made.

Interestingly, pipes, beads, and other ornaments of catlinite become popular with Native Americans in the early 1700s. This brightly colored red, shale-like material, easily carved, is quarried from sites in Minnesota and Wisconsin. The finished products are made near the quarries by the local tribes and traded to eastern tribes. Small numbers of beads and pipes are found on sites in Pennsylvania during the 1600s, but the major

Pottery of the Susquehanna and Delaware basins. Susquehannock pottery; a. Schultz Incised; b. Washington Boro Incised; c. Strickler pedestal. Delaware pottery; d. Munsee Incised; e. Bainbridge Linear; f. brass kettle.

Flintlock muskets were in high demand by Native Americans.

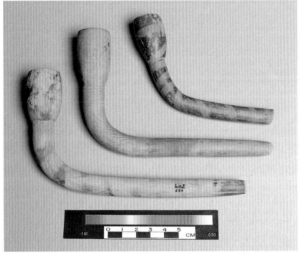

The tulip bowl pipe was a common form during the Contact period.

influx of this material occurs later. The 1700s was a time when many Native Americans in Pennsylvania and adjoining regions could see that their cultures were being destroyed. They began to realize that the Europeans were here to stay and they were going to eventually take all of their land. A nativistic revival movement began in the Midwest to rejuvenate Native American cultures. Tribes began to form alliances with one another to stop the European expansion and to prevent the destruction of Native American societies. Catlinite becomes a symbol of this coalition of Indian tribes and documents the involvement of Pennsylvania Indians in this movement to revitalize Indian culture. Unfortunately, it is too late.

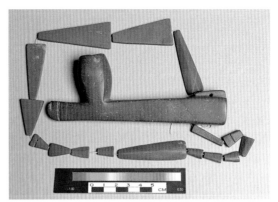

A catlinite pipe and beads. This soft stone was mined in Minnesota and traded to Native Americans in the East.

What People Ate: Subsistence

Farming is the main subsistence pattern and corn, beans, and squash are the main foods. This diet is supplemented by hunting, fishing, and gathering of shellfish and a variety of plant foods. In the Susquehanna drainage basin, slash-and-burn farming is practiced, while in the Delaware basin, domesticated plants are much less important.

The staple diet of the Contact period: corn, beans, and squash—the "three sisters."

The grinding stone was used to process seeds and nuts into a flour.

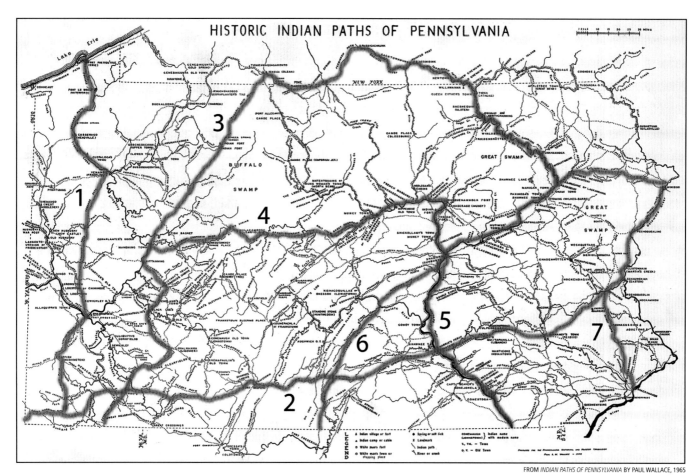

HISTORIC INDIAN PATHS OF PENNSYLVANIA

FROM *INDIAN PATHS OF PENNSYLVANIA* BY PAUL WALLACE, 1965

1. VENANGO
2. RAYSTOWN
3. CATAWBA
4. GREAT SHAMOKIN
5. WYALUSING
6. TUSCARORA/GREAT PATH
7. MINSI

Where People Lived: Settlement Patterns

Habitation sites and villages continue to be near major rivers and in floodplains. In the Susquehanna drainage basin, villages are moved to more fertile soils every fifteen to twenty years. In the Delaware basin, there is little evidence for villages, and their habitation sites seem to move more frequently. Both groups use a variety of hunting and collecting sites that are found throughout upland areas along small streams and at springheads. Villages continue to be the location of farm fields. The village also functions as a base of operations for the exploitation of a wide variety of food resources. Tribal warfare is an issue in the Susquehanna basin, and eventually villages join together numbering nearly 3000 inhabitants in response to raiding by neighboring groups. Trade with the Europeans becomes an important factor in the location and structure of villages. The competition for European goods results in feuding between native tribes. Trade and feuding resulted in increased travel. Footpaths were more heavily traveled and there are several major paths crossing Pennsylvania following the major drainage basins and ridgetops. By the early 1700s, many native populations had been displaced from their traditional homelands and began to migrate into areas not occupied by Europeans, such as the Wyoming Valley north of present-day Wilkes-Barre. This is known as the Refugee Period because of the frequent movements of these displaced groups.

People Living in Groups: Social Organization and Belief Systems

At the beginning of the Contact period, Native American people are living in egalitarian tribal societies. The major themes during this period are trade, warfare, disease, and the resulting displacement of families. There

208

is intensive competition for European trade goods. Native Americans go to great lengths to acquire these goods, including warfare and moving in closer proximity to the Europeans. Trade and warefare enhanced the status of some individuals and this altered the egalitarian family-based social organization in some groups. In Pennsylvania, William Penn purchases land from the tribes and this results in further displacement of families. With increasing numbers of Europeans, disease decimates Native American populations. It is estimated that between 60 to 80 percent of all Native Americans die during this period. The shock to social and religious systems is too great and Native American culture is radically changed. There are very few Native American communities of any size practicing their traditional cultures in Pennsylvania after the Revolutionary War.

Definition

The Contact period is the time when Europeans were first interacting with Native Americans up until the collapse of native cultures in Pennsylvania. It dates between 1550 and 1750 AD and is characterized by the increasing use of European technology by Late Woodland peoples. Eventually, native technology is completely replaced and, soon after this, Native Americans gradually move out of Pennsylvania. Their cultures are radically changed by a variety of factors, such as competition over the fur trade, warfare, disease, and the intrusion of Europeans into Native American lands. Some tribes returned during the French and Indian War, but the effort to restore their traditional values ultimately fails. Some of the last Native American families are removed during Sullivan's campaign along the North Branch of the Susquehanna River during the Revolutionary War.

In this chapter, the presentation will be based on both archaeological research and historic records. This period in the Ohio drainage basin is not well known archaeologically or through historic documents. A few Iroquoian groups are living in far northwestern Pennsylvania, and a group known as the Mingos are referenced as living in the Upper Ohio basin. For the most part, Native American groups traveled through this region, usually on their way out of Pennsylvania, and by the time Europeans arrived, most native populations had already moved out.

Therefore, only cultures in the Delaware and Susquehanna drainage basin will be considered for this period. The Susquehannocks are located primarily in the Susquehanna drainage basin and the Delaware or Lenape are located in the Delaware basin. Extensive archaeology has been conducted on Susquehannock sites and much of what we know is based on these excavations. In contrast, very few Contact period Delaware sites have been excavated. Most of what we know is based on historic records and that does not tell us much about their culture.

This period lasts only 200 years and rather than use the environmental, technological, and social headings used in previous chapters, a geographical and historical approach will be used.

The Delaware

The first Indians encountered by early Dutch and Swedish traders in Pennsylvania were the Delaware, also known as the Lenape. They were the indigenous tribe or local people. Their ancestors lived in the region for hundreds of years or more. As discussed in Chapter 6, the archaeology of these people is not well known, but they seem to have a different type of adaptation than the other major tribes in Pennsylvania. Based on historic accounts, the Delaware Indians grew corn, and this is found at many sites within the region. It does not appear, however, that they farmed in the same way as neighboring tribes. Rather than living in compact villages containing hundreds or thousands of residents, the Delaware frequently lived in small hamlets or scattered farmsteads. Although a few Delaware longhouse settlements, reminiscent of the Susquehannock pattern, have been found, they are very rare. Round or subrectangular houses have also been found. It has been proposed that during the spring and summer, they lived in round houses and moved frequently to exploit a variety of resources. In fall and perhaps winter, families joined together and lived in longhouses. This kind of movement and seasonal merging of families is more similar to a band society than a tribal society.

The Delaware are prominent in the history of William Penn and the founding of Pennsylvania. Penn sought to treat them with fairness, but when he died, that policy changed. They were cheated out of their land holdings and moved from the Delaware Valley by the 1730s. Lands were set aside for them in Chester County, but they remained there only briefly. They moved to western Pennsylvania for a time, but by 1800, they had migrated to Indiana. The main groups are currently living in Oklahoma and Ontario, Canada.

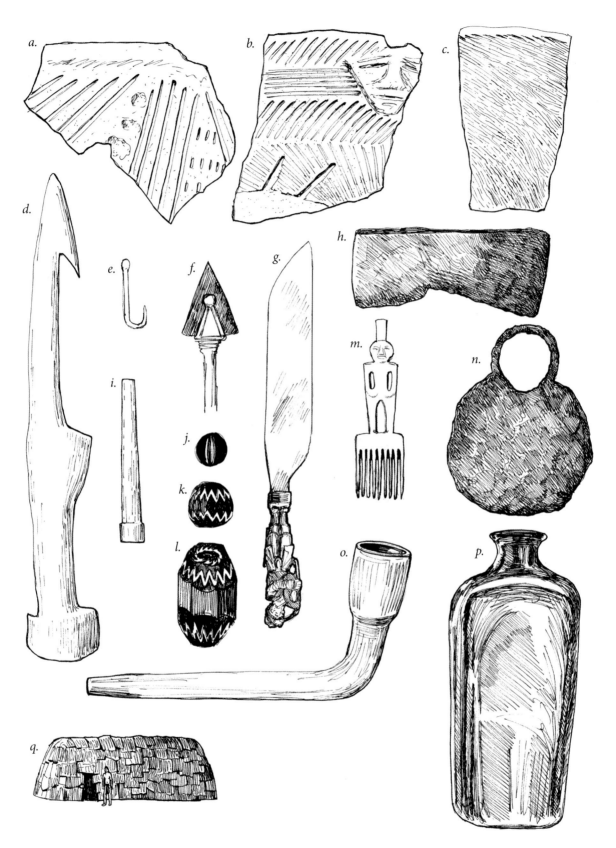

Typical artifacts of the Susquehannock culture: a. Schultz Incised pottery; b. Washington Boro Incised pottery; c. Strickler Cordmarked pottery; d. antler harpoon; e. bone fishhook; f. brass arrowpoint attached to wooden shaft; g. iron knife with pewter handle; h. iron axe; i. antler flint knapping tool; j.–l. glass beads; m. antler comb; n. iron hoe; o. tulip bowl pipe; p. glass wine bottle; q. bark-covered longhouse.

The Susquehannock settlement pattern was similar to the Monongahela annual cycle but the village was much larger, usually including over a thousand men, women, and children. The village served as the agricultural center and as a base for processing foods collected throughout the territory. Hunting and fishing camps were established some distance from the village. Trade with other Native American groups and with the Europeans was important. Males were frequently involved in warfare and trade and not present in the village.

The Susquehannocks

Beginning around 1550, at the dawn of the Contact period, the Susquehannock culture appeared in the lower Susquehanna drainage basin. The Susquehannocks were Iroquoian-speaking and shared many similarities with the Iroquois of New York. It is believed that they moved south from that region. It has been speculated that they were forced out by other Iroquois or, more likely, that they were moving closer to the source of English and Swedish trade goods. The Late Woodland Shenks Ferry culture disappears with the arrival of the Susquehannocks. It is not known if the Susquehannocks conquered the indigenous Shenks Ferry culture or incorporated it into their own culture, or if the Shenks Ferry people simply moved elsewhere. Pottery designs suggest that at least some Shenks Ferry families moved in with the Susquehannocks.

THE STATE MUSEUM OF PENNSYLVANIA/SECTION OF ARCHAEOLOGY

A partially reconstructed longhouse using a post mold pattern from the Strickler site, Lancaster County.

The Susquehannocks lived in large fortified villages, some of which may have contained as many as 3000 people. The villages were composed of longhouses 60 to 80 feet in length. Like the Iroquois, the Susquehannocks were a matrilineal society. The longhouses were divided into compartments occupied by nuclear families related through the female line. The Susquehannocks were farmers and practiced slash-and-burn agriculture. Their villages were moved every fifteen to twenty years to more fertile fields. Their villages all contain evidence of their dependence on domesticated foods in the form of preserved remains of corn, beans, and squash and large storage pits for these foods. It is estimated that more than 60 percent of their diet consisted of corn.

Archaeologists have learned about other dietary habits by examining butchering marks on the bones and the remains found at the bottom of some of the large cooking pots. For animals the size of wild turkeys or smaller, the entire carcass was placed in a pot to boil.

The Susquehannock homeland was in the lower Susquehanna River basin, especially in Cumberland, Dauphin, Lancaster, and York Counties. After European contact, the Susquehannocks engaged in extensive fur trading with the English, Dutch, and Swedes. The archaeology of the Susquehannocks is divided into several phases. Approximately nine villages have been identified covering approximately one hundred fifty years. Several of these are located in the Washington Boro area along the Susquehanna River, south of Columbia, Lancaster County. These sites document the evolution of Susquehannock technology and the group's economic dominance in the region. This is some of the most fertile soil in the United States and it is not surprising that it was intensively used by Native American farmers.

The Susquehannocks controlled the fur trade with the Europeans for nearly a century; however, they were in constant conflict with other Native American tribes, especially the Seneca of western New York, who were jealous of the Susquehannock's control of European goods. Most of the fighting consisted of small skirmishes, but large-scale battles possibly took place with the Seneca in the Washington Boro area and across the Susquehanna River in York County at the Upper (Oscar) Leibhart site (36Yo9). Warfare and disease eventually caught up with the Susquehannocks, and in 1675, approximately five hundred survivors left their village in York County and sought refuge with the English in Baltimore, Maryland. This arrangement ended in disaster when the English laid siege to the Susquehannock village. After escaping the English and with the permission of the Seneca, they soon returned to the lower Susquehanna drainage basin occupying the Lower (Byrd) Leibhart site (36Yo170). Land was set aside for their use in Conestoga Township, Lancaster County, by the colonial government. They did not own the land and they were only allowed to stay as long as they "behaved themselves."

For several decades, the site at Conestoga Town was an important meeting place for Native Americans and the colonial government. The Susquehannocks eventually became known as the Conestoga Indians. As Conestoga Town became less important as a meeting place, the Conestogas blended with the local population and frequently worked for the residents of

Lancaster County. Two weeks before Christmas, in 1763, they were attacked by a vigilante group from Harrisburg known as the Paxton Boys, who had been agitated by Indian attacks from the Ohio Valley. The surviving Conestogas were placed in the Lancaster jail for their own protection, but two days after Christmas, the Paxton Boys returned and killed every man, woman, and child, bringing an end to Susquehannock life and culture.

FROM *EVENTS IN INDIAN HISTORY* BY JAMES WIMER, 1841

The tragic end to the Susquehannocks in Lancaster, December 27, 1763.

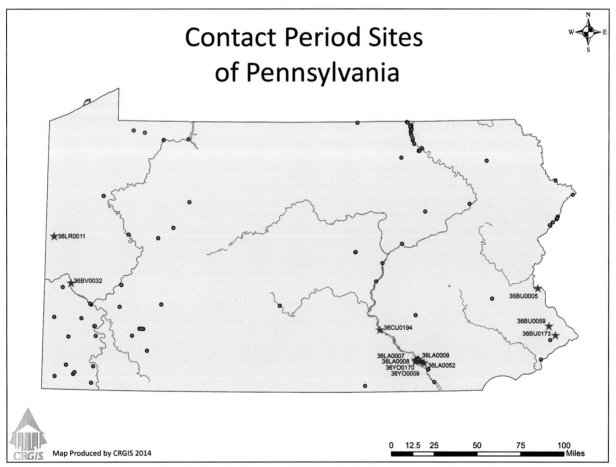

Map illustrating the distribution of Contact period sites in Pennsylvania.

Contact Period Research in Pennsylvania

There are 126 Contact period sites recorded in the PASS files. This period is poorly represented in these files, because the period was brief and it is difficult to recognize these sites. In many ways they are essentially Late Woodland sites with European trade goods. At one time in archaeological research, there was an expectation that trade goods would be common and these sites should be easy to identify; however, after excavating some of these sites, it can be documented that trade goods are common at permanent villages, especially in burials, but not at hamlets or other small communities.

Contact Period Research in the Delaware Drainage Basin

There are 42 Contact period sites recorded in the PASS files in the Delaware drainage basin. Very few of these have been excavated. Considering the prominence of the Delaware tribe in Pennsylvania history, it is ironic that our knowledge of Delaware culture is very poor. In some cases there are historic maps locating sites, but urban expansion has resulted in their destruction. In other cases, they are simply difficult to locate. For example, there are historic references to the Delaware town of Playwicki (36Bu173) and there were several efforts to find the site. When it was eventually located and excavated, the number of European trade goods was very small. The site dates sometime between 1720 and 1740, when much of this area of Bucks County was settled by Europeans; however, there were only three European artifacts: a piece of green bottle glass, a white clay pipe stem and bowl fragments, and a jackknife without the blade. It would appear that a group of Native Americans was primarily using native technology while living in a neighborhood surrounded by Europeans.

In general, throughout the drainage basin sites from this period have been tested but rarely do we get a picture of diet, house types, or social organization. Although not representing the Delaware culture, the Eel Skin Rock Shelter (36Bu59) contains artifacts from this period. In this case, these were Susquehannocks and not Delaware, indicating the pervasive influence of the Susquehannocks. The Overpeck site (36Bu5) is a Delaware habitation possibly with houses. It also contains Susquehannock artifacts, suggesting that the two cultures interacted on a peaceful basis.

Contact Period Research in the Susquehanna Drainage Basin

There are 51 Contact period sites recorded in the Susquehanna drainage basin. A large number of these have been extensively excavated. The excavation of several Susquehannock sites represents some of the largest excavations ever conducted in the state. There are four major excavations and numerous smaller projects. Three of these are located in the Washington Boro area of Lancaster County. The major excavations were conducted by The State Museum of Pennsylvania. The Schultz site (36La7) dates to about 1600 AD and it was occupied for fifteen to twenty years. This site contained a large number of longhouses measuring up to 65 feet in length. The houses were surrounded by a wooden

stockade. The bone and antler artifacts consisted of bone beamers for cleaning hides, bone awls for sewing, and antler flaking tools for sharpening stone arrowpoints, knives, scrapers, and drills. Small triangular arrowpoints are very common. The pottery is abundant and defined as Schultz Incised. This Early Susquehannock type is characterized by elaborate incised triangles on the rims and collars. European trade goods included iron knives and axes, glass beads, and brass ornaments, including tinkling cones. These were worn on clothing and designed to rattle while the person danced. The Susquehannocks traded furs for brass kettles, but at this early stage, they preferred to cut them up into arrowheads and ornaments for their clothing.

The families occupying the Schultz village moved to a new location between 1600 and 1625 about three miles upriver. This is known as the Washington Boro Village (36La8) site. It had a stockade encompassing more than five acres and included as many as 50 houses, 250 families, and more than 1250 people. There was an increase in trade goods. Iron axes and hoes and brass ornaments were common, but earthenware jugs and flintlock guns also appear. Indian-made smoking pipes were common and they frequently had an animal image on the bowl facing the smoker.

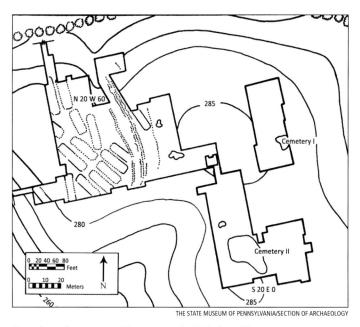

THE STATE MUSEUM OF PENNSYLVANIA/SECTION OF ARCHAEOLOGY

Based on the post mold pattern, the Schultz village was the home of approximately 1200 individuals. It consisted of numerous longhouses surrounded by a wooden palisade.

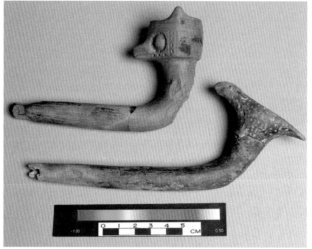

The effigy bowl pipe was used by the Susquehannocks. The effigy always faced the smoker.

The Washington Boro Village probably represents the height of Susquehannock economic power. Indians from all over the region visited this town. Pottery from tribes in the Chesapeake Bay area, Ontario, and as far away as Tennessee has been recovered from this site. This documents their considerable control and influence in the Middle Atlantic region.

The control and influence wielded by the Susquehannocks in the Middle Atlantic region is demonstrated by the three pots below, from left to right, Tennessee, the Chesapeake Bay, and Ontario, Canada. The pot to the left is a classic Washington Boro vessel with a face.

Until recently, archaeologists believed that all of the major Susquehannock villages were known. Some had been destroyed by modern development but at least their location was known; however, while preparing to move a railroad line in the Lemoyne Borough Memorial Park, archaeologists discovered an unrecorded village (36Cn164). It contained longhouses and a stockade. Unfortunately, a large portion of the site had been destroyed by earlier railroad construction and it is not possible to determine its size or the total number of houses. Based on pottery styles, the site seems to date to the Washington Boro Village period. Interestingly, it did not contain the quantity of trade goods found at the Washington Boro site. It did contain large storage pits and quantities of elk bone. Archaeologists hypothesize that this was a small farming village that supported the major village to the south. The Washington Boro Village site was felt to be the more important of the two because it was closer to European trading centers.

After the Washington Boro site was abandoned, the Susquehannocks occupied a series of sites in Lancaster County along the Susquehanna River. By about 1645 they returned to the Washington Boro area and occupied a site adjacent to the Schultz site. This is the Strickler site (36La3) and the third major excavation in the Washington Boro area. The village was over 12 acres in size, with a population of about 2900 residents. Excavations at the Strickler site produced middens and layers of trash that included charred corn cobs and fragments of pumpkins and squash with attached masses of seeds. A wide variety of

THE STATE MUSEUM OF PENNSYLVANIA/SECTION OF ARCHAEOLOGY

Several very large storage pits such as this one were uncovered at the Lemoyne site in Cumberland County.

animal bones with butchering marks was also found. European goods from this site document a significant change in technology, with most of the material remains of European origin. The Susquehannocks modified European goods for their own needs, but the pattern of artifacts and features suggests they continued to maintain many of their own social and religious traditions. It is believed that the Strickler site was visited by members of John Smith's Jamestown Company. Most Native American stockades were circular, but the Strickler site had bastions on two of the stockade corners, which demonstrates a significant European influence.

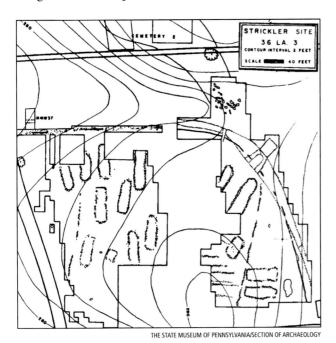

THE STATE MUSEUM OF PENNSYLVANIA/SECTION OF ARCHAEOLOGY

After the Susquehannocks were defeated by the Seneca and forced to leave the region, they eventually returned. Archaeologists call this the Refugee period. Much of their society had been destroyed and they did not have their own land. The colonial government gave them a tract of land in Conestoga Township and they built at least one small village. This is known as Conestoga Town (36La52) and it was excavated by The State Museum in the 1970s. It documents the new lifestyle of the Susquehannocks. There are practically no native-made objects. The longhouse was abandoned and nuclear families lived in simple cabinlike buildings. Their matrilineal social structure was obviously compromised. Christianity and native beliefs blended and the deceased were placed in wooden coffins. This site documents the final disintegration of Susquehannock culture. It was at this site in 1763 that the last of this tribe were killed by the Paxton Boys.

This chalice (Strickler pedestal) was made by a Susquehannock potter and illustrates the influence of Europeans.

THE STATE MUSEUM OF PENNSYLVANIA/SECTION OF ARCHAEOLOGY

Contact Period Research in the Upper Ohio Drainage Basin

There are twenty-three Contact period sites in the Ohio drainage basin recorded in the PASS files. Most of these are trading posts, such as the Penelec site (36Wa152) or Refugee period sites. The Kuskuski site (36Lr11) was a Delaware settlement while they were on their way west. Logstown (36Bv32) was another frequently used stopover site for Native Americans moving west.

The Strickler village was the largest of the Susquehannock towns. It was home to over 2900 individuals. It consisted of numerous longhouses surrounded by at least two wooden palisades.

An Early Contact Period Narrative

Time 350 years ago.

Place The Upper Delaware River Valley.

Climate The "Little Ice Age," 5 degrees cooler and more rain than present.

Flora and fauna A mixed oak, hemlock, and chestnut forest—similar to Pennsylvania at the time of Columbus.

Distinctive artifacts Triangular arrowpoints, well-made pottery with incised lines around the rim, brass artifacts, iron axes, and glass beads.

For all the time and all the places that I, Bilxingkorlac, have lived in my sixty years, I never imagined anyone who was not like us. We are the only people. We are unique. Nobody else could exist who is not just like us. Or so I thought, until I saw a hard blue bead in the Delaware Valley. It was hard like the piece of purple clam shell a man from across several rivers traded to me for a brown stone. The color was deeper, and it was perfectly round with a very tiny hole through it. The next year, a northern man had what I thought was a copper earring shaped into a concentric circle. In a few years, I would see many beads of different colors in the Monongahela Valley. If these were the only strange objects I would ever see, I would still think we were the only people.

I knew something was very different when I traveled to the Susquehanna Valley. In the distant haze, I saw five men walking toward our camp. At first, I thought it was the northerners coming to trade. I had been saving some good things for them. As they got closer, I had a huge shock. They had hair on their faces! Not just a little, they looked like a bear's back.

I have never shown fear to a stranger, but I was very surprised when I saw them for the first time. They spoke a language I had never heard. They smiled, looked happy, and gave us some water from their pottery. Their pottery was clear like still water. I cannot imagine how they could make such a thing. Their water was dark, foul smelling, and made me dizzy, but in a good way. I knew I should offer them something for their gift, but I was so confused from drinking their water. I could not think properly.

Now when I think about it, I am so ashamed. I do not know why I did it. It must have been their water. I had been skinning beaver for several days and had a huge pile of hides. I picked up all the hides and gave them to the strangers. The strangers looked confused, but thanked me very much. They must have been so insulted to get smelly, useless hides, but they were very gracious.

They made a camp close to ours for several weeks. Every day they walked into the woods, but never came back with any food. My brother and I showed them which plants to gather and how to find food. They gave us more of their water, but by now I did not mind the smell so much. I asked where they came from, and they pointed to the rising sun. I do not think so. They probably did not understand the question.

After the strangers had left their camp, we tried to find them. Nobody we spoke to had seen any strangers. This was very odd, because they had to pass through many territories to get to us. Did they avoid all other people and choose us to meet? Did they really come from the sky? Had no one else seen them? My confusion only increased when the children brought us things from their abandoned camp.

I would never go to a stranger's camp so soon after they had left. They might be coming back soon. They might have left their tools behind that they will not need at the next camp. But I forgot all this when I saw what the children had found. The clear pottery was broken into large, sharp pieces. I could make a fine knife from the largest piece. They had been cooking in a large pot that was much harder than pottery. I could not break it. I saw why they left it. There was a hole in the bottom that let the water leak out. There were many other pieces I did not recognize. I kept them because they were so strange.

No wonder they had left. They did not know how to make any tools. There were no broken pieces of stone from making spearheads, knives, and all the tools every man needs. The children found no piles of plant stalks and only a few animal bones. What were these people eating?

After many years, more men with furry faces came to our territory. This time they brought large axes made of a wonderful stone that stayed sharp for many hours. When it became dull, they used a tool to make it sharp again very quickly. They chopped down trees much larger than we ever could. They built houses from these huge logs laid horizontally on the ground instead of vertically. We had always made houses from smaller trees. Even if we could cut down such large trees, we could never have moved them into place. The furry people brought animals bigger than a deer to drag their logs.

I could not understand why they spent so much time making a house. We could never stay in place for a long time, so we never put a lot of effort into making a house. When they had finished making several houses, they made small pens. The pens

ILLUSTRATION BY NANCY BISHOP

had a fence made from the same trees we would have used to make our houses, but shorter. I am sure that any wild animal could get out very easily. The rabbits and woodchucks would tunnel under, and the deer would jump over. Why catch a wild animal, put it in a pen, and then kill it for food the next day?

I was totally amazed at what they found to put into the pens. They had some animals just as furry as their faces. Other animals looked like the wild boars in the forest, but less mean. Another was as agile as a young deer, but very happy to stay in the pen. They even had birds laying eggs and not flying away. How did these people who could not even make a stone tool find such wonderful animals?

Every time I followed the furry men into the forest or showed them how to do simple things that even my children can do, I saw more strange sights and objects. I have to learn more about who they are, where they came from, and why they came here. I am willing to give them something for their information, but they want things from me that they could get for themselves in the forest. An example would be the plants that I put into my smoking pipe. Sometimes I add a few other plants to make them happier.

During the first winter since they built their houses, I brought some dried meat just to see how they were surviving. They invited me into the house, and it was very warm. They had made a fire in a place lined with stone and stacked to the roof. The hole in the roof above the fire drew out all the smoke. My house always filled with smoke and made my eyes burn. They did not have that problem.

I considered the life of the furry men and my own life. I have spent almost sixty years to learn what I have learned, but still my life is very difficult. I never had time to just sit and think and talk the way they do for hours and hours. I have seen their chief yell orders at the other men and they quickly do what they are told. They are trading metal disks for food and tools. They have trained animals to drag huge logs, stay in pens, and give them eggs and milk. They can cut down the biggest trees and split them into pieces small enough for a fireplace. I am getting too old to chase down deer and walk to a new camp every few months. I want to live the life of the furry man. But I do not want the headman yelling at me.

Postscript: The Archaeology of Pennsylvania's Changing Frontier

Frontier is defined as the borderland between two different groups of people. Four hundred years ago, Pennsylvania's frontier was the boundary region between Europeans and Native Americans. Initially, the two groups were separated but exploiting each other for mutual gain. This was followed by a brief period when Native Americans and Europeans occupied the same region, but there continued to be a significant cultural boundary between them. As Europeans increased in numbers, the frontier moved farther west and so did the original residents of the land we call Pennsylvania.

Simply said, contact means any interaction between Native Americans and Europeans. Frequently this took the form of stories of great ships, men riding strange four-legged creatures, exotic goods such as beads, brass kettles, or flintlock muskets that the natives called firesticks, and unfortunately for the Native Americans, disease and warfare. The Contact period was a time of cultural transition, fragmentation, unrest, and the eventual collapse of traditional Native American cultures in Pennsylvania.

One of the first recorded accounts of contact between Europeans and Pennsylvania Indians was in 1608 on the Chesapeake Bay between the Susquehannocks and John Smith of the Virginia Colony. He was very impressed and described them as "great and well proportioned men, are seldom seen, for they seemed like Giants to the English." Based on archaeological evidence, we now know that they were no taller than the average modern-day Europeans; however, they were a formidable tribe that had taken control of the Susquehanna drainage basin and its resources.

The first Europeans must have been a perplexing image to the Indians. They desired European technology but were frequently frightened or abhorred by the Europeans and their culture. In most cases, the desire for European goods won out and, in the early 1600s, a booming exchange of furs for European goods emerged. As noted earlier, historians tell us that the Susquehannocks may have moved south from their homeland in New York to better control the fur trade from competing native groups. They quickly trapped out their own traditional territory and began to trade with Indians in Ohio, New York, and Canada; however, these groups were jealous of the Susquehannock's middleman position, and much of the early Contact period was characterized by intertribal warfare over control of the fur trade, the so-called Beaver Wars of the 1640s. The Seneca of western New York were especially angered and eventu-

ally drove the Susquehannocks out of the drainage, but they quickly became concerned with the vacuum created by the defeat of the Susquehannocks and invited them back as a buffer between the Iroquois homeland and the English in Baltimore.

William Penn arrived in the Commonwealth in 1682, and in his charter he was required to "reduce the Savage Natives by gentle and just manners to the love of civil Societies and Christian Religion." He instituted a different policy compared to most of the other colonies, where the essential goal in dealing with the Indians was to acquire their land. In most cases, whatever the official strategy, the result was warfare and Native Americans were killed or forcibly removed. In Pennsylvania, however, the policy was to treat them fairly and buy their land. This was accomplished through a series of treaties and by 1792, Penn and his descendants had purchased all of what is now known as Pennsylvania.

The Delaware were the first Native groups to be impacted by Penn's policy of "fairness and equality to all." Generally, William Penn was respected by the Delaware, but his agents and descendants were not. The concept of buying land was foreign to most Native Americans, and many of them were bitter and angry by this practice. In particular, the historic Walking Purchase of 1737 enraged the Delaware from an already embittered feeling that they had been cheated and pushed from their lands.

Penn's policies created a time of relative peace. The competition for furs and European goods had essentially passed to the west by the early 1700s. The remaining Susquehannocks resided at Conestoga Town in Lancaster County. Many Delaware had moved west or to the Wyoming Valley above the forks of the Susquehanna. Encouraged by the Iroquois, many small refugee groups such as the Tuscarora, Shawnee, Nanticoke, and Tutelo moved into Pennsylvania.

For example, the Tuscarora were having trouble in their homeland of North Carolina. Regrettably, the English colonists were stealing women and children and selling them as slaves. In June 1710, a delegation of Tuscarora Indians came to deliver a set of wampum belts to the governor of Pennsylvania. The delegation was seeking permission to relocate the tribe to Pennsylvania to avoid a war with colonists in North Carolina. The meeting was held on June 8 at Conestoga Town (36La52), Manor Township, Lancaster County, where representatives sent by Lieutenant Governor Gookin and the Provincial Council met with the Tuscarora.

At this meeting, members of the Iroquois Confederacy invited the Tuscarora to return to their lands in New York. The Tuscarora spoke an Iroquoian dialect and had migrated from New York hundreds of years prior to this meeting. War delayed the move, but following its end in 1713, the tribe began migrating north through the Susquehanna Valley. The Tuscarora Nation was admitted to the Iroquois Confederacy as the sixth nation in 1722, but the move through Pennsylvania lasted until the 1760s.

Mathew Patton was one of the early settlers who began a farm in the 1740s in Franklin County. He was doing so well that he undertook the building a second house when a new conflict began. As France and England expanded their lands in North America, the inevitable conflict between the two European super-powers erupted.

In response to English intrusions in the Upper Ohio Valley, the French built a series of forts in western Pennsylvania, including Fort LeBoeuf south of Lake Erie and the famous Fort Duquesne at the confluence of the Allegheny and Monongahela Rivers. The war began as a result of an expedition led by George Washington. In 1754, he was sent by the Virginia colony to attack Fort Duquesne. On his way, he encountered a French patrol, a fight ensued, and the brother of the French commander-in-chief was killed. Washington knew he was in trouble and hastily built Fort Necessity as a defense against an over-whelmingly larger French force. Unfortunately, he picked a boggy site and it rained during the battle, causing his troop's muskets to misfire and he was forced to surrender. This was the site of the opening battle of the French and Indian War.

When news reached Great Britain, General Edward Braddock was sent to the Ohio Valley with 2100 troops to destroy Fort Duquesne. Eight miles from their objective, Braddock's force was attacked on July 9, 1755, by a smaller but aggressive force of French and Indians. Within five hours the British suffered more than 800 casualties. Braddock was mortally wounded and his army was routed. The catastrophic defeat left settlers of western Pennsylvania unprotected and allowed the Indian allies of the French to initiate a series of raids on settlers in both western Pennsylvania and the Susquehanna Valley.

The French and Indian War served to unify a variety of displaced and fragmented Native American tribes who shared frustration with and anger against the Europeans. Initially, the Delaware were undecided but with intimidation from the French, they eventually took up the hatchet against the English. In one of their early raids, they attacked a series of communities in Franklin and Fulton Counties, killing and capturing more than one hundred people. Mathew Patton's farm witnessed one of these attacks and was burned to the ground.

After Braddock's defeat and several Indian raids, the British built a series of forts along the Susquehanna River. The largest of these was Fort Augusta at Sunbury, with earthen bastions and walls over 200 feet long. Fort Halifax and Fort Hunter, established downriver from Fort Augusta as supply forts, were so positioned because the British felt the war would be fought along the West Branch of the Susquehanna River. As it turned out, most of the fighting took place in the Ohio Valley.

In 1758, with a command of 7000 troops, General John Forbes set out to retake Fort Duquesne. He built a road from Carlisle to the Forks of the Ohio that included the major forts of Bedford, Ligonier, and Pitt. Fort Loudoun served as an important supply depot during this campaign that eventually removed the French from western Pennsylvania. Built in 1756, it is located in Franklin County on the site of Matthew Patton's farm. The design was an interesting adaptation by the Pennsylvania Quaker government to implement a typical English fortification. It included one of Patton's houses as the officers' quarters. The fort was never attacked, but it was the scene of a rebellion in 1765 by local citizens against the harsh treatment by the British garrison. This action is an example of the frustration faced on Pennsylvania's frontier in the mid-1700s and some consider this the first act of the American Revolution.

With the Ohio Valley secure, the British invaded Canada and captured Montreal in 1760. This effectively ended the war on the North American mainland. Known in Europe as the Seven Years' War, it ended in North America with the signing of the Treaty of Paris on February 10, 1763. The Indian allies of the French were dissatisfied with the treaty and offended by the postwar policies of the British. Ottawa chief Pontiac led a series of attacks in the Ohio Valley in May 1763, destroying eight forts and killing thousands of soldiers and settlers. On August 6, a large Indian force was defeated by Colonel Henry Bouquet at the Battle of Bushy Run, ending Pontiac's Rebellion.

As part of the violence, the infamous Paxton Boys from Harrisburg massacred the remaining Susquehannocks (now known as the Conestogas) of Conestoga Manor. During the Revolutionary War, additional savagery was committed by both Native Americans and colonial forces in the Wyoming Valley and this signaled the end of Native American habitation as tribal groups in most of Pennsylvania.

In most of the original colonies, after Native Americans had been decimated by disease and warfare, they were given land. These were the first Indian reservations. With a few exceptions, Pennsylvania did not follow this policy and felt that buying their land was sufficient payment to fulfill the colony's humanitarian duties. The last Native American land in the state was the Cornplanter Grant, which consisted of 600 acres along the Allegheny River near the New York border. This reservation was occupied by Cornplanter, his descendents, and other Indians until 1964, when the remaining residents were relocated upstream in preparation for the construction of the Kinzua Dam. The dam project was strongly opposed by Native Americans and signaled the beginning of a revitalization of Native American culture in America. Although there are not any officially recognized Native American lands in Pennsylvania, many Native Americans continue to live in the state. There have been several attempts to create Indian land for the Delaware, but the state has opposed such initiatives, using the original land treaties as proof of ownership.

The span of time when Native Americans first arrived in North America, and more specifically Pennsylvania, marks a long period of changing cultural adaptations. It also marks the diversity and change of a people. Changes were made in response to human needs, and included changes in response to climate, disease, trade, warfare, and inevitably the interaction with other visitors to the New World— Europeans. This story and progression is chronicled and documented through archaeology. Although the archaeology of Pennsylvania is of one state in our nation, it is the prehistory and history of us as Pennsylvanians. Archaeology serves us this legacy, a legacy that continues to evolve and grow through the discovery, tools, analysis, eyes, hands, and fingers of archaeologists.

AN INDIAN IN THE TWENTY-FIRST CENTURY

Robert Winters

TIME TODAY.

PLACE NORTH AMERICA.

CLIMATE THE EARTH IS WARMING.

FLORA AND FAUNA A MIXED PINE, HEMLOCK, AND CHESTNUT FOREST—MUCH OF WHICH HAS BEEN REPLACED WITH ROADWAYS, VILLAGES, TOWNS, AND CITIES.

DISTINCTIVE ARTIFACTS REENACTMENTS AND EDUCATIONAL EFFORTS TO DISUADE MISUNDERSTANDING AND PREJUDICE.

My tribal name is Sheltowee. I am not a white person writing an imaginary story about being an Indian, I am one. Fifty-two years ago, when I was eight, my grandmother told me I was part Makuchay Shawnee Indian. My mother was upset when she found out I knew and warned me never to say anything about this or people would call me names like "Red Negro." Mom was right. At a Living History event at Fort Loudon, Tennessee, a group of men from the Carolinas called us that and worse. I was singing traditional songs with my Cherokee friends in the original tribal languages when this occurred. The white men were upset because they could not hear some other drunks singing "Danny Boy." This was in 1999. The prejudice against Indians is still out there. The greatest challenges to any Indian in the twenty-first century are not finding food and shelter; instead they are prejudice, stereotyping, and the distortion of our heritage to hype or sell a product.

In the last fifty-two years I have striven to become one thing and one thing only: a Makuchay Shawnee. I have fought prejudice, stereotyping, and cultural distortion. My main tool has been education. I became a cultural anthropologist and archaeologist to be able to do research and separate fact from fiction. I also became a Living History reenactor portraying my Shawnee ancestors in any period to educate the public as to how we looked and lived.

In the beginning, there was very little information and most of it was incorrect. My father, an American of Irish and German ancestry, understood my drive and encouraged it without aggravating my mother's opposition to my heritage. Dad belonged to a Boy Scout organization known as the Order of the Arrow, which had an Indian theme. He never told my mother about this. Dad took me to a two-hundred-year celebration in 1958 of the founding of Pittsburgh at Point State Park. I watched real Indians dancing and playing drums. They had long warbonnets, feather bustles, and heavily beaded garments. Today, I know what's wrong with that picture. They were Lakotas, a western tribe who had no part in the forming of white Pittsburgh. This is one of the great stumbling blocks of any twenty-first-century Indian other than someone of the Plains Tribes. We have to overcome the stereotypes of the Western Great Plains Peoples. There are five hundred tribes and they all do not have warbonnets and feather bustles.

I asked Dad about this, because I had seen the movie *Drums along the Mohawk*, with Henry Fonda, and the Indians in that picture did not look like the Point State Park dancers. Dad lit up and said, "You are right." What he did next was to educate and guide me for the rest of my life. He took me to the Carnegie Museum of Natural History in Pittsburgh, up to the third floor where the Indian exhibits were on display.

I can still recall my first sighting of the Delaware Warrior exhibit, though it was fifty years ago, and I have seen it many times since. "So this is what an Eastern Indian looked like." I was fascinated. The magnetism of that exhibit with a loin-clouted warrior raising a scalp and holding the bloodied knife is just as strong today. The original caption for the exhibit had something to do with the dangers the white settlers faced on the Pennsylvania frontier of the 1750s. The caption changed, becoming more apologetic in explaining that the warrior was defending his homeland against white encroachment. An improvement, yes, but it is not the whole story. The man was fulfilling his destiny as a warrior. The act of scalping has a deep religious aspect that neither caption addresses, even though educated white people wrote the captions. Herein lies a problem between red and white. Red peoples are different, not just in color but in culture. We have different laws, customs, and most of all different religions and religious beliefs. Scalping was originally done to possess the defeated warrior's spirit and strength, thereby empowering the victor. Scalps were decorated and honored with a special song and a dance. What the white educators and the white drunks at Fort Loudon have not realized is that Indians were honoring them in defeat and death with a song. Now there's a radical concept, to honor, not denigrate, an enemy. The third-floor warrior beat a white man, and the Indians beat the whites at Fort Loudon; however, the red people must make amends to the Creator for taking a life, or evil will follow us in this world and the next. You see the truth is a much better story than the museum captions or the white men's attitudes. Education is the key.

Robert Winters with his dog Minque.

This is what it's like to be a half-breed, quarter-breed, eighth-breed, or a full-bred Indian in the twenty-first century. We are the only American minority required to carry a card stating that the bearer is an Indian. In addition, the white government requires the Indian nations to note what percentage an individual is: 100 percent, 50 percent, 12 1/2 percent, and so on. It's like proving a breed of dog in the canine world. This is demeaning, biased, and very prejudicial. If one aspires to prove one's Indian heritage, one must show that percentage of breed. Dog, right? I had to present my heritage back to my great-grandmother in order to get my card. No one in the white world noticed my five unicentric fingerprints that only New World Indians and a group of 300,000 Sino/Malaysians exhibit. No one in the white world examined an X-ray of my skull and found that the bone structures of my ear passages were bent. Indians have a lower position in their skulls for the aural openings than those of white skulls. When the two mix a bending occurs that can cause serious problems with massive ear infections or mastoiditis. This mixing also plays havoc with a person's sinus cavity alignments, which leads to more serious effects from head colds, altitude or depth pressure changes, and a persistent postnasal drip. To the officials, none of these concerns matter, only what percentage of Indian breeding that an individual can document. Even DNA testing is not accepted. Clearly, further education is needed.

I have accepted all this, fought it, climbed over it, dug under it, and somehow got around it. For forty-two years I have made and sold Indian craftwork items. I have researched and furthered my knowledge of North American Indian cultures, particularly the Shawnee and other eastern United States tribes. The items I started making at eighteen years old weren't quite Shawnee. My arrows, for instance, had three feather fletches, each 6 inches long and 22 inches in length. This is a western type. It took me ten years to learn that an eastern Shawnee arrow was much longer and sometimes only had two short fletches 3 inches long. I progressed in spurts with long periods of idle wheel spinning. In the 1960s and '70s, during my formal education period, there were few sources to consult. I was extremely fortunate during this period to be associated with the Section of Man and Recent Invertebrates at the Carnegie Museum of Natural History. Their excellent research libraries enabled me to refine the image of the Delaware Warrior on the third floor. Unfortunately, these libraries are not available to everyone. In the late 1970s and early '80s, I became a field technician and lab assistant for the Anthropology Section at the museum. It was here that I learned how to chip stone tools and gunflints, again by having access to the research library. I worked under or met some of the greatest archaeologists in North America: James Adovasio, James Richardson, and James Swauger. The "Jims" taught me, molded my thinking, and inculcated in me that Indians were people. Indians were resourceful and intelligent, with a cohesive family network superior to any Euro-American. What the "Jims" did was to breathe life into the third-floor warrior through education.

It seems that the educated professionals in the cultural fields of anthropology, archaeology, and sociology are the least prejudiced, most open-minded indviduals, and they disseminate the most accurate information regarding American Indians. But change is still slow and the educators devoted to these fields are buried beneath an avalanche of popular cultural distortion. The base problem is the lack of general education regarding the five hundred tribes of North American Indians present in 1492. In my twelve years of primary and secondary education (1953-65), I was taught about Indians three times. In the first through fourth grades, we had Indians and Pilgrims every November. In the ninth grade, I learned that there were Indians in Pennsylvania. In the eleventh grade, we spent one class period on the French and Indian War and one on the Custer era. It was only in my college anthropological courses that I finally met my ancestors through education. These things are changing in the twenty-first century. My wife, a Cherokee and an elementary school teacher, notes that occasionally an Indian is invited to lecture each class for one period a year. The local high school now has a weeklong program incorporated into the American history course regarding North American Indians; however, not everyone is required to take this course. The image of Indians is brought to the average American citizen by the media with an infusion of mass cultural distortion.

One of the popular Indian images presented by the media today is a blend of cute caricatures or anything "Native American" in concept or design being used to sell a product. Last month as I sat in my doctor's waiting room, I picked up a monthly periodical of some two hundred-plus pages entitled *Cowboys and Indians*. All the salient articles dealt with either the old cowboy period of 1850-1900 or today's cowboys still riding the range in places as far away as Australia. Not one article dealt with Indians, past or present. Two-thirds of the advertisements, however, featured an Indian theme. There were countless sloe-eyed, beautiful Indian women hawking jewelry or fashionable Southwestern apparel. There were pictures of turquoise necklaces and bracelets spilling out of Pueblo pottery and silver buckles and bangles on Navajo rugs, but not one word on the 349 broken treaties that the tribes of America suffer from the United States government. We are bombarded with the cartoons of Chief Wahoo of the Cleveland Indians baseball team. We do the "Tomahawk Chop" of the Atlanta Braves and thrill to the athletes of the Washington Redskins and Florida State Seminoles, who are neither. No sportscaster or network has given even thirty seconds of airtime to explain these names or their origins. The crime that the media has perpetuated is to reduce the history and images of five hundred American Indian tribes to some banal caricature in order to sell a concept or product.

Perhaps thirty thousand people a year stop on the third floor of the museum to see the Delaware Warrior, but any televised game of the Washington Redskins or Cleveland Indians reaches hundreds of thousands of viewers in a single day. Our educators and institutions devoted to cultural education cannot compete. So the popular image of an Indian in the twenty-first century remains some big-nosed guy in a warbonnet swinging a tomahawk and dancing to a drum beat. I strongly believe this reinforces the prejudice against Indians still evident today.

The climate is changing. The tide of prejudice is slowly receding. I believe the main tool that Indians can use against prejudice, stereotyping, and cultural distortion is education. I believe a greater emphasis placed on Indian studies in the primary and secondary educational programs of the United States would be beneficial to all citizens. We are Americans first, and the first Americans laid the groundwork for our nation. Every other group that settled in America has received a place in our studies programs of American history taught in primary and secondary educa-tion. It is time for a full nine-week course to be taught at the high school level regarding the First Americans. Our actual Native American histories are infinitely more exciting than any caricature, cartoon, or stereotype. Teach the truth and the prejudice will eventually disappear. Ne shokway, ne eshway. I have spoken. I am empty.

Epilogue

The story of the first Pennsylvanians has been told from the perspective of more than 16,000 years of changing cultural adaptations. It begins with the Pre-Clovis phase, when glaciers had just receded from northern Pennsylvania and vegetation consisted of an open parkland with a scattering of spruce trees and large expanses of grassland. Megafauna roamed the land. The first humans were living in very small bands of ten to fifteen men, women, and children. Their ancestors had probably come by boat down the west coast of North America from Siberia thousands of years before. Their adaptive strategy was relatively simple. They were foragers, although hunting in this environment probably contributed more than 60 percent of their diet. Their campsites were changed frequently as they moved from one easily exploited food resource to another. The problem with identifying the very first Pennsylvanians is that there were so few of them and they did not use a distinctive set of tools that could be identified with this period. They are practically invisible archaeologically. This period, involving a very low population density, lasted for more than 5000 years.

By 11,200 years ago, evidence of humans appears everywhere south of the glaciers. Maybe the population density reached a level at which they became more archaeologically visible or maybe their sites are easy to identify because they were carrying a very distinctive artifact—the fluted projectile point. Compared to later periods, the population density was relatively low, but the database for the Paleoindian period consists of several well-excavated sites and hundreds of recorded sites. The Paleoindian adaptive strategy seems to have focused on riverine areas and involved frequent moves over long distances to the location of the easily exploitable food resources. A few nut-bearing deciduous trees, such as oak, were now present in the parkland, but hunting continued to contribute more to the diet than gathering. The Paleoindian toolkit was dominated by hunting tools, although nut-gathering and fishing were also part of the subsistence pattern, based on a very few sites that produced food remains. There is a preference for cherts and jaspers and the exclusion of lithic types, such as metarhyolite and quartzite, that were commonly used during later periods. The Younger Dryas climatic episode 10,900 years ago created an even harsher climate, but it does not seem to have had any significant effect on cultural development.

The Younger Dryas ended quickly at 10,100 BP. Temperatures rose and a dense spruce-pine forest moved into the Middle Atlantic region. This represents one of the most dramatic changes in the environment in the past 40,000 years. Interestingly, the cultural changes are minor. The basic Paleoindian adaptive strategy of living on floodplains and moving relatively long distances for food seems to have continued into the Early Archaic period. Fluted points were replaced by notched and serrated projectile points, but a toolkit based on standardized flake tools continued into the Early Archaic period. Nonchert lithic materials, such as metarhyolite and quartzite, were added to the toolkit, but the seasonal round continued to be relatively large and the population density remained low.

At the beginning of Middle Archaic period, a new adaptive strategy was initiated. This was associated with the warm Boreal climatic episode and the emergence of the oak-hemlock forest. The resource-rich forest allowed population density to increase significantly. The new strategy involved the exploitation of a wide variety of food resources available in both riverine and many different upland settings. The bands followed an annual pattern of seasonal movements, returning to the same sites each year. There is an increase in woodworking tools to exploit the hardwood forest, and the standardized flake tools of the Paleoindian/Early Archaic toolkit were replaced by simple generalized flake tools. Lithic preferences are local and the seasonal round decreased in size. Although the population probably tripled in size, the number of people per band was small, indicating there was an increase in the number of bands rather than individual band size.

The Late Archaic period is associated with the warm and wet Atlantic episode, similar to the climate of today. The population density continued to increase and sites are found in many different ecological zones. The relatively generalized technology of the Middle Archaic worked well, but the increasing population could no longer be supported. The Late Archaic period seems to represent an intensification of technological systems in order to increase the quantity of food extracted (or caloric intake) from the environment. A variety of grinding stones for processing nuts and seeds and net sinkers used in fishing appear in the toolkit to make the processing of these foods more efficient. Band size increased and sites were probably being occupied for longer periods. There also seem to be sites that were very large and represent possible meeting places for neighboring bands.

The Sub-Boreal climatic episode began about 4300 years ago and represents a change to a warm dry climate. The change may have been minor, but coupled with the increasing population density, probably represented a crisis in the cultural adaptation. After nearly 4000 years, the Archaic adaptive strategy was no longer viable, mainly because of increased population density. The Transitional period represents a significant change in the manner in which the environment was exploited. There were many technological developments, but for the first time in the archaeological record of Pennsylvania, significant changes in social organization are suggested. Although the specifics are not clear, changes in the way groups were organized and cooperated with one another were now important factors in the efficient exploitation of the environment. These seem to have been successful as the population continued to increase. By the end of this period, the diet was mostly seed plants and a few domesticated plants. When the climate returns to a warm and wet period at 3000 years ago, the adaptive strategy seems to have been able to produce more than sufficient calories and some of the technological and social changes reverse, indicating that the crisis was over.

Beginning at about 3000 years ago, there are significant differences in the archaeological record of the Upper Ohio drainage basin compared to the other basins in Pennsylvania. In the Upper Ohio basin, Early and Middle Woodland groups were on the fringe of Adena and Hopewell influences. Artifacts from these groups appear in the Upper Ohio, but the exact relationship between people in Pennsylvania and the Adena/Hopewell heartland areas in Ohio and Indiana is not well understood. By Middle Woodland times, there is an increasing dependence on corn agriculture and the early dates for this compared to the rest of Pennsylvania are related to the diffusion of this food source from the Lower Ohio basin.

In the Susquehanna and Delaware drainage basins, the Early and Middle Woodland periods are characterized by a variety of projectile point and pottery types that are not particularly distinctive. Therefore, sites are not easily recognized and these periods are very poorly understood. The most commonly studied sites are found in floodplains in a stratified context. The few that have been excavated seem to represent small homesteads of one to three families. Although there is little supporting evidence, based on what we know of the Late Woodland period, it is assumed that population density continues to grow and there was an increased dependence on seed plants and domesticated foods. Corn, however, does not become a common dietary component until Late Woodland times.

By Late Woodland/Late Prehistoric times, 1100 years ago, the archaeological record becomes much more complete. In the Upper Ohio basin, population density had increased to the point where people of the Monongahela culture were living in villages supported by corn, beans, and squash agriculture. The villages contained hundreds of people living in small round houses situated in a circular pattern with an open plaza in the middle. They were practicing slash-and-burn agriculture. This subsistence pattern is frequently associated with intragroup feuding and violence. The stockades surrounding these villages support this interpretation.

In the Susquehanna basin there was an evolution from small farmsteads consisting of one to four houses of the Clemson Island culture to the Shenks Ferry culture eventually occupying circular villages of up to 60 houses surrounded by a wooden stockade. It is assumed they were also involved in intragroup feuding and violence. In the Delaware basin, the evidence for houses and villages is rare. There is ample evidence for corn agriculture, but people remained in small farmsteads and there is no evidence for intragroup feuding.

This was the cultural landscape when the Europeans arrived in North America during the mid-1500s. Two factors dominated the relationship between Native Americans and Europeans—the desire for European goods and disease. The former resulted in the movement of Native Americans to control the fur trade and warfare among the tribes. For example, the Susquehannocks moved to the lower Susquehanna basin in order to get closer to European trade centers. For nearly 100 years, they prospered as middlemen between the English and the more interior tribes. Disease resulted in up to an 80 percent decline in Native American populations and this is reflected in the disappearance of Monongahela villages in the Upper Ohio basin. These two factors, exacerbated by overwhelming numbers of Europeans by the early 1700s and their aggressive policy of land acquisition, resulted in the destruction of Native American culture in Pennsylvania. The Delaware tribe barely survived the diseases and the violence associated with the fur trade, but like so many other tribes, their land was taken and they migrated west to Oklahoma.

Archaeology has been described as constructing a picture puzzle of life in the past. The pieces of the puzzle are artifacts and archaeological sites. Actually, archaeologists reconstruct many puzzles. Each of these is a snapshot of past life. We try to connect these images with explanations or hypothesis of how the pictures change through time. The problem is that many pieces are missing. Many sites have been destroyed by modern construction projects or by natural causes. In this broad-brushed scenario covering Native American cultural evolution in Pennsylvania, there are several major gaps in the story and the following is a brief overview of the most significant missing data. These suggest important avenues for future research.

The understanding of the Pre-Clovis period is severely limited by a lack of data. More sites need to be discovered and meticulously excavated. Unfortunately, the artifact densities from sites of this period are probably too low to be located by state or federal construction project surveys. In addition, most soils dating to this period have been disturbed by modern activities. The Meadowcroft Rockshelter has demonstrated that rock shelters are one place to look. In contrast, floodplains rarely produce soils of this age, and in Pennsylvania are unlikely to be the location of Pre-Clovis sites. Special environments, such as swamps and bogs, have been dated to this period and archaeologists need to examine these settings carefully. Upland settings involving windblown or colluvial soils found at the base of slopes may have the greatest potential to contain undisturbed soils of this age. Although the majority of archaeologists agree that people were here prior to the Clovis phase, there are still only a handful of sites in both North America and South America that can be confidently dated to this period, and this needs to be corrected.

A second issue is diet. Whenever data relevant to this subject is available, its collection for any period should be a high priority. During Paleoindian through the Middle Archaic times, however, dietary remains are especially rare in the Middle Atlantic region. Our reconstructions of prehistoric diet for this period are based on meager remains found in other states and on the idea that whatever foods were available in the region during this time were eaten by people. A major solution to this problem is the systematic collection and analysis of flotation samples, residue analysis, and microwear analysis. These types of investigations can be time consuming and require highly controlled excavation techniques but are absolutely essential to understanding the evolution of past adaptations.

The Transitional period represents significant changes in technology, subsistence patterns, and social organization; however, our understanding of these changes, especially social organization, is minimal. To solve this issue will require a multi-pronged approach, but highly controlled excavations used to examine artifact patterning and the identification of individual occupations or visits are steps in the right direction. Determining the size of separate visits to a site and the number of people present would go a long way in clarifying social organization during this period. Based on ethnographic studies, we have some idea of the size of camps used by foraging bands. Therefore, we need to conduct excavations that represent a reasonable sample of these camps. Whenever undisturbed occupations from this period (or any period) are identified, very large areas approaching 400 square meters should be exposed and the artifacts should be individually mapped to facilitate the analysis of artifact patterning.

The Early and Middle Woodland periods are very poorly documented, especially in the Susquehanna and Delaware basins. This is an incredibly significant period, as it is situated between the major changes of the Transitional period and the complex developments of the Late Woodland period. The generally nondistinctive artifacts from this period have resulted in few occupations being identified. Obviously, we should continue to survey floodplain settings for stratified sites, but this has not been very successful. Sites from this period, however, have been located in upland settings. These have not been identified based on diagnostic artifacts but rather on the radiometric

Overview of Native American Cultural Development in Pennsylvania

Years BP	16,500 BP	11,200 BP	10,900 BP	10,300 BP	10,000 BP	9000 BP
Cultural Period	Pre-Clovis	Clovis	Middle Paleoindian	Late Paleoindian	Early Archaic	Middle Archaic
Diagnostic Artifacts	Miller Lanceolate	Clovis	Debert, Barnes, Crowfield, Holcombe	Dalton, Plano	Palmer, Charleston, Kirk Corner Notched	MacCorkle, St. Albans, LeCroy, Stanly, Neville
Technological Highlights	non-diagnostic tools	fluted points		lanceolate unfluted and basally thinned points	corner-notched and serrated points	bifurcate and stemmed points
Subsistence	hunting contributes 60% to the diet				gathering of roots, seeds, and nuts contributes at least 60% of the diet	
Social Organization	band society					
Climatic Episode	Bölling/Alleröd cool and dry		Younger Dryas cold and dry		Pre-Boreal warm and dry	Boreal warm and dry
Vegetation	spruce-pine parkland				pine-oak forest	

6000 BP	4300 BP	2700 BP	2100 BP	1100 BP	450 BP	200 BP
Late Archaic	Transitional	Early Woodland	Middle Woodland	Late Woodland	Contact	Modern
Otter Creek, Vosburg, Lamoka, Brewerton, Bare Island, Poplar Island, Lackawaxen	Savanna River, Koens-Crispin, Snook Kill, Lehigh, Perkiomen, Susquehanna, Forest Notched, Fishtail, Marcy Creek, Vinette I	Stubenville, Meadowood, Hellgrammite, Half-Moon, Cresap, Robbins, Vinette variants, Adena	Fox Creek, Watson Ware, Raccoon Notched, Jacks Reef, Abbott Zoned, Hopewell, Bushkill Complex	Clemson Island, Owasco, Chance, Shenks Ferry, Overpeck, Levanna & Madison triangles, Monogahela pottery	Susquehannock pottery	
stemmed and notched points, net sinkers, axes, grinding stones, bannerstones	broadspears, fishtails, steatite, early pottery, large FCR features, trade and exchange	pendant, gorget, bola stone, cord-marked pottery, copper tools, burial mounds	netmarked and dentate-stamped pottery, burial mounds	well-made incised pottery, triangular points	European materials	
	Eastern Agricultural Complex hunting, fishing, and more intensive gathering along with gardening			hunting, gathering, fishing; corn, beans, and squash agriculture		
	more structured band society patrilineal?—matrilineal?		tribal organization at least in the Susquehanna and Upper Ohio drainages hamlets—stockaded villages warfare			
Atlantic warm and wet	Sub-Boreal warm and dry	Sub-Atlantic warm and wet	Scandic cool and wet	Medieval warming Little Ice Age		
oak-hemlock forest	oak-hickory forest			oak-hemlock-chestnut forest		

dating of features. The features contain the charcoal for dating but also dietary remains in the form of seeds and nuts. Upland sites confined to plow-zone contexts are frequently considered to have low research value, but these sites need to be more intensively examined for the presence of features. Dating these features will clearly increase our understanding of diet and the use of upland areas during this poorly known period.

Finally, the Late Woodland period documents a complex cultural adaptation and also interactions between different social groups and different tribes. Relatively speaking, we know a great deal about this period partially because of the variety of features—storage pits, processing pits, and post molds—but also because organic remains, such as bone and antler artifacts, food remains, and human remains are more frequently preserved. In the above discussion, changing group behavior and cultural adaptations were emphasized; however, people also existed as individuals in the past. Individuals invented new technologies. Men and women played different roles in effecting change. Individuals controlled or influenced others through their personalities. There is no question that people act in groups and archaeology is most successful at identifying and analyzing group behavior; however, the database from the Late Woodland period, including human DNA, offers the best opportunity to identify individuals in prehistory and their role in cultural change. Being able to include the role of individuals in cultural adaptations will produce a more complete picture of the past.

Archaeologists assume that changes in technology and many social changes require motivating factors. The environment has long been identified as a moti-vating factor in cultural change, but we are learning that there is a complex relationship between the environment and cultural behavior, and that the environment has both a natural and cultural component. As discussed previously, the end of the Younger Dryas did not result in significant cultural changes. There may have been a variety of changes in belief systems as the climate went from cold and dry to a warm, dense spruce forest, but the basic adaptive strategy lasted another thousand years. In another example, the Little Ice Age may have affected the location of Monongahela villages (although that is also debated), but the eastern part of the state seems unaffected by this event.

The archaeology of Pennsylvania represents a great laboratory for testing hypotheses on how cultures evolve and why they changed over the past 16,000 years. Understanding how and why cultures change has a practical application to our own world. For example, the role of population density in cultural change has significant implications considering that human population is currently increasing at an ever-faster rate. Although determining population density is a difficult process that some archaeologists argue is not possible, most agree that population pressure is and was a significant motivating factor in cultural evolution. The changes of the Transitional period and the development of farming in Pennsylvania may well be motivated by increasing population density. Large numbers of students flock to Greece, Italy, Egypt, Central America, and South America to uncover the secrets of "lost civilizations." But when it comes to uncovering the secrets of how and why cultures evolve, Pennsylvania has a great deal to contribute to solving significant research problems that have relevance to our own future.

Glossary

Absolute dating method. A process of dating artifacts or cultural occupations that results in a date of years before the present or calendar years. In Pennsylvania, the most common form is radiocarbon dating. Dendrochronology, or tree ring dating, is another form of absolute dating commonly used in the southwestern United States, where the dry climate allows for the preservation of old trees. See also Relative dating.

AD. *Anno Domini*, or "in the year of the Lord," to count years after the traditionally recognized birth year of Jesus Christ. BC, or "Before Christ" is used to count years before that date.

Adaptation, or adaptive strategy. The process by which a culture exploits their surroundings or environment. Cultural behavior is the basic strategy used by humans to exploit their environment. From an archaeological perspective, it is mainly a combination of social organization, technology, and subsistence patterns. It is a basic theme in archaeological research where archaeologists analyze cultural adaptations in the past and especially why they change.

Aeolian deposit. Soil deposited by wind such as in river valleys where soil is blown off the surrounding ridges. It occurs under dry conditions where there is little or no vegetation. It was common during the Ice Age.

Alluvial deposits. Soils deposited by moving water, such as along rivers and streams. Large rain events cause rivers to overflow and deposit soils on the adjacent floodplains. This is the most common mechanism for the natural burial of artifacts in Pennsylvania.

Anadromous. Fish that live part of their lives in the ocean but migrate up rivers to freshwater to reproduce.

Anthropology. The scientific study of human cultural behavior in all times and places.

Archaeology. The scientific study of past human behavior through the systematic recovery and analysis of material remains. It is one of the four subdisciplines of anthropology.

Archaic period. A division of prehistoric time dating between 10,100 and 4300 BP in Pennsylvania. It is primarily a foraging subsistence pattern involving egalitarian societies. The most distinctive artifacts are a wide variety of spear-points, axes, adzes, net sinkers for fishing, and grinding stones for processing seeds and nuts. Pottery is introduced at the end of this period.

Artifact. The material remains of human behavior. An artifact may be as small as a flake produced while making a stone tool or as large as an entire cooking pot.

Artifact typology. An artifact type is a set of attributes (or characteristics) that are specific to a certain class of artifacts and serve to differentiate that class from all others of similar magnitude. It is common to organize projectile points or pottery styles that are similar in shape or motif and date to the same period into types.

Atlatl. A central Mexican (Nahuat) native word for a spear-thrower. A handheld tool consisting of a long stick with a hook on one end, used to hold a spear that helps to propel the spear with great force. It increases speed and accuracy. It is sometimes used with a stone weight called a bannerstone.

Avocational archaeologists. People without formal education in archaeology who are not paid for the work they perform. Also known as amateur archaeologists, they frequently collect artifacts as a hobby.

Band society. A loosely organized form of human social organization consisting of a family or series of families that usually range from 20 to 50 individuals. A band society occupies a specific territory, although membership is easily and frequently changed. Decisions are based on group consensus. There are few strict rules of behavior although peer pressure is very effective in reducing "bad" behavior.

Baton. Also known as a soft hammer, it is used in shaping stone tools and can be made of antler, bone, or wood, such as hickory, ash, or oak. A baton typically produces wide thin flakes that function to thin projectile points or other biface forms.

Biface. A flaked stone tool that has two edges and two "faces" (i.e., a front and a back). A biface is flaked on both faces. Typically, projectile points and knives are types of bifaces. *See also* Uniface.

Bioturbation. A form of ground disturbance caused by a burrowing animal or the roots of plants growing in the soil. Although usually minimal, it is a natural activity that occurs at most sites. It displaces artifacts from their original culturally determined pattern, making it more difficult to interpret a site. The term is most frequently used when the process has been extreme and there is evidence for substantial movement of artifacts from their original place in the soil.

BP. Years before present, based on 1950 AD.

Carbon dating, or C-14 dating. See Radiocarbon dating.

Colluvial deposit, or slope wash. Soil deposited by gravity; usually found at the bottom of hill slopes. A rock slide is an extreme example.

Conchoidal fracture. A specific type of breakage pattern characteristic of rocks that are chipped and shaped into stone tools. Rocks that have a conchoidal fracture break like glass. Rocks that break in a conchoidal pattern break in a controlled and predictable manner.

Contact period. A division of time that denotes the period of interaction between Native Americans and Europeans. Some archaeologists use this term to cover the time from the earliest appearance of European trade goods in the region (including trade with Indian middlemen). Other archaeologists use this term to apply only to the time when Europeans were physically in the region, using the term Protohistoric for the time when European trade goods are present in the region. The Protohistoric period in the Susquehanna Valley begins at about 1550 when European trade goods first appear. The Contact period begins about 1609 when members of the Jamestown colony begin to write about the Susquehannocks based on actual contact.

Context. The three-dimensional location of an artifact or feature in relation to all of the artifacts, features, and ecofacts around it, including the soil in which it was deposited.

Culture. An anthropological concept that represents humanity's technological, social, and ideological adaptation to the environment. Culture is learned and shared by a group. Overall it is a strategy for exploiting the environment. An archaeological culture is defined as a similar set of artifacts found at several sites, covering a restricted region and limited time span.

Cultural anthropology. The holistic study of human group behavior. It is one of the four subdisciplines of anthropology.

Curation. The process of managing, preserving, and interpreting archaeological collections, typically after they have been removed from the ground. It is one of the primary functions of museums.

Debitage. The collective term that refers to the sharp-edged material remaining after a stone tool is made through the process of knapping. Flakes are produced when a core is shaped into tool or blank or a tool is sharpened.

Dendrochronology. The dating of artifacts using tree rings. It requires a series of trees that cover a period dating from the present to the past. Rings vary in width based on changes in climate, such as precipitation and temperature. A master sequence of rings is compared to archaeological wood specimens, thereby accurately dating any associated artifacts. Unfortunately, in the Middle Atlantic region, wood is rarely preserved in sufficiently large pieces to develop a master sequence and therefore this method is rarely used.

Diagnostic artifact. A style of artifact that is consistently dated to a relatively specific period using absolute dating methods, such as radiocarbon dating. This type of artifact is used to date human occupations when no other dating methods are available.

Drainage basin. A land region from where a flowing body of water receives water runoff and groundwater flow. It is similar to the concept of a river valley, but it includes all the upland areas, such as ridges and mountains, from which water drains into a specific valley. They can range in size from the Susquehanna drainage basin to very small perennial streams.

Eastern Agricultural Complex. A term that applies to a group of plants first domesticated and used in the Midwest, such as squash, marsh elder, chenopodium, sunflower, maygrass, little barley, and knotweed. One or more of these plants was probably grown in gardens in Pennsylvania by Early Woodland times.

Ecofact. The material remains of the environment used to recreate past climates, flora, and fauna. Preserved bone, partially burned plant parts such as seeds or charcoal, and pollen grains are examples used from archaeological contexts. Clusters of rounded river cobbles reflect river conditions and flow velocities and are therefore ecofacts.

Egalitarian societies. Social systems in which all individuals are of relatively equal status. There are few differences in wealth or material goods and everyone has equal access to resources. The main social roles are headman and shaman. There are few benefits from either of these roles. It is believed that most Native American groups throughout prehistory in Pennsylvania were egalitarian.

Erosion. The removal of soil by water or wind. High winds or floodwaters can wash soil and artifacts from archaeological sites, essentially destroying the sites.

Ethnographic analogy. Using modern cultures to compare and interpret archaeological situations or remains.

Feature. The remains of human activity, similar to an artifact; features cannot be physically removed from an archaeological site and instead must be mapped and described by archaeologists. In Pennsylvania, these typically consist of hearths, storage pits, wells, privies, and post molds.

Fire-cracked rock (FCR). Angular or fractured pieces created when rock is heated in a fire. Usually found in cooking hearths, in stone boiling pits, or as a scatter across a living floor. The largest FCR features are associated with the Transitional period.

Flint knapping. The process of making stone tools by chipping or removing small flakes. This can be accomplished by indirect percussion using a punch or direct percussion using a soft hammer, baton, or hard hammer using a stone. Flakes can also be removed by means of pressure using an antler pressure flaker. *See also* Toolstone.

Flotation. An archaeological data recovery method for collecting small organic materials, such as seeds, nuts, and charcoal, by immersing soil samples in water and collecting the lighter organic remains that float. This is called the light fraction. The heavy fraction sinks to the bottom and can contain small stone artifacts such as flakes, glass beads, or other nonorganic objects.

Floodplain. The topographic setting found along rivers and streams that forms from water-deposited soils, primarily from repeated flooding events. This landform is generally flat but may include a series of steplike terraces that represent flood episodes when the river was at a higher level of deposition. The soils are usually well drained and fertile. They were a favorite topographic setting for Native American occupations throughout prehistory.

Foraging. A term used to describe a subsistence pattern whereby food is provided by a combination of hunting animals, fishing, shellfish collecting, and gathering seeds, roots, nuts, fruits, and leaves of wild plants. In this book, it is synonymous with the term *hunting and gathering*.

Friable. A term used to describe pottery that is easily broken into small pieces. Early Woodland pottery is generally friable and therefore rarely found in large pieces.

Geoarchaeology. The study of archaeology using the methods of geology and other earth sciences.

Glacier. A massive ice formation caused by an increase in precipitation and a decrease in temperatures in the northern latitudes, which results in more snowfall in the cold seasons than melting in the warm seasons. This results in an accumulation of snow; once the snow accumulates to hundreds of feet, it turns to ice and the ice flows downhill by gravity.

Hammerstone. Also known as a hard hammer, used in the early stages of stone tool manufacture. Typically used to break large blocks of stone into smaller pieces that can be worked into tools. Hammerstones usually are hard dense stones such as quartzite, sandstone, or basalt.

Historical archaeology. The archaeological excavation, analysis, and interpretation of material remains dating to a time when the cultures under examination are associated with written records.

Inorganic artifacts. Materials such as stone and pottery that are not biological in origin; they were never alive. These are known as nonperishable items in that they preserve forever.

In situ. A Latin phrase meaning "in place." An artifact that has not been moved since it was originally dropped by a person is said to be *in situ*. This prase is very important to the interpretation of artifact patterning. Typically, artifacts in deeply buried, stratified sites are *in situ*, whereas artifacts in a plowzone are not *in situ* and have been moved by plowing.

Linguistics. The study of human language including its structure, history, and diversity, along with how language influences cultural behavior and how behavior influences language. It is one of the four subdisciplines of anthropology.

Megafauna. Large mammals over 90 pounds in weight that lived during the Pleistocene epoch. These animals evolved to large sizes because it is easier to maintain body heat in a large body size. Mammoth, mastodon, bison, horse, giant sloth, giant beaver, musk ox, saber-toothed tiger, and dire wolf, all now extinct, are examples, and their remains have been found in Pennsylvania or adjacent states.

Midden. An organic-rich feature created through human behavior generally consisting of food remains and other organic and nonorganic materials. Usually found in layers of a site that have been occupied for a relatively long period of time. Sometimes it is the result of organic material accumulating in surface depressions of a village.

Matrilineal social organization. A social system that traces kinship through female relatives related by blood. Inheritance of land and ceremonial knowledge is through the female line. In societies where matrilineal characteristics are strongly expressed, such as Iroquoian tribes, tribal leaders were appointed by the senior females of the family. The longhouse in Susquehannock villages was occupied by a group of sisters, female cousins, and their families related by blood to an ancestral female. This form of kinship is common among slash-and-burn agriculturalists.

New World. The continents of North and South America after discovery by Europeans.

Old World. The continents of Europe, Asia, and Africa.

Organic artifacts. Tools and ornaments made from materials that are organic in nature (once alive), such as wood, bone, antler, horn, shells, wood, leaves, and other plant parts.

Paleoindian period. This division of prehistoric time dates from the first humans entering the New World during the Ice Age approximately 17,000 years ago and ends with the appearance of a modern climate around 10,100 years ago. Primarily a foraging subsistence pattern was practiced by egalitarian societies. During this period in Pennsylvania, hunting probably contributed more food than the gathering of plants. The most distinctive artifact of this period is the fluted projectile point.

Paleontology. The study of past animal and plant life. These are usually preserved as fossils in rock.

PASS number. The Pennsylvania Historical and Museum Commission's Bureau for Historic Preservation maintains a record of all archaeological sites for which they have received information from other archaeologists and the general public. This is a geographic information–based system that includes electronic map information and information on the associated artifacts. This database is named the Pennsylvania Archaeological Site Survey (PASS) file.

Patrilineal social organization. A social system that traces kinship through male relatives related by blood. Inheritance of land and ceremonial knowledge is through the male line. This form of kinship is common among slash-and-burn agriculturalists but also hunter-gatherers.

Physical anthropology. The study of human cultural behavior emphasizing the study of human physical remains. This includes the study of human evolution, human biological variation, forensics, and the study of our nearest relatives, the primates. It is one of the four subdisciplines of anthropology.

Post molds. A type of feature that represents the remains of a wooden post that had been set into the ground. It could be part of a tent, house, stockade, drying rack, or some other type of structure. Post molds form when the post rots in place or the post is pulled from the ground and organically rich topsoil fills the empty space, forming a dark stain in the lighter undisturbed subsoil.

Prehistoric archaeology. Archaeological excavation, analysis, and interpretation of material remains dating to a time when the cultures being examined are not associated with written records. Ninety-eight percent of human culture occurred during prehistoric times.

Protohistoric. This is similar to the term "Contact period." It is the period of Native American culture dating to the time when written records were incomplete and/or biased. Strictly defined, the Contact period is the time when Europeans were initially meeting Indians. The Protohistoric period is when Native peoples are receiving European goods from other Native middlemen.

Provenience. The three-dimensional location of an artifact or feature on a site.

Radiocarbon dating. An absolute dating method based on measuring the decay of carbon 14 to nitrogen. It is accurate between approximately 300 and 50,000 years ago. It produces a date before the present (based on the year 1950) in radiocarbon years. Although radiocarbon years were once thought to equal calendar years (365 days in length) it is now known that they do not and, in fact, vary slightly in length; however, using a correction formula, radiocarbon years can now be calibrated to calendar years.

Relative dating. A method of dating artifacts or archaeological occupations that simply results in determining that one occupation is older than another. Stratigraphic analysis is the most common form of relative dating. The basic concept is that artifacts or occupations that are deeper in the ground and lower in the soil profile are older than those above them. This is the most common form of dating. *See also* Absolute dating.

Riverine. The ecological setting surrounding rivers. It is similar to the term *valley*. This geographic setting contains many different food resources and was a favored location for villages and base camps.

Rock shelter. A rock overhang most frequently found along hillsides. It provides shelter from wind and rain. They may be very large in size, protecting hundreds of square feet, or only large enough for two people. In Pennsylvania, rock shelters usually have been used by Native Americans at some point in the past and they have been termed "prehistoric motels." They are significant archaeological resources because they are relatively dry compared to open-air sites, allowing for better organic preservation. They are also frequently stratified, providing for a better archaeological context. They are complicated to excavate, however, and many have been destroyed through poor excavation techniques and looting.

Settlement pattern. The study of the distribution of archaeological sites. This usually involves an analysis of their topographic and ecological settings. In some studies the goal is to develop predictive models on where sites are located and how they can be found. In other studies, the goal is to study all of the different sites that were used during a single period. The distribution of sites reflects the different types of resources that were being exploited and the manner in which the environment was being exploited. Changes in the distribution of sites over time may represent changes in the adaptive strategy.

Site. A concentration of artifacts that can be separated from other concentrations.

Slash-and-burn farming, or swidden agriculture. A farming method involving the clearing of forests by burning down the trees and planting the crops in the ashes of the nutrient-rich soil. It does not involve plowing of the soil or artificial fertilization. The fertility of the soil decreases significantly with each annual use. In Pennsylvania, after approximately five years of use, new fields were cleared and the process was repeated. Eventually, the fertile fields within approximately a two-mile radius become exhausted and the entire village moves.

Stratigraphy. The layers of soil and rock in the earth. Layers are formed based on changes in the depositional environment and postdepositional changes in the layers, such as the washing away of organic matter. Archaeologists excavate a site by following one layer of soil at a time.

Surface sites, or plowzone sites. Archaeological sites located in an unstratified context close to the existing ground surface, commonly found in plowed fields. Artifacts from several different periods or occupations are frequently mixed together. This is the most common type of site recorded in Pennsylvania.

Toolkit. The combination of implements used by an individual or a culture to exploit their environment.

Toolstone. Rock suitable for making tools, usually glass-like in structure, with predictable breakage patterns; it is hard, relatively homogenous, and free of other minerals and impurities.

Transitional period. This division of prehistoric time dates between 2700 and 4300 BP. The climate was warm and dry and this caused periodic reductions in food resources. This period is characterized by a distinctive set of artifacts that includes broadspears, steatite bowls, the earliest fired-clay pottery, and large fire-cracked rock features. Jasper and metarhyolite were traded over large areas. Foraging was the primary subsistence pattern but the gardening of chenopodium, maygrass, and little barley may also have been taking place.

Tribal society. A form of social organization structured by kin (family) groups. The families trace their ancestry to a common, sometimes mythical being. Frequently, they are further organized along male or female ancestry. Membership is less flexible than in band societies. Group decisions are based on a consensus among the families. This form of social organization is most commonly associated with agriculture during the Woodland period although it was probably much older.

Uniface. A chipped stone tool that is only worked or shaped on one surface. These are the most common types of stone tools. *See* Biface.

Upland. This topographic term refers to the ridges and hills above the valley floor. These areas usually do not contain the variety of food resources available in the valleys, but on a seasonal basis, nuts in the fall or deer in the winter were exploited by Native Americans. Stone for making tools was also frequently found in upland settings.

Use-wear patterns. When stone tools are repeatedly used, their edges become damaged and "dull." The damage consists of tiny flakes being removed from the tool's edge or polish and microscopic striations or lines. An analysis of these markings under a microscope (100x–400x) can reveal the direction in which the tool was used and the types of material on which it was used. Use-wear markings can be employed to identify meat-cutting knives, scrapers used on dry hides, scrapers used on fresh hides, or tools used for carving wood, antler, and bone. Microwear analysis is very useful in identifying the activities that were undertaken at an archaeological site.

Water-screening. An archaeological field method used to recover small organic and nonorganic materials. Typically, soil is washed through a fine mesh screen, with holes 1/16 inch square, revealing small flakes or beads of a minute size. This is a very effective artifact recovery method but requires lots of time, effort, and water.

Waste flakes. The pieces of stone that result from the production of stone tools. These can vary in size but are usually less than 2 inches long. They are one of the most common artifacts at Native American sites and are useful in the analysis of stone tool technology.

Woodland period. This division of prehistoric time dates between 2700 BP and 1550 AD. It is the time when Native American societies became more dependent on domesticated plants and farming. Fired-clay pottery was more commonly used, improving in quality and becoming highly decorated. By the end of this period, most groups in Pennsylvania were living in tribal rather than band societies.

References and Additional Reading

A. D. Marble & Company

2003   *Archaeological and Geological Study of Shriver Chert in Snyder and Union Counties, Pennsylvania: Alternative Mitigation for the Troxell Site (36SN91),* Vol. 1. Report to the Pennsylvania Department of Transportation, District 3-0.

2003   *Alternative Mitigation to the Interstate Fairgrounds Site (36Br210) Athens Bridge Replacement Project,* Vol. 1. Report to the Pennsylvania Department of Transportation, District 3-0.

Adovasio, James M., J. D. Gunn, J. Donahue, and Robert Stuckerrath

1975   "Excavations at Meadowcroft Rockshelter, 1973–1974: A Progress Report." *Pennsylvania Archaeologist* 45(3):1–30.

Adovasio, James M., and Jake Page

2002   *The First Americans: In Pursuit of Archaeology's Greatest Mystery.* Random House, NY.

Affleck, Richard M.

2002   *At the Sign of the King of Prussia.* Pennsylvania Historical and Museum Commission for the Pennsylvania Department of Transportation, Harrisburg, PA.

Binford, Lewis R.

1965   "Archaeological Systematics and the Study of Cultural Process." *American Antiquity* 31 (2 Part 1):203–210.

Boyd, Varna G., and Kathleen A. Furgerson

1999   *The Mystery of the Monongahela Indians.* Project mitigation for the Pennsylvania Department of Transportation, District 9-0. Greenhorne & O'Mara, Inc.

Braun, Esther K., and David P. Braun

1994   *The First Peoples of the Northeast.* Moccasin Hill Press, Lincoln, MA.

Burkett, Kenneth

1999   "Prehistoric Occupations at Fishbasket." *Pennsylvania Archaeologist* 69(1):1–100.

2012   "Fishbasket." orgsites.com/pa/redbankarch/_pgg3.php3, accessed February 2014.

Cadzow, Donald A.

2001   *Petroglyphs in the Susquehanna River near Safe Harbor, Pennsylvania.* Pennsylvania Historical and Museum Commission, Harrisburg, PA.

Callahan, Errett

1979   "The Basics of Biface Knapping in the Eastern Fluted Point Tradition: A Manual for Flintknappers and Lithic Analysts." *Archaeology of Eastern North America* 7:1–180.

Carr, Kurt W.

1989   "The Shoop Site: 35 Years After." In: *New Approaches to Other Pasts,* edited by W. Fred Kinsey and Roger Moeller, 5–28. Archaeological Services, Bethlehem, CT.

Carr, Kurt W., and Jenny Keller

1998   *The Development of Prehistoric Settlement Pattern Research Priorities in Pennsylvania.* Pennsylvania Historical and Museum Commission, Harrisburg, PA.

Carr, Kurt W., and James M. Adovasio

2002   "Paleoindians in Pennsylvania." In: *Ice Age Peoples of Pennsylvania,* edited by Kurt W. Carr and James M. Adovasio, 1-50. Pennsylvania Historical and Museum Commission, Harrisburg, PA.

Custer, Jay F.

1996   *Prehistoric Cultures of Eastern Pennsylvania.* Pennsylvania Historical and Museum Commission, Harrisburg, PA.

2001   *Classification Guide for Arrowheads and Spearpoints of Eastern Pennsylvania and the Central Middle Atlantic.* Pennsylvania Historical and Museum Commission, Harrisburg, PA.

Custer, Jay F., Scott C. Watson, and Daniel Bailey

1996   "A Summary of Phase III Data Recovery Excavation at the West Water Street Site (36Cn175), Lock Haven, Clinton County, Pennsylvania." *Pennsylvania Archaeologist* 66(1):1–53.

Deetz, James

1967   *Invitation to Archaeology.* Natural History Press, Garden City, NY.

1977   *In Small Things Forgotten: The Archeology of Early American Life.* Anchor Press, Garden City, NY.

Dent, Richard J., Jr.

1995   *Chesapeake Prehistory: Old Traditions, New Directions*. Plenum Press, NY.

Engelbrecht, William

2003   *Iroquoia: The Development of a Native World*. Syracuse University Press, Syracuse, NY.

Fagan, Brian M.

2000   *Ancient North America: The Archaeology of a Continent*. 3rd ed. Thames & Hudson, London.

Gardner, William M.

1989   "An Examination of Cultural Change in the Late Pleistocene and Early Holocene (ca 9200 to 6800 B.C.)." In: *Paleoindian Research in Virginia: A Synthesis*, edited by J. M. Wittkofski and T. R. Reinhart, 5–51. Special Publication No.19 of the Archaeological Society of Virginia.

Gardner, William M., and Robert A. Verrey

1979   "Typology and Chronology of Fluted Points from the Flint Run Area." *Pennsylvania Archaeologist* 49 (1–2):13–46.

Grumet, Robert S.

1995   *Historic Contact: Indian People and Colonists in Today's Northeastern United States in the Sixteenth Through Eighteenth Centuries*. University of Oklahoma Press, Norman.

Hatch, James W.

1993   *Research into the Prehistoric Jasper Quarries of Bucks, Lehigh and Berks Counties, Pennsylvania*. Report submitted to the Pennsylvania Historical and Museum Commission, Harrisburg, PA.

Heberling, Scott D., and William M. Hunter

2006   *On the Road: Highways and History in Bedford County*. Pennsylvania Historical and Museum Commission for the Pennsylvania Department of Transportation, Harrisburg, PA.

Heisey, Henry W., and J. Paul Witmer

1962   "Of Historic Susquehannock Cemeteries." *Pennsylvania Archaeologist* 32(3–4):99-130.

Holmes, William H.

1897   *Stone Implements of the Potomac Chesapeake Tidewater Province*. Fifteenth Annual Report, Bureau of Ethnology, 1893–1894:13–152

Justice, Noel D.

1995   *Stone Age Spear and Arrow Points of the Midcontinental and Eastern United States*. Indiana University Press, Bloomington.

Kelly, Robert L., and David Hurst Thomas

2012   *Archaeology: Down to Earth*. 6th ed. Thomson and Wadsworth. Belmont, CA.

Kent, Barry C.

1980   *Discovering Pennsylvania's Archeological Heritage*. Pennsylvania Historical and Museum Commission, Harrisburg, PA.

1984   *Susquehanna's Indians*. Pennsylvania Historical and Museum Commission, Harrisburg, PA.

Kent, Barry C., Ira F. Smith, and Catherine McCann, eds.

1971   *Foundations of Pennsylvania Prehistory*. Pennsylvania Historical and Museum Commission, Harrisburg, PA.

Kingsley, Robert G., James A. Robertson, and Daniel G. Roberts

1990   *The Archaeology of the Lower Schuylkill River Valley in Southeastern Pennsylvania*. Philadelphia Electric Company, Philadelphia.

Kinsey, W. Fred, III, ed.

1972   *Archaeology in the Upper Delaware Valley: A Study of the Cultural Chronology of the Tocks Island Reservoir*. Pennsylvania Historical and Museum Commission, Harrisburg, PA.

Kinsey, W. Fred, and Jeffrey R. Graybill

1971   "Murry Site and Its Role in Lancaster and Funk Phases of Shenks Ferry Culture." *Pennsylvania Archaeologist* 41(4):7-43.

Kraft, Herbert C.

1974   *A Delaware Indian Symposium*. Pennsylvania Historical and Museum Commission, Harrisburg, PA.

2001   *The Lenape-Delaware Indian Heritage: 10,000 B.C. to A.D. 2000*. Lenape Books, Elizabeth, NJ.

Lantz, Stanley

1984 "Distribution of Paleo-Indian Projectile Points and Tools from Western Pennsylvania: Implications for Regional Differences." *Archaeology of Eastern North America* 12:210–230.

Letts, Cali A., Jeanne M. Moe

2009 *Project Archaeology: Investigating Shelter.* Montana State University, Bozeman.

MacDonald, Douglas H.

2002 *Pennsylvania Archaeological Data Synthesis: The Upper Juniata River Sub-Basin 11 (Watersheds A–D).* GAI Consultants, Inc. mitigation report.

2003 *Pennsylvania Archaeological Data Synthesis: The Raccoon Creek Watershed.* Report submitted by GAI Consultants, Inc. to the Pennsylvania Department of Transportation, District 11-0.

Mayer-Oakes, William J.

1955 *Prehistory of the Upper Ohio Valley: An Introductory Archeological Study.* Carnegie Museum, Pittsburgh, PA.

McConaughy, Mark A.

2011 "Burial Ceremonialism at Sugar Run Mound (36WA359), a Hopewllian Squawkie Hill Phase Site, Warren County, Pennsylvania." *Midcontinental Journal of Archaeology* 36(1):73–104.

McConaughy, Mark A., and Janet R. Johnson

2003 "Sugar Run Mound (36Wa359) and Village (36Wa2): Hopewell/Middle Woodland in Warren County, Pennsylvania." In: *Foragers and Farmers of the Early and Middle Woodland Periods*, edited by Paul Raber and Verna Cowin, 101–116. Pennsylvania Historical and Museum Commission, Harrisburg, PA.

McNett, Charles W.

1985 "The Shawnee-Minisink Site: An Overview." In: *Shawnee-Minisink: A Stratified Paleoindian Archaic Site in the Upper Delaware Valley of Pennsylvania*, edited by C. W. McNett, 321–326. Academic Press, Orlando.

Means, Bernard K.

2007 *Circular Villages of the Monongahela Tradition.* University of Alabama, Tuscaloosa.

Mercer, Henry Chapman

1885 *The Lenape Stone, or the Indian and the Mammoth.* Putnam Press. New York.

Michels, Joseph W.

1994 "Excavations at the Sheep Rock Shelter (36Hu1): An Historical Review." *Pennsylvania Archaeologist* 64 (1):28–40.

Michlovic, Michael G.

1976 "Social Interaction and Point Types in the Eastern United States." *Pennsylvania Archaeologist* 46 (1–2):13–16.

Miller, Patricia E.

2004 *Plow Zone Archaeological Sites in the Commonwealth of Pennsylvania: Characterization and Context.* KCI Technologies report to Pennsylvania Historical and Museum Commission, Harrisburg, PA.

2009 *The Wallis Site: The Archaeology of a Susquehanna River Floodplain at Liverpool, Pennsylvania.* Pennsylvania Historical and Museum Commission for the Pennsylvania Department of Transportation, Harrisburg, PA.

O'Brien, Greg

2008 *The Timeline of Native Americans; The Ultimate Guide to North America's Indigenous Peoples.* Thunder Bay Press, San Diego.

Orlandini, John

2008 *The Ancient Native Americans of the Wyoming Valley: 10,000 Years of Prehistory.* Self-published, Shavertown, PA.

2008 *Indians, Settlers, and Forgotten Places in the Endless Mountains.* Self-published, Shavertown, PA.

Pevarnik, George L., and Joseph R. Blondino

2010 *Towards a Baseline Lithic Atlas for the Marshalls Creek Chert Quarry Archaeological District, Upper Delaware Valley of Pennsylvania.* Report for Cultural Heritage Research Services, Inc. and the Pennsylvania Department of Transportation, Harrisburg, PA.

Raber, Paul A.

2007   *Connecting People and Places: The Archaeology of Transportation at Lewistown Narrows.* Pennsylvania Historical and Museum Commission for the Pennsylvania Department of Transportation, Harrisburg, PA.

2008   "The Mykut Rockshelter, 36Hu143: An Upland Hunting/Butchering Station in Central Pennsylvania." *Archaeology of Eastern North America* 36:25-62.

Raber, Paul A., Patricia E. Miller, and Sarah M. Neusius, eds.

1998   *The Archaic Period in Pennsylvania: Hunter-Gatherers of the Early and Middle Holocene Period.* Pennsylvania Historical and Museum Commission, Harrisburg, PA

Raber, Paul A., and Verna L. Cowin, eds.

2003   *Foragers and Farmers of the Early and Middle Woodland Periods in Pennsylvania.* Pennsylvania Historical and Museum Commission, Harrisburg, PA.

Reinhart, Theodore R., and Mary Ellen N. Hodges, eds.

1990   *Early and Middle Archaic Research in Virginia: A Synthesis.* Special Publication No. 22 of the Archeological Society of Virginia.

1991   *Late Archaic and Early Woodland Research in Virginia: A Synthesis.* Special Publication No. 23 of the Archeological Society of Virginia.

1992   *Middle and Late Woodland Research in Virginia: A Synthesis.* Special Publication No. 29 of the Archeological Society of Virginia.

Rieth, Christina B., ed.

2008   *Current Approaches to the Analysis and Interpretation of Small Lithic Sites in the Northeast.* New York State Museum Bulletin Series 508, New York State Education Department.

Ritchie, William A.

1961   *A Typology and Nomenclature for New York Projectile Points.* New York State Museum and Science Service, Bulletin No. 384, Albany, NY.

1969   *The Archaeology of New York State.* Natural History Press, Garden City, NY.

Sassaman, Kenneth E.

1999   "A Southeastern Perspective on Soapstone Vessel Technology in the Northeast." In: *The Archaeological Northeast,* edited by Mary Ann Levine, Kenneth E. Sassaman, and Michael. S. Nassaney, 75-95. Bergin and Garvey, Westport, CT.

Smith, Shelley J., Jeanne M. Moe, Kelly A. Letts, and Danielle M. Paterson

1996   *Intrigue of the Past: A Teacher's Activity Guide for Fourth though Seventh Grades.* Bureau of Land Management, Anasazi Heritage Center, Dolores, CO.

Snow, Dean R.

1980   *The Archaeology of New England.* Academic Press, NY.

1996   *The Iroquois.* Blackwell, Malden, MA.

Stanford, Dennis, and Bruce Bradley

2012   *Across Atlantic Ice: The Origins of American Clovis Culture.* University of California Press, Oakland.

Stewart, R. Michael

1995   *Phase III Data Recovery, Shermans Creek Site (36Pe2), Perry County, Pennsylvania.* Prepared for Texas Eastern Transmission Corporation, Houston, TX.

2002   *Archaeology: Basic Field Methods.* Kendall/Hunt Publishing Company, Dubuque, IA.

Sullivan, Lynne P., and S. Terry Childs

2003   *Curating Archaeological Collections: From the Field to the Repository.* Archaeologists Toolkit 6, Alta Mira Press, Lanham, MD.

Tantaquidgeon, Gladys

1972   *Folk Medicine of the Delaware and Related Algonkian Indians.* Pennsylvania Historical and Museum Commission, Harrisburg, PA.

Truncer, James

2004   *Steatite Vessel Manufacture in Eastern North America.* BAR International Series 1326.

Turnbaugh, William A.

1975   *Man, Land, and Time: The Cultural History and Demographic Patterns of North-Central Pennsylvania.* Unigraphic, Evansville, IN.

Vento, F. J.

1994   *Genetic Stratigraphy: The Model for Site Burial and Alluvial Sequences in Pennsylvania.* Report submitted to the Grants Office of the Bureau for Historic Preservation, Harrisburg, PA.

Wall, Robert D., and Hope E. Luhman

2003   *A Bridge to the Past.* Pennsylvania Historical and Museum Commission for the Pennsylvania Department of Transportation, Harrisburg, PA.

Wall, R. D., R. M. Stewart, J. Cavallo, D. McLearen, R. Foss, P. Perazio, and J. Dumont

1996   *Prehistoric Archaeological Synthesis.* Trenton Complex Archaeology: Report 15. The Cultural Resource Group, Louis Berger & Associates, East Orange, NJ. Prepared for the Federal Highway Administration and the New Jersey Department of Transportation, Bureau of Environmental Analysis, Trenton.

Wallace, Paul A. W.

1999   *Indians in Pennsylvania.* Pennsylvania Historical and Museum Commission, Harrisburg, PA.

Witthoft, J.

1952   "A Paleo-Indian site in Eastern Pennsylvania: An Early Hunting Culture." *Proceedings of the American Philosophical Society* 96(4):464–495.

Wittkofski, J. Mark, and Theodore R. Reinhart, eds.

1994   *Paleoindian Research in Virginia: A Synthesis.* 2nd ed. Special Publication No. 19 of the Archeological Society of Virginia.

Index

A

244